China's Remarkable Economic Growth

China's Remarkable Economic Growth

John Knight and Sai Ding

OXFORD
UNIVERSITY PRESS

OXFORD
UNIVERSITY PRESS

Great Clarendon Street, Oxford, OX2 6DP,
United Kingdom

Oxford University Press is a department of the University of Oxford.
It furthers the University's objective of excellence in research, scholarship,
and education by publishing worldwide. Oxford is a registered trade mark of
Oxford University Press in the UK and in certain other countries

First Edition published in 2012

Impression: 1

British Library Cataloguing in Publication Data

Data available

Library of Congress Cataloguing in Publication Data

Data available

ISBN 978-0-19-969869-1

Printed in Great Britain
on acid-free paper by
Clays Ltd St Ives plc

Preface

This book is written by an economist near the end of his career and another near the start of hers. John Knight began his research in the 1960s, when many African colonies were achieving independence, and there was a new determination to accelerate their pace of economic development. It was natural for an aspiring development economist to be drawn into research on African economies. By 1990 the high hopes for Africa had proved unfounded, and his initial optimism had given way to pessimism, partly because it seemed then that the underlying problems were intractable, being as much political as economic. China, by contrast, was just opening up to foreign researchers, it was increasingly possible to apply the conventional tools of economic analysis, and the emerging economic reforms already suggested that growth would be rapid and that China would become a major economy within a very few decades. Thus, when the opportunity arose for him to conduct research on the Chinese economy, he leaped at it. For two decades his main research interest has been the Chinese economy and its transition towards becoming a market economy.

Over that period he has been engaged in answering several questions concerning the labour market, the rural–urban divide, rural–urban migration, income distribution, education, subjective well-being, and poverty in China. However, the biggest questions, subsuming all others, concern the remarkable rate of economic growth that China has achieved over the reform period: why, how, and with what consequences? It is one of the most exciting and challenging issues that a contemporary economist can address. He decided to take this daunting bull by the horns.

When John Knight began to conduct research on China, the research results and understanding that were then available to western scholars were very limited. Since then the literature on the Chinese economy has grown at an exponential rate even faster than that of the Chinese economy itself—reflecting the increasing availability of good data, the expanding number of well-trained Chinese economists, and the growing bandwagon of foreign economists who have become interested. Nevertheless, whether our criterion is the importance of the questions to be answered or the potential to help improve economic welfare, the Chinese economy remains vastly under-researched by comparison with more advanced economies. The explanation for this misallocation of resources is probably to be found in the sociology of the economics profession and the resultant research incentives.

Sai Ding, who is now a lecturer at Glasgow University, joined the project as a post-doctoral research officer at Oxford University, after initial training at Nankai University in Tianjin and doctoral research at Birmingham University. Although she was new to research on the Chinese economy, over the course of three years we have jointly produced three articles on cross-country and cross-province growth regressions and another on investment in China. These appear in suitably amended form as the five chapters of Part II, representing what is perhaps the core of the book (Chapters 4–8). We indicate in each of Parts I–IV whether that part is the result of joint or single authorship.

Maynard Keynes once remarked that economists should write articles on specific topics, not books; advice which fortunately he did not always observe himself. It is a great advantage of journal publication that one's research comes under close scrutiny through the peer review process, and can benefit greatly from it. Our aim has been to publish the more original parts of the book in this way and then to rewrite the material for the book both so that it can reach a broader readership and so that it can fit into the theme of the book. The hope is that the whole will add up to more than the sum of its parts. This follows the same format as was used in John Knight's two previous books on China, both with Lina Song: *The Rural–Urban Divide: Economic Disparities and Interactions in China* (1999), and *Towards a Labour Market in China* (2005).

Despite our attempt to develop a theme, we have written the book in such a way that each chapter is fairly self-contained. The one exception is that the methodological Chapter 5 is a necessary building block for the substantive Chapters 6 and 7. Our approach would enable a reader with specific interests to select particular chapters—although it would be useful to read the final, concluding Chapter 13 first so as to provide context.

Many acknowledgements and thanks are due. The research on which the book is based was supported by a substantial grant from the Leverhulme Trust (the funded project bears the same title as the book) and two grants from the Nuffield Foundation under its Small Grant Scheme. We thank these bodies for their financial support and for the confidence that they have shown in the research.

We are grateful to the copyright holders of the following journals for permitting us, with acknowledgement, to present, in suitably revised form, work that has appeared in their journals: Sai Ding and John Knight, 'Can the augmented Solow model explain China's remarkable economic growth? A cross-country panel data analysis', *Journal of Comparative Economics*, 37 (2009) (Chapter 4); Sai Ding and John Knight, 'Why has China grown so fast? The role of physical and human capital formation', *Oxford Bulletin of Economics and Statistics*, 73, 2 (2011) (Chapters 5 and 6); John Knight and Sai Ding, 'Why does China invest so much?', *Asian Economic Papers*, 9, 3 (2010) (Chapter 8); John Knight, Deng Quheng and Li Shi, 'The puzzle of migrant labour shortage and rural labour surplus in China', *China Economic Review*, 22, 3 (2011) (Chapter 9); John Knight, 'Reform, growth and inequality in China', *Asian Economic Policy Review*, 3, 1 (2008) (Chapter 10); John Knight and Ramani Gunatilaka, 'Does economic growth raise happiness in China?', *Oxford Development Studies*, 39, 1 (2011) (Chapter 11); and John Knight and Wei Wang, 'China's macroeconomic imbalances: causes and consequences', *The World Economy* (2011) (Chapter 12).

Chapter 9 is based on a paper published jointly with Deng Quheng and Li Shi. A version of Chapter 11 appeared as a journal article written with Ramani Gunatilaka. Part of Chapter 12 is based on a joint publication with Wei Wang. John Knight thanks his co-authors for allowing results of their joint research to be included in this volume.

Prototypes of various chapters have been presented at seminars in the Universities of Essex, Fudan, Johannesburg, Kansai, Macau, Nottingham, Oxford, Peking, Stellenbosch, and Western Ontario, and in Beijing Normal University and Chinese University of Hong Kong, and at conferences or workshops in Beijing, Brighton, Durham, Frankfurt, Guildford, Helsinki, Nottingham, Oslo, Oxford, San Francisco, Shanghai, Stockholm, Tokyo and Warwick. We are grateful to the organizers and participants for providing us with these opportunities to obtain helpful feedback on the research from experts.

Among the numerous colleagues and friends whom we wish to thank for helpful interest and advice on the research are Magnus Blomstrom, Deng Quheng, Dick Easterlin, Markus Eberhardt, Belton Fleisher, Xiaolan Fu, Ramani Gunatilaka, Hal Hill, Huang Yiping, Anke Hoeffler, Geeta Kingdon, Fung Kwan, Li Shi, Cyril Lin, Guy Liu, Meng Xin, Riaxin Minami, Jim Mirrlees, Albert Park, Qiao Tongfeng, Gus Ranis, Lina Song, Francis Teal, Jon Temple, John Toye, Wang Wei, Wang Xiaolu, Wing Thye Woo, Adrian Wood, Yao Yang, Yu Yongding, Linda Yueh, and Zhang Xiaobo.

We also thank the Department of Economics, University of Oxford, for hosting the research, even after John Knight had retired from his post in September 2008; and to David Hendry, Ann Gibson, Claire Brunt, and Gillian Coates for ensuring that the project ran smoothly.

Sai Ding is grateful for the support of the Department of Economics in the University of Glasgow.

The collegiality of the Fellowship of St Edmund Hall, Oxford has been, as always, a powerful support. John Knight has benefited also from his membership of the China Growth Centre at St Edmund Hall.

Contents

Part I Introduction
John Knight

Part II The Determinants of China's Economic Growth
Sai Ding and John Knight

Contents

Part III The Consequences of China's Economic Growth
John Knight

Part IV Conclusion
John Knight

List of Figures

List of Tables

List of Tables

Part I
Introduction

John Knight

1

Setting the Stage

For the period 1960–1980 we observe, for example, India 1.4 percent a year, . . . South Korea 7.0 percent, . . . an Indian will on average be twice as well off as his grandfather, a Korean 50 times . . . The consequences for human welfare involved in questions like these are simply staggering: once one starts to think about them, it is difficult to think of anything else.

(Lucas 2002: 20–1)

1.1 The Issues

China's economic growth has been remarkable. Over three decades of economic reform, from 1978 to 2008, the annual growth of output per capita averaged 8.7%. Such is the power of compound interest that this means that output per capita increased more than twelve times during that period. The effect on poverty was dramatic: over 250 million people were lifted out of dollar-a-day poverty (Ravallion and Chen 2007).

Table 1.1, comparing China with selected countries over the period since 1980, shows that China achieved consistently high output growth of over 10% per annum in each of the three decades, whereas the world economy as a whole grew consistently at about 3% per annum. The mature economies—such as the United States, Japan, and the United Kingdom—grew at a modest pace, not exceeding 4% per annum on average. We see that the Russian economy collapsed after its overnight economic transition but recovered respectably after 2000. India's economy grew by almost 6% per annum in the two decades up to 2000, and growth rose to almost 8% per annum after 2000 as the pace of its economic reform and marketization quickened: India might come to rival China's dynamism in the coming decade. Both South Korea (9% per annum) and Taiwan (8% per annum) grew rapidly during the 1980s but their growth slowed down as their economies matured. The city states of Hong Kong and Singapore also grew annually at over 6% in the first decade of the table but their growth similarly

Table 1.1. The annual average percentage rates of growth in real GDP, 1978–2007, selected countries

Country	1980–90	1990–2000	2000–7
World	3.1	2.9	3.2
China	10.2	10.6	10.3
United States	3.0	3.5	2.6
Japan	4.0	1.1	1.7
United Kingdom	3.2	2.7	2.6
Russia	1.9	−4.7	6.6
India	5.8	5.9	7.8
South Korea	9.4	5.8	4.7
Taiwan	7.9	6.4	3.8
Singapore	6.4	7.6	5.8
Hong Kong	6.9	3.6	5.2
Vietnam	.	7.9	9.8
Botswana	10.3	6.0	5.3

Source: World Bank, *World Economic Indicators*; Taiwan, *Taiwan Statistical Yearbook*.

decelerated. Vietnam, reforming later than China, managed almost 8% per annum in the decades after 1990. Another small and resource-rich economy, Botswana, achieved over 10% per annum growth in the 1980s, but that high growth could not be sustained.

Earlier, Japan had managed rapid growth for a considerable time, averaging 8% per annum from 1952 to 1980, but there was a slowing down in the 1980s, and since its financial crash at the end of the 1980s the Japanese economy has stagnated. Similarly, South Korea had a spell of fast growth (9% per annum) during its most successful period of export-led industrialization 1965–90, and the same can be said of Taiwan (9% per annum) over the period 1960–90.[1] However, it appears that China is the only country which has consistently achieved very high growth since 1980. This feat is even more exceptional because, apart from India, it is the only heavily populated and poorly resourced country among the front runners.

China's rate of growth during the reform period really is remarkable. It deserves to be researched and understood. Why did it happen? How did it happen? Can it be evaluated? Can it continue? These are among the most important questions that a contemporary economist can ask. They are the subject of this book.

1.2 China's Economic History

Adam Smith, relying on travellers' reports, wrote in *The Wealth of Nations*:

China has long been one of the richest, that is, one of the most fertile, best cultivated, most industrious, and most populous countries in the world. It seems, however, to have been long stationary. (Smith 1776: 73)

Table 1.2. Real income per capita and its growth in China and Europe in the long run

	China	Europe	Ratio Europe/China
Real income per capita (1990 US$)			
1280	600	500	0.83
1700	600	870	1.45
1820	600	1129	1.88
1952	537	4374	8.15
1978	979	10,860	11.09
1995	2,653	13,951	5.26
Growth in real income per capita (% per annum)			
1280–1700	0.0	0.1	
1700–1820	0.0	0.2	
1820–1952	–0.8	1.0	
1952–1978	2.3	3.6	
1978–1995	6.0	1.5	

Source: Maddison (1998: tables 1.3, 2.1, 2.2c).

Maddison (1998) confirmed that at times in past centuries China was techno-logically sophisticated and achieved a high level of income per capita. Farm productivity in the fertile areas of China, such as the Yangtze delta, was high enough to support a high population density. However approximate might be Maddison's pre-twentieth century estimates, they suggest that China and Europe were roughly on a par for several centuries prior to the nineteenth century, in an era when economic growth was negligible (Table 1.2). Over the following one and a half centuries, China's income per capita fell somewhat as the imperial system decayed and socio-political stability was lost, whereas Europe's living standard benefited from the industrial revolution and the cumulative process of economic growth that it generated. Europe had developed arrangements in which capitalism and innovation could flourish but China had not.

The table suggests that the Chinese economy did not achieve sustained growth of income per capita until the second half of the twentieth century, initially during the period of central planning up to 1978 (2.3% per annum, measured in 1990 US dollars) and then, even more rapid, during the period of economic reform up to 1995 (6.0% per annum).

It was in China that printing, the magnetic compass, and gunpowder were invented. Needham, in his monumental volumes on science and technology in China, posed a puzzle—why did the industrial revolution not first occur in China? Indeed, all the preconditions appeared to be in place in the fourteenth century.

It is arguable that China's failure to grow rapidly prior to the mid-twentieth century was due to the imperial system of governance (Maddison 1998; Acemoglu 2009: 807). For a millennium of imperial rule China was governed by an educated bureaucracy. The society was hierarchical, with a sharp divide between the educated elite (the mandarins and the gentry) and the masses. China's authoritarian political institutions normally regulated economic activity very tightly, including both internal and external trade. The bureaucrats were essentially rent seekers: they squeezed the profits of enterprise and restricted the entry of new entrepreneurs who might adopt and exploit new technologies in a process of creative destruction. Broad-based property rights and contracting institutions were not developed. An autonomous middle class was not allowed to emerge as a force for economic and political change. The type of education received and the prevailing mindset generally did not encourage scientific enquiry. Lin (1995) argues that the imperial examination system ensured that the most able people underwent a classical, Confucian education leading on to governance, and had no time or incentive to pursue science.

Contrast this picture of a dictatorial system with the picture of rapid economic growth that has been achieved since the start of economic reform under the current, no less dictatorial, system. It seems that authoritarianism itself is a guarantee neither of economic stagnation nor of sustained economic progress. Much depends on the quality and the objectives of the rulers. One of the questions to be addressed in this book is: what is the underlying political economy of China's recent remarkable economic growth?

1.3 The Data

Should China's officially reported growth rate be believed? Is it not too good to be true? These questions have produced a vigorous academic debate in recent years, at times verging on the polemical because of the unwillingness of the National Bureau of Statistics (NBS) to explain in sufficient detail the sources, methods, and assumptions on which its estimates of GDP and GDP growth are based. Two scholars (Angus Maddison and Thomas Rawski) have argued that GDP and its growth have been overestimated at certain times. Another (Carsten Holz) has normally defended the official estimates.

The NBS faces two main problems in estimating China's total output. They are associated with China's rapid economic growth and its transition from a centrally planned to a market economy. One is the difficulty of recording the many new economic activities as they emerge; the other is the danger that administratively gathered statistics are distorted by reporting incentives. The former can lead to underestimation of output and its growth; it has been argued that the latter has led to overestimation.

Under central planning the problems of statistical reporting were particularly severe, partly because the administratively gathered statistics were inappropriate for the estimation of GDP and partly because the NBS was disbanded and statistical collection did not take place for several years during the Cultural Revolution (Maddison 2006). However, we concentrate here on the period of economic reform, from 1978 onwards. Maddison (1998) argued that the official estimate of real GDP growth between 1978 and 1995 (9.9% per annum) was too high, and estimated that the true figure was 7.5% per annum. The discrepancy (–2.4% per annum) was attributed mainly to an exaggeration of the real growth of industry and services owing to the use of too low a price deflator. Holz (2006a) criticized the basis of Maddison's revisions, a criticism which elicited a defence Maddison (2006) and a subsequent response (Holz 2006b).

In the mid-1990s there was a growing sense that local officials were falsifying the statistics that they reported, and that this led to an exaggeration of local growth rates. Many statistics still relied on the administratively based traditional reporting system. The authoritarian 'developmental state' placed great importance on achieving growth targets. This produced an incentive for local officials to overstate local economic performance in order to avoid criticism or gain promotion. Evidence consistent with this hypothesis was the fact that the sum of province GDPs reported by provincial branches of the NBS exceeded the national GDP that the central office of the NBS reported, being 19% higher in 2004.

The problem led the top leadership to take action in 1997: it instituted investigations of statistics gathering and warned of punishments for falsification. The problem should have declined after 1997, partly for this reason and partly because since 1996 the NBS has been moving from the system of administrative data collection towards one based on sample surveys and periodic census benchmarking. Nevertheless, Rawski (2001) claimed that GDP growth was greatly exaggerated in the period 1997–2001, explaining this in terms of incentives for false reporting and political pressures on the NBS. According to the NBS, real GDP rose by 35% over those four years; according to Rawski, the rise was no more than 11%. His test and revision were based on the expected relationships between GDP growth and the growth of certain variables that should bear a strong relationship with GDP growth, such as industrial energy use, air travel, and consumer prices. However, Holz (2003) was not persuaded by this revision, pointing instead to problems with these test variables, and Lin (2004) reconciled the evidence in terms of changes in the economy.

In 2006 the NBS undertook a benchmark revision of the GDP series from 1993 onwards, on the basis of the 2004 economic census, which covered industry and services. As a result the 2004 GDP was revised upwards by 17%, largely on account of a revision of value added in services. Thus, contrary to expectations, the revision validated the aggregated provincial GDP estimates and cast doubt on the previously reported national estimate. The revision raised the growth rate of real GDP over the period 1993–2004 from 9.4% to 9.9% per annum. However, Holz (2008) queried the accompanying upward revision of price deflators and calculated, therefore, that the revised growth rate might actually be underestimated by 0.8% per annum, in which case the true growth rate over this period would be 10.7% per annum.

In summary, there are good reasons to expect errors in the estimation of China's GDP and its growth. The economy has developed and evolved rapidly and the statistical services have had to develop and evolve rapidly to keep pace. The NBS is a much stronger organization now than it was at the start of economic reform. It is likely that there are inconsistencies in coverage and definitions over time, and it is possible that, initially at least, estimates of GDP growth in particular years were exaggerated. Much depends on the professionalism of the NBS leadership, and its ability, despite the opaqueness of its operations, to make reasoned and accurate adjustments to data when likely errors are perceived to arise.

Our reading of the literature leads us to conclude that China's GDP and its growth, as most recently revised, are probably not systematically biased upwards, and certainly not by a significant amount. China does indeed have a remarkably high rate of economic growth, which needs to be explained.

1.4 The Methodology

Economic growth is one of the most difficult phenomena for economists to understand. At the theoretical level, many models of economic growth are available as a framework for applied analysis. However, the models tend to contain a limited number of variables, and these are normally the proximate determinants of economic growth. They are probably not the underlying determinants. It might be necessary to go behind the proximate determinants if we are to understand why China has grown so fast. This could be particularly important in the case of a transition economy. In the movement from a centrally planned economy towards a market economy, many institutional variables are changing rapidly, in a way which would not be true of advanced market economies. Growth models are generally concerned to explain the outward shift of the production frontier. However, economic transition is likely to involve a movement towards the production frontier as well as an outward shift of the production frontier.

No single methodological approach on its own can explain something as complicated as economic growth. Accordingly, we adopt and encompass several approaches: economic theory, economic history, institutional evolution, and econometric analysis. We regard this as a particular strength of our contribution. It corresponds closely to what Rodrik (2003) has termed 'analytic narrative', that is, a country study which is explicitly informed and framed by growth theory and growth econometrics. However, whereas Rodrik's objective is primarily to improve our understanding of economic growth using the country analytic narrative as a backdrop and secondarily to understand the growth of the country being studied, our priorities are reversed.

1.5 Outline of the Book

We start by outlining the various approaches to explaining economic growth—theoretical models, empirical estimates, and non-economic considerations—that will frame our explanation of China's growth (Chapter 2). We then describe and explain the process of economic transition in China, the evolution of institutions and policies, and their interactions with the economic growth that the reforms unleashed (Chapter 3).

The framework provided by these two very different perspectives helps with the interpretation of the econometric analysis that forms the core of the book (Part II, Chapters 4–7). Chapter 4 places China in international perspective by estimating cross-country growth equations. Chapter 5 explains the econometric model which is used to examine the determinants of China's growth by means of cross-province growth regressions. Chapter 6 then explores the contributions of physical and human capital investment, and Chapter 7 the contributions of three forms of structural change which occurred as China reformed and developed: sectoral change from agriculture to industry, ownership change from state to private ownership, and change in economic openness as China engaged with the rest of the world. One of the proximate determinants of China's growth is the remarkably high investment rate, which itself needs to be explained. This is done in Chapter 8.

Economic growth on its own should not be accepted as a central goal of economic policy without an evaluation of its consequences. Part III considers some of the consequences of China's economic growth. Whereas China was a supreme example of a labour-surplus economy when economic reform began, an important issue—with implications for income inequality and poverty—is examined in Chapter 9: is China running out of unskilled labour? Income inequality rose rapidly over the period of economic reform: to what extent was this rise due to economic growth and the policies that generated growth (Chapter 10)? Chapter 11 explores a new topic for China, based on our own survey research: does economic growth raise happiness in China? Some other important consequences of rapid growth are discussed in Chapter 12.

In the concluding Part IV, Chapter 12 considers the prospect for China's continued rapid economic growth. It examines the various factors that might slow down the growth rate, including whether the current serious macroeconomic imbalances of the Chinese economy are sustainable and whether the social costs and adverse consequences of rapid growth will bring it to an end. Chapter 13 summarizes the argument of the book and draws the evidence together so that the whole can be greater than the sum of the parts. The importance placed on China's underlying political economy provides a unifying theme. The chapter appraises China's remarkable growth in retrospect.

Note

1. The earlier figures are taken from International Monetary Fund, *International Financial Statistics Yearbook*, and Taiwan, *Taiwan Statistical Yearbook*.

References

Acemoglu, Daron (2009), *Introduction to Modern Economic Growth*, Princeton: Princeton University Press.

Holz, Carsten (2003), 'Fast, clear and accurate: how reliable are China's output and economic growth statistics?', *The China Quarterly*, 173: 122–63.

——(2006a), 'China's reform period economic growth: how reliable are Angus Maddison's estimates?', *Review of Income and Wealth*, 52, 1: 85–119.

——(2006b), 'China's reform period economic growth: how reliable are Angus Maddison's estimates? Response to Angus Maddison's reply', *Review of Income and Wealth*, 52, 3: 471–5.

——(2008), 'China's 2004 economic census and 2006 benchmark revision of GDP statistics: more questions than answers?' *The China Quarterly*, 193: 150–62.

Lin, Justin Yifu (1995), 'The Needham puzzle: why the industrial revolution did not originate in China', *Economic Development and Cultural Change*, 43, 2: 269–92.

——(2004), 'Is China's growth rate real and sustainable?', *Asian Perspective*, 28, 3: 5–29.

Lucas, Robert E. (2002), *Lectures on Economic Growth*, Cambridge, Mass.: Harvard University Press.

Maddison, Angus (1998), *Chinese Economic Performance in the Long Run*, Paris: Development Centre of the Organization for Economic Co-operation and Development.

——(2006), 'Do official statistics exaggerate China's GDP growth? A reply to Carsten Holz', *Review of Income and Wealth*, 52, 1: 121–6.

Ravallion, Martin, and Shaohua Chen (2007), 'China's (uneven) progress against poverty', *Journal of Development Economics*, 82, 1: 1–42.

Rawski, Thomas (2001), 'What is happening to China's GDP statistics?', *China Economic Review*, 12: 347–54.

Rodrik, Dani (2003), 'Introduction: what do we learn from country narratives?', in Dani Rodrik (ed.), *In Search of Prosperity: Analytic Narratives on Economic Growth*, Princeton: Princeton University Press.

Smith, Adam (1776), *Inquiry into the Nature and Causes of the Wealth of Nations*, London: Dove (4th edn., 1826).

2

Approaches to Understanding Economic Growth

The objective in this chapter is to provide a framework for understanding the chapters to come. The reader is likely to be familiar with much of the material but, because the approaches are broad and varied, possibly not all of it. The chapter encompasses models of economic growth, empirical approaches to economic growth, the relationships between the literatures on economic growth and on economic development, and the relationships between economic growth and economic inequality.

2.1 Models of Economic Growth

Economic growth became a central concern of economists in the period after the Second World War. Starting with Harrod (1939), Domar (1946), Solow (1956), and Kaldor (1957), the initial emphasis was placed on the development of growth theory. This involved the construction of formal models using a small number of precisely defined economic variables in order to illuminate aspects of the growth process. There was little resort to empirical testing of the models other than by reference to a set of 'stylized facts' about growth.

This is not the place to set out the details of the different growth models: these can be found in the many textbooks on economic growth, development economics, and macroeconomics (for instance, Acemoglu 2009; Aghion and Howitt 2009; Jones 1998; Ray 1998; Romer 1996; and Ros 2000). However, it will be helpful to remind the reader of the questions, assumptions, and predictions of the various sorts of model as a guide to understanding the chapters to come.

The most influential of these early models was the so-called neoclassical, or Solow, model of growth (Solow 1956). Based on a conventional production function and thus on the assumption of diminishing returns to each factor of production, the model derived powerful conclusions. Starting from a low level of output per worker, saving and investment take place and the capital–labour ratio, and thus the output–labour ratio, rises. The economy experiences diminishing returns to capital: the marginal product of capital, and thus the market-determined rate of profit on capital, falls. The economy eventually reaches a long-run equilibrium level of output per worker. This level can be raised only as a result of technical progress, assumed to be set exogenously. In equilibrium, therefore, growth of output per worker is determined outside the model.

A prediction of the Solow model is that each economy will tend towards its own long-run equilibrium level of output per worker, and that those which are further away from their 'steady states' will grow faster. The implication is that there will be 'conditional convergence', that is, standardizing for differences in saving rate, depreciation rate, labour force growth, and rate of technical progress, economies will converge.

The speed of convergence makes a great difference to the way in which the model is to be viewed. Sato (1966), assuming 'plausible' values of the parameters and applying simulation methods to the neoclassical model, found that an economy might take generations to reach its stable equilibrium in response to a parameter change. Thus, analysis of the transition to steady-state growth might be more relevant than that of the steady state itself.

Two pieces of evidence contributed to dissatisfaction with the Solow model. One was the failure of economies in recent years to converge not only absolutely but also conditionally (summarized in Ray 1998: 74–84): the growth rates of different countries varied greatly. The other was the relative constancy of the output–capital ratio over time in many countries: diminishing returns to capital would lower the output–capital ratio unless there was precisely offsetting technical progress. The assumption that the rate of technical progress is exogenous to the model was also seen as a limitation. These considerations led to the development of a new wave of growth models based on assumptions that were regarded as more realistic. Having the property that the rate of growth of output per worker is determined within the model, they are generally known as endogenous growth models. There are three main (albeit overlapping) forms of endogenous growth model: relating to human capital, to technical progress, and to externalities.

We start with the first of these, explored by Lucas (1988) and others: the recognition that investment can take the form either of physical capital or of human capital. The complementarity between these two factors of production might help to keep up the ratio of output to physical capital in the process of economic growth, but there would still be diminishing returns to capital as a whole in the presence of a further factor of production, such as unskilled labour or land, unless it was in unlimited supply.

An early advance in dealing with technical progress was to recognize that much technical knowledge is embodied in capital goods: investment can thus be the vehicle of technical progress. This led to the development of vintage models of capital, in which technical knowledge is embodied in new plant and machinery and each successive vintage of capital involves technical improvement (Solow 1959; Kaldor and Mirrlees 1962). Romer (1990) placed emphasis on research and development as the determinant of technical progress. Human capital can be employed either in the production of goods or in the production of knowledge. Thus, the rate of technical progress depends on the level of human capital and the proportion that is employed in research and development activities. A distinction is made between the production of knowledge and its diffusion. The diffusion of new knowledge throughout the economy generates technical progress but, unless invention can be protected by property rights, early diffusion can blunt the incentive to invest in knowledge production.

Some growth models (for instance, Mankiw et al. 1992) contain the strong assumption that, on account of the diffusion of knowledge, technical progress occurs at the same rate in all countries. By contrast, Grossman and Helpman (1991) argued that technical progress is not the same in all countries owing to the different capacities of different countries to assimilate existing technologies. According to Romer (1993), ideas can be expensive to produce but cheap to use: the importance of such economies of scale can enable larger countries to grow faster.

The notion that positive economic 'externalities' (benefits to society as a whole which are not taken into account by individual decision makers) can play a role in economic growth has a long history, going back to Adam Smith (1776). Young (1928) argued that there exist economies of scale at the macroeconomic level which promote economic growth. The view that technological know-how and know-why are built up in the process of production itself was developed theoretically by Arrow (1962), with his notion of 'learning by doing', and empirically by Lall (1992), who examined the determinants of firms' technological capabilities. This sort of argument was formalized by Romer (1986), who treated technical progress as a positive externality generated by the total capital stock of the economy. The assumption is that there are constant or diminishing returns to scale for individual producers but increasing returns to scale for the economy as a whole. Through its effect on technical progress, capital accumulation can offset the effect of diminishing returns to capital and raise output per worker. Even if human capital is not formally employed in research and development activities, education can help people to produce new ideas. It is thus possible for the stock of human capital in the economy to generate externalities which raise the rate of technical progress.

Externalities can take the form of complementarities. If a person acts in a particular way, this can increase the incentive of others to act similarly. For instance, assume that the expected profitability, and thus investment, of each firm is raised by high investment in the economy as a whole. Moreover, if individual investment bears a non-linear relationship to the economy-wide anticipated investment rate—being insensitive at low and at high anticipated rates—there is the possibility of more than one self-fulfilling outcome. For instance, there can be one stable equilibrium in which investment is generally low and another stable equilibrium in which it is generally high (illustrated in Ray 1998: 114–16). Such forces open the possibility of vicious and virtuous cycles of investment and growth.

2.2 Empirical Approaches to Economic Growth

The improvement in the quantity and quality of growth-related data within countries and the increasing availability of multi-country data sets, together with advances in econometric methodology, have made possible, and indeed have invited, quantitative research on the determinants of economic growth within and across economies. A great many studies have appeared, using different methodologies and often obtaining divergent results. The diversity of conclusions about the causes of growth suggests that empirical growth research should be approached with caution albeit not scepticism.

Three main methodologies are used: growth accounting, estimation based on formal growth models, and open-ended growth equations. None is clearly superior to the others. Each has its strengths and weaknesses. Each is more appropriate for answering certain growth questions than are the others. It is possible that more can be learned by trying all three approaches than by adopting only one approach. We discuss each in turn.

Growth-accounting methodology, going back to Denison (1966), has been much used, although with varying degrees of sophistication. It is particularly helpful if the research objective is to estimate the contribution to growth of each of the factors of production, and of the residual contribution, known as 'total factor productivity' (TFP) growth, which is often equated with technical progress. However, growth accounting is open to three main criticisms. It requires the measurement of capital stock and capital consumption, and assumptions about the parameter which governs the contributions of each factor, often equated with its share of income. The residual need not represent technical progress alone or at all: it might be seen as 'a measure of our ignorance' (Abramovitz 1956: 11), including contributions from economies of scale, structural change, resource reallocation, and measurement error. It is arguable that technical progress and investment cannot be meaningfully separated: much technical progress requires embodiment in capital goods and new investment normally involves technical improvement (Scott 1989).

Structural growth modelling provides empirical tests of the theoretical models of growth, so indicating whether their simplifying assumptions are valid and illuminating of the growth process. However, the empirical specifications include only the variables contained in the theoretical models and generally exclude many variables that can have a causal effect on economic growth. The variables which are normally included may well be the proximate determinants, but they themselves may need to be explained in terms of the underlying determinants of growth. For this reason, even the seminal work by Mankiw et al. (1992) and the literature which it spawned can be seen as providing only a partial explanation of the growth process.

Initiated by Barro (1991), informal growth regressions possess the advantage over growth accounting and structural growth modelling in that they permit the introduction of explanatory variables which represent the underlying as well as the proximate determinants of growth. This is also their disadvantage: any plausible variable can be included in the regression equation. It raises the issue of 'model uncertainty'. Researchers are apt to include whichever variables they wish to investigate but to exclude other variables that are potentially important and which, if excluded, might bias the results. The required solution to this problem is the use of recently developed approaches to model selection, such as extreme bounds analysis, Bayesian model averaging analysis, and general-to-specific analysis.

Underlying all empirical approaches to explaining the determinants of economic growth is the need to establish that the explanatory variables in equations predicting the growth rate have a causal effect on growth and are not merely statistical associations. This is important both for understanding the true processes at work and for making proposals for policy interventions. The problem is that some of the explanatory variables may be 'endogenous', that is, determined within the system. The definition of an endogenous variable is that it is correlated with the error term in the equation. The correlation might arise because causation runs from the dependent variable to the explanatory variable in question or because one or more unobserved variables affect both the dependent and the explanatory variable.

There are various ways of addressing endogeneity in the context of economic growth. One is to look for 'natural experiments', such as the exogenous division of Korea into North and South. It is more likely in such circumstances that the causal effect of governance and institutions on growth can be established. Another is to analyse panel data and to eliminate 'fixed effects', that is, to discard the influence of the unobserved characteristics of countries or regions by examining how their growth rates and their observed explanatory variables change over time. Yet another is to find 'instruments' for the potentially endogenous explanatory variables, that is, to find variables that are well correlated with the explanatory variable but do not enter into the determination of economic growth. By predicting the endogenous variable using the instrument, it is possible to isolate exogenous variation in the endogenous variable and thus to identify its causal effect on the growth rate. Our data sets and growth equations lend themselves to the instrumenting of potentially endogenous independent variables by means of 'system generalized method-of-moments' (system GMM) estimation techniques (as developed by Arellano and Bover 1995; Blundell and Bond 1998).

2.3 Economic Growth and Economic Development

It is an important question: do the approaches to understanding economic growth that are described above apply equally to rich and poor countries? Most growth models have been formulated with advanced economies and analytical tractability in mind. Hicks (1965: 3–4) expressed doubt that the growth theory of the time was relevant to the economics of underdevelopment. As Temple (2005) noted, economic development involves a transition from one form of economy to another that is very different, and stylized growth models generally do not address such transitional issues.

A basic distinction between advanced and backward economies lies in the efficiency of resource allocation. In the former, resources are normally fully employed and market forces ensure that the returns to the factors of production tend to be the same across sectors. In the latter, there is often unemployment or underemployment of labour and large sectoral variation in the returns to the factors of production. This led Arthur Lewis (1954) to formulate a theory of economic development with surplus labour. Economic growth takes the form of the transfer of labour from the rural, agricultural, subsistence sector, where it is underemployed and can be withdrawn without the loss of output, to the urban, industrial, capitalist sector, where the wage is set at a subsistence level. Capital accumulation in the latter sector is governed by saving out of profits; it need not be subject to diminishing returns if more labour can be employed without opportunity cost. The withdrawal of rural labour eventually begins to raise the marginal product of labour and household income in agriculture, a process that is assisted by an improvement in the terms of trade between agriculture and industry, and urban wages begin to rise in response to market scarcity. The economy moves from the classical stage to the neoclassical stage of the development process. The economy becomes less dualistic and the fruits of economic development are spread more widely.

When Lewis (1955) published *The Theory of Economic Growth*, his book was neither about theory (in the conventional sense of the formal modelling of economic variables) nor only about economic growth (as opposed to the broader notion of economic development). The factors which figure prominently in most growth models of course appeared, but they were not the only players. No less weight was given to issues which growth theorists often take for granted. These included the will to economize, reflected in economic objectives and attitudes; economic institutions, involving the rights and freedoms which mould economic incentives; and issues of governance and government.

Like the classical economists such as Smith (1776), Lewis was willing to cross the conventional disciplinary boundaries in order to understand why and how economic growth takes place. By contrast, possibly in the pursuit of rigour and with stable advanced economies in mind, most growth theorists have tended to be narrow and 'economistic'. However, some economists, through a growing interest in the role of institutions and of political economy in the development process, have recently taken a more classical approach to explaining economic growth. The two sub-disciplines—economic growth and development economics—have moved closer together.

Research on economic development is increasingly engaged with questions of political economy, institutional structures, and forms of governance (for instance, surveyed in Adam and Dercon 2009). The reward structures facing economic actors play a part in shaping whether they undertake investment in technology, fixed capital, and human capital. The reward structures in turn are determined by economic and political institutions, such as contract enforcement, law and order, public infrastructure, corruption, and political resistance to economic change. When variables reflecting such issues are included in informal growth regressions, it is commonly found that 'institutions matter', and more so than geography or culture (for instance, Rodrik et al. 2004). They might be thought of as the underlying determinants of economic development; they have been referred to as 'the complex sociological tangle ... the residual of the formal economist's intellectual advance' (Toye 2007). It remains true, however, that 'the political economy of growth is in its infancy' (Acemoglu 2009: 874).

Is there a trade-off between economic growth and democratic institutions? Democratic competition might reduce corruption and improve the quality of economic policies but it might also generate pressure groups, policy deadlocks, and short-term electioneering. However, dictatorships, as well, have to appease various constituencies in order to remain in power. The empirical evidence fails to establish a robust relationship (Alesina and Perotti 1994; Aghion and Howitt 2009: ch. 17). There is huge variation in the economic quality of dictatorships—varying from kleptocracies to authoritarian 'developmental states'. The latter group has included East Asian states which, not content with just making market corrections, have intervened to 'govern the market', for instance in their stress on education and on promoting industrialization. Their growth-oriented policies might stem from external threats to the regime—as was arguably the case in South Korea and Taiwan (Amsden 1989; Wade 1990). Democracies tend to produce less extreme outcomes.

In principle, political instability can create economic insecurity and hence reduce investment and so also growth. Slow growth in turn can breed political instability, thus creating a vicious circle. This is more likely the poorer is the country as poverty appears to contribute to political instability. By contrast, Huntington (1968) has argued that social unrest can be fomented by rapid economic growth: aspirations are raised and new demands are generated. This is a particular problem if countries lack the institutions to cope with the structural and social transformation and social turmoil that often accompany economic growth. There is some cross-country evidence that political instability (as measured by indicators of country risk, such as risk of expropriation and lack of contract enforceability, rather than actual or attempted violent regime change) has a negative effect on both investment and growth (Knack and Keefer 1995).

Acemoglu et al. (2005) developed a theoretical and empirical case that differences in economic institutions are the fundamental cause of differences in economic development because they determine the incentives of and the constraints on economic actors. However, economic institutions are endogenous. There is generally a conflict over the social choices which mould institutions, ultimately resolved in favour of groups with greater political power. Economic institutions promote economic growth when the political institutions allocate power to groups with interests in broad-based property rights enforcement, when they create effective constraints on those holding power, and when there are relatively few economic rents to be captured by them.

In similar vein, Lin (2009) stressed government as the most important institution in a developing country: its policies shape the quality of other institutions and the incentive structure in the economy. However, he differed from Acemoglu et al. (2005) when he considered the relative importance of political pressures and ideology as determinants of government policies. Like Keynes (1935), he placed greater weight on ideas than on vested interests. Ideology provided his explanation of why unsuccessful 'comparative advantage defying' policies were generally pursued in the early post-war period; and also of why there was a drastic reversal of policies as the 'prevailing social thinking' swung towards the 'Washington consensus'—again often unsuccessful because insufficient regard was paid to the problems that had previously been created.

The potential importance of the state is well recognized in the economic development literature. The term 'developmental state', coined by Johnson (1982) to characterize Japan in the early post-war period, has been used to describe states which actively, resolutely, and successfully pursue economic growth. Some other East Asian countries have been placed in the same category, including South Korea and Taiwan. There can be differences among developmental states and over time in the degree of democracy or dictatorship, the nature and extent of state intervention in the economy, and the strength of industrial policy. However, they all share an overriding policy objective to achieve rapid economic growth by means of active state policies, and success in meeting that objective.

Political economy cannot be ignored. The motivations of rulers are important determinants of the pace of economic development. Whether a country is a failing state, is gripped by development-defying ideology, or is a developmental state matters a great deal. It is arguable that at different times in the twentieth century China experienced all three of these conditions. It is a recurrent theme of this book that during the period of economic reform China has been a developmental state.

2.4 Economic Growth and Inequality

There is a considerable literature—both theoretical and empirical—about the effect of economic growth on income inequality, and also about the effect of inequality on economic growth. There are reasons why income inequality is likely to increase as the economy grows. The transfer of labour from the larger, low-income, rural sector to the smaller, high-income, urban sector raises overall inequality in household income per capita, and this is accentuated if the urban sector has a more unequal distribution of income (Kuznets 1955). Change in the composition of the labour force towards more education can have the same effect (Knight and Sabot 1983). The nature both of the production function and of technical progress in the expanding urban sector can raise the returns to physical and human capital. Moreover, credit constraints tend to disequalize the ownership of these factors among households. The immaturity of markets involves great heterogeneity of the returns to the same factor across an undeveloped economy (Banerjee and Duflo 2005).

Income inequality may begin to fall at a higher level of income, so creating an inverse U-shaped relationship between income per capita and income inequality. The 'Kuznets effect' goes into reverse as the urban sector becomes predominant, and the greater marketization that occurs with economic growth tends to equalize the return to each factor throughout the economy. The socio-political changes that accompany economic development—including more democratic governance—may help to reduce inequality through government policy interventions.

The empirical testing of the causal effect of income level on income inequality shows the inverse U-shaped relationship to be weak or non-existent across countries (summarized by Ray 1998: 201–9). The relationship from growth to inequality might be better examined by means of country studies over time.

There are some reasons why income inequality can boost the rate of economic growth and other reasons why it can have a retarding effect. In classical accounts of economic growth it is only capitalists and rentiers who save (Eltis 2000: ch. 10). Thus, if labour receives only a small share of national income, this implies a high saving rate and so permits a high investment rate. The modern approach is to examine the household propensity to save at different levels of income: this may rise with income level. It is possible, therefore, that the national saving and investment rates increase as economic growth occurs.

19

An unequal distribution of income and wealth is likely to mean that many households lack collateral and are subject to credit constraints, and therefore cannot grasp opportunities for investment, whether in business or in education (for instance, Banerjee and Newman 1993). A high degree of inequality in a society might slow down growth by creating a demand for redistribution of income and wealth, particularly if it leads to socio-political instability that reduces business confidence and so deters investment, or if it is met by high taxation of marginal income (for instance, Alesina and Rodrik 1994).

The effect of inequality on growth has to be decided empirically. Cross-country studies suggest that the growth rate is negatively affected by the initial inequality of income and of wealth (summarized in Ray 1998: 220–3). Alesina and Perotti (1996) identified social discontent and socio-political instability as the channel through which this effect operates. It is likely, however, that the differences in history, natural resources, institutions, governance, and culture in each country are important in moulding these relationships, so that country studies are also required.

2.5 Looking Ahead

Economists should be humble in trying to explain a phenomenon as complex as economic growth in poor economies. After a comprehensive evaluation, Acemoglu (2009: 873) was driven to conclude that 'we are far from understanding the process of economic development and the structural transformation that it involves'. Nevertheless, the framework provided in this chapter is helpful in understanding the analysis to come.

The institutional Chapter 3 examines the processes by which economic governance and policies evolved over the period of economic reform. The cross-country analysis of Chapter 4 is based on the Solow model augmented by the introduction of both human capital and sectoral transfer. The cross-province analysis of Chapters 5–7 involves the estimation of informal growth regressions that contain as explanatory variables initial income level (as a measure of conditional convergence), physical capital, human capital (both as a stock, to proxy externalities, and as a flow), labour transfer from a low- to high-productivity sector, and proxies for institutional change. Chapter 8 considers why diminishing returns to capital have not damped down China's remarkably high rate of capital accumulation. Chapter 10 examines China's economic development within the framework of the Lewis model and enquires whether China is running out of surplus labour. Knowledge of the possible relationships between economic growth and economic inequality is required in Chapter 11, which asks why inequality has risen so rapidly in China.

There are various possible approaches to the study of economic growth in China. Each is helpful but none is sufficient on its own. For that reason, we make an attempt to combine economic theory, quantitative analysis, economic history, institutional analysis, and political economy. The hope is that the whole will be greater than the sum of the parts. The breadth of our approach is a distinctive feature of this book.

References

Abramovitz, Moses (1956), 'Resource and output rends in the United States since 1870', *American Economic Review*, 46, 2 (May): 5–23.

Acemoglu, Daron (2009), *Introduction to Modern Economic Growth*, Princeton: Princeton University Press.

——S. Johnson, and J. A. Robinson (2005), 'Institutions as the fundamental cause of long-run growth', in P. Aghion and S. N. Durlauf (eds.), *Handbook of Economic Growth, Vol. 1, Part A*, Amsterdam: Elsevier Science: 385–472.

Adam, Christopher, and Stefan Dercon (2009), 'The political economy of development', *Oxford Review of Economic Policy*, 25, 2: 173–89.

Aghion, Philippe, and Peter Howitt (2009), *The Economics of Growth*, Cambridge, Mass: The MIT Press.

Alesina, Alberto, and Roberto Perotti (1994), 'The political economy of growth: a critical survey of the recent literature', *World Bank Economic Review*, 8, 3: 351–71.

——————(1996), 'Income distribution, political instability and investment', *European Economic Review*, 40: 1203–28.

——and Dani Rodrik (1994), 'Distributive politics and economic growth', *Quarterly Journal of Economics*, 109, 2 (May): 465–90.

Amsden, Alice (1989), *Asia's Next Giant: South Korea and Late Industrialization*, New York and Oxford: Oxford University Press.

Arellano, M., and O. Bover (1995), 'Another look at the instrumental variable estimation of error-components models', *Journal of Econometrics*, 68, 1 (July): 29–51.

Arrow, Kenneth J. (1962), 'The economic implications of learning by doing', *Review of Economic Studies*, 29, 3 (June): 155–73.

Banerjee, Abhijit, and Esther Duflo (2005), 'Growth through the lens of development economics', in P. Aghion and S. N. Durlauf (eds.), *Handbook of Economic Growth, Vol. 1, Part A*, Amsterdam: Elsevier Science: 473–544.

——and A. Newman (1993), 'Poverty, incentives and development', *American Economic Review*, 84, 2 (May): 211–15.

Barro, Robert (1991), 'Economic growth in a cross-section of countries', *Quarterly Journal of Economics*, 106, 2: 407–43.

Blundell, R., and S. Bond (1998), 'Initial conditions and moment restrictions in dynamic panel data models', *Journal of Econometrics*, 87, 1 (August): 115–43.

Denison, Edward F. (1966), *Why Growth Rates Differ*, Washington, DC: The Brookings Institution.

Domar, Evsey D. (1946), 'Capital expansion, rate of growth, and employment', *Econometrica*, 14, 2 (April): 137–47.

Eltis, Walter (2000), *The Classical Theory of Economic Growth*, 2nd edn., Basingstoke: Palgrave.

Grossman, G., and Helpman, E. (1991), *Innovation and Growth in the Global Economy*, Cambridge, Mass.: The MIT Press.

Harrod, R. F. (1939), 'An essay in dynamic theory', *Economic Journal*, 49, 193 (March): 14–33.

Hicks, J. R. (1965), *Capital and Growth*, Oxford: Clarendon Press.

Huntington, Samuel (1968), *Political Order in Changing Societies*, New Haven, Conn.: Yale University Press.

Johnson, Chalmers (1982), *MITI and the Japanese Miracle: The Growth of Industrial Policy 1925–1975*, Stanford, Calif.: Stanford University Press.

Jones, Charles I. (1998), *Introduction to Economic Growth*, New York: Norton and Company.

Kaldor, Nicholas (1957), 'A model of economic growth', *Economic Journal*, 67, 268 (December): 591–624.

——and James Mirrlees (1962), 'A new model of economic growth', *Review of Economic Studies*, 29, 3 (June): 174–92.

Keynes, J. M. (1935), *The General Theory of Employment, Interest and Money*, London: Macmillan.

Knack, Stephen, and Philip Keefer (1995), 'Institutions and economic performance: cross-country tests using alternative institutional measures', *Economics and Politics*, 7, 3: 207–27.

Knight, J. B., and R. H. Sabot (1983), 'Educational expansion and the Kuznets effect', *American Economic Review*, 73, 5: 1132–6.

Kuznets, Simon (1955), 'Economic growth and income inequality', *American Economic Review*, 45, 1 (March): 1–28.

Lall, Sanjaya (1992), 'Technological capabilities and industrialization', *World Development*, 30, 2: 165–96.

Lewis, W. Arthur (1954), 'Economic development with unlimited supplies of labour', *The Manchester School*, 22: 139–91.

——(1955), *The Theory of Economic Growth*, London: George Allen and Unwin.

Lin, Justin (2009), *Economic Development and Transition: Thought, Strategy and Viability*, Cambridge: Cambridge University Press.

Lucas, Robert E. (1988), 'On the mechanics of economic development', *Journal of Monetary Economics*, 22, 1 (July): 3–42.

Mankiw, N. Gregory, David Romer, and David N. Weil (1992), 'A contribution to the empirics of economic growth', *Quarterly Journal of Economics*, 107, 3: 407–37.

Ray, Debraj (1998), *Development Economics*, Princeton: Princeton University Press.

Rodrik, Dani, Arvind Subramanian, and Francesco Trebbi (2004), 'Institutions rule: the primacy of institutions over geography and integration in economic development', *Journal of Economic Growth*, 9, 2: 131–66.

Romer, David (1996), *Advanced Macroeconomics*, New York: McGraw-Hill.

Romer, Paul (1986), 'Increasing returns and long run growth', *Journal of Political Economy*, 94, 5 (October): 1002–37.

——(1990), 'Endogenous technological change', *Journal of Political Economy*, 98, part 1: S71–101.

——(1993), 'Idea gaps and object gaps in economic development', *Journal of Monetary Economics*, 32, 3 (December): 543–73.

Ros, Jaime (2000), *Development Theory and the Economics of Growth*, Ann Arbor: University of Michigan Press.

Sato, K. (1966), 'On the adjustment time in neoclassical growth models', *Review of Economic Studies*, 33, 3 (July): 263–8.

Scott, Maurice (1989), *A New View of Economic Growth*, Oxford: Clarendon Press.

Smith, Adam (1776), *An Inquiry into the Nature and Causes of the Wealth of Nations*, London, Dove (4th edn., 1826).

Solow, Robert M. (1956), 'A contribution to the theory of economic growth', *Quarterly Journal of Economics*, 70, 1: 65–94.

——(1959), 'Investment and technical progress', in K. Arrow, S. Karlin, and P. Suppes (eds.), *Mathematical Methods in the Social Sciences*, Stanford, Calif.: Stanford University Press: 89–104.

Temple, Jon (2005), 'Dual economy models: A primer for growth economists', *The Manchester School*, 73, 4: 435–78.

Toye, John (2007), 'Solow in the tropics', University of Oxford, mimeo.

Wade, Robert (1990), *Governing the Market: Economic Theory and the Role of Government in East Asian Industrialization*, Princeton, NJ: Princeton University Press.

Young, Allyn (1928), 'Increasing returns and economic progress', *Economic Journal*, 38, 152 (December): 527–42.

3

The Evolution of Institutions and Policies

3.1 Introduction

Over three decades China has undergone a remarkable process of institutional and policy change. It has made the transition from being a centrally planned and controlled economy towards becoming a market economy—although the transition remains incomplete in several dimensions. It has been a process of evolution and gradualism, in contrast with the abrupt economic change, or 'big bang', that accompanied political collapse in the countries of the former Soviet Union. It has generally been one of evolving response—well described as 'crossing the river by feeling for the stones'—rather than the implementation of an articulated grand plan.

At the start of economic reform in 1978, China was gripped by an awful set of 'initial conditions'. The country was poor, overpopulated, and short of human capital and natural resources. The prevailing ideology was hostile to markets and opposed to radical reform. Institutions and policies were wholly inappropriate, giving rise to very inefficient incentive structures.

It would be naive for us to concentrate on the far bank of the river, that is, to judge the reform process against a best-practice set of institutions that would provide the rule of law, security of property, enforceability of contracts, and competitive markets. It is indeed unlikely that this was the goal that the initial reformers had in mind. A 'big bang' reform would have been economically disruptive and politically unacceptable. It is more relevant to examine how China went about crossing the river.

The crossing was gradual, exploratory, pragmatic, path dependent, and context specific. Transitional institutions were created and allowed to evolve as the economy changed and grew. The process was governed by three criteria: it had to start by tweaking the initial conditions; it had to be efficiency enhancing; and it had to be interest compatible, both for the Chinese Communist Party (CCP) and for groups which might otherwise obstruct the reforms (Qian 2003). We illustrate below how these criteria were met.

This chapter provides a brief economic history of the transition to a market economy in China. There are three main but related objectives. One is to go beyond the description of events and to consider the causal processes at work: how one reform and the economic response to it required yet another reform, and so on. The second is to examine how the process of transition interacted with the process of economic growth: how transition promoted growth and how growth in turn promoted transition. The underlying hypothesis is that a combination of institutional and policy changes and the economic responses placed China on a path of cumulative causation involving rapid economic growth. The third objective is to understand the political economy that underlay the reform policies.

We begin, in Section 3.2, with a brief account of the period of central planning. Section 3.3 examines the evolution of rural reform, and Section 3.4 does the same for urban reform. Section 3.5 considers those aspects of policies and institutions that relate to the economy as a whole. Section 3.6 examines the underlying political economy of the economic reform process. Section 3.7 draws conclusions about the relationships between policies and institutions, on the one hand, and economic growth, on the other hand, and explains how the results of this chapter will inform the analysis of later chapters.

3.2 Central Planning

The legacy left by China's command economy to its reform economy must be understood. The initial conditions affected all aspects of the reform process. When China embarked on its journey—one of 'crossing the river by feeling for the stones'—the riverbank that it left behind had a far-reaching impact on the crossing.

The rural sector

The rural and the urban sectors, being compartmentalized and separated except through the intermediation of the state (Knight and Song 1999), require separate discussion. We begin with the rural sector. On taking power in 1949, the CCP confiscated land from rich peasants and landlords and redistributed it to poor and landless households. The land reform of 1950–3 was enormously popular: it gave the state legitimacy and formed bonds of support for the new government. The subsequent gradual collectivization of agriculture therefore encountered no serious resistance from the majority of peasants. The apparent success of this collectivization and the need to extract more agricultural surplus for industrialization emboldened the leadership to go further and to establish people's communes. All factors of production were collectively owned, private plots of land were abolished, and households were remunerated less according to their work and more according to their need.

Simultaneously, the leadership embarked on a 'Great Leap Forward'. Poor management of the communes, the leadership's exhortation to produce 'backyard' iron and steel, the lack of individual incentives to work the land, and three successive years of bad weather resulted in a rural crisis. It is estimated that as many as 45 million (8.2% of the rural population) died as a result of the ensuing famine (for instance, Dikötter 2010: 333). The famine raged for three years without public recognition that it was occurring. Even the leadership, being fed exaggerated reports of commune production, were initially ignorant of the calamity. Comparing the Indian and Chinese famines, Dreze and Sen (1989: 210–15) attributed the disaster partly to the CCP's monopoly of power and control of the press. The brunt of the famine was borne by the peasants: the state procurement of food grains was not reduced. It is unclear how far this was due to deliberate protection of urban-dwellers and how far due to exaggerated harvest reports at a time of ideological fervour.

The remaining years of the Maoist era were characterized by the social upheaval of the 'Cultural Revolution' of 1966–76, and by an emphasis on self-reliance for the communes. The high mandatory targets for grain production and the stress on local self-reliance on grain meant that the benefits of producing high-value crops and of local specialization in farming activities were lost. Nevertheless, various technological improvements were made in agriculture: the irrigated area rose from 30% of cultivated land in 1952 to 45% in 1978, there was increased use of electricity and of chemical fertilizer, and high-yielding seed varieties spread rapidly (Lin 1994: 36–8).

Despite these advances, agriculture performed badly during the period of the communes. The state failed to solve the problems of incentives, monitoring, and supervision (Lin 1990). According to Wen (1989), total factor productivity in agriculture was lower in 1977 than it had been in 1952. Farm output did little more than keep up with the growth of population. For instance, the availability of grain per person in the country as a whole rose by only 0.4% per annum over the period 1952–78 (Knight and Song 1999: 32).

It is possible to give an economic interpretation to the thrust of rural economic policy during the period of central planning. The leadership gave priority to rapid urban industrialization, and saw the rural sector as the source of marketed and investible surplus for that industrialization. Farmers have incentives to produce more and to market more of their produce if prices are raised. However, the state relied on coercion rather than incentives to secure the harvest. It introduced compulsory procurement of peasant output at low prices and imposed collectivization to acquire greater control over the surplus. This 'price scissors' policy kept down agricultural prices in relation to industrial prices, so permitting lower wages and higher surpluses in the state-owned industrial sector (Knight 1995; Knight and Song 1999: ch. 7).

However, this economic interpretation is narrow and incomplete. Politics, not economics, was in command. There was extreme politicization of economic decision making, with extensive use of simple directives and slogans, and replacement of economic criteria by ideological values. The formation of the communes provided political and social control, and enabled the leadership to pursue political objectives such as egalitarianism and collective rather than individual behaviour and way of life.

Although initially voluntary, collectivization became coercive. Probably with the creation of the communes in 1958, and certainly with the disastrous Great Leap Forward that ensued, the partnership between the state and the peasants dissolved. Peasant dissatisfaction swelled during the Cultural Revolution but without serious consequences for the state. The state was unusually strong and rural society was unusually weak: organizations that might compete with government—such as clans, private companies, and religious organizations—did not exist.

The urban sector

The new government took over many factories but initially allowed the private sector to continue. However, a radical policy shift in 1955–6 brought an abrupt move to public ownership, and the urban private sector was extinguished. China now had a 'command economy'.

In the period of central planning, the primary objective of economic policy was rapid urban industrialization. China's leaders followed the Soviet model. The planners neglected labour-intensive industrial sectors suitable for China's abundant labour supply, and instead gave priority to heavy industry such as metals, materials, and chemicals. Production was to meet domestic demand: this was to be inward-looking industrialization. In contrast to the successful East Asian economies of that period, there was no attempt to exploit opportunities for light manufactures or for exports.

A system of central planning was set up. The planners issued commands that assigned production targets to enterprises and directly allocated both factors of production and produced inputs to them. Prices were used not to direct resource allocation but to channel resources to government and to heavy industry. The state-owned enterprises (SOEs) had very little autonomy: they could not adjust their labour forces, nor could they retain any of their profits. Market performance did not drive investment decisions: the banks were merely intermediaries between the planners, responsible for allocating funds, and the enterprises. The CCP strengthened control over the SOEs through its power over managerial careers.

The government adopted a system of bureaucratic allocation of labour and of administered wages (Knight and Song 1999: ch. 2). The huge pre-liberation wage differences were greatly reduced. After the wage reform of 1956 only minor differences were permitted in the national wage scale. Egalitarianism ruled, and the productive characteristics of workers were not rewarded. Especially during the Cultural Revolution, 'brain workers' were paid no more than 'hand workers'. At that time, the need for material incentives was played down, and premiums and bonuses based on work performance were abolished. Wages were unrelated to labour allocation.

After 1957 the state labour bureaux exercised a virtual monopoly over the allocation of urban labour. The initial assignment to a job was very important: the first job was often the last. Job rights were fully entrenched. The security and dignity provided by employment were regarded as valuable ends in themselves. Almost all state employees, and many employees of large collectives, enjoyed an 'iron rice bowl'—lifetime tenure of the job at a relatively high wage in an enterprise providing a mini welfare state. The workplace (*danwei*) was normally responsible for the housing, pensions, and medical treatment of its employees, and often provided other social services as well.

The state was concerned with the socio-political consequences of urban unemployment. Its treatment of rural migrants contrasted starkly with its treatment of urban-born workers. Rural–urban migration was very strictly controlled and restricted: only particular categories of rural workers, such as university graduates or retired soldiers, were allowed to settle in the cities, and even temporary rural–urban migration ('floating') was in general not permitted over much of the central planning period. It was effectively prevented by the payment of rural people according to the work point system (keeping workers in the commune) and the monopolized state distribution of food and other living requirements only to registered urban residents (so excluding rural people from the cities).

Administrative labour allocation encouraged overmanning. Under pressure to alleviate urban unemployment, the state labour bureaux expected work units to accept labour beyond their economic requirements. The need to provide employment generally diminished the incentive to use it more efficiently and thus to raise labour productivity.

3.3 Rural Reform

We divide the discussion of rural economic reform into two parts: the initial, sharp, and momentous changes in the period 1978–85, and the slower, more gradual changes that occurred after 1985.

The initial reforms, 1978–1985

The sector most urgently requiring reform was the long-stagnating farm sector. Agriculture had become the bottleneck: rapid growth of the economy could not be achieved without an acceleration of agricultural growth. However, continued coercion of the peasants was rejected. It was conceived both to have failed and to be politically dangerous. We examine three aspects of the 1978–85 rural reforms: the restoration of household production, the reform of marketing to create price incentives for production, and the development of enterprise and markets.

The initial reforms, announced in 1978, involved a shift from heavy to light industry in order to provide 'incentive goods', a raising of farm prices to provide production incentives, and a lowering of the level of the commune accounting unit, again to provide incentives. The rural reforms rapidly outstripped these measures. The peasants interpreted them as a signal that change was possible, and the reform initiative passed from the state to the peasants. They pushed the reforms further than they were meant to go. They were permitted to do so because the new goal of economic growth effectively increased peasant power.

This was not organized power; the peasants were not a pressure group. They took the initiative through individual, atomized behaviour. Because state policy had been uniformly imposed, they responded in identical ways in overwhelming numbers but as unorganized individuals. Both poor peasants (who were hungry) and rich peasants (whose consumption was capped) wanted to take advantage of the new political climate. They acted in concert. The rural reforms were that rare economic event, a 'Pareto improvement', benefiting almost all rural people. The national leadership appeared to lose control of the pace and nature of reform.

In many regions of China the peasants led the state in the creation of family farms. Spontaneous experiments were permitted in the initiating provinces (Anhui and Sichuan); in some other provinces (such as Hubei) the experiments involved secrecy and conflict. Peasants throughout much of China were attracted to family farming because it seemed to offer higher incomes, security, and independence. Village cadres sensed a new confidence in peasants, and experienced peasant hostility if they failed to uphold peasant interests: they often colluded with the peasants.

The move to the household production unit proceeded very rapidly because farmers found that it was economically successful. The institutional change from the collective system to the 'household responsibility system' raised total factor productivity (TFP) growth in agriculture (Lin 1992). Also, the new incentives for farmers to invest also meant that mechanical power was sharply increased (Naughton 2007: 263). Decollectivization thus had a dramatic, albeit a once-for-all, effect on farm production and income. The household responsibility system, first officially banned and then tolerated, had by the mid-1980s become official policy, to be followed uniformly throughout China.

On the one hand, the reform leaders dared not risk the uncooperative hostility of the peasants; on the other hand, political caution was required. This was partly to gauge the economic success of the experimentation, and partly because there were cracks in the reform coalition—factional and bureaucratic rivalries. The reformers could not mobilize constituencies within the state apparatus strong enough to initiate bold agricultural policy changes (Kelliher 1992: 71–5).

The state introduced two main pricing reforms: higher procurement prices from 1979 to 1981, and the easing of mandatory procurement in 1985. Peasants responded to the price incentives by increasing production and switching away from grain to the more profitable crops. A free market price for extra-quota production developed, which, except in bumper years, was normally above the procurement price. 'Contract purchasing' was introduced in 1985, by which government would negotiate purchase prices before each planting season, and which established a dual system in which some sales were governed by the market and others by the state.

The privatization and marketization of rural China was a process of cumulative causation which government could not control. When one aspect of economic life was reformed, gains in efficiency were impeded unless other aspects of economic life were allowed to follow. Consider four aspects: land tenure, credit, labour, and entrepreneurship.

Land was allocated on a leasehold basis to households within each village normally according to the number of household members. The initial short-term contracts were replaced in 1984 by leasehold contracts of fifteen years or more. This was a necessary consequence of the need to provide incentives for long-term farm investments. Gradually peasants came to treat their land as private property: the need for farm credit and off-farm employment opportunities caused them to lease it, rent it, hire labour to work it, and to use it as security for loans. Local communities were allowed to work out their own solutions to the need to transfer land among households; in many cases such transfers involved payment of rents. Nevertheless, the evolution of markets for land, in particular, was a long and drawn-out process. It was held back by the insecurity of land property rights.

Once the household became the production unit it was inevitable that capital and labour markets would follow. The inadequacy of the official financial system in providing credit to farmers caused a private credit market to spring up. The state tacitly accepted this development, despite the high rates of interest charged on unsecured loans. Similarly, a market for hired labour emerged, in response to the needs of private businesses for labour and of poor, underemployed peasant households for employment.

When the restraints on non-agricultural activities were relaxed a new entrepreneurial class began to form. Many of the new entrepreneurs were former cadres. They were in a good position to take over the former collective enterprises, and through connections they had access to credit, information, and telephones.

Other new business people were young and relatively well educated. The state aligned itself with the new entrepreneurial class partly to promote rural development and partly to retain its power. A new social basis of power was needed because of the widespread indifference of rural people to the CCP. The state targeted the economic leaders—entrepreneurs and successful farmers—who had the greatest stake in the reform policies. The party welcomed them into official positions, so that economic leaders tended also to be the political leaders. Their influence over the villagers was strengthened through patron–client relationships (Oi 1989: ch. 9).

The backdrop to this period was high underemployment, albeit disguised, and rapid growth of the population and labour force. With little unutilized arable land available, this growth of population posed a severe threat to living standards. Nevertheless, the institutional changes produced a sharp improvement of the lot of rural-dwellers. Agricultural production grew by more than 6% per annum, and there was a remarkable growth in employment in township and village (TVE) enterprises: from 28 million to 79 million over the seven years (16% per annum) (Knight and Song 1999: 40). The dynamism of the TVE sector reflects the unleashing of previously pent-up entrepreneurial talent and the initial market disequilibrium that stemmed from the planners' neglect of light manufactures.

Gradualist reforms, 1986–

We trace the evolution of policy towards the rural areas as it affects farm prices and production, farm land markets, rural industry, and rural–urban migration. In the 1980s urban ration prices were well below procurement prices. As the average producer price rose, so the cost of food subsidies given to urban workers also rose. Urban food subsidies escalated to exceed 10% of government budget revenue in 1985 (Knight and Song 1999: 37). The phasing out of mandatory procurement required increases either in the prices or in the subsidies of urban food consumption. Government was dependent on the urban state-owned and collective enterprises for much of its revenue, and therefore needed to keep those workers contented (Lin 1994: 62). The state accorded priority to urban people because 'any display of discontent on their part is far more dangerous to the regime than localized peasant uprisings, easily dispersed by the authorities' (Aubert 1990: 28). Accordingly, in 1985 the decision was taken to avoid further increases in agricultural purchasing prices (Ash 1993: 32), a decision that was more or less adhered to until 1991. For a few years after 1985 agricultural production grew more slowly.

With the urban population subdued after the massacre of civilians in 1989, it was safer to raise the urban selling prices of grain. In 1992, the government ended the subsidy on grain. The dual system continued but grain procurement shrank rapidly and the state purchasing prices approached market prices. The gradual withdrawal of government from the market for food was facilitated by the rapid increase in urban real wages in the 1990s. By the year 2000 the transition to competitive product markets for food was essentially complete. The trade liberalization of agricultural markets required by China's accession to the WTO in 2001 had important implications. It enabled China to specialize within agriculture according to its comparative advantage, for instance importing more bulk, land-intensive cereal products and exporting more labour-intensive horticultural products.

Because there was no formal land register and property rights remained unclear, the development of land markets was slow. In the late 1990s, when government policy became more favourable to migration and also to comprehensive marketization, policy makers turned their attention to improving the efficiency and volume of land rental markets. This culminated in legislation in 2003 which made property rights clearer. Land registers were to be built up and villagers were instructed to sign new land contracts with thirty-year lease terms. Rental markets grew, especially in the commercialized coastal provinces.

The rural population of China peaked in the mid-1990s. Between 1995 and 2008 the rural population fell by 138 million (16%) (NBS 2009: 89). This was partly due to the effect of the one-child family policy, introduced at the start of economic reform, and partly to urbanization. The institutions were now in place to facilitate the consolidation of plots as village populations declined. Indeed, the new institutions reduced the opportunity cost of migration and so accelerated the outflow of rural people—especially of young people, many of whom turned their backs on farming. It had become easier also to rationalize landholdings in pursuit of economies of scale and greater specialization in crop production.

Despite the potential economic benefits of according formal ownership rights—strengthening incentives to make long-term investments in the land and assisting farm consolidation—China's leaders remained unwilling to privatize farm land. Guaranteed access to land provides security for rural households. It enables surplus labour to be absorbed with least economic hardship and least political instability.

Between 1978 and the mid-1990s the township and village enterprises (TVEs) were the most dynamic part of the economy. In this experience, China is probably unique among developing countries. Whereas employment in TVEs was 28 million in 1978, it was 140 million in the temporary peak year 1996 (NBS 2009: 113). In addition to the contribution that the TVEs directly made to economic growth, they played a driving role in China's economic reform. The entry of TVEs provided competition for the state-owned enterprises (SOEs) and urban collective enterprises (UCEs). They brought prices into line with costs. They challenged, competed away, and dissolved the industrial monopoly held by the state sector, which had to become more efficient to survive. Thus, TVEs drove forward the process of marketization in the economy as a whole.

Several factors account for the remarkable success of rural industrialization. The initial opportunity arose from the artificial conditions that were being imposed on the economy. Whereas the urban areas continued to be rigidly controlled throughout the 1980s, rural enterprise was relatively uncontrolled, being outside the planning system. Of crucial importance was the fact that TVEs faced factor prices that reflected China's factor endowment. Wage costs were about one-half of those in SOEs, and capital—with funding available only at market rates of interest or at the high opportunity cost of internally generated funds—was expensive. However, credit constraints were eased by the rural credit cooperatives that expanded rapidly as rural household savings rose, and these institutions lent a high proportion of their funds locally. Reflecting their choice of both products and production methods, the labour–capital ratio of TVEs was nine times that of SOEs. Rural industry was concentrated in coastal and suburban areas which provided a reasonable infrastructure and access to markets, including much sub-contracting from SOEs. TVEs were initially very profitable: they were able to fill the market niches—mainly light consumer manufactures—that had been neglected by the planners, and—sometimes with enterprise, knowledge, and finance from Hong Kong and the Chinese diaspora—to export unskilled-labour-intensive manufactures in which China's factor endowments provided a comparative advantage. Thus, they shared the monopoly rents of SOEs in some activities and earned high profits in the product markets that contained unsatisfied consumer demand.

The institutional framework was favourable. The decentralization of economic powers to local governments gave local governments incentives to raise revenues by owning, encouraging, and taxing local economic activities. The profitable opportunities were to be found in industry rather than agriculture. In 1985 Chen Yun complained that 'No industry, then no money' had overwhelmed the adage 'No grain, then no stability' (Hua et al. 1993: 180). Local governments were not only supporters of TVEs but normally the de facto owners. Because state taxes of TVEs were low and profits high, local governments were able to raise 'extra-budgetary revenue'. Local governments were willing to act as guarantors of TVEs, so giving them a degree of access to bank funding, but this represented a form of insurance from the community rather than the creation of soft budget constraints. Unlike the state sector, there was organizational diversity—private households (e.g. Wenzhou), government ownership (backward areas), true worker cooperatives (Sunan), and foreign ownership (the Pearl River delta)—varying across different areas to suit local conditions.

Originally the sector was called the TVE sector because there was much township or village involvement. The distinction between the local government ownership and private ownership is unclear because local government ownership might simply be nominal—private ownership remained ideologically unsafe—or local governments might own shares in private firms. National ideological constraints were relaxed over the 1990s, and the taboos against private business were gradually lifted. It became politically easier for townships and villages to privatize their enterprises. Whereas public ownership initially protected and fostered rural industry, changes in the economic environment reduced its benefits and increased its costs. There was a gradual process of privatization which became dramatic after the mid-1990s.

By the mid-1990s the supernormal profits of the 1980s had been competed away, and the rapid growth of the sector came to an end. As a result of the economic reforms in urban China, TVEs faced tougher competition from urban firms, both the reforming SOE sector and the new private sector. More powerful incentive systems were required to reward TVE managers. As markets developed, the supportive and protective role of local governments became less important. The stronger market for managers encouraged their full or partial ownership of the enterprise. Very often the transfer of ownership involved 'insider privatization'.

The structure of rural industry changed in the 2000s—becoming technologically more advanced, achieving economies of scale, developing industrial clusters, and extending inter-regional markets. These changes, and the improvement in incentives and efficiency resulting from privatization, allowed the rural industrial sector to grow; employment in the sector reached 182 million in 2008 (NBS 2009: 113).

During the commune period the state constructed an 'Invisible Great Wall' that divided rural and urban China, a wall that was maintained but became more permeable during the reform period. Rural–urban migration grew in importance with economic reform. The phenomenon can be viewed either from a rural or an urban perspective: here we explore the former.

There are two forms of migration in China, which must be clearly distinguished. There is *hukou* migration, which is permanent, and non-*hukou* migration—known as 'floating'—which has normally been temporary. Permanent migration was, and still is, controlled through the residence registration (*hukou*) system. Any change of residence registration required official approval. The main ways for a rural person to get registered urban status are to acquire higher education, retire from the military, or have farmland taken over for urban use. Since possession of a *hukou* gives entitlement to local resources, there is an incentive for local governments to exclude outsiders from their resources. This was more important in the early years of economic reform, when food rationing and food subsidies were still in place, than in the later years. Permanent movements between rural localities are somewhat more easily permitted than movements from rural to urban areas and particularly to the big cities. Restrictions on *hukou* migration remain in place. If rural people have a choice, the choice is normally between remaining in the village and migrating out on a temporary basis.

Rural households might prefer temporary to permanent migration because it ensures that a household retains the economic security (access to farmland and house land) and the close social ties provided by the village. However, temporary migration also serves public policy. Urban settlement poses a greater threat to social stability than does temporary urban residence: an economic downturn would mean that many of the unemployed could be returned to and absorbed into the rural economy. Moreover, the rural supply price of a single temporary migrant is likely to be lower than that of a permanent migrant household: the abundant supply of cheap temporary migrant labour has been conducive to rapid urban economic growth.

3.4 Urban Reform

Only in the mid-1980s, when the major rural reforms had been made, did government turn seriously to urban reform. The initial objective was to reduce the inefficiency of the, then ubiquitous, state sector. We examine two related aspects of urban reform, the state-owned enterprises and the urban labour market.

Enterprise reform

China has become the industrial workshop of the world in just three decades of economic reform. Between 1978 and 2008 industrial production grew on average by 11% per annum. Industry has been transformed from being a state-owned enterprise sector at the heart of the centrally planned command economy to becoming an increasingly corporatized and privatized enterprise sector subject to widespread product market competition. We examine the various institutional and policy changes that lay behind this transformation and provided the incentives that made it possible.

Under central planning, the SOEs were multifunctional units in a hierarchical bureaucracy. Managers had little autonomy and low reward. Their task was to fulfil plan targets and tend to their workplace (*danwei*) community, and their incentives to achieve efficiency in production were weak. Industrial reform can be divided into two stages, distinguished by a crisis that occurred in the mid-1990s.

The first stage involved only minor and gradualist reforms within the existing system. Initial SOE reform comprised increasing product market competition both from the rapidly expanding TVE sector and from within, and increasing managerial autonomy and incentives. One form that the greater autonomy took was the introduction of the dual price system, which permitted enterprises to sell their marginal production at market prices. The dual price system had the political advantage that producers could face efficient incentives at the margin without resistance from the planning bureaucracy. China could in that way 'grow out of the plan' (Naughton 1995). One form of the stronger incentives was the rise in the proportion of enterprise profits that could be retained for discretionary use, from under 10% about 1980 to over 50% about 1990. However, industry remained state owned and largely state controlled.

Two developments lay behind the later, more radical institutional reforms of the SOE sector. One was the perceived need to make managers more accountable as they acquired more discretionary powers. The enactment of the Company Law of 1994 was crucial. It provided a legal framework for corporatizing SOEs. Once an SOE was a corporation it could diversify its ownership and could even be privatized. The Company Law also created a common legal framework for the different ownership forms, so helping to level the playing field on which they competed. The ownership structure of Chinese industry changed remarkably. In 1985 the SOEs accounted for 65% of industrial output, the collective sector, comprising TVEs and urban collective enterprises (UCEs), for 32%, and other firms for only 3% (NBS 1999: 36). In 2008 (when the distinctions among ownership forms had become blurred), SOEs and solely state-funded corporations accounted for 13% of industrial output, jointly owned corporations (normally having state participation and control) 18%, domestic private enterprises 27%, foreign enterprises 30%, the collective sector 2%, and others 10% (NBS 2009: 487). The 2008 distribution actually understates the importance of the private sector and TVEs as it includes only enterprises with revenue above ¥5 million.

Under central planning the SOEs had been highly profitable. This was achieved by means of the planners' 'price scissors' policies—keeping food prices and thus industrial wages down and industrial prices up—and by the lack of product market competition (Knight 1995; Knight and Song 1999). The second main reason for more radical industrial reform was the declining profitability of the state-owned sector in the face of intensifying product market competition. Competition became possible among SOEs under the dual price system, as well as with TVEs. For instance, a survey conducted by the World Bank in the mid-1990s found that over 90% of SOEs reported having complete autonomy in selling, production, and purchasing, and over 75% in pricing their products (OECD 2002: 165). The profitability of the SOE sector collapsed. In 1985 the profits of state-owned industries were 19% of the net value of fixed assets, and the losses of the loss-making enterprises (LMEs) represented 4% of the profits of the profit-making enterprises (PMEs); in 1995 (the worst year) the corresponding figures were 4 and 49%, respectively (Knight and Song 2005: 24). Having been 8% of GDP a decade before, the profit of state industry was then little more than 1% (Naughton 2007: 305).

The state was forced to act, both to protect its dwindling revenue and to provide the funds required to maintain high investment and rapid economic growth. Many SOEs were closed down and many were privatized. 'Overmanning' had previously been permitted and even encouraged by governments preferring to keep unemployment disguised in the factories rather than open on the streets. The remaining SOEs were now required drastically to reduce their employment levels. Between 1995 and 2000, employment of 'staff and workers' (corresponding to permanent employees) in the combined SOE and UCE sector fell by 34%, and employment in manufacturing 'urban units' fell by 40% (NBS 2009: 14, 26–7). Since some of this fall might have been due to ownership reclassification, it is helpful also to consider the number of workers retrenched. By the end of 2000, the gross figure for the accumulated laid-off workers exceeded 60 million, representing 40% of the staff and workers who had been at risk (Knight and Xue 2006: table 6). Local governments owned most of the SOEs that were closed or privatized. Central government held onto its large SOEs in the protected and profitable sectors such as energy, communications, armaments, and natural resources.

During the 1990s an important strategic decision was made for China to enter the World Trade Organization (WTO). Accession took place in 2001 but years of prior preparation and negotiation were required. The trade regime had to be liberalized and foreign direct investment welcomed. There is evidence that the decision was taken in order to force the pace of urban economic reform, so that China could both comply with the requirements for WTO membership and compete successfully against foreign competition (Branstetter and Lardy 2008: 650).

With profits and government revenue down, SOEs and state-dominated corporations had increasingly to turn to the state-owned banks (SOBs) for finance. Despite the new discipline imposed by the product market, there was an expectation that the banks would support loss-making SOEs or corporations under state control. The spur to managerial efficiency was blunted by the expectation and the experience of soft budgets, and by the government's willingness to write off bad debts of SOEs and SOBs as the number of non-performing loans (NPLs) mounted. Only in the 2000s did budgets begin to harden.

Economic reform measures were often interrelated and complementary. The new wave of enterprise reforms in the late 1990s was assisted by other reforms, including bank reform, labour market reform, social security reform, and housing privatization. The latter three reforms were necessary for the traditional Chinese *danwei* to discard its non-core function of providing a mini welfare state for its worker community.

Despite the improvement in managerial incentives for efficiency, corporate governance in the part of the industrial sector that continued to be under state control remained inadequate (Naughton 2007: 319–23). Market-based oversight was weak because stock markets played a limited role. Control-based oversight was ineffective because of weak monitoring by banks and potential conflicts of objectives between the overseeing bodies and the CCP. Product market competition continued to be the main constraint on managerial behaviour. Enterprise reform remained incomplete, so providing scope for further improvements in the productive efficiency of Chinese industry.

Labour market reform

Under central planning, China did not possess a 'labour market'. Instead there was a bureaucratic system of labour allocation and wage determination. The early labour market reforms involved granting greater managerial autonomy in matters of employment, for instance, abandoning the system of labour allocation, allowing real wages to rise, introducing performance-related wage incentives, and permitting more temporary migration according to the excess demand for urban labour as the demand for workers outpaced the urban-born labour supply.

An urban labour market was not swept into being by a process of cumulative causation of the sort that had characterized the rural reform process. Urban reform was impeded by the systemic nature of the problem: reform of one aspect required consistent reform of other aspects. For labour market reform to be successful, there had also to be concurrent reform of, for instance, enterprise management, housing, social services, pensions, and unemployment insurance. A worker losing a job had to give up much more than the job: he lost the mini welfare state provided by the *danwei*. This made workers reluctant to quit, and employers reluctant to dismiss them. Attempts to achieve a more flexible labour market would meet resistance from urban workers unless interrelated problems were solved together. Urban reform required a strategic plan for making the transition 'across the river', with many stones being felt for at the same time.

In the mid-1990s the important decision was made to reform the SOEs and to force mass redundancies. This effectively required the creation of a labour market. The Labour Law of 1994 was a landmark because it attempted to provide a framework within which the labour market could operate. The distinction that had been made earlier between 'permanent' and 'contract' urban workers now became important: only the former were eligible for *xia gang* redundancy payments. Labour market forces were felt by particular sections of the urban labour force—new entrants and retrenched workers—whereas permanent workers who kept their jobs were protected from the market. The great majority of new entrants found employment in the non-state sector, where market forces operated more freely (Knight and Song 2005: 24). Market forces cannot influence wages unless labour is mobile or potentially mobile. Labour mobility across employers grew but did so only slowly. A survey of urban workers in 1999 found that 78% of respondents had held only one job and a further 16% two jobs (Knight and Song 2005: 136). Nevertheless, the emerging labour market pressures raised the Gini coefficient of wage inequality among urban *hukou* employees, from 0.24 (adjusted for comparability) in 1988, to 0.33 in 1995, and to 0.37 in 2002. Similarly, the returns to the productive characteristics of workers, such as education, rose over time, and they rose by more in the more marketized coastal provinces. However, growing wage segmentation by ownership form, by enterprise profitability, and by province suggests that labour market reform remained incomplete (Knight and Song 2008).

Until the mid-1990s the *danwei* carried the administrative and financial burden of urban social welfare, and these arrangements tied workers to their employers. The new principle then introduced was that the employer, the employee and the state should share financial responsibility for social protection, that the funds should be pooled and administered at provincial, prefectural, or city level, and that the system should be extended beyond the state sector. The process of transfer to the new principle began in the mid-1990s, with the reforms proceeding at different paces in different areas and aspects. These included unemployment insurance, health care, pensions, and housing. For instance, the sale of public housing was sanctioned in 1994, and this popular development proceeded so rapidly that eight years later 80% of urban households owned their own houses.

Governments at various levels permitted the orderly inflow of rural–urban migrants to fill the increasing number of residual jobs available for them in the urban areas. However, the residence registration (*hukou*) system remained in place. It was therefore very difficult for migrants to become permanent urban residents, especially of the larger cities. This policy helped China to avoid the growth of urban poverty and slums that is characteristic of many developing countries. Thus, government might well have perceived it as a way of providing protection against social instability. Nevertheless, the continued treatment of rural *hukou* holders as second class citizens in the cities—placing them at a disadvantage in access to jobs, social security, education for their children, and housing—has been a source of discontent among them.

3.5. Economy-Wide Reform

We consider five reforms that applied to the economy as a whole: the reform of the legal system, educational policy, financial policy, fiscal policy, and the trade regime.

Law reform

An efficient market system requires that economic agents be confident of a reasonable return on their investments and of the reliability of their business agreements. In many economies this is achieved through the rule of law—governing property and contracts. China began its transition to a market economy without the rule of law, and yet it managed to grow rapidly. What is the explanation for this puzzle?

Under central planning, government direction, supervision, and conflict resolution was all-important: the state provided economic agents with the confidence and security that their limited autonomy required. However, as the economy 'grew out of the plan' and became more marketized, the need emerged either for the legal institutions commonly found in market economies or for functional substitutes. Clarke et al. (2008) argue that the substitutes were more important than the law. Confidence came from the social relationships (*guanxi*) that are important in Chinese society and help to create trust, and from the state's focus on economic growth objectives. There was an implicit political guarantee of property and contract rights that arose from the incentive system facing local officials.

A legal system nevertheless gradually grew out of the system of administrative directions. There was a need early on to bring regularity to government operations, which suffered from particularistic bargaining, for instance between SOEs and their superior bodies. As the market economy and the private sector developed, so the need for legal regulation grew. For instance, a contract law (1981 and 1999), a company law (1994), a policy declaration of rule according to the law (1999), and an expropriation and compensation law (2004) were introduced as and when the need became compelling. It is arguable that the law followed rather than led the market (Clarke et al. 2008: 399).

It remains the state's view that the legal system is a tool of governance and control. The courts are not independent of government at different levels (Clarke et al. 2008: 395–6). China has managed to grow rapidly despite having a legal system which emerged and evolved only in response to economic growth and transition, and which remains imperfect and merely complementary to alternative ways of ensuring business confidence and investment.

Educational policy

Even in a well-functioning market economy there are reasons why education cannot safely be left to the market. The long-term investment nature of educational expenditure and the inability to use the resultant human capital as security for a loan produce underinvestment—all the more so in poor countries. Government expenditures or subsidies are required.

Government was largely responsible for educational provision and funding under central planning. Despite impressive progress in the provision of primary education in the command economy, by the census year 1982 only 1% of the population aged 15 and over possessed tertiary education, 10% upper middle and 24% lower middle schooling, 31% primary schooling, and 34% no formal education (Naughton 2007: 196). The comparable figures for 2008 were 7%, 14%, 41%, 31%, and 7% respectively (NBS 2009: 100–1). The stock of educated adults changes more slowly than the flow: in the 2000s the policy objective of universal enrolment in basic education (nine years, corresponding to primary plus lower middle school) had been fairly widely achieved, even in poor rural areas (Knight et al. 2009).

A remarkable expansion of tertiary education commenced in 1999. In 1998 tertiary enrolment was 3.4 million and in 2008 it was 20.2 million (NBS 2009: 795). The fact that the additional supply of tertiary places was met by a corresponding demand, despite declining subsidies for students, indicates the high private value placed on education in China. The explanation is partly cultural but also economic. Whereas 'brain workers' were paid no more than 'hand workers' under central planning, the private return on a year of education rose from 3.6% in 1988 to 7.2% in 2002 as market forces were increasingly felt in the urban labour market (Appleton et al. 2005).

Various educational problems remain, particularly in rural China where (until the mid-2000s) fiscal decentralization gave rise to an educational poverty trap involving both the quantity and quality of education (Knight et al. 2009, 2010). Nevertheless, the emphasis placed by both the government and the people of China on educational investment over the reform period created a human capital infrastructure for sustained economic growth.

Financial reform

Under central planning, China's financial system was simply the state banking sector. This in turn merely provided trade credit: investment was decided by the planners and funded by the government budget; the banks simply served as conduits for this funding. The financial system has lagged behind the rest of the economy in the transition process. It continues to be dominated by the banking sector. This in turn remains heavily protected and regulated, and is largely under state ownership or control. The banks under the state have given preference to the state sector, so requiring other firms to rely mainly on retained profits or informal sources of funds for their investments. Stock markets exist but remain hobbled by governance and transparency problems.

There are several reasons why the financial sector has lagged behind. One is that the banking system was used to ease the process of transition and to keep it on track. Bank finance propped up loss-making SOEs, so protecting their employees. A further reason for the banks' continued inefficiency was their lack of banking skills and business orientation. Yet another was their political subordination: some projects were funded for political reasons. Non-performing loans burgeoned; in the late 1990s they accounted for 40% of total loans. The banks were technically insolvent, and 'woefully unsuited for the demands of a sophisticated market economy' (Naughton 2007: 460).

In 1998 government began to recapitalize the state banks, setting up state-run asset management companies which bought the banks' bad debts at face value and auctioned them at low prices. The proportion of NPLs fell over the 2000s, but mainly because government had assumed much of their bad debts. The bailout weakened the incentive for the banks to reform. The main reasons why banking efficiency began to improve was the entry of new banks and the greater competition that this produced, and a reduction in political interference on lending.

The continuing inadequacy of the financial sector presents a puzzle: how could China's economy invest so much and grow so rapidly without a modern financial system? The answer provided by Allen et al. (2008) is that the financial system has done enough not to slow down the growth of the non-state sector, largely because informal financial channels have filled the gap. In particular, the (fastest-growing) private and hybrid sectors funded their investment through retained profits.

Fiscal reform

Under central planning, the SOEs did nearly all the saving. They handed over their profits to the government, which planned and carried out most of the investment. This represented a transfer within the state sector, for which a tax system was largely irrelevant. The state budget (whether revenue or expenditure) represented 34% of GDP in 1978. However, this proportion fell consistently, to a trough of 11% in the crisis years 1994–6.

The fiscal erosion had several causes. A profit retention policy for SOEs, which was intended to strengthen their incentives to be efficient, was introduced in the 1980s, and the retention rate rose over time. The emerging non-state sector largely escaped taxation, and its growth therefore reduced revenue as a proportion of GDP. Increased competition from TVEs and among SOEs reduced SOE profits and thus taxable capacity, and forced government to subsidize loss-making SOEs. Under the system in which local government collected taxes and transferred much of the revenue to central government, local governments lacked incentives to collect revenue unless they would benefit; this became a problem as central government control was loosened.

Sweeping changes were made to the tax system in 1994 in response to the fiscal crisis. The revenue-remittance system, which had worked in the command economy, was replaced with a more conventional one. Different taxes were assigned to central and local government, tax sharing was introduced on a formulaic basis, and new taxes—such as value added tax on all enterprises—were introduced. The restructuring of intergovernmental fiscal relations raised the central government's share dramatically, so increasing its power both economically and politically. The new tax system gradually raised public revenue as a proportion of GDP, reaching 18% in 2005.

Nevertheless, local governments retained fiscal incentives to raise revenue by promoting local economic growth: they were entitled to the revenue from some taxes and to share the revenue from others. They also retained 'extra-budgetary funds', for instance levies and fees for local public services. The proliferation of such taxes in rural China, some apparently unjustified, was a source of peasant discontent. In the 2000s central government reduced the scope for rural revenue raising and it increased transfers from higher to lower levels of government, for instance by abolishing agricultural tax and introducing free rural basic education. These moves can be seen as part of the new policies for a 'harmonious society'.

Trade reform

China's command economy was one of the most closed economies in the world. The ratio of trade (exports plus imports) to GDP was less than 10%. There was a centrally controlled foreign trade monopoly and an inconvertible currency. The domestic economy was isolated from the world economy, and any goods that were traded had to be repriced. China then enjoyed few of the potential gains from trade. Yet in the 2000s China achieved a degree of openness that is exceptional for such a large country and economy. The ratio of trade to GDP exceeded 58%. Being labour abundant, land scarce, and capital scarce, China's ability to exploit its comparative advantage through trade had produced a great economic benefit.

How was this transformation achieved? There was a gradual sequencing. The first step was to liberalize export processing while maintaining protection of domestic markets. Four 'special enterprise zones' for export processing were set up at the start of economic reform. The national trading system was liberalized in 1984, and the overvalued yuan was depreciated. A dual exchange rate system was introduced, with production outside the plan receiving a depreciated, market-driven exchange rate. Trade was de-monopolized: there were twelve trading firms in 1978 but 800 in 1985 (Branstetter and Lardy 2008: 635). However, the system of tariffs and non-tariff barriers still protected domestic production against imports: the average nominal tariff was 43% in 1992.

In the mid-1990s the leadership took the momentous decision to prepare China for WTO accession. China began to liberalize trade in order to meet the stringent conditions for WTO membership. Tariffs and non-tariff barriers were dramatically reduced, and the exchange rate was unified. In 1999 the nominal tariff rate was down to 17%, and in 2005—four years after WTO accession—it had reached 9% (Naughton 2007: 391). By 2001 35,000 companies were permitted to engage in foreign trade (Branstetter and Lardy 2008: 635).

3.6 The Political Economy of Economic Reform

The origins of reform

Among the successes of central planning was the high investment rate that had been achieved: gross fixed investment as a proportion of GDP averaged 27% in the decade prior to reform. Industry grew rapidly but the concentration on heavy industry—often capital intensive and technologically demanding—meant that much of that investment was used inefficiently. Another success was the provision of socialized consumption—basic education and basic health care—in both town and countryside, well in advance of other poor developing countries (Knight and Song 1999: chs. 4, 5).

Against these successes, there were several failures. The system of central planning involved much obvious microeconomic inefficiency. This was apparent in all areas of the economy, not least in the organization of production and the use of labour. At the macroeconomic level, the various attempts that had been made to speed up development had produced overshooting, and in each case the economy floundered. There was virtual stagnation of real private consumption. In 1977 real wages of urban workers were 103% of their 1952 levels (Knight and Song 1999: 45). Takahara (1992: 62, 66) describes widespread unrest among urban workers in the years 1975–7, reflecting grassroots discontent at the long stagnation of real wages. According to Kelliher (1992: 9), 'despite Mao's lifelong dedication to peasant interests, the government eventually became all but deaf to peasant complaints of deprivation'. By 1978 discontent was widespread in the countryside. The growth of industrial employment was not rapid enough to reduce the extent of underemployment, which continued to grow and was an overwhelming feature of both rural and urban China.

In his later years Mao Zedong was a great obstacle to China's economic development. On his death in 1976 the way was open for a change in policy. There was a reordering of objectives from the political to the economic. The new leadership, under Deng Xiaoping, was intent on economic reform. There were three likely reasons.

First and foremost, the loss of political legitimacy during the years of economic stagnation, the Great Leap Forward, and the Cultural Revolution required an improvement in living standards to restore and solidify political support for the CCP. It was necessary to promote economic development in order to provide a new form of legitimacy for the regime. Failure to reform would mean economic stagnation, social tension, and political decline.

A second consideration was new awareness of the West's prosperity and of the greater success of some East Asian countries, including Taiwan, Hong Kong, and South Korea. If they could achieve rapid economic growth by harnessing the market and pursuing outward-looking, open economy policies, might not China also become more successful if it were to move towards similar policies?

Third, the trauma of the Cultural Revolution had the effect of weakening the capacity for central planning, so that an initial attempt after Mao's death in 1976 to restore growth by means of an ambitious ten-year plan rapidly floundered. It led to the decision (at the Fourth Plenum of December 1978) to adopt a new, albeit yet uncharted, economic policy.

The fact that the system concentrated discretionary power at the top provided the scope for at least gradual reform. The leadership embarked on two important reform programmes: not only economic but also political reform, that is, reform of state and party. As early as 1980, Deng Xiaoping called for reform of the leadership system towards greater professionalism through the use of educational qualifications, cadre training, and an incentive system that rewarded the achievement of state objectives and involved performance evaluation in career promotion.

Over the years, the party and state bureaucrats and SOE managers were moulded to meet CCP objectives, to which the achievement of economic growth was central (Naughton 1995). By these means administrative reform kept pace with economic reform. Not only did the bureaucracy normally not hold back economic reform but also it was often willing and able to lead economic reform.

The processes of reform

Unlike the former Soviet Union, China underwent economic reform with only this minor political change. Also unlike the former Soviet Union—where drastic economic reform followed swiftly on drastic political change—China embarked on gradual, step-by-step economic reform. Reform proceeded by a series of positive feedback loops, so enabling the reform leaders both to consolidate their power and to push the reforms forward. How was this achieved?

Given that the leadership now gave the highest priority to the achievement of economic growth, it had to ensure that the economic transition from plan to market would be politically possible. It was necessary to manage the major redistribution of power and funds involved in economic reform (Shirk 1993). The groups that stood to benefit from the reforms had to be motivated and the groups that stood to lose had to be made ineffective. Various institutional changes were needed to alter the incentives of bureaucrats so as to favour acceptance, even pursuit, of economic reform.

The reform leaders needed to build up a reform coalition. They developed their powers of patronage, which stemmed from the hierarchical control over much of the economy and from the *nomenklatura* system of official appointments. Increasingly, officials' remuneration and promotion were dependent on their fulfilment of the reform objectives. As market opportunities were created, access to the new sources of income could be made available through patronage. There is evidence that the incentive system did indeed promote growth. Li and Zhou (2005) found for the period 1979–95 that the promotion of top province leaders depended on the growth success of the province over their period of tenure. Similarly, the development of local fiscal powers to retain revenue (initially through the growth of 'extra-budgetary revenue') provided incentives at all levels of local government to promote local economic development. Again, there is some supporting empirical evidence. Jin et al. (2005) found that in the decade 1982–92 the 'contractual revenue retention rate' of provincial governments was positively associated with faster development of the non-state sector and more reform of the state sector.

In the early years reform was assisted by a decentralization of decision making and a transfer of powers to local officials and managers, so producing lower level patronage relations within the hierarchical system via 'particularistic contracting'.

This web of patronage enabled officials to obtain loyalty and support from subordinates in exchange for advantageous contracts. The early introduction of the dual-track pricing system had the virtue of avoiding opposition from planners and managers and yet harnessing the market for improved resource allocation.

Another facilitator of the reform process was gradual political institutionalization, that is, movement towards a system governed by rules, clear lines of authority, and collective decision making (Shirk 1993). Over the reform years the CCP developed a sophisticated system of decision making, succession, and cadre promotion. This institutionalization was functional for economic growth (Yao 2010).

One of the benefits of gradualism was that policy makers could learn from experimentation and experience. Another was that economic actors had time to adapt to markets and to change their attitudes. For instance, SOE managers learned to cope with new market competition and to find ways of benefiting from market opportunities. The growth of the non-state sector drew resources away from SOEs. Not only did non-state managers themselves have stronger profit incentives but also their competition strengthened the incentives of SOE managers.

Naughton (2008) distinguishes two distinct political periods. In the first (1978–93) power at the top was fragmented. There were many 'veto players' who could protect their constituencies, so making reform difficult. This was the period of 'reform without losers': policy had to follow a narrow and unopposed path.

At the end of the first period, SOEs and urban workers remained protected and were still untouched by economic reform. By the second period (from 1993 onwards), many of the revolutionary elders had died off. Power was now less fragmented. Policy making could become more decisive, and reform-related costs could be imposed on some of the losing groups. Moreover, the emerging mid-1990s crisis facing the SOEs and government revenue and threatening to stop rapid economic growth forced bolder action upon the leadership.

A broad process of comprehensive reform was initiated. It was necessary to tackle several problems together, for instance the reform of SOEs, urban workers, social security, migration, government revenue, the foreign exchange rate, and trade. The absence of any one of these reforms had the potential to make some of the others ineffective. The reforms were assisted by a feedback loop: the more rapid growth of output and government revenue that they produced made it easier for the state to compensate the losers. The reforms and their success developed new and expanding patronage resources for the CCP, and broadened the reform coalition.

Why was reform successful?

He and Yao (2009) pose the fundamental question underlying our account of the process of economic reform and institutional change. Why did Chinese leaders manage not only to adopt but also to maintain growth-oriented policies whereas many other developing countries have not done so? The authors argue that a socially unequal society often contains elite groups having overwhelming economic and political advantages, and that government is likely to form an alliance with the elites. They attribute underdevelopment in some societies to their unequal social structures. By contrast, in a socially equal society, no group has overwhelming advantage over the others, so that rebellions or revolutions by the unfavoured groups become credible threats if government favours some groups. It is more likely to produce a 'disinterested government'—one which does not represent the interests of particular social groups and is not captured by any social groups.

The authors attribute China's economic success to having a disinterested government. During the second period of economic reform, the CCP resisted the pressures which arose when economic reforms hurt particular interest groups. The reason for this was the social equality that had been inherited from the period of central planning, despite the economic failures of that dark time. The egalitarian social structure and the absence of social classes that the reform leadership inherited reduced the incentives of the CCP to rely on narrow support to maintain its power. The party aligned its own interests with, and tied its hold on power to, economic growth.

He and Yao (2009) provide examples to show that the CCP has resisted pressures from social groups. These interest groups might emerge as a result of the reforms and might then stall further reform. As an example they cite the dual track pricing system which, by permitting free market prices for production beyond the plan quota, provided market incentives at the margin without dismantling the planning apparatus. However, the existence of two prices unintentionally created opportunities for rent seeking by those with access to supplies at the lower quota prices. A powerful bureaucratic group emerged with an interest in maintaining the partially reformed system. Nevertheless, the leadership continued with the marketization process, which eventually competed away the rents arising from the dual track system.

A second example cited is the reform and privatization of the SOEs. Both involved heavy initial labour redundancies while disguised unemployment was eliminated from firms. The support of the urban working class was put at risk. The authors interpret the government's handling of this issue as reflecting its determination to continue with economic reform while introducing policies to assist the laid-off workers and relying on economic growth to provide them with alternative employment in the longer term.

The authors are at their most contentious when they discuss the existence of the rural–urban divide—so large as to make China an international outlier. They suggest that differential productivity—for instance, strong agglomeration effects favouring city development—is more important than differential political power as the explanation for the divide. They recognize that the lack of democracy enables government to ignore the numerical predominance of the rural population, but point to the 'harmonious society' policies introduced, albeit belatedly, to promote rural development. In criticism of the disinterested government hypothesis, this unfavoured majority group was surely too weak to be a 'credible threat' (in the terminology of the authors). Moreover, it can be argued that the relative lack of political power of the rural majority was functional for China's rapid economic growth.

The interpretation in terms of disinterested government underplays the role of dictatorship as opposed to democracy. China's authoritarian rule was functional for the implementation of the pro-growth policy of the reform period. The political strength of party and state avoided the potentially growth-retarding effects of popular pressures for redistribution that are often felt in more democratic societies. Government was able to take a longer-term view than is generally possible in democratically governed societies. Authoritarian rule is not a guarantee of fast economic growth, as China's earlier history under the CCP reveals, and democracy is not a guarantee of slow economic growth, as India's recent history illustrates. However, authoritarian rule combined with overriding growth objectives undoubtedly helped the Chinese economy to grow rapidly after 1978.

Stalled transition?

The underlying political economy has had adverse as well as favourable effects. It is arguable that in the process of concentrating so exclusively on economic growth the government distorted the economy in various ways and aggravated structural imbalances (Huang 2009; Yao 2010). We return to this issue in Chapter 12 in our consideration of the prospects for China's future economic growth. Here we consider the corollary argument, attributed to Huang (2009), that the concentration on policies to promote growth has stalled the transition to a market economy. In essence it is that there has been asymmetry in China's reform of product and factor markets, and that the reform of factor markets involves a trade-off between growth and other economic objectives.

Apart from a few remaining cases of price regulation—such as oil, gas, and electricity—product markets are now fairly free of state intervention. The tradeable sector has become sufficiently important for international prices—along with the exchange rate—to be influential in the determination of many goods prices. Except for certain oligopolistic industries still mainly under state ownership and control—such as energy, communications, and banking—product markets are now fairly competitive. By contrast, factor markets remain undeveloped, regulated, and distorted. Huang (2009) attributes this to the state's overwhelming growth objective. Consider each factor market in turn.

Although urban *hukou* workers are not effectively unionized, the factory operatives among them generally receive wages that are above the market-clearing level. For instance, Knight and Li (2005) and Knight and Song (2008) found evidence that enterprises shared profits informally with urban *hukou* workers. Although the *danwei*-based social security provision was dismantled, it was replaced by employer contributions to broader, sometimes city-wide, schemes which ensure that urban formal sector employees generally enjoy social welfare coverage. On average the cost of such schemes adds at least a third to payrolls (Huang 2009: 11). The situation faced by rural–urban migrant workers is very different. They are prevented by the state's household registration (*hukou*) system from competing effectively with urban workers: there is a segmented urban labour market. The wages of rural–urban migrants are governed primarily by market forces. Being normally short-term employees on one-year contracts, they are generally not covered by social security provision: their payroll cost to employers would otherwise rise substantially. The growth of the urban economy in recent years has relied heavily on an increasing number, and proportion, of rural–urban migrants. The household registration system has helped to maintain the practice of temporary migration, or 'floating'. As long as the influx of rural–urban migrants is into relatively unskilled jobs requiring little training, the system—however inequitable—is economically efficient and growth enhancing.

The capital market remains distorted. China has a 'repressed financial system' with regulated interest rates, credit rationing, and government influence on credit allocation. Financial intermediation remains highly dependent on the banks, in particular the large state-owned or state-controlled banks (SOBs), which are still saddled with non-performing loans (NPLs). The formal sector, and in particular the SOE sector, has preferential access to credit, and smaller private firms are neglected. The repressed financial system was functional in promoting high investment and growth when the urban economy was dominated by SOEs, but it no longer serves the purpose of promoting rapid and efficient growth— nowadays growth is rapid despite the financial repression (Allen et al. 2008). The timidity of the reform measures so far might be explained by the need to protect the vulnerable SOBs.

Land is owned by the state in the cities and by the local community in the countryside. Agricultural and unutilized land requires government approval if it is to be reclassified for industrial use. There is no market price involved if land is sold for industrial use: the price is normally set by government departments. In order to attract investment, it is common for local governments to underprice land for sale or use. This is one of several subsidies offered in the competition to attract industrial development to a locality.

Although not a primary factor of production, the environment is utilized in production and can thus be viewed as an input into the production process. China has introduced a series of environmental laws and regulations but their enforcement has been weak because governments have prioritized economic growth. The pollution of air, water, and land is a visible result of China's economic growth. Since producers generally do not fully compensate for the damage they do to the environment, their production costs are lowered and short-term growth is promoted. However, long-term growth is endangered.

For illustrative purposes, Huang (2009: 15–6) made a very rough estimate of the costs of distorted factor markets, by converting them into production subsidy-equivalents. These include the non-payment of social welfare contributions for rural–urban migrant workers, the sale of farm land for industrial use at below market price, the rise in interest rates that would result from financial market liberalization, the lower domestic price in relation to the international price of oil, and an official estimate of the cost of uncompensated environmental damage. On that basis the production subsidy-equivalent amounts to 7% of GDP. This subsidy-equivalent can be seen as the consequence of the overriding priority that has been given to economic growth objectives. The subsidy policies that are used to promote economic growth come at a cost to society in the form of worsened income distribution, especially for rural households, and deteriorated environment.

3.7 Conclusion

When the Chinese economy was centrally planned, institutions and policies were inefficient both in a static and a dynamic sense. Economic growth was achieved only through rapid, enforced capital accumulation, mainly in heavy industry. The incentive structure was very weak and unsuited for the transition to a market economy. Transition proceeded slowly and experimentally, departing gradually from the initial conditions. It was governed by two criteria: the reforms had to be efficiency enhancing and they had to be interest compatible. The underlying political economy was therefore important to the process. The fact that government gave the highest priority to economic growth was crucial.

There were two ways in which institutions and policies could be reformed. One was through an initial policy stimulus generating an economic response, which in turn generated a policy response, thus setting in train a process of cumulative causation. This describes well the rural reform that took place between 1978 and 1985 and the early urban reform that improved the efficiency of the state sector without changing the system. The other way was by means of simultaneous and complementary strategic reform measures designed to overcome the problem of systemic equilibrium. This describes the urban reform that took place in the new economic and political circumstances of the decade after 1993.

The three stages of economic reform can be illustrated in a simple diagram (Figure 3.1). On the horizontal axis is an index of economic reform (m) (with the

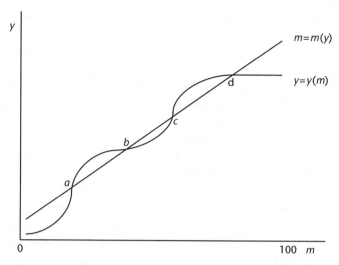

Figure 3.1 Relationships between economic reform (*m*) and economic growth (*y*)

transition from a planned to a market economy varying from 0 to 100%). The vertical axis measures output (*y*). Although the policy objective is growth, rather than level, of output, the analysis is clearer using level and standardizing for the exogenous determinants of growth. The effect of successful reform in encouraging further reform is depicted by the curve *m* = *m*(*y*), here assumed to be a linear relationship. The effect of reform on output is depicted as *y* = *y*(*m*). The crucial assumption is that it is non-linear, for reasons to be explained.

There are four equilibrium points: *a*, *b*, *c*, and *d*. Points *a* and *c* are unstable equilibria, and points *b* and *d* are stable. We start at point *a*, the politically imposed central planning condition. A marginal reform, moving the economy to the right of *a*, generates greater output, which in turn encourages more reform, and so on: the economy moves by a cumulative but piecemeal process to a new equilibrium at *b*. This analysis describes the rural reforms of the period 1978–85 and the early urban reforms 1985–93.

Marginal reform beyond *b* is unsuccessful: the induced increase in output is insufficient to generate more reform and instead there is a reversion to point *b*. The problem is akin to 'the theory of the second best' in welfare economics, according to which the removal of one market distortion is not necessarily welfare improving in the presence of other market distortions. In our case, owing to the systemic nature of the reform problem, one reform is unsuccessful unless it is accompanied by certain related reforms. Successful reform at this stage requires a non-marginal transition to point *c* or beyond. This analysis corresponds to the broad and strategic urban reforms of the decade after 1993.

Beyond *c* the reform process continues until point *d* is reached. The curve *y* = *y* (*m*) is assumed to be horizontal at *d*. Output is now maximized: transition to a fully marketized economy requires a reweighting of the social welfare function by introducing other objectives as well as output. This analysis illustrates the possibility that the transition to a fully marketized economy is currently stalled.

Consider how the arguments and conclusions of this chapter will be drawn upon in subsequent chapters. Chapters 6 and 7, which deal with cross-province growth regressions for China, introduce some of the variables discussed above and measure their contribution to China's growth. These include human capital, ownership change, trade liberalization, and labour market change. In explaining the determinants of the investment rate in Chapter 8, we examine how institutional reform, substitutes for legal rights, and confidence in government growth objectives and policies contribute to China's high investment rate. In Chapter 12, which considers whether China's high growth rate is sustainable, we draw on the institutional and political analysis of this chapter to examine whether China's 'developmental state' might come to an end. The underlying political economy of China is the common thread that runs through the book.

References

Allen, Franklin, Jun Qian, and Meijun Qian (2008), 'China's financial system: past, present, and future', in Loren Brandt and Thomas Rawski (eds.), *China's Great Economic Transformation*, Cambridge and New York: Cambridge University Press.

Appleton, Simon, Lina Song, and Qingjie Xia (2005), 'Has China crossed the river? The evolution of wage structure in China', *Journal of Comparative Economics*, 33, 4: 644–63.

Ash, Robert F. (1993), 'Agricultural policy under the impact of reform', in Y. Y. Kueh and Robert F. Ash (eds.), *Economic Trends in Chinese Agriculture*, Oxford: Clarendon Press.

Aubert, Claude (1990), 'The agricultural crisis in China at the end of the 1980s', in Jørgen Delman, Clemens Østergaard, and Flemming Christiansen (eds.), *Remaking Peasant China*, Aarhus: Aarhus University Press.

Branstetter, Lee, and Nicholas Lardy (2008), 'China's embrace of globalization', in Loren Brandt and Thomas Rawski (eds.), *China's Great Economic Transformation*, Cambridge and New York: Cambridge University Press.

Clarke, Donald, Peter Murrell, and Susan Whiting (2008), 'The role of law in China's economic development', in Loren Brandt and Thomas Rawski (eds.), *China's Great Economic Transformation*, Cambridge and New York: Cambridge University Press.

Dikötter, Frank (2010), *Mao's Great Famine: The History of China's Most Devastating Catastrophe, 1958–62*, London: Bloomsbury.

Dreze, Jean, and Amartya Sen (1989), *Hunger and Public Action*, Oxford: Clarendon Press.

He Daxing and Yang Yao (2009), 'Equality, the disinterested government, and economic growth: the case of China', China Center for Economic Research, Peking University, Working Paper Series No. E2009004, June.

Hua Sheng, Zhang Xuejun, and Luo Xiaopeng (1993), *China: From Revolution to Reform*, London: Macmillan.

Huang, Yiping (2009), 'China's great ascendancy and structural risks: consequences of asymmetric market liberalization', Peking University, China Center for Economic Research, Working Paper No. E2009003, June.

Jin Hehui, Yingyi Qian, and Barry Weingast (2005), 'Regional decentralization and fiscal incentives: federalism, Chinese style', *Journal of Public Economics*, 89, 9–10: 1719–42.

Kelliher, Daniel (1992), *Peasant Power in China: The Era of Rural Reform, 1979–1989*, New Haven: Yale University Press.

Knight, John (1995), 'Price scissors and intersectoral resource transfers: who paid for industrialization in China?', *Oxford Economic Papers*, 47, 1: 117–35.

——and Li Shi (2005), 'Wages, firm profitability and labor market segmentation in China', *China Economic Review*, 16, 3: 205–28.

————and Deng Quheng (2009), 'Education and the poverty trap in rural China: setting the trap', *Oxford Development Studies*, 37, 4 (December): 311–32.

——————(2010), 'Education and the poverty trap in rural China: closing the trap', *Oxford Development Studies*, 38, 1 (March): 1–24.

——and Lina Song (1999), *The Rural-Urban Divide: Economic Disparities and Interactions in China*, Oxford: Oxford University Press.

————(2005), *Towards a Labour Market in China*, Oxford: Oxford University Press.

————(2008), 'China's emerging urban wage structure, 1995–2002', in Björn Gustafsson, Li Shi, and Terry Sicular (eds.), *Inequality and Public Policy in China*, Cambridge: Cambridge University Press: 221–42.

——and Xue Xinjun (2006), 'How high is urban unemployment in China?', *Journal of Chinese Economic and Business Studies*, 4, 2 (July): 91–107.

Li Hongbin and Zhou Li-an (2005), 'Political turnover and economic performance: the incentive role of personnel control in China', *Journal of Public Economics*, 89, 9–10: 1743–62.

Lin, Justin Yifu (1990), 'Collectivization and China's agricultural crisis in 1959–1961', *Journal of Political Economy*, 98 (December): 1228–52.

——(1992), 'Rural reforms and agricultural growth in China', *American Economic Review*, 82, 1: 34–51.

——(1994), 'Chinese agriculture: institutional changes and performance', in T. N. Srinivasan (ed.), *Agriculture and Trade in China and India*, San Francisco: International Center for Economic Growth.

National Bureau Of Statistics [NBS] (1999), *Comprehensive Statistical Data and Materials on Fifty Years of New China*, Beijing: China Statistics Press.

——(2009), *China Statistical Yearbook*, Beijing: China Statistics Press.

Naughton, Barry (1995), *Growing Out of the Plan: Chinese Economic Reform, 1978–1993*, Cambridge: Cambridge University Press.

——(2007), *The Chinese Economy. Transitions and Growth*, Cambridge, Mass.: The MIT Press.

——(2008), 'A political economy of China's economic transition', in Loren Brandt and Thomas Rawski (eds.), *China's Great Economic Transformation*, New York: Cambridge University Press.

Oi, Jean C. (1989), *State and Peasant in Contemporary China*, Berkeley and Los Angeles: University of California Press.

Organization For Economic Cooperation And Development [OECD] (2002), *China in the World Economy: The Domestic Challenges*, Paris: OECD.

Qian, Yingyi (2003), 'How reform worked in China', in Dani Rodrik (ed.), *In Search of Prosperity: Analytic Narratives on Economic Growth*, Princeton: Princeton University Press.

Shirk, Susan L. (1993), *The Political Logic of Economic Reform*, Berkeley and Los Angeles: University of California Press.

Takahara, Akio (1992), *The Politics of Wage Policy in Post-Revolutionary China*, London: Macmillan.

Wen, Guangzhong James (1989), 'The current land tenure and its impact on long term performance of the farming sector: the case of modern China', Ph.D. diss., University of Chicago.

Yao Yang (2010), 'A Chinese way to democratization?', *China: An International Journal*, 8, 2 (September): 330–4.

Part II
The Determinants of China's Economic Growth

Sai Ding and John Knight

4

China in a Cross-Country Growth Perspective

4.1 Introduction

According to official Chinese statistics, the average growth rate of GDP over the three decades 1979–2009 was 9.7% per annum. Despite the controversy over the reliability of the official figures of real output growth, discussed in Chapter 1, the fact that China's growth has been remarkably rapid is beyond dispute. Very few countries, and none as important as China, have been able to match that pace of sustained economic growth. What can we learn about the causes of China's success by comparing China with other countries?

While China's growth over the reform period has received much attention in the economic literature, research has tended to focus on relatively narrow issues such as growth convergence or divergence among provinces, cross-province growth variation, and the role of particular variables, all of which are based on data for China alone. Although these studies are relevant to an understanding of growth patterns within China, they can only hint at why China as a whole could grow so rapidly, and at the key factors driving the persistent growth disparity between the Chinese and other economies.

This chapter attempts to fill the gap in the literature by incorporating China into a cross-country growth study. Its novelty and contribution lie in the following three aspects. First, the empirical growth model that we adopt is based on the neoclassical, or Solow, growth model but it is augmented by human capital and it allows for cross-country differences in productivity growth as measured by structural change. Unlike the growth-accounting approach, it is a useful means of estimating growth in aggregate efficiency without using capital stock data, thus avoiding making strong assumptions about unknown parameters of production functions. The structural model used in this chapter also reduces the problem of model uncertainty that is faced by informal growth regressions.

Secondly, our econometric methodology involves extending the previous cross-section work of Temple and Wößmann (2006) to the dynamic panel-data context, in which the unobserved country-specific effects and potential endogeneity and measurement error of regressors are controlled for. By classifying countries at similar levels of development into the same sample, we control partially for the differences in technology and institutions and so alleviate the problem of parameter heterogeneity. Robust regression techniques are used to isolate the influence of potential outliers so that we are able to concentrate on the most coherent part of the data set. Our efforts in jointly dealing with the problems of omitted variables, parameter heterogeneity, measurement error, endogenous regressors, and influential outliers can provide new and more reliable insights into the empirical relationships that explain country differences in growth rates.

Thirdly, in order to explain China's relative growth success, we use the estimated equation to decompose the sources of differences in growth rates between China and other countries. To our knowledge, this is the first attempt to explain China's exceptional growth performance by means of cross-country growth regressions.

The chapter is organized as follows. Section 4.2 provides some background on China's growth performance by placing it in comparative perspective. Section 4.3 briefly summarizes the neoclassical growth theory and its empirical formulation in a cross-country growth context. Section 4.4 describes the data and sample classification and Section 4.5 discusses our econometric methodology. In Section 4.6 we set out and interpret the estimation results, and in Section 4.7 we provide an explanation of China's absolute and relative growth rate on the basis of the model predictions. Section 4.8 draws conclusions. An appendix provides technical details for readers interested in methodological issues.[1]

4.2 Background to China's Growth

Figure 4.1 reflects China's rapid growth of GDP per capita, averaging 8.8% per annum over the period 1978–2009. The figure also shows a cyclical pattern of growth, more marked in the first and second stages of reform than in the third stage. Three peaks are evident, in 1984–5, 1992–3, and 2007–8, respectively reflecting the outcome of agricultural reforms, the green light given to capitalism, and the recent economic boom. The growth rate troughed in 1989–90 owing to a surge of inflation and social unrest. The adverse impact of Asian financial crisis during the period 1997–9 and the decline in external demand as a result of the recent global economic recession are also evident.

Our broad hypothesis in this chapter is that the reforms created institutions and incentives which improved both static allocative efficiency and dynamic factor accumulation. Growth was also facilitated by the absorption of the abundant resource, labour, into the expanding, more productive, activities. There was drastic movement towards the economy's production frontier and dramatic movement of the frontier. It is plausible that together they were responsible for China's remarkably high rate of economic growth over the reform period.

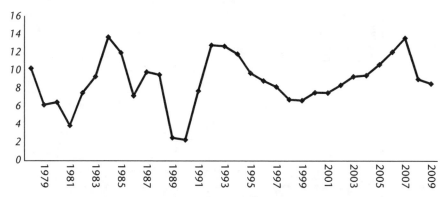

Figure 4.1 Annual percentage growth rates of GDP per capita in China, 1978–2009
Data source: World Bank, *World Development Indicators*, 2010 database.

We compare China with the main regions of the world economy in Table 4.1. We do so in terms of variables that suggest specific hypotheses for testing. The table provides information at ten-year intervals over the period 1980–2009, the average for that period, and the change between 1980 and 2009. For China, as for other countries, our measure of GDP is based on the World Bank's constant price (year 2000) US dollar equivalents, rather than official Chinese statistics, for the purpose of international comparison.

China's annual average growth of GDP per capita over the thirty years (8.9%) is five times that of the high-income economies (1.8%), and is much higher than that of Sub-Saharan Africa and Latin America and the Caribbean (0.2% and 0.9% respectively). China's sustained growth rate is indeed remarkable.

In 1980 China had a lower level of GDP per capita than any of the regions included in the table, although by 2000 it had overtaken South Asia and Sub-Saharan Africa. The intuition is that China, still under central planning, was initially further away from its equilibrium GDP per capita, and that forces of convergence would thus enable it to grow relatively fast. This hypothesis requires testing.

China's growth performance has been associated with an extremely high investment rate. Gross capital formation as a proportion of GDP (averaging 38.8%) is remarkable for such a poor country, reflecting high household and enterprise saving rates and large capital inflows. We see that the four other regions managed to invest only about 20% of their GDP. A large part of the answer to the question 'why does China grow so fast?' might be 'because it invests so much'. That must be a core hypothesis of our enquiry.

Rapid economic growth was inevitably associated with rapid structural change in the Chinese economy, as industrialization proceeded. There is a huge rural–urban income divide in China, which provides a strong incentive for rural workers to migrate out of agriculture (Knight and Song 1999). We calculate that even in

Table 4.1. International comparison of key variables

	1980	1990	2000	2009	Average during 1980–2009	Change between 1980 and 2009
GDP per capita growth rate per annum (%)						
China	6.46	2.29	7.64	8.54	8.85	2.08
South Asia	3.87	3.42	2.36	6.55	3.87	2.68
Sub-Saharan Africa	1.07	-1.76	0.79	-0.78	0.23	-1.85
Latin America and the Caribbean	3.87	-1.39	2.41	-3.03	0.95	-6.90
High-Income Economies	0.46	2.26	2.83	-3.95	1.76	-4.41
GDP per capita per annum (constant 2000$)						
China	186.44	391.65	949.18	2206.26	795.76	2019.82
South Asia	235.32	327.86	449.60	712.62	400.95	477.30
Sub-Saharan Africa	589.60	530.75	515.38	620.01	539.84	30.41
Latin America and the Caribbean	3565.73	3258.70	3852.41	4823.19	3950.02	1257.46
High-Income Economies	17304.14	21916.68	26368.33	26888.71	22119.68	9584.57
Share of gross capital formation in GDP (%)						
China	35.19	34.74	32.76	47.66	38.76	12.47
South Asia	18.73	22.83	23.53	33.19	24.35	14.46
Sub-Saharan Africa	24.76	17.75	17.28	20.79	19.12	-3.97
Latin America and the Caribbean	24.54	19.39	21.07	19.99	20.44	-4.55
High-Income Economies	24.62	22.94	22.03	17.23	21.62	-7.39
Share of agriculture in GDP (%)						
China	30.09	27.05	14.83	10.35	20.78	-19.74
South Asia	37.15	30.67	24.16	18.33	26.47	-18.82
Sub-Saharan Africa	18.72	19.61	18.49	13.07	17.62	-5.65
Latin America and the Caribbean	10.16	8.97	6.67	6.07	7.81	-4.09
High-Income Economies	3.97	2.81	1.79	1.47	2.53	-2.50

Population growth rate per annum (%)						
China	1.25	1.47	0.71	0.51	1.06	-0.74
South Asia	2.46	2.14	1.83	1.47	1.92	-0.99
Sub-Saharan Africa	3.11	2.88	2.49	2.47	2.72	-0.64
Latin America and the Caribbean	2.31	1.84	1.51	1.10	1.67	-1.21
High-Income Economies	0.84	0.84	0.82	0.63	0.70	-0.21
Average years of schooling over age 15 (year)						
China	4.77	5.85	6.36	8.17	6.89	3.40
South Asia	2.48	3.24	3.76	5.63	4.38	3.15
Sub-Saharan Africa	2.24	2.93	3.40	5.41	4.15	3.17
Latin America and the Caribbean	4.86	5.54	6.18	8.42	6.98	3.56
High-Income Economies	7.82	8.64	9.30	10.62	9.60	2.80
Average annual growth rate of average years of schooling (%)						
China	1.66	3.36	0.78	0.28	0.88	-1.38
South Asia	6.31	3.73	1.96	0.50	1.87	-5.81
Sub-Saharan Africa	3.48	2.97	1.27	0.59	1.53	-2.89
Latin America and the Caribbean	2.65	1.41	0.93	0.36	0.96	-2.29
High-Income Economies	2.01	1.36	0.71	0.14	0.66	-1.87

Data source: Human capital variables are from Barro and Lee (2010); and other variables are from World Bank, *World Development Indicators* 2010 Database. The Barro and Lee data are provided at five-year intervals, so that for the year 2009, we use the reported 2010 human capital data instead.

2000 the ratio of GDP per worker in non-agriculture to that in agriculture was 4.9 in China, higher than in any other region except Sub-Saharan Africa (5.7). The share of agriculture in GDP fell from 30.1% (higher than elsewhere) in 1980 to only 10.4% in 2009. The fall (by 19.7 percentage points) was greater than in other regions; indeed, beyond South Asia, the fall was less than six percentage points in the slow-growing regions of the world. The change in China's sectoral composition of output involved the reallocation of labour from low average labour productivity (and possibly zero marginal labour productivity) agriculture to high-productivity industry.

China has implemented a draconian population policy since the late 1970s. Despite the controversy over the humanity of the 'one-child family policy', it has been efficient in reducing fertility and slowing down the rate of population growth. This reduced the pressure on the land and on other scarce resources. By contrast, other regions of the developing world have experienced higher rates of population growth. We hypothesize that China's growth of GDP per capita benefited from its restrictive population policy.

Human capital can raise the individual productivity of workers and improve the adaptability, allocative efficiency, and technical level of an economy. Using the Barro and Lee (2010) data on international educational attainment, we find that China's average years of schooling in the population aged over 15 (6.9 years) was much lower than that of high-income economies (9.6 years), but higher than that of South Asia (4.4 years) and Sub-Saharan Africa (4.2 years), and on a par with that of Latin America and the Caribbean (7.0 years) over the period 1980–2009. The pattern of annual growth rate of average years of schooling shows opposite results: the average annual growth rate of China (0.9%) was faster only than that of high-income economies (0.7%) and slower than those of other developing country groups. Therefore, we expect that China's rapid economic growth relative to other developing countries is partly due to the level of education, while that relative to the high-income economies can be partly explained by the growth rate of human capital over the reform period.

4.3 Augmenting the Solow Model

There is an enormous literature on cross-country growth research. One type of cross-country growth regressions is based on structural growth models. In their influential work, Mankiw, Romer, and Weil (1992), hereafter MRW, found that a neoclassical model with exogenous technology and diminishing returns to capital provides an excellent explanation for international income disparities, that is, about 80% of the cross-country variation in income per capita can be explained by accumulation of human and physical capital. Their cross-section analysis has been extended to a panel-data framework by researchers using various estimation methods to deal with the problems of omitted variables, endogenous regressors, and measurement error.[2] By contrast, others have found evidence against neoclassical growth models and for endogenous growth models, in which capital is an input to the production technology for innovations and long-run differences in productivity are endogenous.[3] A major criticism of structural growth models is that variables which plausibly affect growth are left out.

Other methodological approaches are possible. One is to use ad hoc informal growth regressions incorporating a wide range of variables (Barro 1991). However, this approach presents the estimation challenges described in Chapter 2 above. The cross-country growth-accounting approach tends to focus on the role of technological progress in determining economic growth. Klenow and Rodríguez-Clare (1997) claim that total factor productivity (TFP) growth accounts for 90% of the international variation in output growth. Particularly sharp rejections of the importance of capital accumulation also come from Hall and Jones (1999) and Easterly and Levine (2001). However, the methods and results of growth accounting are open to the criticisms listed in Chapter 2.

In this chapter we choose to estimate structural growth regressions, building on the Solow growth model. We augment the Solow model with human capital, and we also incorporate structural change terms.

Starting with the framework of MRW, the dynamics of a country's growth rate towards the steady state can be expressed as[4]

$$
\ln\left(\frac{Y(t)}{L(t)}\right) - \ln\left(\frac{Y(0)}{L(0)}\right) = -\theta \ln\left(\frac{Y(0)}{L(0)}\right) + \theta \frac{\alpha}{1-\alpha} \ln(s)
$$
$$
-\theta \frac{\alpha}{1-\alpha} \ln(n+g+\delta) + \theta \ln A(0) + gt,
$$

(4.1)

where Y is output, L is labour (growing exogenously at rate n), $Y(t)/L(t)$ and $Y(0)/L(0)$ are output per worker at time t and at some initial date respectively; $A(0)$ is the initial level of efficiency and A grows exponentially at rate g as a result of labour-augmenting technical progress; s is the constant fraction of output that is saved and invested; δ is the depreciation rate of physical capital; α is the elasticity of output with respect to physical capital; $\theta = 1 - e^{-\lambda t}$, where λ is the rate of convergence, given by $\lambda = (n+g+\delta)(1-\alpha)$. Thus, the growth of income per worker is a function of the initial level of income and the determinants of the ultimate steady state.

In order to capture the explicit role of human capital, MRW augmented the Solow model by including accumulation of human capital as well as physical capital. They provided two possible ways of examining the effect of human capital on economic growth. The first is to estimate the reduced form of the model augmented by inclusion of human capital accumulation. Approximating around steady state, MRW showed that growth of output per worker in this model is given by

$$\ln\left(\frac{Y(t)}{L(t)}\right) - \ln\left(\frac{Y(0)}{L(0)}\right) = -\theta\ln\left(\frac{Y(0)}{L(0)}\right) + \theta\frac{\alpha}{1-\alpha-\beta}\ln(s_k) + \theta\frac{\beta}{1-\alpha-\beta}\ln(s_h)$$
$$-\theta\frac{\alpha+\beta}{1-\alpha-\beta}\ln(n+g+\delta) + \theta\ln A(0) + gt,$$
(4.2)

where s_k and s_h are the fractions of income invested in physical capital and human capital respectively. The convergence rate is given by $\lambda = (n+g+\delta)(1-\alpha-\beta)$, where β is the elasticity of output with respect to human capital. The assumption $\alpha+\beta < 1$ implies that there are decreasing returns to capital as a whole.

MRW's second way of expressing the role of level of human capital in determining economic growth is

$$\ln\left(\frac{Y(t)}{L(t)}\right) - \ln\left(\frac{Y(0)}{L(0)}\right) = -\theta\ln\left(\frac{Y(0)}{L(0)}\right) + \theta\frac{\alpha}{1-\alpha}\ln(s_k) - \theta\frac{\alpha}{1-\alpha}\ln(n+g+\delta)$$
$$+\theta\frac{\beta}{1-\alpha}\ln(h^*) + \theta\ln A(0) + gt,$$
(4.3)

where h^* is the steady-state level of human capital. Note that these alternative regressions predict different coefficients on the saving and population growth variables in the augmented Solow model.

A major criticism of MRW's specification is their assumption of a common exogenous rate of technological progress.[5] MRW's justification is that technology, as a public good, is freely available to individuals and can be transferred instantaneously across national borders. However, this assumption contradicts the fact that diffusion of new technology can be costly or time consuming, especially for developing countries. Therefore, it is arguable that models for growth in GDP per worker should allow productivity growth to vary across countries.

Temple and Wößmann (2006) developed an empirical model to examine the impact of labour reallocation on aggregate productivity growth. They augmented the conventional growth regressions based on the MRW framework so as to allow for structural change. Their basic idea is that changes in the structure of employment will raise aggregate productivity when the marginal product of labour varies across sectors. If the marginal product of labour is lower in agriculture, then the movement of agricultural workers to non-agricultural sectors will raise total output. Since this additional output is produced without change in the total input of capital and labour, the reallocation of labour raises aggregate productivity. They also predict a convex relationship between growth and structural change. The intuition is that the growth impact of a given extent of structural change will be greatest in those countries experiencing more rapid structural change, as these are also the countries in which the intersectoral wage differential is greatest.

Temple and Wößmann (2006) extended MRW's model by including the structural change terms to proxy the varying productivity growth across countries in a cross-section framework as follows:

$$\ln\left(\frac{Y(t)}{L(t)}\right) - \ln\left(\frac{Y(0)}{L(0)}\right) = w + \frac{t(k-1)}{1-\alpha-\beta} MGROWTH + \frac{tk\phi}{(1-\alpha-\beta)\psi} DISEQ + \theta\gamma'X - \theta\ln\left(\frac{Y(0)}{L(0)}\right)$$

(4.4)

where X is a vector of explanatory variables including rates of saving, physical and human capital accumulation. $MGROWTH$ and $DISEQ$ are the first set of structural change variables, derived from the assumption that the labour share in output is the same across provinces. The alternative formulation is to substitute $MGROWTH2$ and $DISEQ2$ in equation (4.4) in place of $MGROWTH$ and $DISEQ$. $MGROWTH2$ and $DISEQ2$ are the second set of structural change variables, based on the assumption that all provinces have the same Cobb–Douglas technologies in agriculture. $MGROWTH$ and $MGROWTH2$ are the linear terms reflecting changes of employment in the non-agricultural sector; $DISEQ$ and $DISEQ2$ are the quadratic terms capturing the convexity effect.[6] Thus, the specification of equation (4.4) is a hybrid of the Solow model with an aggregate production function and a two-sector framework with sectoral product differentials.

4.4 Data and Sample

Our empirical analysis is based on several data sets of worldwide aggregate series, including Penn World Table (PWT), World Bank World Development Indicators (WDI), and Statistical Database of the Food and Agriculture Organization of the United Nations (FAO). Given the presence of cyclical effects as shown in Figure 4.1, we opt for non-overlapping five-year time intervals, which are less sensitive to temporary factors associated with business cycles. The sample period we choose is 1980–2004, corresponding roughly to the reform period in China.

We employ real GDP chain per worker (RGDPWOK) from PWT 6.2, which is adjusted for purchasing power parities (PPPs) and constant price. PPPs are believed to be superior to exchange rates when comparing real incomes and growth rates across countries, as the use of commercial exchange rates tends to overstate the magnitude of income disparities (Temple 1999a; Bosworth and Collins 2003). However, there is concern about the PPP estimates for China[7] and no consensus on the reliability of China's GDP figures from various sources.[8] To address the potential measurement error problems we run a large number of sensitivity tests of the robustness of our findings.

The dependent variable is the change in the logarithm of real GDP per worker at five-year intervals, and the initial level of income on the right-hand side is measured by real GDP per worker data, starting in 1980, 1985, . . . and ending in 2000. We prefer the per worker variable to the per capita variable because the Solow model is based on a Cobb–Douglas production function in which only the economically active population is involved.

Following MRW and others,[9] we proxy the share of saving by the share of investment in real GDP, which can be obtained from PWT 6.2. The time series are averaged over each five-year interval. Heston and Sicular (2008) argued that conversion to a common price base may lower the capital formation proportions for China. We therefore conduct a sensitivity test using China's official data of the investment share in real GDP to check whether our results are robust.

WDI (September 2006 edition) data on total population and fraction of the population in the age group 15–64 allow us to calculate the working-age population for each country. The average rate of growth of the workforce is computed as the difference between the natural logarithms of the working-age population at the end and beginning of each period and dividing this difference by the number of years.

Rather than follow MRW, Caselli et al. (1996), and Bond et al. (2001) in using the secondary-school enrolment rates to proxy the rates of investment in schooling, we rely on the average level of human capital data provided by Barro and Lee (2001). Both Gemmell (1996) and Temple (1999a) argued that school enrolment rates may conflate human capital stock and accumulation effects and can be a poor proxy for either. The human capital measure that we use is average years of schooling in the population aged over age 15, which provides a direct measure of the stock of human capital at five-year intervals. For our sensitivity tests we adopt Wang and Yao's (2003) estimates of average years of schooling in China. They argued that the number of graduates from the educational system is a more accurate flow measure than the enrolment rates used by Barro and Lee (2001), and accordingly used each year's school graduates to obtain the addition to the human capital stock.

The FAO provides annual data on total labour force and agricultural labour force respectively, making the calculation of agricultural share of employment possible for most countries. Comparing the employment data for China from FAO with those from *China Labour Statistical Yearbook* compiled by the National Bureau of Statistics of China (NBS), we find a large discrepancy between these two sources (see Table A4.1 in the appendix to this chapter). The FAO data correspond closely in most years to the NBS data for total rural employment (including rural non-agricultural employment, amounting to 170 million in 2000). The origin of the FAO's error is probably the official classification of all rural people (including rural non-farm employment, for example, workers in the township and village enterprises) as the 'agricultural population' under central planning, implying that the error is China-specific. We therefore use the NBS data for agricultural labour force in our analysis. Brandt et al. (2008) argued that the NBS employment data series contains a major discontinuity in 1990, and that it too may underestimate the rate of decline in the primary sector labour force. Given the important role of structural change variables played in this model, we adopt Brandt et al.'s data as a further sensitivity test. The annual data on agricultural share of value added are available from WDI. The quinquennial beginning-period data on both employment share and value added share for each country are used to construct the structural change terms.

We consider three samples of countries in this chapter.[10] Sample I comprises all countries available from PWT 6.2 except those receiving a grade 'D' in terms of data quality. As pointed out by MRW, the problem of measurement error is likely to be extremely serious for these countries and variables can be badly measured. By eliminating these least reliable data from our sample, we are left with a sample of 146 developed and developing countries.

Sample II contains all developing countries and four East Asian Tigers[11] in our non-grade-D sample. Temple (1999a) mentioned that integrating developed and developing countries in a single empirical framework is not without its problems since institutions and growth processes in developing countries can be different from those in countries already near the technological frontier. We incorporate four East Asian Tigers into this sample because China shares some economic growth patterns with these countries owing to cultural similarities, geographic location, and similar economic development strategies. This sample contains 111 countries after excluding OECD and non-OECD high-income economies from Sample I.

Sample III comprises sixty-one large developing countries (with populations of more than five million) and four East Asian Tigers, where grade D data are also excluded. These countries are likely to have much in common with China. By grouping countries with similar features into the same sample, we expect to control at least partly for the differences in technology and institutions and to alleviate the problem of parameter heterogeneity.

4.5 Empirical Methodology

It is difficult to judge whether countries are in their steady states. Use of the growth equation rather than the income equation permits us to take account of transitional dynamics through the inclusion of initial income. Our empirical analysis will therefore focus on the growth equation. The growth regression approach encounters the omitted variable problem associated with the unobservable initial level of technology. In a single cross-section growth regression, this omitted $A(0)$ term is left within the residual term. Since variations in technical efficiency across countries are likely to be correlated with other explanatory variables, estimates of regressors in a conditional convergence regression are biased and inconsistent. Panel-data methods make it possible to control for the unobserved country-specific effect by treating initial efficiency as a time-invariant fixed effect and eliminating its influence through a time-dimensional transformation. Another advantage of the panel over the cross-section regression is the alleviation of the endogeneity problem through the inclusion of lags of regressors as instruments. We therefore rely on panel-data methods to estimate the cross-country growth regressions.

Following Bond et al. (2001), our equations (4.1), (4.2), (4.3), and (4.4) can be generalized in the following panel-data model

$$\Delta y_{i,t} = (\alpha - 1)y_{i,t-1} + x'_{i,t}\beta + \eta_i + \gamma_t + \nu_{i,t} \quad , \tag{4.5}$$

for $i = 1, \ldots\ldots N$ countries and $t = 2, \ldots\ldots T$ periods, where $\Delta y_{i,t}$ is the log difference in real GDP per worker over a five-year period, $y_{i,t-1}$ is the logarithm of real GDP per worker at the beginning of each period, and $x_{i,t}$ is a vector of other characteristics measured either at the beginning of each period or as an average over each five-year period, including physical and human capital accumulation, population growth, and structural change variables. In this chapter, we maintain the MRW idea of a common world technology trend representing advancement of knowledge, but we allow for the variation in productivity growth associated with structural change. In addition, the unobserved heterogeneity in the initial level of efficiency is picked up by the country-specific effects, η_i. The time dummy, γ_t, is expected to capture productivity changes that are common to all countries. Both the country-effects and time-effects may also reflect country-specific and period-specific components of measurement errors (Bond et al. 2001).

Estimating equation (4.5) is equivalent to estimating a dynamic panel-data model with a lagged dependent variable on the right-hand side as

$$y_{i,t} = \alpha y_{i,t-1} + x'_{i,t}\beta + \eta_i + \gamma_t + \nu_{i,t}, \tag{4.6}$$

for $i = 1, \ldots\ldots N$ countries and $t = 2, \ldots\ldots T$ periods. In the context of cross-country growth regressions, our data are characterized by a large number of countries N over a small number of averaged periods T.

The presence of country-specific effects, η_i, implies several econometric problems related to the estimation of dynamic panel-data models. The correlation between the lagged dependent variable and the time-invariant country-specific effects renders the OLS estimator biased and inconsistent. In the cross-country growth regressions, the OLS estimate of the coefficient of initial income term, $\hat{\alpha}$, is likely to be biased upward owing to the positive correlation between $y_{i,t-1}$ and η_i (Hsiao 1986). For the fixed effects estimator, the within-groups transformation wipes out the time-invariant η_i, but $(y_{i,t-1} - \bar{y}_{i-1})$, where $\bar{y}_{i-1} = \sum_{t=2}^{T} (y_{i,t-1}/(T-1))$, can still be correlated with $(\nu_{i,t} - \bar{\nu}_{i,})$ even if the $\nu_{i,t}$ are not serially correlated. Nickell (1981) showed that the unbiasedness and consistency of within-groups estimator in a dynamic panel will depend upon T being large. However, in the typical growth regression with small T, the estimate of the coefficient of initial income term, $\hat{\alpha}$, is likely to be seriously biased downwards (Nickell 1981). This is due to the negative correlation between the transformed lagged dependent variable and the transformed error term.

The growth regression that uses the 'first-differenced generalized method-of-moments (GMM)' estimator is firstly differenced to eliminate the effect of initial efficiency; secondly, lagged levels of the right-hand-side variables are used as instruments in the first-differenced equations. However, Bond et al. (2001) showed that the first-differenced GMM estimator is subject to a large downward finite sample bias particularly when the number of time-series observations is small, as the lagged levels of variables are only weak instruments for subsequent first-differences. Instead, they recommended using a 'system GMM' estimator with superior finite sample property developed by Arellano and Bover (1995) and Blundell and Bond (1998). By adding the original equation in levels to the system, these authors found dramatic improvement in efficiency and significant reduction in finite sample bias through exploiting these additional moment conditions. Bond et al. (2001) also claimed that the potential for obtaining consistent parameter estimates even in the presence of measurement error and endogenous right-hand-side variables is a considerable strength of the GMM approach in the context of empirical growth research. As a consequence, a panel-data system GMM estimator will be our preferred estimation method.

Detection of outliers is important in the cross-country growth regression when a large number of heterogeneous countries are included in the sample (Temple 1999b). In the dynamic panel-data framework the use of a lagged dependent variable guarantees that an outlier in the dependent variable will also show up as a bad leverage point in the independent variables. Temple (1999a) suggested that single-case diagnostics[12] are likely to miss groups of outliers or wrongly identify representative observations as outlying. Therefore, we rely on the robust regression technique, iteratively reweighted least squares (RWLS), to identify possible outliers and then omit these from our estimation. RWLS assigns a different weight to each observation with zero or lower weights given to observations with large residuals. By removing 13 unrepresentative observations from our sample (with weights less than 0.5), we restrict the influence of outliers and focus on the most coherent part of the data set.

4.6 Empirical Results

We start by estimating the textbook Solow model as described by equation (4.1) in Table 4.2. Note that all estimated standard errors are corrected for heteroskedasticity and time dummies are included in each regression. In the system GMM estimation initial level of income is treated as a predetermined variable and both investment rates and population growth rates are treated as potentially endogenous variables. Since the p values of over-identifying tests may be inflated when the number of moment conditions is large (Bowsher 2002), we restrict the number of instruments used for each first-differenced equation by including a subset of

Table 4.2. The textbook Solow model

	Sample I: 146 countries			Sample II: 111 countries			Sample III: 61 countries		
	OLS	Within Groups	System GMM	OLS	Within Groups	System GMM	OLS	Within Groups	System GMM
Constant	0.181** (0.081)	2.962** (0.438)	0.826** (0.380)	0.292** (0.114)	2.988** (0.477)	0.813* (0.462)	0.256 (0.215)	1.883** (0.595)	0.727 (0.475)
$\ln(Y_{i,t-1})$	−0.051** (0.008)	−0.307** (0.042)	−0.145** (0.029)	−0.046** (0.009)	−0.318** (0.047)	−0.110** (0.051)	−0.074** (0.011)	−0.284** (0.057)	−0.176** (0.057)
$\ln(s_{it})$	0.124** (0.015)	0.114** (0.034)	0.256** (0.048)	0.118** (0.016)	0.106** (0.039)	0.237** (0.048)	0.154** (0.020)	0.171** (0.050)	0.198** (0.047)
$\ln(n_{it} + g + \delta)$	−0.029 (0.036)	0.117** (0.047)	0.025 (0.116)	0.025 (0.038)	0.131** (0.045)	0.129 (0.144)	−0.045 (0.085)	−0.096 (0.109)	−0.159 (0.141)
R^2	0.239	0.359		0.218	0.358		0.339	0.381	
m_1			−3.73 [0.000]			−3.28 [0.001]			−2.64 [0.008]
m_2			−0.53 [0.598]			−0.73 [0.468]			−1.20 [0.231]
Hansen test p value			0.213			0.290			0.364
Difference Sargan p value			0.637			0.675			0.261
Implied λ	0.009	0.073	0.031	0.009	0.077	0.023	0.015	0.067	0.039
Adding-up restriction p value	0.018	0.000	0.037	0.001	0.001	0.011	0.245	0.543	0.798
No. of observations	511	511	511	368	368	368	230	230	230

Note: Heteroskedasticity-consistent standard errors are in parentheses; the test statistics for first and second order correlation are given by m_1 and m_2 respectively and the p-values are in brackets. In the system GMM estimation, $\ln(Y_{i,t})$ is treated as predetermined variable; $\ln(s_{it})$ and $\ln(n_{it} + g + \delta)$ are treated as endogenous variables; $g + \delta$ is assumed to be equal to 0.05; λ is the convergence rate; the adding-up restriction refers to the hypothesis that the coefficients of investment and population growth rate are equal in magnitude but opposite in sign as predicted by equation (4.1); and ** and * indicate that the coefficient is significantly different from zero at the 5 and 10% significance level respectively.

instruments for each predetermined or endogenous variable. After applying a correction to the two-step covariance matrix derived by Windmeijer (2005), we find very similar results obtained from the one-step and two-step GMM estimators. Therefore we report only the heteroskedasticity-robust one-step system GMM results.

The coefficients on initial income have the expected negative sign and are highly significant for all three samples using various estimation methods, indicating strong evidence of conditional convergence. Hence a lower starting value of real income per worker tends to generate a higher growth in GDP per worker, once the determinants of steady states are controlled for. Consistent with the prediction of Bond et al. (2001) and Hoeffler (2002), we find that our system GMM estimator yields a consistent estimate of $\hat{\alpha}$ which lies in between the upper bound provided by the OLS estimator and lower bound given by the within-groups estimator.

The investment rate has a significantly positive effect on the growth of GDP per worker in all regressions even after controlling for unobserved country-specific effects and allowing for the likely endogeneity of investment.[13] However, we fail to identify a significantly negative correlation between population growth and the growth of income per worker. The restriction that the coefficients of the investment and population growth variables are equal in magnitude but opposite in sign is rejected in Samples I and II. Moreover, the estimated elasticity of output with respect to capital (α) obtained from a restricted version of equation (4.1) is found to be above 0.5 for all three samples, which is higher than the model-suggested-value of capital share of income, 0.33. Therefore, for reasons similar to those of MRW, we reject the textbook Solow model based on the results in general and those of system GMM in particular.

We move on to introduce the Solow model augmented with human capital. The role of education in determining economic growth is a matter of dispute in the cross-country growth empirics. MRW found a significantly positive effect of human capital on growth, while other studies (Benhabib and Spiegel 1994; Pritchett 1999) claimed that increases in measured educational attainment are not causally related to output growth, especially in developing countries.

In Table 4.3, we estimate equation (4.2) which incorporates the log difference of average years of schooling as a proxy for the accumulation of human capital, as well as equation (4.3), which includes the logarithm of average years of schooling as a measure of the level of human capital respectively. In addition, following the argument of Gemmell (1996) that both larger stock and faster growth of human capital can raise output growth, we test a third specification which augments the Solow model with both the stock and accumulation of human capital.

From now on, we report only the results of system GMM estimation. We treat the initial level of human capital as a predetermined variable and the growth rate of human capital as a potentially endogenous variable, as fast-growing economies are likely to devote a higher proportion of their resources to educational

Table 4.3. System GMM estimation of the augmented Solow model with human capital

	Sample I: 146 countries			Sample II: 111 countries			Sample III: 61 countries		
	(1)	(2)	(3)	(1)	(2)	(3)	(1)	(2)	(3)
Constant	−0.442 (0.330)	−0.699** (0.340)	−0.351 (0.301)	−0.213 (0.324)	−0.402 (0.298)	−0.163 (0.342)	−0.177 (0.328)	−0.359 (0.243)	−0.144 (0.315)
$\ln(Y_{i,t-1})$	−0.092** (0.029)	−0.087** (0.022)	−0.101** (0.025)	−0.085** (0.033)	−0.061** (0.029)	−0.075** (0.029)	−0.075** (0.038)	−0.059** (0.027)	−0.093** (0.028)
$\ln(s_{it})$	0.173** (0.042)	0.139** (0.039)	0.121** (0.032)	0.157** (0.038)	0.146** (0.033)	0.132** (0.029)	0.137** (0.038)	0.122** (0.037)	0.116** (0.032)
$\ln(n_{it} + g + \delta)$	−0.348** (0.131)	−0.461** (0.156)	−0.346** (0.127)	−0.239** (0.119)	−0.253** (0.107)	−0.181 (0.133)	−0.218** (0.117)	−0.269** (0.089)	−0.263** (0.087)
$\ln(h_{it})$	0.014 (0.044)		0.084** (0.041)	0.053 (0.045)		0.086** (0.041)	0.028 (0.051)		0.073** (0.036)
$\Delta\ln(h_{it})$		0.241 (0.159)	0.258* (0.141)		0.219 (0.146)	0.189 (0.127)		0.011 (0.159)	0.077 (0.102)
Joint significance test for $\ln(h_{it})$ & $\Delta\ln(h_{it})$			5.51 [0.064]			5.49 [0.064]			5.66 [0.059]
m_1	−3.70 [0.000]	−4.05 [0.000]	−4.18 [0.000]	−3.63 [0.000]	−3.72 [0.000]	−4.00 [0.000]	−2.68 [0.007]	−2.64 [0.008]	−2.80 [0.005]
m_2	−1.03 [0.301]	−1.12 [0.262]	−1.11 [0.265]	−1.11 [0.269]	−1.02 [0.308]	−1.03 [0.303]	−0.82 [0.414]	−0.90 [0.371]	−0.94 [0.348]
Hansen test p value	0.365	0.610	0.963	0.998	0.992	0.998	0.999	0.999	0.999
Difference Sargan p value	0.430	0.492	0.476	0.870	0.833	0.701	0.707	0.933	0.999
Implied λ	0.019	0.018	0.021	0.018	0.013	0.016	0.016	0.012	0.020
Adding-up restriction p value	0.198	0.734		0.517	0.529		0.497	0.458	
No. of observations	378	375	375	266	263	263	184	184	184

Note: Heteroskedasticity-consistent standard errors are in parentheses; the test statistics for first and second order correlation are given by m_1 and m_2 respectively and the *p*-values are in brackets; $\ln(Y_{i,t-1})$ and $\ln(h_{i,t})$ are treated as predetermined variables; $\ln(s_{i,t})$, $\ln(n_{i,t} + g + \delta)$ and $\Delta\ln(h_{i,t})$ are treated as endogenous variables; $g + \delta$ is assumed to be equal to 0.05; λ is the convergence rate; when the growth rate of human capital is included, the adding-up restriction refers to the hypothesis that the three coefficients other than the one on lagged output sum to zero; when the level of human capital is included, the restriction is that the coefficients on the rates of investment and population growth are opposite in sign and equal in absolute value; and ** and * indicate that the coefficient is significantly different from zero at the 5 and 10% significance level respectively.

investment. We find that when the two human capital variables enter the Solow formulation individually, neither of them proves to be significant. This is consistent with the many studies that have failed to find a robust correlation between educational attainment and output growth. However, when we simultaneously incorporate the stock and accumulation of human capital into the regressions, the level of human capital becomes highly significant and positive for all samples; moreover, Wald tests suggest strong evidence of joint significance of both human capital variables even in Samples II and III, containing only developing countries. Hence, our results provide support for a role of both the initial stock and subsequent growth of human capital in fostering output growth even in less developed countries.

Compared with the textbook Solow model, inclusion of human capital in the regressions leads to several major changes. First, the population growth term, which has previously been wrongly signed, becomes negative and strongly significant for almost all regressions and samples. Second, these unrestricted regressions do not lead to rejection of the adding-up hypotheses as predicted by equation (4.2) and (4.3). Moreover, in the restricted models, the calculated physical capital's share of income (α) and human capital's share of income (β) suggest $\alpha + \beta < 1$, so implying decreasing returns to the set of reproducible factors of production, a key assumption of the Solow model. In brief, all results suggest better performance of the augmented Solow model with human capital than of the textbook one.

We further supplement the augmented Solow model with the structural change terms to test whether labour reallocation makes a significant contribution to economic growth. Table 4.4 presents the system GMM results with the first set of structural change terms, MGROWTH and DISEQ. Because periods of more rapid economic growth are also periods of expanding opportunity for rural workers and of rapid structural transformation, we treat both the linear and non-linear structural change terms as potentially endogenous variables.[14] In line with the findings of Temple and Wößmann (2006), whereas MGROWTH and DISEQ are not individually significant, we find for all samples that they are jointly significant according to the Wald test.

The results become even better when we add instead the second set of structural change terms, MGROWTH2 and DISEQ2, into the cross-country growth regressions. The alternative set of structural change variables captures structural change in both employment and total value added.[15] In Table 4.5, not only are both structural change terms jointly significant but also the non-linear term, DISEQ2, itself remains highly significant and positive in every regression. Each structural change term is strongly significant in the two developing country samples. Reflecting the very different sectoral structures and patterns of structural change in developed and developing countries, our results show that the role of structural change in determining economic growth is stronger in the case of developing

Table 4.4. System GMM estimation of the augmented Solow model with human capital and the first set of structural change terms

	Sample I: 146 countries			Sample II: 111 countries			Sample III: 61 countries		
	(1)	(2)	(3)	(1)	(2)	(3)	(1)	(2)	(3)
Constant	-0.408* (0.246)	-0.661** (0.259)	-0.406 (0.294)	-0.016 (0.389)	-0.184 (0.345)	-0.147 (0.306)	-0.212 (0.271)	-0.166 (0.272)	-0.057 (0.276)
$\ln(Y_{i,t-1})$	-0.113** (0.018)	-0.095** (0.017)	-0.085** (0.023)	-0.118** (0.024)	-0.095** (0.018)	-0.085** (0.024)	-0.101** (0.021)	-0.101** (0.018)	-0.096** (0.023)
$\ln(s_h)$	0.206** (0.035)	0.206** (0.032)	0.113** (0.026)	0.176** (0.030)	0.192** (0.028)	0.116** (0.026)	0.148** (0.031)	0.153** (0.028)	0.109** (0.027)
$\ln(n_{it} + g + \delta)$	-0.345** (0.090)	-0.404** (0.096)	-0.312** (0.114)	-0.237** (0.114)	-0.242** (0.103)	-0.216** (0.095)	-0.296** (0.080)	-0.285** (0.078)	-0.245** (0.079)
$\ln(h_{it})$	0.045 (0.032)		0.067** (0.033)	0.071** (0.038)		0.071** (0.035)	0.022 (0.041)		0.053* (0.033)
$\Delta\ln(h_{it})$		0.057 (0.076)	0.166 (0.108)		0.026 (0.078)	0.092 (0.083)		0.057 (0.102)	0.062 (0.088)
MGROWTH	0.561 (1.130)	0.475 (1.194)	1.225 (1.109)	0.413 (1.145)	0.369 (1.173)	1.225 (0.928)	1.135 (0.902)	0.701 (1.046)	0.397 (0.879)
DISEQ	2.484 (3.184)	2.916 (3.177)	2.057 (3.055)	2.971 (2.974)	3.457 (3.099)	2.074 (2.568)	2.484 (2.624)	3.841 (3.062)	3.732 (2.473)
Joint significance test for $\ln(h_{it})$ & $\Delta\ln(h_{it})$			4.98 [0.083]			4.57 [0.101]			2.74 [0.255]
Joint significance test for MGROWTH & DISEQ	7.18 [0.028]	8.54 [0.014]	20.67 [0.000]	9.56 [0.008]	9.72 [0.008]	23.11 [0.000]	17.00 [0.000]	15.91 [0.000]	18.51 [0.000]
m_1	-3.69 [0.000]	-3.81 [0.000]	-4.29 [0.000]	-3.45 [0.000]	-3.56 [0.000]	-3.76 [0.000]	-2.90 [0.004]	-2.91 [0.004]	-2.89 [0.004]
m_2	-0.83 [0.408]	-1.07 [0.284]	-1.17 [0.240]	-0.96 [0.337]	-1.11 [0.266]	-1.12 [0.264]	-0.75 [0.456]	-0.85 [0.393]	-0.90 [0.366]
Hansen test p value	0.595	0.532	0.999	0.982	0.990	0.999	0.999	0.999	0.999
Difference Sargan p value	0.200	0.336	0.707	0.359	0.326	0.999	0.985	0.991	0.999
Implied λ	0.024	0.020	0.018	0.025	0.020	0.018	0.021	0.021	0.020
No. of observations	373	370	370	261	258	258	179	179	179

Note: MGROWTH and DISEQ are treated as endogenous variables; other definitions are the same as in previous tables.

Table 4.5. System GMM estimation of the augmented Solow model with human capital and the second set of structural change terms

	Sample I: 146 countries			Sample II: 111 countries			Sample III: 61 countries		
	(1)	(2)	(3)	(1)	(2)	(3)	(1)	(2)	(3)
Constant	−0.235 (0.274)	−0.659** (0.276)	−0.156 (0.251)	0.036 (0.380)	−0.386 (0.310)	0.166 (0.341)	0.169 (0.306)	−0.155 (0.286)	0.395 (0.262)
$\ln(Y_{i,t-1})$	−0.106** (0.029)	−0.107** (0.021)	−0.106** (0.029)	−0.093** (0.029)	−0.071** (0.016)	−0.081** (0.028)	−0.107** (0.027)	−0.094** (0.022)	−0.118** (0.021)
$\ln(s_{h2})$	0.153** (0.032)	0.135** (0.037)	0.120** (0.028)	0.139** (0.029)	0.138** (0.029)	0.114** (0.028)	0.096** (0.031)	0.096** (0.035)	0.105** (0.027)
$\ln(n_{it} + g + \delta)$	−0.297** (0.159)	−0.513** (0.119)	−0.276** (0.133)	−0.170 (−0.149)	−0.241* (0.125)	−0.087 (0.134)	−0.197** (0.101)	−0.314** (0.125)	−0.133* (0.082)
$\ln(h_{it})$	0.066** (0.033)		0.089** (0.034)	0.066** (0.036)		0.078** (0.037)	0.068* (0.037)		0.064** (0.026)
$\Delta\ln(h_{it})$		0.110 (0.111)	0.159 (0.124)		0.088 (0.101)	0.120 (0.118)		−0.035 (0.132)	0.045 (0.075)
MGROWTH2	1.333 (1.167)	1.029 (0.936)	1.262 (1.086)	1.533 (1.228)	1.699* (0.985)	1.467 (1.129)	2.732** (1.071)	3.092** (1.152)	2.941** (0.696)
DISEQ2	0.143** (0.062)	0.223** (0.061)	0.188** (0.069)	0.118** (0.059)	0.111** (0.057)	0.131** (0.056)	0.196** (0.058)	0.214** (0.061)	0.226** (0.054)
Joint significance test for $\ln(h_{it})$ & $\Delta\ln(h_{it})$			6.72 [0.035]			4.74 [0.093]			6.61 [0.037]
Joint significance test for MGROWTH2 & DISEQ2	9.09 [0.011]	17.85 [0.000]	12.80 [0.002]	8.34 [0.015]	10.40 [0.006]	9.53 [0.009]	13.83 [0.001]	14.73 [0.001]	36.77 [0.000]
m_1	−3.74 [0.000]	−3.82 [0.000]	−3.99 [0.000]	−3.54 [0.000]	−3.41 [0.001]	−3.69 [0.000]	−2.66 [0.008]	−2.48 [0.013]	−2.56 [0.010]
m_2	−0.92 [0.360]	−1.06 [0.288]	−1.01 [0.314]	−0.96 [0.337]	−1.06 [0.287]	−0.96 [0.338]	−0.77 [0.442]	−0.82 [0.414]	−0.78 [0.433]
Hansen test p value	0.538	0.986	0.873	0.968	0.999	0.999	0.999	0.999	0.999
Difference Sargan p value	0.246	0.393	0.395	0.437	0.969	0.899	0.979	0.997	0.999
Implied λ	0.022	0.023	0.022	0.020	0.015	0.017	0.023	0.020	0.025
No. of observations	355	352	352	250	247	247	170	170	170

Note: MGROWTH2 and DISEQ2 are treated as endogenous variables; other definitions are the same as in previous tables.

countries. In addition, the persistently significant *DISEQ2* term further justifies the hypothesis that the growth effect of structural change is non-linear.

Inclusion of the second set of structural change terms further improves the performance of the human capital variables. There is now a significant and positive association between cross-country differences in the initial endowment level of education and subsequent output growth even when the stock of human capital enters the regression on its own. Besides, all other parameters are correctly signed and highly significant in every regression. There is also no evidence of second order serial correlation in the first-differenced residuals, and neither the Hansen test nor the Difference Sargan test rejects the validity of the instruments. All this suggests that our system GMM estimators are consistent. The estimated convergence rate, λ, remains stable at around 2% per annum for each sample, which is consistent with the evidence commonly found in the cross-country growth literature (for instance, Bond et al. 2001; Barro and Sala-i-Martin 2004).

In brief, our system GMM results strongly support the extended version of the augmented Solow model with both human capital and structural change. The movement of labour across sectors is basic to the process of economic growth and development, and this needs to be captured in the cross-country growth regressions.

4.7 Explaining China's Relative Performance

The good performance of the augmented Solow model with structural change allows us to predict China's growth rate and to examine the reasons why China has grown faster than other countries. The prediction is made by introducing China's values of the explanatory variables into the estimated equation. The model that we employ for prediction is the one augmented by both level and growth rate of human capital as well as structural change terms given in Table 4.4. We choose the estimates of Sample III when we compare China with Sub-Saharan Africa and opt for Sample I when we later account for the predicted growth difference between China and all other country groups in the world. Our results remain robust when the sensitivity tests described in section 4.4 are conducted.[16]

Table 4.6, using PWT 6.2, shows that the actual average annual growth rate of output per worker in China over the period 1980–2004 was 7.2%. Our model predicts that output per worker in China grew at an average rate of 6.3% per annum, implying an unexplained residual of 0.9% per annum. Given the average prediction standard error of 0.7%, China's annual growth rate falls within the 95% confidence interval for the prediction.[17] The part of the unexplained residual that is not due to measurement error might represent the remaining improvement in allocative and technical efficiency that is not accounted for by the model— resulting, for instance, from economic reforms and marketization. Thus China's

Table 4.6. Growth predictions for China and growth difference predictions between China and Sub-Saharan Africa

Variable	(1) Parameter estimates	(2) Mean value of China (per annum)	(3) Mean value of SSA (per annum)	(4) Mean difference (China vs SSA)	(5) Difference in predicted growth (China vs SSA)	(6) Percentage of total predicted growth difference (China vs SSA)
				(4) = (2) − (3)	(5) = (1) * (4)	
$\ln(Y_{i,t-1})$	−0.096	1.554	1.655	−0.101	0.010	17.2
$\ln(s_{it})$	0.109	0.662	0.386	0.276	0.030	53.7
$\ln(n_{it} + g + \delta)$	−0.245	−0.760	−0.704	−0.056	0.014	24.3
$\ln(h_{it})$	0.052	0.345	0.232	0.113	0.006	10.6
$\Delta\ln(h_{it})$	0.062	0.015	0.016	−0.001	0.000	−0.2
MGROWTH	0.397	0.011	0.004	0.007	0.003	4.9
DISEQ	3.733	0.001	0.000	0.001	0.004	7.3
Actual annual growth rate/growth rate difference		0.072	0.004	0.068		
Predicted annual growth rate/growth rate difference		0.063	0.007	0.056		
Residual		0.009		0.012		

Note: This is based on Sample III estimation. The predicted growth for China equals the sum of all contributions to growth by the regression variables including constant and time dummies. The difference in the sample means of a variable between regions X and Y equals the average value in region X minus the average value in region Y; the difference in predicted growth between region X and Y attributable to a certain variable is equal to the difference in the sample means of that variable between region X and Y times the estimated coefficient on that variable from the regression; the total difference in predicted growth between region X and Y equals the sum of the differences in predicted growth attributable to all variables contained in the regression including constant and time dummies.

growth is due to a combination of both pushing out the production frontier and moving towards the frontier. Our augmented Solow model—capturing initial income, investment, population growth, level and growth of human capital, as well as structural change—is successful in predicting China's growth rate.

A meaningful decomposition of China's absolute growth rate is not possible owing to the negative convergence term (comparing initial output with zero output) and the logarithmic form of some explanatory variables, but a decomposition of China's relative growth is informative. Table 4.6 presents a detailed decomposition of the differences in the growth predictions for China and Sub-Saharan Africa. We choose Sub-Saharan Africa for research focus as a country group that is representative of least developed countries in 1980 (of which China was one) and which subsequently experienced growth failure. The actual and predicted annual growth difference between China and Sub-Saharan Africa are 6.8% and 5.6% respectively, that is, the unexplained residual is 1.2% per annum. When the predicted growth difference is decomposed, we find that capital investment is the most important component (accounting for 54% of the total).

Capital accumulation has traditionally been viewed as an inferior source of growth, in that capital deepening is subject to diminishing returns and will eventually run out of steam. This has not been true for China's high investment rates for two reasons. Firstly, investment is a major carrier of structural change: structural transformation requires investment in new, normally high-productivity activities. In China, employment growth in the high-productivity industrial and service sectors is determined by the rate of investment in those sectors. The new job opportunities are largely filled by migrant workers from the low-productivity agricultural sector. Secondly, the slow convergence rate predicted by our model, roughly 2% per annum, implies that the average time an economy spends to cover half of the distance between its initial position and its steady state is about thirty-five years. Therefore, given the diminishing returns to investment, the role of capital accumulation in driving economic growth can persist for decades during the economic transition to the long-run equilibrium.

The role of capital accumulation in driving economic growth in East Asia has been emphasized in several influential studies. For instance, Krugman (1994) argued that the 'myth of East Asia's growth miracle' lay in a mobilization of resources and an extraordinary growth in inputs rather than gains in efficiency. Young (1995) adopted the growth-accounting approach and identified the fundamental role played by factor accumulation in explaining the growth of four East Asian tigers. Our results are in line with these findings but add to the literature by highlighting the role of capital accumulation for China in the context of cross-country growth regressions.

As far as other variables are concerned, the fact that the average growth rate of human capital in China was slightly below that in Sub-Saharan Africa over the period 1980–2004 leads us to predict that their growth difference would be smaller by 0.2%. Contributions to that difference came from China's slower population growth (24%), higher level of human capital (11%), conditional convergence gain (17%), and its more dramatic structural change (12%).

Using this methodology we are able to account for the predicted growth differences between China and other major country groups as shown in Table 4.7, based on estimates of Sample I. Growth prediction for China and growth difference prediction between China and Sub-Saharan Africa are also reported as a robustness check: we find that our prediction results remain stable when different sample estimates are employed. Our main findings for the other country groups are as follows.

Firstly, conditional convergence, the basic property of the Solow model, has considerable explanatory power for the growth difference across countries, ranging from 21% between China and South Asia to 93% between China and the high-income economies.

Secondly, China invests more than other economies, which accounts for more than 40% of the predicted growth difference between China and both East Asia and the Pacific and also South Asia, and 28% in the case of Latin America and the Caribbean. By stimulating structural change, high investment rates are not only a cause of economic growth but also a symptom of productivity improvement.

Thirdly, reallocation of labour from low- to high-productivity sectors is another source of China's economic growth. The joint contribution of the linear and non-linear structural change terms to the predicted growth difference ranges from 12% between China and Latin America and the Caribbean to 22% between China and the high-income economies. The role of the structural change terms is consistent with the common view (for instance, World Bank 1993; Young 1995) that an important part of productivity growth in low-income economies is attributable to improvement in allocative efficiency through intersectoral reallocation of labour from agriculture to industry.

Fourthly, the slower population growth rate of China contributes a little to its growth difference with other developing countries (accounting for 7% of the predicted difference between China and Latin America and the Caribbean; 3% in the case of South Asia; and 1% for East Asia and the Pacific).

Fifthly, the level of human capital explains 16% of the predicted growth difference between China and South Asia. Compared with most other country groups shown in Table 4.7, the level of human capital in China is still quite low.

Lastly, the growth rate of human capital contributes positively to the predicted growth difference of China with the high-income economies, but its contribution is tiny (1%).

Table 4.7. Growth predictions for China and growth difference predictions between China and other country-groups

Variable	Parameter estimates	Mean value of China	Percentage Components of the Difference in Predicted Growth Rates						
			China vs All Other Countries	China vs High-Income Economies	China vs All Other Developing Countries	China vs Sub-Saharan Africa	China vs Latin America and the Caribbean	China vs East Asia and the Pacific	China vs South Asia
$\ln(Y_{i,t-1})$	-0.085	1.554	64.8	93.4	46.9	24.8	52.6	46.8	21.2
$\ln(s_{it})$	0.113	0.662	25.8	10.9	31.3	42.9	27.5	40.7	40.8
$\ln(n_{it}+g+\delta)$	-0.313	-0.760	-13.1	-47.1	-3.6	24.2	7.2	1.0	3.4
$\ln(h_{it})$	0.067	0.345	-1.8	-11.0	2.8	10.8	-0.2	-2.9	16.2
$\Delta\ln(h_{it})$	0.165	0.015	-0.7	1.0	-1.4	-1.7	0.0	-0.4	-6.1
MGROWTH	1.225	0.011	13.3	19.8	11.0	10.9	10.3	13.7	13.8
DISEQ	2.057	0.001	2.3	2.6	2.1	2.9	1.8	3.7	3.5
Actual annual growth rate/growth rate difference		0.072	0.061	0.058	0.059	0.066	0.067	0.051	0.044
Predicted annual growth rate/growth rate difference		0.067	0.056	0.052	0.056	0.064	0.061	0.044	0.049
Residual		0.005	0.005	0.006	0.003	0.002	0.006	0.007	-0.005

Note: This is based on Sample I estimation. All other countries consist of 145 countries in Sample I except China. All other countries consist of 145 countries in Sample I except China, which also includes Europe and Central Asia that is not reported in this table; the high-income economies include 39 high-income OECD and non-OECD members; All other developing countries consist of 106 countries except China; Sub-Saharan Africa includes 26 countries; Latin America and the Caribbean contains 26 countries; East Asia and the Pacific comprises 14 countries excluding China; and South Asia includes 7 countries.

4.8 Conclusion

We have examined the role of the augmented Solow model in explaining China's remarkable economic growth rate, both absolute and relative to the rest of the world. Following Temple and Wößmann's (2006) introduction of two sectors into the model, we allowed productivity growth to vary across countries. We extended their cross-section analysis to a dynamic panel-data analysis using a robust and consistent system GMM estimator. We showed the value of cross-country comparative analysis in our attempt to explain China's remarkable economic growth.

Firstly, we found that the extended version of the augmented Solow model provides a good explanation of China's economic growth, that is, China's annual growth rate of GDP per worker (7.2%) falls within the 95% confidence interval for its predicted value (6.3%). The unexplained residual might represent China's efficiency gains from economic reform and marketization that are not captured by the structural change terms.

Secondly, our model is a valuable means of understanding the large and persistent differences in growth rates between China and other countries. China's relatively good performance is mainly due to accumulation of physical capital, conditional convergence, improvements in factor productivity through structural change, and slower population growth. The level of human capital contributes to the growth difference between China and other developing countries, but not the growth of human capital. There is room for China to expand its investment in human capital. Our identification of this set of variables provides a framework for the development of growth-promoting policies.

China's experience shows that rapid growth is indeed possible despite starting with imperfect institutions, provided that the government addresses the institutional obstacles to growth as they become apparent. The reform of rural and urban institutions from 1978 onwards loosened various binding constraints on growth and helped unleash previously untapped market forces. The preferred model captures the effects of factor accumulation and structural change.

Our analysis is silent on the role of several underlying and policy-relevant variables such as institutions, research, and development, financial depth and openness of the economy, each of which is potentially important in the growth process (see, for instance, Quah 2000). However, data requirements favour a cross-province rather than a cross-country analysis of such variables. We turn to this analysis in Chapters 5, 6, and 7. Moreover, since some variables in our growth equations, such as the rate of physical capital accumulation, may themselves need to be explained if we are to discover the ultimate drivers of growth (see, for instance, Blomström et al. 1996), it is sensible also to investigate their determinants in China. This is the subject of Chapter 8.

APPENDIX 4.1

Table A4.1. Employment data for China

	FAO Data			NBS Data			Brandt, Hsieh and Zhu (2008) data		
	Total labour force (10,000 persons)	Labour force in agriculture (10,000 persons)	Share of agricultural labour force (%)	Total employment (10,000 persons)	Employment in agriculture (10,000 persons)	Share of agricultural employment (%)	Total employment (10,000 persons)	Employment in primary sector (10,000 persons)	Share of primary sector employment (%)
1978	52,946	39,565	74.73	40,152	28,318	70.53	46,843	32,445	69.26
1979	54,017	40,017	74.31	41,024	28,634	69.80	47,967	31,416	65.50
1980	55,104	40,718	73.89	42,361	29,122	68.75	49,397	30,593	61.93
1981	56,258	41,459	73.70	43,725	29,777	68.10	51,039	29,890	58.56
1982	57,429	42,209	73.50	45,295	30,859	68.13	52,618	29,138	55.38
1983	58,636	42,980	73.30	46,436	31,151	67.08	54,117	28,338	52.36
1984	59,897	43,787	73.10	48,179	30,868	64.07	55,810	27,634	49.51
1985	61,224	44,636	72.91	49,873	31,130	62.42	57,551	26,946	46.82
1986	62,630	45,538	72.71	51,282	31,254	60.95	59,151	27,704	46.84
1987	64,106	46,485	72.51	52,783	31,663	59.99	60,744	27,726	45.64
1988	65,618	47,452	72.30	54,334	32,249	59.35	62,240	28,232	45.36
1989	67,116	48,404	72.12	55,329	33,225	60.05	63,561	29,913	47.06
1990	68,563	49,312	71.92	64,749	34,117	52.69	64,749	30,107	46.50
1991	69,524	49,652	71.42	65,491	34,956	53.38	65,491	30,044	45.88
1992	70,413	49,928	70.91	66,152	34,795	52.60	66,152	29,943	45.26
1993	71,248	50,151	70.39	66,808	33,966	50.84	66,808	29,219	43.74
1994	72,056	50,343	69.87	67,455	33,386	49.49	67,455	28,155	41.74
1995	72,858	50,518	69.34	68,065	33,018	48.51	68,065	27,759	40.70
1996	73,657	50,678	68.80	68,950	32,909	47.73	68,950	26,827	38.91
1997	74,446	50,820	68.26	69,820	33,095	47.40	69,820	26,734	38.29
1998	75,223	50,939	67.72	70,637	33,232	47.05	70,637	26,625	37.69
1999	75,979	51,034	67.17	71,394	33,493	46.91	71,394	25,991	36.41
2000	76,711	51,100	66.61	72,085	33,355	46.27	72,085	25,446	35.30

Notes: NBS data are from *China Labour Statistical Yearbook* (2003), compiled by National Bureau of Statistics of China (NBS) and Ministry of Labour and Social Security of China; NBS definition of agricultural employment is the number of employment in farming, forestry, animal husbandry, and fishing. FAO data are from Statistical Database of the Food and Agriculture Organization of the United Nations. FAO definition of labour force in agriculture (economically active population in agriculture) is that part of the economically active population engaged in or seeking work in agriculture, hunting, fishing or forestry; and FAO definition of total labour force (economically active population) is the number of all employed and unemployed persons (including those seeking work for the first time).

APPENDIX 4.2. MODEL DERIVATIONS

The textbook Solow model

By assuming diminishing returns to capital and exogenous rates of saving, population growth and technological progress, the Solow (or neoclassical, or exogenous) growth model predicts that the long-run economic growth rate is exogenously determined by the rate of technological progress and that adjustment to stable steady-state growth is achieved by endogenous changes in factor accumulation. Cobb–Douglas production function with constant returns to scale can be written as

$$Y = K^{\alpha}(AL)^{1-\alpha} \qquad 0 < \alpha < 1, \tag{A4.1}$$

where Y is output, K is capital, L is labour, A is labour-augmenting technological progress, and α is the share of capital in total output. L and A are assumed to grow exogenously at rates n and g respectively, so that $L(t) = L(0)e^{nt}$ and $A(t) = A(0)e^{gt}$. Assuming that s is the constant fraction of output that is saved and invested, and defining output and stock of capital per unit of effective labour as $y = Y/AL$ and $k = K/AL$, respectively, the evolution of k is given by

$$\dot{k} = sy - (n+g+\delta)k = sk^{\alpha} - (n+g+\delta)k, \tag{A4.2}$$

where δ is the rate of depreciation. It is evident that k converges to its steady-state value

$$k^{*} = \left(\frac{s}{n+g+\delta}\right)^{\frac{1}{1-\alpha}} \tag{A4.3}$$

The steady-state capital–labour ratio is related positively to the saving rate and negatively to the population growth rate. Solving the equation for the steady state, substituting (A4.3) into the production function and taking logs, gives steady-state income per worker as

$$\ln\left(\frac{Y^{*}}{L}\right) = \ln A(0) + gt + \frac{\alpha}{1-\alpha}\ln(s) - \frac{\alpha}{1-\alpha}\ln(n+g+\delta) \tag{A4.4}$$

In the Solow version of the neoclassical model, the steady-state income level of a country is thus determined by the country's saving and labour force growth rates and parameters of technology.

MRW assumed that efficiency growth (g) and depreciation rate of capital (δ) are the same across countries, but allowed the initial level of efficiency $A(0)$ to vary randomly across countries owing to differences in resource endowments, technology, institutions, climate, and so on. In order to capture the different initial levels of efficiency across countries, MRW assumed that

$$\ln A(0) = a + \epsilon, \tag{A4.5}$$

where a is a constant and ε is a country-specific shock. Then the empirical specification of steady-state income per worker is

$$\ln\left(\frac{Y^*}{L}\right) = a + \frac{\alpha}{1-\alpha}\ln(s) - \frac{\alpha}{1-\alpha}\ln(n+g+\delta) + \epsilon \tag{A4.6}$$

Differences in the steady-state income levels across countries are thus controlled for by the inclusion of saving and population growth rate variables in the regression. Equation (A4.6) assumes that all countries are currently in their steady states or that departures from steady states are random across countries. However, it is of more interest to consider the equation describing the out-of-steady-state growth behaviour.

Let y^* be the steady-state level of income per effective labour given by equation (A4.6), and let $y(t)$ be the actual value at time t. Approximating around the steady state, the speed of convergence is given by $d\ln y(t)/dt = \lambda[\ln(y^*) - \ln y(t)]$, where λ is the rate of convergence, given by $\lambda = (n+g+\delta)(1-\alpha)$. Then it implies

$$\ln y(t) = (1 - e^{-\lambda t})\ln(y^*) + e^{-\lambda t}\ln y(0), \tag{A4.7}$$

where $y(0)$ is income per effective labour at some initial date. Subtracting $\ln y(0)$ from both sides and substituting for y^* leads to the following approximation

$$\ln y(t) - \ln y(0) = -\left(1 - e^{-\lambda t}\right)\ln y(0) + \left(1 - e^{-\lambda t}\right)\frac{\alpha}{1-\alpha}\ln(s) - \left(1 - e^{-\lambda t}\right)\frac{\alpha}{1-\alpha}\ln(n+g+\delta)$$
$$\tag{A4.8}$$

Equation (A4.8) is formulated in terms of income per effective labour, whereas in implementation it has to be reformulated in terms of income per worker. Substituting the following expression for income per effective labour

$$\ln y(t) = \ln\left(\frac{Y(t)}{L(t)}\right) - \ln A(0) - gt \tag{A4.9}$$

into equation (A4.8) gives

$$\ln\left(\frac{Y(t)}{L(t)}\right) - \ln\left(\frac{Y(0)}{L(0)}\right) = -\theta\ln\left(\frac{Y(0)}{L(0)}\right) + \theta\frac{\alpha}{1-\alpha}\ln(s) - \theta\frac{\alpha}{1-\alpha}\ln(n+g+\delta) + \theta\ln A(0) + gt,$$
$$\tag{A4.10}$$

where $\theta = 1 - e^{-\lambda t}$ and λ is the rate of convergence. Thus, in the Solow model the growth of income per worker is a function of the initial level of income and the determinants of the ultimate steady state.

The augmented Solow model with human capital

In order to capture the explicit role of human capital in determining economic growth, MRW augmented the Solow model by including accumulation of human capital as well as physical capital. The Cobb–Douglas production function is specified as

$$Y = K^\alpha H^\beta (AL)^{1-\alpha-\beta} \quad 0 < \alpha + \beta < 1, \tag{A4.11}$$

where H is the stock of human capital, β is the share of human capital in total output, and all other variables are defined as before. The assumption $\alpha + \beta < 1$ implies that there are decreasing returns to capital as a whole. MRW assumed that the fractions of income invested in physical capital and human capital are constant at the rates of s_K and s_h respectively, and that both types of capital depreciate at a common rate δ. The evolution of the economy is determined by

$$\dot{k} = s_k y - (n+g+\delta)k = s_k k^\alpha h^\beta - (n+g+\delta)k \tag{A4.12a}$$

$$\dot{h} = s_h y - (n+g+\delta)h = s_h k^\alpha h^\beta - (n+g+\delta)h, \tag{A4.12b}$$

where $y = Y/AL$ $k = K/AL$, and $h = H/AL$ are quantities per effective unit of labour. Solving these equations for steady state gives

$$k^* = \left(\frac{s_k^{1-\beta} s_h^\beta}{n+g+\delta} \right)^{\frac{1}{1-\alpha-\beta}} \quad \text{and} \quad h^* = \left(\frac{s_k^\alpha s_h^{1-\alpha}}{n+g+\delta} \right)^{\frac{1}{1-\alpha-\beta}}. \tag{A4.13}$$

Substituting (A4.13) into the production function and taking logs gives steady-state income per worker as

$$\ln \left(\frac{Y^*}{L} \right) = \ln A(0) + gt + \frac{\alpha}{1-\alpha-\beta} \ln (s_k) + \frac{\beta}{1-\alpha-\beta} \ln (s_h) - \frac{\alpha+\beta}{1-\alpha-\beta} \ln (n+g+\delta). \tag{A4.14}$$

Approximating around steady state, MRW showed that growth of output per worker in this model is given by

$$\ln \left(\frac{Y(t)}{L(t)} \right) - \ln \left(\frac{Y(0)}{L(0)} \right) = -\theta \ln \left(\frac{Y(0)}{L(0)} \right) + \theta \frac{\alpha}{1-\alpha-\beta} \ln (s_k)$$
$$+ \theta \frac{\beta}{1-\alpha-\beta} \ln (s_h) - \theta \frac{\alpha+\beta}{1-\alpha-\beta} \ln (n+g+\delta) + \theta \ln A(0) + gt, \tag{A4.15}$$

where $\theta = 1 - e^{-\lambda t}$ and the convergence rate is given by $\lambda = (n + g + \delta)(1 - \alpha - \beta)$.

MRW also presented an alternative way to express the role of human capital in determining economic growth. Combining (A4.14) with the equation for the steady-state level of human capital given in (A4.13) yields an equation for economic growth per worker as a function of the rate of investment in physical capital, the rate of population growth, and the level of human capital as

$$\ln\left(\frac{Y(t)}{L(t)}\right) - \ln\left(\frac{Y(0)}{L(0)}\right) = -\theta\ln\left(\frac{Y(0)}{L(0)}\right) + \theta\frac{\alpha}{1-\alpha}\ln(s_k) - \theta\frac{\alpha}{1-\alpha}\ln(n+g+\delta)$$

$$+ \theta\frac{\beta}{1-\alpha}\ln(h^*) + \theta\ln A(0) + gt,$$

(A4.16)

where h^* is the steady-state *level* of human capital as defined by equation (A4.13).

The augmented Solow model with structural change

Temple and Wößmann (2006) developed an empirical model to examine the impact of labour reallocation on aggregate productivity growth and they augmented the conventional growth regressions based on the MRW framework so as to allow for structural change. It is a general equilibrium model of production with two sectors and two factors. Total output is given by

$$Y = \frac{Y_a + qY_m}{\Omega(1,q)},$$

(A4.17)

where q is the relative price of the urban sector good; Y_a and Y_m are output quantities in agriculture and non-agriculture; and $\Omega(1,q)$ is a GDP price deflator.

The production function in each sector has constant returns to scale and is given by

$$Y_a = A_a F(K_a, L_a),$$

(A4.18a)

$$Y_m = A_m G(K_m, L_m),$$

(A4.18b)

where A_a and A_m are TFP in agriculture and non-agriculture respectively. Assuming that workers are paid their marginal products gives $w_a = A_a F_L$ and $w_m = qA_m G_L$, where w_a and w_m are wages in agriculture and non-agriculture respectively; and the L subscript denotes the partial derivative with respect to labour. Capital also receives its marginal product in both sectors, that is, $A_a F_K = qA_m G_k = r$, where r is the rental rate on capital and the K subscript is the partial derivative with respect to capital.

This model assumes that any observed effects of reallocation arise because of marginal product differentials and that the propensity to migrate depends on the ratio of wages in the two sectors. Migration will cease when the intersectoral wage ratio falls to a level denoted by k, so the long-run migration equilibrium is $w_m = kw_a$, where $k \geq 1$.

The relationship between the extent of structural change and wage ratio can be expressed as

$$x = \frac{p}{1-p} = \psi\left(\frac{w_m}{kw_a} - 1\right),$$

(A4.19)

where p is the migration propensity, defined by $p = -\Delta a/a$, where a is the share of agricultural employment in total employment; and ψ is the speed of adjustment to the long-run equilibrium. The 'odds ratio' for migration is increasing in the wage gap between the two sectors. Rearranging (A4.19) gives

$$\frac{w_m}{w_a} = k\left(1 + \frac{1}{\psi}\frac{p}{1-p}\right), \tag{A4.20}$$

so the extent of current wage ratio can be deduced using information on the observed pace of structural change. In this model, the wage differential varies across countries according to the value of p.

By assuming that the speed of adjustment (ψ), the equilibrium differential (k) and the labour share in total output $(\phi = (w_a L)/Y)$ are constant across economies, Temple and Wößmann (2006) derived the following expression for the aggregate Solow residual

$$\frac{\dot{Z}}{Z} = s(t)\frac{\dot{A}_a}{A_a} + (1 - s(t))\frac{\dot{A}_m}{A_m} + (k-1)\phi(1-a)\frac{\dot{m}}{m} + k\phi\frac{1}{\psi}\frac{p}{(1-p)}(1-a)\frac{\dot{m}}{m}, \tag{A4.21}$$

where $s(t)$ is the nominal output share for agriculture at time t, or $s(t) = Y_a/(Y_a + qY_m)$; ϕ is the labour share in total output, or $\phi = (w_a L)/Y$; and m is the share of non-agricultural employment in total employment, or $m = 1 - a$.

In the presence of an intersectoral wage differential, the aggregate Solow residual can thus be decomposed as a weighted average of the sectoral TFP growth rates plus the 'growth bonus' obtained by reallocating labour to a sector where its marginal product is higher. Since the migration propensity p is related to the extent of structural change as measured by $\dot{m}/m$, equation (A4.21) implies a convex relationship between growth and structural change. The intuition is that the growth impact of a given extent of structural change will be greatest in those countries experiencing more rapid structural change, as these are also the countries in which the intersectoral wage differential is greatest. Note that the two structural change terms in equation (A4.21) will disappear when there is no wage differential in equilibrium, $k = 1$, and the adjustment process in response to disequilibrium is instantaneous, $\psi \to \infty$.

Since it was not possible to measure capital stocks at the sectoral level, Temple and Wößmann (2006) treated sectoral TFP as unobservable and relied on a vector V to capture the cross-section variation in aggregate TFP growth that is not due to structural change, as follows

$$\frac{\dot{Z}}{Z} = \beta'V + (k-1)\phi MGROWTH + k\phi\frac{1}{\psi}DISEQ, \tag{A4.22}$$

where V is a vector of determinants of aggregate TFP growth including initial level of aggregate TFP and regional differences in technology and institutions proxied by regional dummies; and the structural change terms are defined as

$$MGROWTH = (1-a)\frac{\dot{m}}{m} \approx \Delta m \tag{A4.23a}$$

$$DISEQ = \frac{p}{1-p}(1-a)\frac{\dot{m}}{m} \approx \frac{p}{1-p}\Delta m. \tag{A4.23b}$$

Temple and Wößmann (2006) then extended MRW's model by including the structural change terms derived above to proxy the varying productivity growth across countries. Given the Cobb–Douglas production technology in equation (A4.11), TFP growth is equal to the growth rate of efficiency (g) times the exponent on the efficiency index ($1 - \alpha - \beta$). In the presence of wage differentials, TFP growth is a function of structural change terms as shown in equation (A4.22). Then the extension of MRW's model takes the form

$$\ln\left(\frac{Y(t)}{L(t)}\right) - \ln\left(\frac{Y(0)}{L(0)}\right) = w + \frac{t(k-1)}{1-\alpha-\beta}MGROWTH + \frac{tk\phi}{(1-\alpha-\beta)\psi}DISEQ + \theta\gamma'X - \theta\ln\left(\frac{Y(0)}{L(0)}\right),$$
$$\tag{A4.24}$$

where X is a vector of explanatory variables including rates of saving, physical and human capital accumulation. Thus, the specification of equation (A4.24) is a hybrid of the Solow model with an aggregate production function and a two-sector framework with sectoral product differentials.

When replacing the assumption that the labour share in output, ϕ, is the same across countries by an assumption that all countries have the same Cobb–Douglas technologies in agriculture, Temple and Wößmann (2006) constructed a second set of structural change terms

$$MGROWTH2 = (1-a)\frac{s}{a}\frac{\dot{m}}{m} \tag{A4.25a}$$

$$DISEQ2 = \frac{p}{1-p}(1-a)\frac{s}{a}\frac{\dot{m}}{m,} \tag{A4.25b}$$

where s is the share of agriculture in total value added. This alternative set of structural change terms adds s/a, that is, the share of agriculture in value added divided by the share of employment.

Notes

1. We draw on Ding and Knight (2009).
2. For instance, by Islam (1995), Caselli et al. (1996), Bond et al. (2001), and Hoeffler (2002).
3. Including Lichtenberg (1993), Howitt (2000), and Bond et al. (2010).
4. See Appendix 4.2 for a detailed derivation of the model.
5. Made, for instance, by Easterly and Levine (2001), Gundlach (2007), Klenow and Rodríguez-Clare (1997), and Mcquinn and Whelan (2007).
6. See Appendix 4.2 for precise definitions of the structural change variables.

7. In the 'Treatment of China in PWT 6', Heston pointed out that the basis for PPP estimates for China is very little improved over previous versions of PWT. The World Bank and IMF recently revised downward their estimates for China's PPP-based GDP by around 40%, based on new statistical calculations of PPP exchange rates published in December 2007 by the International Comparison Program (ICP). Since our focus is growth rather than level of income, we expect the impact of any inaccuracy of the PPP figures to be relatively minor in our research.

8. Discussed in Chapter 1.

9. Islam (1995), Caselli et al. (1996), and Hoeffler (2002).

10. Full lists of countries included in the different samples are provided in table A2 in the Appendix of Ding and Knight (2009).

11. Hong Kong, Taiwan, South Korea, and Singapore.

12. Such as Cook's distance measure, the Studentized distance residuals, and DFFITS.

13. In our system GMM estimation the original investment variables lagged by ten-year and fifteen-year periods are used as instruments in the first-differences equations, and first-differenced investment variables lagged by five-year period are used as additional instruments in the levels equations.

14. The levels of structural change variables lagged by ten-year and fifteen-year periods are used as instruments in the first-differences equations, and first-differenced structural change variables lagged by five-year period are used as additional instruments in the levels equations.

15. The definitions of MGROWTH2 and DISEQ2 are provided in Appendix 4.2.

16. We ran a large number of sensitivity tests for China using Brandt et al.'s (2008) employment data, China's official real GDP data, China's official data of investment over GDP, Wang and Yao's (2003) human capital data, and a sub-sample test for the period 1980–94 when the reliability of China's GDP data is less subject to dispute. Our results proved to be consistent and robust.

17. This is calculated based on the mean value of the prediction for each five-year interval.

References

Arellano, Manuel, and Olympia Bover (1995), 'Another look at the instrumental variable estimation of error-components models', *Journal of Econometrics*, 68: 29–52.

Barro, Robert (1991), 'Economic growth in a cross section of countries', *Quarterly Journal of Economics*, 106, 2: 407–43.

——and Jong-wha Lee (2001), 'International data on educational attainment: updates and implications', *Oxford Economic Papers*, 3: 541–63.

————(2010), 'A new data set of educational attainment in the world, 1950–2010', NBER Working Paper No. 15902.

——and Xavier Sala-i-Martin (2004), *Economic Growth* (2nd edn.). Cambridge, Mass.: The MIT Press.

Benhabib, Jess, and Mark Spiegel (1994), 'The role of human capital in economic development: evidence from aggregate cross-country data', *Journal of Monetary Economics*, 34, 2: 143–73.

Blomström, Magnus, Robert Lipsey, and Mario Zejan (1996), 'Is fixed investment the key to economic growth?', *Quarterly Journal of Economics*, 111, 1: 269–76.

Blundell, Richard, and Stephen Bond (1998), 'Initial conditions and moment restrictions in dynamic panel data models', *Journal of Econometrics*, 87, 1: 115–43.

Bond, Stephen, Anke Hoeffler, and Jonathan Temple (2001), 'GMM estimation of empirical growth models', CEPR Discussion Paper No. 3048.

——Asli Leblebicioglu, and Fabio Schiantarelli (2010), 'Capital accumulation and growth: a new look at the empirical evidence', *Journal of Applied Econometrics*, 25, 7: 1073–99.

Bosworth, Barry, and Susan Collins (2003), 'The empirics of growth: an update', *Brookings Papers on Economic Activity 2003*, 2: 113–79.

Bowsher, Clive (2002), 'On testing overidentifying restrictions in dynamic panel data models', *Economics Letters*, 77: 211–20.

Brandt, Loren, Chang-Tai Hsieh, and Xiaodong Zhu (2008), 'Growth and structural transformation in China', in Loren Brandt and Thomas Rawski (eds.), *China's Great Economic Transformation*, Cambridge and New York: Cambridge University Press: 683–728.

Caselli, Francesco, Gerardo Esquivel, and Fernando Lefort (1996), 'Reopening the convergence debate: a new look at cross-country growth empirics', *Journal of Economic Growth*, 1: 363–89.

Ding, Sai, and John Knight (2009), 'Can the augmented Solow Model explain China's remarkable economic growth? A cross-country panel data study', *Journal of Comparative Economics*, 37: 432–52.

Easterly, William, and Ross Levine (2001), 'It's not factor accumulation: stylized facts and growth models', *World Bank Economic Review*, 15: 177–219.

Gemmell, Norman (1996), 'Evaluating the impacts of human capital stocks and accumulation on economic growth: some new evidence', *Oxford Bulletin of Economics and Statistics*, 58, 1: 9–28.

Gundlach, Erich (2007), 'The Solow model in the empirics of growth and trade', *Oxford Review of Economic Policy*, 23, 1: 25–44.

Hall, Robert, and Charles Jones (1999), 'Why do some countries produce so much more output per worker than others?', *Quarterly Journal of Economics*, 114, 1: 83–116.

Heston, Alan, and Terry Sicular (2008), 'China and development economics', in Loren Brandt and Thomas Rawski (eds.), *China's Great Economic Transformation*, Cambridge and New York: Cambridge University Press: 27–67.

Hoeffler, Anke (2002), 'The augmented Solow model and the African growth debate', *Oxford Bulletin of Economics and Statistics*, 64, 2: 135–58.

Howitt, Peter (2000), 'Endogenous growth and cross-country income differences', *American Economic Review*, 90, 4: 829–46.

Hsiao, Cheng (1986), *Analysis of Panel Data*, Cambridge: Cambridge University Press.

Islam, Nazrul (1995), 'Growth empirics: a panel data approach', *Quarterly Journal of Economics*, 110, 4: 1127–70.

Klenow, Peter, and Andrés Rodríguez-Clare (1997), 'A neoclassical revival in growth economics: has it gone too far?', *NBER Macroeconomics Annual*, 12: 73–103.

Knight, John, and Lina Song (1999), *The Rural–Urban Divide: Economic Disparities and Interactions in China*, Oxford: Oxford University Press.

Krugman, Paul (1994), 'The myth of Asia's miracle', *Foreign Affairs*, 73, 6: 62–79.

Lichtenberg, Frank (1993), 'R&D investment and international productivity differences', in H. Giersch (ed.), *Economic Growth in the World Economy*, Tübingen: J. C. B. Mohr: 89–110.

Mcquinn, Kieran, and Karl Whelan (2007), 'Solow (1956) as a model of cross-country growth dynamics', *Oxford Review of Economic Policy*, 23, 1: 45–62.

Mankiw, Gregory, David Romer, and David Weil (1992), 'A contribution to the empirics of economic growth', *The Quarterly Journal of Economics*, 107: 407–37.

Nickell, Stephen (1981), 'Biases in dynamic models with fixed effects', *Econometrica*, 49, 6: 1417–26.

Pritchett, Lant (1999), 'Where has all the education gone?', *World Bank Economic Review*, 15, 3: 367–91.

Quah, Danny (2000), 'Cross-country growth comparison: theory to empirics', LSE Department of Economics Working Paper.

Temple, Jonathan (1999a), 'The new growth evidence', *Journal of Economic Literature*, 37, 1: 112–56.

——(1999b), 'A positive effect of human capital on growth', *Economics Letters*, 65: 131–4.

——and Ludger Wößmann (2006), 'Dualism and cross-country growth regressions', *Journal of Economic Growth*, 11: 187–228.

Wang, Yan, and Yudong Yao (2003), 'Sources of China's economic growth, 1952–1999: incorporating human capital accumulation', *China Economic Review*, 14: 32–52.

Windmeijer, Frank (2005), 'A finite sample correction for the variance of linear efficient two-step GMM estimators', *Journal of Econometrics*, 126: 25–51.

World Bank (1993), *The East Asian Miracle: Economic Growth and Public Policy*, Oxford: Oxford University Press.

Young, Alwyn (1995), 'The tyranny of numbers: confronting the statistical realities of the east Asian growth experience', *Quarterly Journal of Economics*, 110, 3: 641–80.

5

The Basic Cross-Province Growth Equation

5.1 Introduction

In this and the next two chapters, we conduct cross-province panel-data analysis to explain why China as a whole, and indeed all its provinces, has grown so fast. This chapter provides the base which can then be built on in Chapters 6 and 7.

This cross-province approach can be justified from both an economic and a statistical perspective. Firstly, although all provinces have grown rapidly by international standards, we are able to exploit the variations in province growth rates to explain the determinants of China's growth. Even though each province would correspond to a country in most other parts of the world, they have certain characteristics in common. All provinces are part of the 'developmental state' in which, since 1978, rapid economic growth has received primacy at all levels of government. They are all subject to central government policies with regard to foreign trade, family planning, macroeconomic management, financial policies, etc. Nevertheless, some provinces reformed and marketized earlier and further than others. Moreover, there are province differences in openness to foreign trade, natural increase in population, level of economic activity, and the investment–output ratio. To illustrate, if China's high growth is mainly due to the high average rate of investment in physical and human capital, it is informative to use province differences in investment to investigate what the effect on China's growth rate would be if it had the much lower investment rate typical of other poor countries.

Secondly, the analysis of provincial time-series data expands our sample size substantially. It reveals more information about the various determinants of growth than would an aggregate time-series analysis. Moreover, the province-level data may well be more reliable. In 2006 China's National Bureau of Statistics (NBS) undertook a benchmark revision of national income and product accounts statistics based on the 2004 economic census. This revision validates the pre-economic census provincial aggregate output values and invalidates the corresponding national figures (Holz 2008).

Economists are better able to analyse the direct than the indirect determinants of growth, and yet these conventional variables may simply represent associations that are themselves to be explained by causal processes. There are three possible empirical approaches: growth accounting, structural growth modelling, and informal growth regression. Each has its strengths and weaknesses; each deserves to be explored. In contrast to the former two, the third approach permits the introduction of some explanatory variables that represent the underlying as well as the proximate causes of economic growth. That is well suited to our purposes and is therefore used in Chapters 5–7.

A feature of our study is to use recently developed approaches to model selection in order to construct empirical models based on robust predictors. There are many growth theories and few grounds on which to choose among them. The issue of model uncertainty has attracted much research attention in the context of cross-country growth regressions. However, to the best of our knowledge, it has been largely ignored in cross-province growth studies of China, that is, the existing literature has not explicitly or systematically considered the issue of model selection before any investigation of particular causes of China's growth.

In this chapter, we first use two leading model-selection and model-averaging approaches, Bayesian model averaging and the automated general-to-specific approach, to examine the association between the growth rate of real GDP per capita and a large range of potential explanatory variables. These include the initial level of income, fixed capital formation, human capital formation, population growth, the degree of openness, institutional change, sectoral change, financial development, infrastructure, and regional advantage. The variables flagged as being important by these procedures are then used in formulating our baseline model, which is estimated using panel-data 'system generalized-method-of-moments' (GMM) to address the problems of omitted variables, endogeneity, and measurement error of regressors. The robustness of the selected models and the contribution of main variables will be examined in Chapters 6 and 7, with the former focusing on the proximate determinants of growth and the latter focusing on the underlying factors.

Section 5.2 explains and justifies our empirical methodology. Section 5.3 discusses the data set and provides summary statistics. In Section 5.4 we report the model-selection results, and in Section 5.5 the specification and results of the baseline equation. Section 5.6 summarizes and concludes.[1]

This is necessarily a technical chapter, providing the methodology and paving the way for the two chapters that follow. Since the methodology has passed the test of a peer-reviewed journal publication (Ding and Knight 2011), the reader who is willing to take the technicalities on trust may wish to concentrate on the concluding Section 5.6.

5.2 Methodology

We draw on the relevant literatures to explain and justify our methodology. This concerns the choice of informal growth regressions, the method of dealing with model uncertainty, and the panel-data estimation approach. We begin by explaining why we choose to adopt the informal growth regression approach.

In the cross-country analysis of Chapter 4 we found that the Solow model augmented by both human capital and structural change provides a fairly good account of China's remarkable growth performance. Moreover, five factors—conditional convergence from a low income level, high physical capital formation, high level of human capital, rapid structural change away from agriculture, and slow population growth—made the main contributions to China's relative growth success. These pointers set the scene for the current cross-province analysis. However, structural growth modelling of this sort might leave out important underlying causes of growth. At least some of these variables can be incorporated in informal growth regressions.

There is a large literature on cross-province growth regressions for China. Two empirical approaches have been used: either some version of the neoclassical growth model, often in the form of the augmented Solow model as developed by Mankiw, Romer, and Weil (1992) (henceforth MRW), or informal growth regressions[2] that contain among other variables the explanatory variables in which the researcher is most interested. Different periods are analysed, although most are confined to the period of economic reform, from 1978 onwards. The methods of analysis vary in sophistication, from cross-section OLS to panel-data GMM analysis. The research covers a broad range of factors relating to variation in growth among Chinese provinces, such as convergence or divergence, physical and human capital investment, openness, economic reform, geographical location, infrastructure, financial development, labour market development, spatial dependence, and preferential policies.[3] An underlying problem in all the research is the difficulty in establishing causal relationships as opposed to mere associations.

These studies often use an assortment of economic theories to motivate a variety of variables that are included in the cross-province (or cross-city) growth regressions, and then test the robustness of their conclusions to the addition of an ad hoc selection of further controls. Although each study may present intuitively appealing results, none has directly posed the general question: can the variations in growth highlighted by cross-province growth regressions explain why the economy as a whole has grown so fast? Moreover, no systematic consideration has been given to uncertainty about the regression specification, with the implication that conventional methods for inference can be misleading.

Another strand of growth research on China adopts the growth-accounting approach to break down the observed growth of GDP into components associated with changes in factor inputs and in production technologies.[4] Average annual total factor productivity (TFP) growth in China for the reform period is found to range from a high of 3.9% to a low of 1.4% in these studies. This disconcertingly wide variation is partly the result of the different assumptions made.

Brandt et al. (2008) argued that conventional growth accounting based on aggregate data for China cannot capture the effects of structural change, in particular labour reallocation from the agricultural to the non-agricultural sector and from the state to the non-state sector. In their growth accounting estimates for the period 1978–2004, they incorporated three sectors and found that the contribution of structural change to annual output growth was 2.3 percentage points, of which transfer from the state to the non-state sectors accounted for 1.8 percentage points and that from agriculture to non-agriculture 0.5 percentage points.

The growth-accounting approach involves measuring the capital stock and making assumptions about unknown parameters such as output elasticities and capital depreciation rates. Two further arguments make us disinclined to use growth accounting. First, when the TFP growth is measured as a residual, that is, as the growth rate in GDP that cannot be accounted for by the growth of the observable inputs, it should not be equated with technological change. It covers many factors such as structural change, improvement in allocative efficiency, economies of scale, and any misspecification of the production function. This is particularly true for China: according to Borenzstein and Ostry (1996), technological progress in China has been substantially lower than TFP growth, with the difference representing structural change and unmeasured input growth. Second, technological change and investment may not be separable in reality, that is, changing technology requires investment, and investment inevitably involves technological change. For instance, in Chapter 4 we argued that investment is a major carrier of structural change in China: structural transformation requires investment in new, normally high-productivity, activities. Employment growth in the high-productivity industrial and service sectors is determined by the rate of investment in those sectors, and the new job opportunities are largely taken by migrant workers from the low-productivity agricultural sector.

There is no single explicit theoretical framework to guide empirical work on economic growth. The neoclassical model predicts that the long-run growth rate is determined by the rate of exogenous technological progress, and that adjustment to stable steady-state growth is achieved by endogenous changes in factor accumulation. It is silent on the determinants of technological progress. Endogenous growth theory concentrates on technological progress and emphasizes the role of learning by doing, knowledge spill-over, research and development, and education in driving economic growth.[5] Because the theories are not mutually exclusive, the problem of model uncertainty concerning which variables should be included to capture the underlying 'data generation process' presents a central challenge for empirical growth analysis.

This issue gained increasing attention after the seminal work of Levine and Renelt (1992). The authors applied an extreme bounds analysis (EBA) to cross-country growth regressions and investigated the robustness of a large number of variables that were found in the literature to be correlated with growth. This work was further extended by Sala-i-Martin (1997) and Temple (2000). Other econometric and statistical methods have been developed and applied to handle model uncertainty, among which Bayesian model averaging[6] and the general-to-specific approach[7] are among the most influential. In this chapter we adopt the Bayesian model averaging (BMA) and general-to-specific (GETS) approaches to consider the association between GDP per capita growth rates and a wide range of potential explanatory variables. The purpose of the first-stage model selection is to provide guidance on the choice of variables to include in the subsequent panel-data analysis.

The basic idea of BMA is that the posterior distribution of any parameter of interest is a weighted average of the posterior distributions of that parameter under each of the models with weights given by the posterior model probabilities. Thus a natural way to think about model uncertainty is to admit that we do not know which model is 'true' and, instead, attach probabilities to different possible models. By treating parameters and models as random variables, the uncertainty about the model is summarized in terms of a probability distribution over the space of all possible models. The idea of the GETS procedure is to specify a 'general unrestricted model' (GUM), which is assumed to characterize the essential data generation process, and then to 'test down' to a parsimonious encompassing and congruent representation based on the theory of reduction. The specific regression is a valid restriction of the general model if it is statistically well specified and also encompasses every other parsimonious regression. One attractive feature of the automatic procedure of model selection is argued to be the huge efficiency gain.

Each of the two procedures has comparative advantages and disadvantages in dealing with model uncertainty. For example, one key disadvantage of BMA is the difficulty of interpretation, that is, parameters are assumed to have the same interpretation regardless of the model in which they appear; in addition, it does not lead to a simple model, making the interpretation of results harder (Chatfield 1995). Criticisms of GETS modelling commonly concern the problems of controlling the overall size of tests in a sequential testing process and of interpreting the final results from a classical viewpoint (Owen 2003). Hence, the joint application of BMA and GETS model-selection procedures in this chapter is designed to combine the strengths of both methods and to circumvent the limitations of each to some extent. A discussion of the two methods is provided in an appendix to Ding and Knight (2011).

Since neither method can handle the problem of endogenous regressors during the model-selection process, no causal interpretation can be attached to the results at this stage. We therefore adopt a two-stage testing approach to solve this problem. When a subset of variables is identified as receiving the greatest support from the underlying data according to the model-selection results, a further panel-data analysis is conducted to investigate the deeper determinants of provincial GDP per capita growth. Although cross-section regression has the advantage of focusing on the long-run trends of economic growth, panel-data methods can control for omitted variables that are persistent over time, and can alleviate measurement error and endogeneity biases by use of lags of the regressors as instruments (Temple 1999).

It is a challenge to estimate a short dynamic panel with fixed effects and multiple endogenous regressors, especially when the number of cross-sections is relatively small. Several econometric problems require attention. For instance, the correlation between the lagged dependent variable and the time-invariant region-specific effects renders the OLS estimator biased and inconsistent (Hsiao 1986). In the cross-country or cross-province growth regressions, the OLS estimate of the coefficient of initial income term is likely to be biased upward (Bond et al. 2001; Hoeffler 2002). Nickell (1981) showed that the within-groups estimator will be biased for fixed T (number of time periods) and large N (number of cross-sections). Although the bias diminishes with T, for the typical growth regression with small T, the within-groups estimate of the coefficient of the initial income term is likely to be seriously biased downwards. This problem also applies to the instrumental variable methods based on fixed effects.

The system GMM estimator for dynamic panels has become popular in the empirical growth literature in order to overcome this bias and also to address the problems of endogeneity and mismeasurement. It combines the standard set of equations in first-differences with suitably lagged levels as instruments, with an additional set of equations in levels with suitably lagged first-differences as instruments. By adding the original equation in levels to the system and exploiting these additional moment conditions, Arellano and Bover (1995) and Blundell and Bond (1998) found a dramatic improvement in efficiency and a significant reduction in finite sample bias compared with first-differenced GMM. However, caution is needed in applying system GMM to our study. First, the instrument proliferation problem is likely to be severe when the cross-section dimension is small. According to Bowsher (2002) and Roodman (2009), as T rises, the instrument count can easily grow large relative to the sample size, so making some asymptotic results about the estimators and related specification tests misleading. Second, cross-sectional error dependence can lead to serious problems in the estimation of short dynamic panels. Sarafidis and Robertson (2009) demonstrate that under cross-sectional error dependence, the GMM estimator is inconsistent as $N \to \infty$ for fixed T, which holds for any lag length of the instruments used.

To address the instrument proliferation problem, we adopt two ways of restricting the number of instruments used in our system GMM estimation. The first is to collapse the instrument sets, that is, the GMM estimator is based on one instrument per variable instead of one instrument for each variable at each period. The second approach is to use only certain lags instead of all possible lag lengths for instruments in each first-differenced equation. For example, for potentially endogenous variables, levels of that variable lagged by ten-year, fifteen-year, and twenty-year periods are used as instruments in the first-differenced equations, and first-differenced variables lagged by a five-year period are used as additional instruments for the levels equations. Following the suggestion of Roodman (2009), we report the number of instruments generated for our regressions together with the Hansen and Difference Sargan statistics. Regarding the second problem, we include time-specific effects in our regressions to capture common variations in the dependent variable and to reduce the asymptotic bias of the estimator in the presence of cross-sectional error dependence. All the standard errors are robust to heteroskedasticity and clustering on province.

5.3 The Data

The original sample consists of a panel of thirty provinces with annual data for the period 1978–2007.[8] The data come mainly from *China Compendium of Statistics 1949–2004*, compiled by the National Bureau of Statistics of China. The data for 2005–7 are obtained from the latest issues of *China Statistical Yearbook*. The reliability of Chinese official macroeconomic data is often under dispute. One important issue is the problem of data inconsistency over the sample period. For example, GDP figures for the years 2005–7 were recompiled on the basis of China's 2004 economic census, while corresponding provincial data for earlier years remain unrevised. Another problem is data non-comparability across provinces. Take population as an example: the household registration population figure is provided for some provinces, whereas for others only permanent population data are available. In addition, the substantial 'floating population' of temporary migrants is not fully accounted for by the population data. These discrepancies can result in measurement error problems and may call into question the reliability of our estimation results. Therefore, we use a number of 'cleaning rules' (see the appendix in Ding and Knight 2011) to get rid of potential outliers for each variable, and we employ the panel-data system GMM estimator to deal with potential mismeasurement.

Our first-stage model-selection analysis is based on cross-section data, in which observations (other than initial income level) are averaged over the entire sample period. For the subsequent panel-data study, we opt for non-overlapping five-year time intervals, a choice which has been widely used in the cross-country growth literature.[9] On the one hand, by comparison with the yearly data, the five-year average set-up alleviates the influence of temporary factors associated with business cycles. On the other hand, we are able to maintain more time-series variation than would be possible with a longer-period interval. There are thus six time periods (T), corresponding to the five-year intervals (1978–82, 1983–87, ..., 2003–7), and there are thirty cross-sections (N), corresponding to the thirty provinces.

All the variables are calculated in 1990 constant prices, the price indices being province specific.[10] The dependent variable is the growth rate of real GDP per capita. The provincial growth rates are shown in Table 5.1. The annual average per capita growth rate of all thirty provinces over the entire reform period was 7.7%, with an average value of 8.1% for the coastal provinces and 7.5% for interior provinces. China's economic reform generated across-the-nation rapid growth, that is, both the coastal and inner regions grew fast by international standards. However, that a growth disparity did exist is indicated by the 4% average growth difference between the highest growth province (Zhejiang) and the lowest one (Gansu) over the full sample period. Table 5.1 also reveals interesting time patterns in China's growth. Rapid growth occurred in the first decade, slowed down in the second decade, and accelerated in the third decade. In the period 1998–2007, the growth disparity across provinces became smaller and even the slowest-growing province (Yunnan) managed an average rate of 8.2% per annum.

The explanatory variables can be broadly classified into ten categories: initial level of income, physical capital formation, human capital formation, population growth rate, degree of openness, pace of economic reform or institutional change, sectoral change or degree of industrialization, infrastructure, financial development, and geographic location. A geographical distinction is made between 'coastal' and other provinces. This classification follows that of the literature, the underlying rationale being that the provinces deemed to be coastal have

Table 5.1. Descriptive statistics of provincial GDP per capita growth rates

	Full-sample period	Sub-sample periods		
	1978–2007	1978–1987	1988–1997	1998–2007
All provinces (30 provinces)	0.077	0.072	0.054	0.106
	(0.037)	(0.027)	(0.031)	(0.032)
Coastal provinces (11 provinces)	0.081	0.078	0.061	0.119
	(0.033)	(0.027)	(0.030)	(0.028)
Interior provinces (19 provinces)	0.075	0.073	0.055	0.109
	(0.038)	(0.026)	(0.032)	(0.034)
Highest growth province	0.103	0.112	0.108	0.131
	(0.024)	(0.001)	(0.046)	(0.055)
Lowest growth province	0.061	0.019	0.011	0.082
	(0.049)	(0.007)	(0.007)	(0.040)

Notes: Mean values and standard deviations (in parentheses) are provided; coastal provinces consist of Liaoning, Hebei, Tianjin, Shandong, Jiangsu, Shanghai, Zhejiang, Fujian, Guangdong, and Hainan, plus Beijing; and interior provinces include Anhui, Gansu, Guangxi, Guizhou, Heilongjiang, Henan, Hubei, Hunan, Inner Mongolia, Jiangxi, Jilin, Ningxia, Qinghai, Shaanxi, Shanxi, Sichuan, Tibet, Xinjiang, and Yunnan; for the full-sample period, the highest growth province was Zhejiang, and the lowest growth province was Gansu; for the three sub-sample periods, Zhejiang, Fujian, Shaanxi were the highest growth provinces respectively, and Shanghai, Tibet, Yunnan were the corresponding lowest growth provinces.

advantages in the form of lower-cost access to markets (see Appendix 5.1 for detailed definitions).

5.4 Model-Selection Results

The prospects for selecting a good model depend primarily on the adequacy of the general unrestricted model as an approximation to the data generation process (Doornik and Hendry 2007). A poorly specified general model stands little chance of leading to a good 'final' specific model. We consider ten different groups of explanatory variables, and rely (albeit sufficiently loosely) on growth theory and previous empirical findings to guide the specification of the general model. One important issue is that variables within each category are highly correlated, which may cause problems if all variables are simultaneously included in one general regression. The strategy we adopt is to select one or two representative variables from each range (based on existing empirical literature and correlation results) to form the basic general model, and then to test for the robustness of the model-selection results using other variables left in each group. Throughout this section, when we refer to growth we shall, unless indicated otherwise, mean average annual growth of real GDP per capita ($g_{i,\,t}$).

We start from a general model that includes thirteen explanatory variables and searches for statistically acceptable reductions of this model. The included variables are the logarithm of initial level of income ($lny_{i,t-1}$), ratio of fixed capital formation over GDP (fcf/GDP), secondary school enrolment as a proportion of the total population (stu_{SEC}/pop), ratio of students enrolled in higher education to students enrolled in regular secondary education ($stu_{HIGH}/stu_{REGSEC,}$), population natural growth rate ($popngr$), ratio of exports to GDP ($export/GDP$), the SOE share of industrial output (ind_{SOE}/ind_{TOTAL}), change in non-agricultural share of employment ($MGROWTH$), degree of industrialization ($deofin$), railway density ($railway/area$), ratio of business volume of post and telecommunications to GDP ($post\&tele/GDP$), and a coastal dummy ($dumcoastal$).

We first use BMA to isolate variables that have a high posterior probability of inclusion. In Table 5.2 we present a summary of the BMA results, where the posterior probability that the variable is included in the model, the posterior mean, and the posterior standard deviation for each variable are reported. Owing to the difficulty of interpreting parameters in economic terms when the conditioning variables differ across models, our emphasis here lies on the posterior probability of inclusion for each variable, that is, the sum of posterior model probabilities for all models in which each variable appears. Given that the prior probability of a variable being in the true model is set at 0.5, its robustness may be assessed in terms of how the data update this prior. We therefore refer to a specific variable as being important if the posterior probability of inclusion is greater than

0.5. The results indicate a possibly important role for the initial level of income, the SOE share of total industrial output, secondary school enrolment, fixed capital formation, and population growth.

We then conduct an automatic model-selection exercise using the GETS methodology. Starting from the same general model and searching for statistically acceptable reductions, the software package *Autometrics* arrives at a final model with a set of explanatory variables broadly similar to those highlighted by the BMA analysis. The OLS estimation of the final specific model is reported in Table 5.3. We find that growth in GDP per capita is negatively associated with the initial

Table 5.2. Bayesian model averaging (BMA) model-selection results

Regressor	Posterior probability of inclusion	Posterior mean	Posterior standard deviation
Constant	100.0	0.223	0.036
$lny_{i,t-1}$	100.0	−0.021	0.005
ind_{SOE}/ind_{TOTAL}	100.0	−0.064	0.013
stu_{SEC}/pop	100.0	0.483	0.135
fcf/GDP	69.2	0.035	0.031
$popngr$	59.9	−0.859	0.917
stu_{HIGH}/stu_{REGSEC}	36.3	0.024	0.041
$export/GDP$	27.6	0.007	0.015
$railway/area$	20.2	−0.020	0.056
$loan/GDP$	8.5	−0.001	0.003
$dumcoastal$	8.4	0.001	0.002
$MGROWTH$	7.7	−0.005	0.136
$post\&tele/GDP$	6.9	−0.002	0.025
$deofin$	5.6	−0.001	0.004

Notes: Estimation is based on cross-sectional data; dependent variable: growth rate of real provincial GDP per capita.

Table 5.3. General-to-specific (GETS) model-selection results

Regressor	Coefficient	Standard error	t-value	t-probability	Partial R^2
Constant	0.249	0.029	8.35	0.000	0.752
$lny_{i,t-1}$	−0.025	0.004	−5.45	0.000	0.564
fcf/GDP	0.059	0.021	2.86	0.009	0.262
stu_{SEC}/pop	0.418	0.122	3.44	0.002	0.339
$popngr$	−1.823	0.701	−2.60	0.016	0.227
$export/GDP$	0.025	0.018	1.43	0.167	0.081
ind_{SOE}/ind_{TOTAL}	−0.055	0.012	−4.31	0.000	0.446
Sigma	0.006	RSS	0.001	R^2	0.845
F(6,23)	20.97 [0.000]	LogLik	115.804	AIC	−7.197
Normality test		$\chi^2(2) = 1.872$ [0.393]			
Testing for heteroscedasticity		F(12,10) = 0.558 [0.832]			

Notes: This is the OLS estimation of final specific model based on cross-sectional data, T = 30; dependent variable: growth rate of real provincial GDP per capita; RSS: residual sum of squares; F(6,23): joint significance test; LogLik: log-likelihood; and AIC: Akaike's information criterion.

income level, population growth, and the SOE share of industrial output, whereas fixed capital investment and secondary school enrolment are positively correlated.

The major difference between the results of the two methods lies in the role of exports in explaining cross-province growth rates, that is, despite the statistical insignificance, exports as a proportion of GDP is retained by GETS in the final specific model, but BMA analysis flags the export ratio as potentially unimportant (with a posterior inclusion probability of 28%). Other variables such as sectoral change, infrastructure, and financial development are identified as unimportant predictors of economic growth by both model-selection methods. However, this outcome may simply reflect the highly endogenous nature of these variables, which cannot be accounted for at the model-selection stage. We will re-examine the role of some of these variables in determining output growth in the panel-data context in Chapter 7.

5.5 The Baseline Model

Using the model-selection results, delivered by BMA and GETS, and various panel-data techniques, we estimate the baseline model (Table 5.4). Consistent with the

Table 5.4. Panel-data estimation of the selected baseline model

Regressors	OLS	Within Groups	IV (2SLS)	SYS-GMM	SYS-GMM
$lny_{i,t-1}$	−0.035**	−0.061**	−0.074**	−0.046**	0.036**
	(0.004)	(0.012)	(0.018)	(0.007)	(0.004)
fcf/GDP	0.074**	0.067**	0.227**	0.093**	
	(0.016)	(0.026)	(0.100)	(0.026)	
stu_{SEC}/pop	0.463**	0.035	0.898*	1.008**	
	(0.139)	(0.253)	(0.500)	(0.284)	
$popngr$	−3.095**	−3.843**	−3.475*	−4.057**	
	(0.597)	(1.162)	(2.078)	(1.036)	
$export/GDP$	0.027**	0.005	0.075	0.044**	
	(0.011)	(0.016)	(0.061)	(0.018)	
ind_{SOE}/ind_{TOTAL}	−0.052**	−0.053**	0.017	−0.054**	
	(0.011)	(0.025)	(0.084)	(0.021)	
R^2	0.746	0.784			
AR(2) p value				0.866	0.811
Hansen p value			0.352	0.665	0.362
Dif Sargan p value				0.249	0.966
No. of observations	150	150	149	150	150

Notes: Five-year interval panel data is used for estimation and all time dummies are included but not reported to save space; standard errors are in parentheses, which are heteroskedasticity-consistent and clustering on province; in both the IV and system GMM estimation, $lny_{i,t-1}$ is treated as predetermined, *popngr* is treated as exogenous, and all other variables are treated as endogenous; ** and * indicate that the coefficient is significantly different from zero at the 5 or 10% significance level respectively.

prediction of Bond et al. (2001) and Hoeffler (2002), we find that our system GMM estimator yields a consistent estimate of the coefficient on the initial level of income which lies in between the upper bound provided by the OLS estimator and the lower bound given by the within-groups estimator. The instrumental variable method (IV-2SLS) yields an estimate of the initial level of income even lower than that of within-groups, indicating the potential bias of this kind of fixed-effect estimator in short dynamic panels. Thus, the panel-data system GMM with a restricted instrument set is our preferred estimation method.

Interestingly, the GMM results support the model selected by the GETS procedure, that is, the ratio of exports to GDP appears positive and significant. Controlling for other explanatory variables, the initial level of income is found to have a negative effect on subsequent provincial growth rates, providing evidence of conditional convergence over the reform period. The estimated coefficient implies that a one percentage point lower initial level of GDP per capita raises the subsequent growth rate of GDP per capita by 0.05 percentage points. As we explained in Chapter 2, conditional convergence is an implication of the neoclassical growth model, deriving from the assumption of diminishing returns to capital accumulation. The controls imply that the provinces have different steady states, and that convergence will lead them to their respective steady-state levels of income per capita. Despite the challenge posed by endogenous growth theory, the neoclassical paradigm of conditional convergence is widely supported by empirical evidence in both the cross-country growth literature[11] and the cross-province growth literature on China.[12]

It is notable that when we exclude other control variables and regress the growth rate on the initial income per capita alone, the coefficient becomes significantly positive, indicating absolute divergence. Table 5.4 shows the coefficient on initial income per capita in this specification to be 0.036 (significant at the 5% level), whereas it is –0.046 (significantly negative at the 5% level) in the baseline model. Our findings of conditional convergence and absolute divergence reveal an interesting growth pattern in China: poor provinces grew less rapidly than rich ones, but they tended to converge in a relative sense towards their own steady state. One possible explanation for conditional convergence is that relatively poor provinces have lower stocks of physical and human capital, so that the marginal product of capital is higher for them. Another explanation might lie in the central government's regional development policies. During the period 1978–93, fiscal decentralization reform gave provincial governments more discretionary power in tax administration and revenue collection. The 'fiscal contracting system' reduced the central government's share of revenue and curtailed fiscal transfers away from rich and towards poor provinces (Raiser 1998; Knight and Li 1999). In 1994, the 'tax assignment system' reform strengthened the central government's fiscal capacity, which enabled it to promote economic development in poor regions such as the western provinces and minority areas. From about 1998 onwards there was a fiscal redistribution towards poor provinces (Wong and Bird 2008: 456). This might help to explain the convergence between lowest and highest growth provinces in recent years (Table 5.1).

Fixed capital formation is an important determinant of China's growth: a one percentage point rise in the ratio of fixed capital formation to GDP in a province raises its growth rate of GDP per capita by 0.1 percentage points. Human capital investment appears also to be important, that is, a one percentage point increase in the secondary school enrolment ratio is associated with a higher growth rate of GDP per capita by 0.3 percentage points. Since both physical and human capital accumulation are the focus of Chapter 6, detailed discussion will follow in that chapter.

The increase in population has a negative consequence for growth: reducing the rate of population growth by 0.1 percentage points is associated with an increase in GDP per capita growth of 0.4 percentage points. A rapid population growth rate involves a cost, that is, faster growth of the labour force means more capital has to be used to equip the growing labour force, and hence there is less scope for capital deepening, with resultant slower growth of capital per worker and thus output per worker. Within the standard Solow model, slower population growth implies a higher equilibrium level of output per worker and capital per worker. This means that if two provinces have the same initial income level, but one has a lower population growth rate, it will grow more quickly than the other as they move towards their equilibrium growth rates. Whatever its effect on current well-being, by slowing down the growth of population and reducing the strain on resources, China's 'one-child family' policy, introduced in the late 1970s, has a positive impact on the growth of GDP per capita.

Exports are conducive to provincial growth: a one percentage point increase in the ratio of exports to GDP leads to an increase in GDP per capita growth of 0.08 percentage points. According to the report of the Commission on Growth and Development (2008), a flourishing export sector is an important ingredient of high and sustained growth, especially in the early stages. In endogenous growth theory, international trade, especially exports, is viewed as an important source of human capital augmentation, technological change, and knowledge spill-over across countries (Grossman and Helpman 1995). China's open-door policy, adopted after 1978, created an excellent opportunity to exploit its comparative advantage in labour-intensive manufacturing industry, making exports a driver of China's growth. We shall explore more deeply the effect of the economy's greater openness on its growth in Chapter 7.

The SOE share of industrial output has a significant and negative impact on output growth: a decrease of one percentage point in this variable raises the GDP per capita growth rate by 0.04 percentage points. This variable is a proxy for the pace of economic reform or institutional change. In the mid-1980s, SOEs were given successively greater autonomy in production and a greater share of the profits they generated through a variety of profit remittance contracts and management responsibility systems. However, owing to the principal-agent problem inherent in state ownership, the effect of the industrial reform in improving the efficiency and profitability of SOEs remained limited. By contrast, non-state-owned enterprises such as collectively owned rural township and village enterprises in the 1980s and domestic and foreign privately owned industrial enterprises in the 1990s grew rapidly in response to market opportunities and better incentive structures. Therefore, the declining share of SOEs in industrial output is conducive to the growth of GDP per capita. This effect is examined in detail in Chapter 7.

There is no evidence of second order serial correlation in the first-differenced residuals, and neither the Hansen test nor the Difference Sargan test rejects the validity of instruments. In brief, our system GMM results favour the model selected by the GETS procedure and highlight the role of conditional convergence, physical and human capital formation, population growth, degree of openness, and ownership type in determining the economic growth of Chinese provinces.

5.6 Conclusion

In this chapter we have attempted to answer a broad question: why has China grown so fast? The economies of all provinces grew rapidly by international standards over the period of economic reform, but there is sufficient variation in growth among the thirty provinces to permit a cross-province analysis. Our choice of the informal growth regression instead of the growth-accounting or structural growth modelling approach allows us to consider both the proximate and the underlying determinants of growth in China.

Growth empirics has been heavily criticized because of the inherent model uncertainty. This uncertainty arises because theoretical guidance on variable selection and measurement is lacking. The problem has been widely recognized in the cross-country growth literature but largely ignored when modelling economic growth in China. In this chapter we attempted to fill the gap in the literature by adopting two recently developed approaches to model selection, BMA and GETS, to tackle model uncertainty. This enabled us to choose from a wide range of candidate predictors of China's economic growth. The first-stage model-selection results identified a role for conditional convergence, physical and human capital formation, population growth, degree of openness, and ownership in determining output growth across China's provinces.

The endogeneity of regressors constitutes another serious problem in growth regressions. Many of our explanatory variables have to be considered endogenous: physical and human capital accumulation, openness, institutions, and so on. To solve that problem, in the second-stage model estimation we adopted the system GMM estimator for dynamic panels.

Among results of the baseline model, three major findings relate to capital accumulation: there is conditional convergence among provinces, and both physical and human capital investments promote economic growth. They are consistent with the implications of the transitional dynamics of neoclassical growth theory. Such transitional movement is indeed to be expected given the likely disequilibrium of the Chinese economy at the start of economic reform. Our evidence of conditional convergence implies that each province is converging towards its equilibrium steady state. It might, however, have other explanations, for example, that convergence reflects the effects of fiscal transfers from the central government to poor provinces and minority areas. The growth impacts of physical and human capital accumulation are in line with the conditional convergence argument. An alternative interpretation of the positive effects of investment, drawing on endogenous growth theory, is that it has generated not only capital accumulation but also technological progress. This interpretation is examined further in Chapter 6.

The results of the baseline equation imply also that China's 'one-child family' policy helped to promote the growth of output per capita. Two measurable indicators of institutional and policy change—the opening up of the economy and the privatization of production—had significant and substantial effects on the growth rate. These structural changes, implying that China had started from a position of much inefficiency and well within its production frontier, are examined in more detail in Chapter 7.

APPENDIX 5.1   DETAILED VARIABLE DEFINITIONS

Variable	Definition	Units
Dependent variable		
$g_{i,t}$	Growth rate of real provincial GDP per capita	proportion
Independent variables		
$lny_{i,t-1}$	Logarithm of beginning-period real GDP per capita	1990 RMB
fcf/GDP	Fixed capital formation to GDP	proportion
stu_{SEC}/pop	Students enrolled in secondary education/Year-end total population	proportion
stu_{HIGH}/stu_{REGSEC}	Students enrolled in higher education/Students enrolled in regular secondary education	proportion
popngr	Population natural growth rate = Birth rate – death rate	proportion
export/GDP	Ratio of exports to GDP (Exports converted to RMB using official exchange rate from IFS, IMF)	proportion
ind_{SOE}/ind_{TOTAL}	Output value of state-owned enterprises/Gross industrial output value	proportion
MGROWTH	Linear sectoral change term: Change of non-agricultural share of employment	proportion
deofin	Degree of industrialization (Gross industrial output value/(Gross industrial output value + Gross agricultural output value))	proportion
railway/area	Mileages of railways per square kilometre (Total railway length/Area)	proportion
post&tele/GDP	Business volume of post and telecommunication/GDP	proportion
dumcoastal	A dummy variable which is equal to one for coastal provinces (Liaoning, Hebei, Tianjin, Shandong, Jiangsu, Shanghai, Zhejiang, Fujian, Guangdong, and Hainan, plus Beijing), and zero otherwise.	0 or 1

Note: All the variables are calculated in 1990 constant prices and price indices are province specific.

Notes

1. This chapter draws on Ding and Knight (2011).
2. For instance, Barro (1991), and Barro and Sala-i-Martin (2004).
3. For example, Chen and Fleisher (1996), Li et al. (1998), Raiser (1998), Chen and Feng (2000), Démurger (2001), Bao et al. (2002), Brun et al. (2002), Cai et al. (2002), Jones et al. (2003), Hao (2006), Yao (2006), Guariglia and Poncet (2008), and Fleisher et al. (2010).
4. For instance, Borenzstein and Ostry (1996), Hu and Khan (1997), Woo (1998), Wang and Yao (2001), Young (2003), and Brandt et al. (2008).
5. For instance, Lucas (1988) and Romer (1990).
6. See Raftery (1995), Fernández et al. (2001), and Sala-i-Martin et al. (2004).
7. See Hendry and Krolzig (2004), and Hoover and Perez (2004).

8. China is administratively decomposed into thirty-one provinces, minority autonomous regions, and municipalities. Since Chongqing became a municipal city in 1997, we combine Chongqing with Sichuan for the period 1997–2007, so making it consistent with earlier observations.

9. For instance, Islam (1995), Bond et al. (2001), and Ding and Knight (2009).

10. The deflator is the provincial consumer price index (CPI). It is widely believed that China's implicit GDP deflator based on the Material Product System approach has understated inflation in China, therefore exaggerating real GDP growth (Wu 1997; Maddison 1998; Woo 1998; Rawski 2001). Using a different approach, Maddison (1998) predicts that the average annual real GDP growth rate for China is 2.4 percentage points below the official one. His GDP figure has been accepted internationally by the Penn World Tables and the World Bank. However, that figure is national rather than province specific. According to Wu (1997) and Holz (2006), a simple and relatively acceptable approach to deriving China's real GDP growth rate is to use the official CPI as a single deflator. Both authors show that the use of price indices instead of the official implicit deflators gives a figure for China's real growth rate that is similar to that of Maddison. For this reason we deflate the nominal GDP and other variables for each province by province-specific CPI. There are no provincial price data for Tibet for the period 1978–89; we use the national price index instead.

11. For example, MRW (1992), Islam (1995), Bond et al. (2001), and Ding and Knight (2009).

12. For example, Chen and Fleisher (1996), Chen and Feng (2000), and Cai et al. (2002).

References

Arellano, Manuel, and Olympia Bover (1995), 'Another look at the instrumental variable estimation of error-components models', *Journal of Econometrics*, 68: 29–52.

Bao, Shu Ming, Gene Hsin Chang, Jeffrey Sachs, and Wing Thye Woo (2002), 'Geographic factors and China's regional development under market reforms, 1978–1998', *China Economic Review*, 13: 89–111.

Barro, Robert (1991), 'Economic growth in a cross section of countries', *Quarterly Journal of Economics*, 106: 407–43.

——and Xavier Sala-i-Martin (2004), *Economic Growth* (2nd edn.). Cambridge, Mass.: The MIT Press.

Blundell, Richard, and Stephen Bond (1998), 'Initial conditions and moment restrictions in dynamic panel data models', *Journal of Econometrics*, 87: 115–43.

Bond, Stephen, Anke Hoeffler, and Jonathan Temple (2001), 'GMM estimation of empirical growth models', CEPR Discussion Paper No. 3048.

Borenzstein, Eduard, and Jonathan Ostry (1996), 'Accounting for China's growth performance', *American Economic Review*, 86, 2: 224–8.

Bowsher, Clive (2002), 'On testing overidentifying restrictions in dynamic panel data models', *Economics Letters*, 77: 211–20.

Brandt, Loren, Chang-tai Hsieh, and Xiaodong Zhu (2008), 'Growth and structural transformation in China', in Loren Brandt and Thomas Rawski (eds.), *China's Great Economic Transformation*, Cambridge and New York: Cambridge University Press: 683–728.

Brun, Jean-françois, Jean-louis Combes, and Mary-françoise Renard (2002), 'Are there spillover effects between coastal and noncoastal regions in China?', *China Economic Review*, 13: 161–9.

Cai, Fang, Dewen Wang, and Yang Du (2002), 'Regional disparity and economic growth in China: the impact of labor market distortions', *China Economic Review*, 13: 197–212.

Chatfield, Chris (1995), 'Model uncertainty, data mining, and statistical inference', *Journal of the Royal Statistical Society*, 158: 419–44.

Chen, Baizhu, and Yi Feng (2000), 'Determinants of economic growth in China: private enterprise, education and openness', *China Economic Review*, 11: 1–15.

Chen, Jian, and Belton Fleisher (1996), 'Regional income inequality and economic growth in China', *Journal of Comparative Economics*, 22: 141–64.

Commission On Growth and Development (2008), *The Growth Report: Strategies for Sustained Growth and Inclusive Development* (Conference edn.).

Démurger, Sylvie (2001), 'Infrastructure development and economic growth: an explanation for regional disparities in China', *Journal of Comparative Economics*, 29: 95–117.

Ding, Sai, and John Knight (2009), 'Can the augmented Solow model explain China's economic growth? A cross-country panel data analysis', *Journal of Comparative Economics*, 37, 3: 432–52.

——(2011), 'Why has China grown so fast? The role of physical and human capital formation', *Oxford Bulletin of Economics and Statistics*, 73, 2: 141–74.

Doornik, Jurgen, and David Hendry (2007), *PcGive 12 Volume I: Empirical Econometric Modelling*, London: Timberlake Consultants Press.

Fernández, Carmen, Eduardo Ley, and Mark Steel (2001), 'Model uncertainty in cross-country growth regressions', *Journal of Applied Econometrics*, 16: 563–76.

Fleisher, Belton, Haizheng Li, and Min Qiang Zhao (2010), 'Human capital, economic growth, and regional inequality in China', *Journal of Development Economics*, 92, 2: 215–31.

Grossman, Gene, and Elhanan Helpman (1995), *Innovation and Growth in the Global Economy*. Cambridge, Mass.: MIT Press.

Guariglia, Alessandra, and Sandra Poncet (2008), 'Could financial distortions be no impediment to economic growth after all? Evidence from China', *Journal of Comparative Economics*, 36, 4: 633–57.

Hao, Chen (2006), 'Development of financial intermediation and economic growth: the Chinese experience', *China Economic Review*, 17: 347–62.

Hendry, David, and Hans-Martin Krolzig (2004), 'We ran one regression', *Oxford Bulletin of Economics and Statistics*, 66: 799–810.

Hoeffler, Anke (2002), 'The augmented Solow model and the African growth debate', *Oxford Bulletin of Economics and Statistics*, 64, 2: 135–58.

Holz, Carsten (2006), 'China's reform period economic growth: how reliable are Angus Maddison's estimates?', *Review of Income and Wealth*, 52, 1: 85–119.

——(2008), 'China's 2004 economic census and 2006 benchmark revision of GDP statistics: more questions than answers?', *China Quarterly*, 193: 150–63.

Hoover, Kevin, and Stephen Perez (2004), 'Truth and robustness in cross-country growth regressions', *Oxford Bulletin of Economics and Statistics*, 66: 765–98.

Hsiao, Cheng (1986), *Analysis of Panel Data*, Cambridge: Cambridge University Press.

Hu, Zuliu, and Mohsin Khan (1997), 'Why is China growing so fast?' *International Monetary Fund Staff Papers*, 44, 1: 103–31.

Islam, Nazrul (1995), 'Growth empirics: a panel data approach', *The Quarterly Journal of Economics*, 110: 1127–70.

Jones, Derek, Cheng Li, and Ann Owen (2003), 'Growth and regional inequality in China during the reform era', *China Economic Review*, 14: 186–200.

Knight, John, and Li Shi (1999), 'Fiscal decentralization: incentives, redistribution and reform in China', *Oxford Development Studies*, 27: 5–32.

Levine, Ross, and David Renelt (1992), 'A sensitivity analysis of cross-country growth regressions', *American Economic Review*, 82: 942–63.

Li, Hong, Zinan Liu, and Ivonia Rebelo (1998), 'Testing the neoclassical theory of economic growth: evidence from Chinese provinces', *Economics of Planning*, 31: 117–32.

Lucas, Robert (1988), 'On the mechanics of economic development', *Journal of Monetary Economics*, 22: 3–42.

Maddison, Angus (1998), *Chinese Economic Performance in the Long Run*, Paris: Development Centre of the Organization for Economic Cooperation and Development.

Mankiw, Gregory, David Romer, and David Weil (1992), 'A contribution to the empirics of economic growth', *The Quarterly Journal of Economics*, 107: 407–37.

Nickell, Stephen (1981), 'Biases in dynamic models with fixed effects', *Econometrica*, 49, 6: 1427–36.

Owen, Dorian (2003), 'General-to-specific modelling using Pcgets', *Journal of Economic Surveys*, 17: 609–27.

Raftery, Adrian (1995), 'Bayesian model selection in social research', in Peter Marsden (ed.), *Sociological Methodology*, Cambridge: Blackwell.

Raiser, Martin (1998), 'Subsidising inequality: economic reforms, fiscal transfers and convergence across Chinese provinces', *Journal of Development Studies*, 34: 1–26.

Rawski, Thomas (2001), 'What is happening to China's GDP statistics?', *China Economic Review*, 12: 347–54.

Romer, Paul (1990), 'Are non-convexities important for understanding growth?' *American Economic Review*, 80: 97–103.

Roodman, David (2009), 'A note on the theme of too many instruments', *Oxford Bulletin of Economics and Statistics*, 71, 1: 135–58.

Sala-i-Martin, Xavier (1997), 'I just ran two million regressions', *American Economic Review*, 87: 178–83.

——Gernot Doppelhofer, and Ronald Miller (2004), 'Determinants of long-run growth: a Bayesian averaging of classical estimates (BACE) approach', *American Economic Review*, 94, 4: 813–35.

Sarafidis, Vasilis, and Donald Robertson (2009), 'On the impact of error cross-sectional dependence in short dynamic panel estimation', *Econometrics Journal*, 12: 62–81.

Temple, Jonathan (1999), 'The new growth evidence', *Journal of Economic Literature*, 37: 112–56.

——(2000), 'Growth regressions and what the textbooks don't tell you', *Bulletin of Economic Research*, 52, 3: 181–205.

Wang, Yan, and Yudong Yao (2001), 'Sources of China's economic growth, 1952–99: Incorporating human capital accumulation', World Bank Policy Research Working Paper No. 2650.

Wong, Christine, and Richard Bird (2008), 'China's fiscal system: a work in progress', in Loren Brandt and Thomas Rawski (eds.), *China's Great Economic Transformation*, Cambridge and New York: Cambridge University Press: 429–66.

Woo, Wing Thye (1998), 'Chinese economic growth: sources and prospects', in Michel Fouquin and Françoise Lemoine (eds.), *The Chinese Economy*. London: Economica.

Wu, Harry (1997), 'Measuring China's GDP', Briefing Paper Series No. 8, Department of Foreign Affairs and Trade, Australia.

Yao, Shujie (2006), 'On economic growth, FDI and exports in China', *Applied Economics*, 38: 339–51.

Young, Alwyn (2003), 'Gold into base metals: productivity growth in the People's Republic of China during the reform period', *Journal of Political Economy*, 111: 1220–61.

6

The Role of Physical and Human Capital Formation

6.1 Introduction

It is widely thought that China's exceptional growth performance over the past three decades is most fundamentally a reflection of the high investment rates that have characterized the economy. As Figure 6.1 illustrates, real gross capital formation over the entire reform period averaged a fairly steady 38% of real GDP (*gcf/GDP*), which is very high by international standards. The rate of gross fixed capital formation (*fcf/GDP*) has increased significantly in recent years, rising from an average of 29% between 1978 and 1993 to an average of 37% thereafter. Inventory accumulation amounted to, on average, 6% of GDP (*inven/GDP*). It peaked at the

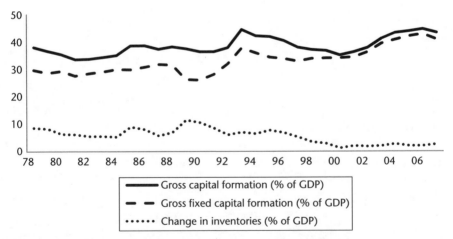

Figure 6.1. Gross capital formation and its composition, 1978–2007.
Data source: World Bank, *World Development Indicators* (June 2009 edition).

end of the 1980s, reflecting the severe economic recession, and declined gradually thereafter thanks to the process of marketization. Hence, it is not implausible to hypothesize that China's growth success is mainly investment driven and that a major part of the answer to the question 'why does China grow so fast?' is simply 'because it invests so much' (Naughton 2007; Riedel et al. 2007).

This chapter leads on from the two preceding chapters. In Chapter 4 we showed that the rate of gross fixed capital formation in China has been very high by international standards, and that it has accounted for much of China's superior growth performance. We also showed that China's high initial level of human capital stock also contributed to her fast growth relative to other developing countries, although the growth of human capital did not make a contribution. In Chapter 5 the baseline equation to explain growth across China's provinces indicated that the ratio of physical investment to GDP was important for growth, as was secondary school enrolment, our proxy for the growth of human capital. Our focus in this chapter is on the growth impact of various types of physical and human capital investment. Our key question is: which types matter?

Using the baseline model arrived at in Chapter 5, we examine the contribution to economic growth of various types of physical investment (Section 6.2) and various types of education (Section 6.3). In Section 6.4 some counterfactual simulations are conducted in an attempt to answer the underlying question: can the cross-province growth regressions help us to understand why China as a whole has grown so fast? Section 6.5 briefly analyses the factors that permit China's rapid capital accumulation. Section 6.6 summarizes and concludes.[1]

6.2 Physical Capital Accumulation

There is substantial empirical evidence in the cross-country growth literature that capital accumulation has a positive and significant effect on growth. For instance, Levine and Renelt (1992), applying Extreme Bounds Analysis (EBA) to examine the cross-country relationship between economic growth and a large set of variables, found almost all their results to be fragile except for the positive correlation between the share of investment in GDP and the growth rate. Adopting an alternative, less restrictive, version of EBA, Sala-i-Martin (1997) confirmed an important, positive, and robust relationship of both equipment investment and non-equipment investment with the growth rate of output per capita.

Making either cross-section or time-series studies, Mankiw, Romer, and Weil (hereafter MRW) (1992), Islam (1995), Caselli et al. (1996), and Bond et al. (2001) reported evidence that investment affects the level of output per worker in the steady state or the transitional growth rate while the economy converges to its steady state. However, because empirical specifications in these studies are derived from Solow-type models in which the steady-state growth rate is assumed to be exogenous, the question of whether investment affects the long-run growth rate of output per worker cannot be addressed.

The recent work by Bond et al. (2010) fills this gap in the literature. After controlling for cross-country heterogeneity in all parameters and allowing for cross-country dependence in the error terms in the growth equation, they find that investment as a share of GDP has a large and statistically significant effect not only on the level of output per worker but, more importantly, on the long-run growth rate. They claim their results to be in line with the prediction of endogenous growth models in which capital is used as an input in the production of innovations, so contributing to long-term economic growth.

By contrast, Blomström et al. (1996) argued that fixed investment does not cause economic growth: they found that growth induces subsequent capital formation more than capital formation induces subsequent growth. In an influential review of the recent empirical literature, Easterly and Levine (2001) concluded that 'the data do not provide strong support for the contention that factor accumulation ignites faster growth in output per worker'. The cross-country growth literature therefore remains controversial.

Many studies of growth in China have adduced evidence of investment-driven growth. For example, using an augmented Solow model, Li et al. (1998) find for the period 1978–95 that both the level and the growth rate of GDP per capita are higher in the provinces with more investment in physical and human capital, as well as lower population growth and greater economic openness. Adopting a spatial lag model for the period of 1978–98, Ying (2003) concludes that the growth of capital stock, non-farm labour force, manufactured products, and FDI are important sources of provincial output growth. By contrast, using aggregate time-series data over the period 1990–2003, Qin et al. (2006) confirm the existence of a long-run positive relationship between investment and growth but find that causality runs from the latter to the former, that is, output growth drives investment demand. Again, there is no consensus on the investment-growth nexus in the literature on China.

Although our own baseline equation does provide support for a causal positive effect of investment on provincial growth rates, the relationship therefore deserves closer scrutiny to further our understanding of the causal mechanisms at work. Controlling for the set of variables selected in the baseline model, we focus on the impact of various types of physical investment on GDP per capita growth. Because the association between investment and growth does not prove causality, all measures of physical capital formation are treated as endogenous variables in our system GMM estimation. To save space, we report only the coefficients of interest along with relevant specification tests.

We first decompose total investment in fixed assets ($finv_{TOTAL}/GDP$) into investment in capital construction ($finv_{CC}/GDP$), investment in innovation ($finv_{INNO}/GDP$), and investment in other fixed assets ($finv_{OTHER}/GDP$) in Panel 1 of Table 6.1.[2] We find that the former three have positive and significant impacts on growth, whereas the last appears insignificant. These results highlight the role of investment spending on capital construction and technological innovation in promoting growth, and imply that fixed investment in other areas such as the real estate sector and natural resource exploitation is not growth enhancing, possibly because the full effects are longer term. Moreover, the growth impact of investment in innovation is much greater than that of total investment in fixed assets and that of investment in capital construction: a one percentage point rise in the innovation investment ratio is associated with 0.3 percentage point higher growth rate of GDP per capita. Although, according to Scott (1989, 1993), almost every investment is bound up with technological change, our 'investment in innovation' variable is particularly likely to identify productivity-enhancing innovation. Our finding suggests that the contribution which investment

Table 6.1. The growth impact of physical capital formation

Panel 1. Investment in capital construction, in innovation, and in other fixed assets

	$finv_{TOTAL}/GDP$	$finv_{CC}/GDP$	$finv_{INNO}/GDP$	$finv_{OTHER}/GDP$
Coefficients	0.184** (0.042)	0.174** (0.047)	0.277** (0.082)	0.077 (0.111)
AR(2) p value	0.636	0.778	0.810	0.911
Hansen p value	0.108	0.100	0.261	0.167
Dif Sargan p value	0.607	0.862	0.367	0.922
No. of instruments	26	26	26	26
No. of observations	150	150	150	150

Panel 2. Total investment in fixed assets: by ownership classification

	$finv_{SOE}/finv_{TOTAL}$	$finv_{COL}/finv_{TOTAL}$	$finv_{PRIV}/finv_{TOTAL}$
Coefficients	−0.129** (0.026)	−0.077 (0.111)	0.197** (0.096)
AR(2) p value	0.610	0.919	0.953
Hansen p value	0.167	0.172	0.193
Dif Sargan p value	0.393	0.586	0.791
No. of instruments	26	26	26
No. of observations	149	149	149

Panel 3. Domestic vs foreign investment

	$finv_{DOM}/GDP$	fdi/GDP	$finv_{DOM}$	fdi
Coefficients	0.227** (0.025)	−0.181 (0.052)	0.002** (0.001)	0.008* (0.005)
AR(2) p value	0.488	0.131	0.145	0.856
Hansen p value	0.811	0.689	0.697	0.697
Dif Sargan p value	0.728	0.293	0.354	0.365
No. of instruments	41	41	41	41
No. of observations	150	149	150	149

Notes: Panel-data system GMM results are reported; standard errors are in parentheses, which are heteroskedasticity consistent and clustering on province; the control variables are those selected by the model selection procedures, that is, $lny_{i,t-1}$, stu_{SEC}/pop, $popngr$, $export/GDP$ and ind_{SOE}/ind_{TOTAL}, in which $lny_{i,t-1}$ is treated as predetermined, $popngr$ is treated as exogenous, and all other variables are treated as endogenous; time dummies are included; ** and * indicate that the coefficient is significantly different from zero at the 5 or 10% significance level respectively.

can make to technological progress is a powerful driver of growth. China began economic reform from a position far below the technological frontier. In a transition economy, much investment is necessary to maintain the value of the firm in response to a violent process of obsolescence created by new products, new production processes, and huge changes in relative prices. Our results provide evidence that investment, and investment-driven improvements, in technology are important for China's growth.

We then classify investment in fixed assets according to ownership: investment spending by SOEs ($finv_{SOE}/finv_{TOTAL}$), collectively owned enterprises ($finv_{COL}/finv_{TOTAL}$), and private enterprises ($finv_{PRIV}/finv_{TOTAL}$) in Panel 2 of Table 6.1. Since these variables may contain information similar to our proxy for the extent of economic reform, the SOE share of industrial output (ind_{SOE}/ind_{TOTAL}), we drop that term in these regressions. We find that the share of investment made by SOEs has a significantly negative effect on growth: a decrease in the SOE share of fixed investment by one percentage point is associated with an increase in GDP per capita growth of 0.13 percentage points. This result is consistent with the widespread perception that the efficiency of investment in the SOEs is far below that in the non-state sector, so that the growth rate of GDP per capita should fall as the SOE share of investment rises (for instance, Brandt and Zhu 2000). Consequently, the recent decline in the SOE share of fixed investment is a positive development. The coefficient on the share of investment by collective firms appears insignificant. The collective economy consists of both township and village enterprises (TVEs) and urban collectives firms (UCEs). The former are generally said to have been dynamic, especially in the 1980s, whereas the latter are run by local governments and still suffer from the disincentives associated with soft budget constraints and principal-agent problems. Hence, the impact of collective firms on growth is ambiguous.

The share of private-sector investment affects growth positively: a one percentage point increase in this variable is associated with an increased growth rate of 0.20 percentage points. The expansion of private sector investment has a favourable impact, in line with the evidence that the average return on investment in the private sector is higher than that in the SOEs (Riedel et al. 2007: 40–2). Our evidence thus supports the view that the private sector is the driving force in the Chinese economy. It is therefore beneficial that the centre of gravity of the economy has been shifting from the state to the private sector.

A caveat is in order: in the late 1990s some SOEs were corporatized, and would have been reclassified as private, although the state, being the major shareholder, generally retained control. Insofar as the most profitable or promising SOEs were listed, the results are likely to exaggerate the incentive effects of different ownership status.

A major imbalance in the allocation of resources between the public and private sectors remains. For example, bank loans constitute an important part of investment financing only for the relatively inefficient and unprofitable SOEs, while private firms are discriminated against by the formal financial system and rely predominantly on their 'own funds' to finance investment.[3] The estimates imply that financial sector reform would raise the growth rate further.

Finally, we attempt to distinguish the role of domestic investment ($finv_{DOM}/GDP$) and foreign direct investment (fdi/GDP) in driving China's growth. Ideally, we would choose measures of the stock of FDI, but in the absence of such data at the provincial level, the flows of FDI are adopted. FDI can contribute to growth by bringing not only capital but also a familiarity with foreign production techniques, overseas markets, and international supply chains to the host country. However, empirical evidence of knowledge or productivity spill-overs from FDI is rather mixed. For instance, Javorcik (2008) utilized survey data to examine various channels through which the entry of multinationals affects domestic enterprises in the same industry or in upstream or downstream sectors in the Czech Republic and Latvia. She found both positive and negative effects of foreign entry on domestic producers, depending on host country conditions and the type of FDI inflows.

In the China literature the aggregate growth impact of FDI is commonly found to be positive. For instance, Wei (1995) investigated the effect of China's open door policy using city-level data sets and found that higher rates of FDI were related to faster growth of income per capita in the late 1980s. Similar findings were obtained by Jones et al. (2003), who tested the Solow model augmented by FDI with city-level data for the decade 1989–99. Using quarterly national data from the years 1981–97, Liu et al. (2002) showed that, in a time-series cointegration framework, there is a long-run bidirectional causal relationship among growth, imports, exports, and FDI. From a cross-province panel-data analysis for the period 1978–2000, Yao (2006) found that both exports and FDI have a strong and positive effect on economic growth. Our hypothesis is therefore that a unit of FDI is more important for growth than a unit of domestic investment on account of techno-logical transfers and knowledge spill-overs.

Domestic investment has a positive influence on growth, that is, an increase in domestic investment of one percentage point raises GDP per capita growth by 0.2 percentage points (Panel 3, Table 6.1). Surprisingly, we find no evidence of a significant and positive impact of FDI. One possible explanation of our finding lies in variable specification. The share of FDI grew steadily throughout the 1980s but never exceeded 1% of GDP (Figure 6.2), and it was highly concentrated in four Special Economic Zones in Guangdong and Fujian provinces. Deng Xiaoping's 'southern tour' in the spring of 1992 unleashed a surge of inward FDI in China, which reached its peak of 6.2% of GDP in 1994. Since 1995, the share of FDI in GDP has drifted downwards because China's GDP growth has been more rapid than the growth of FDI inflow. This may partly explain the insignificant and negative coefficient of the FDI term.

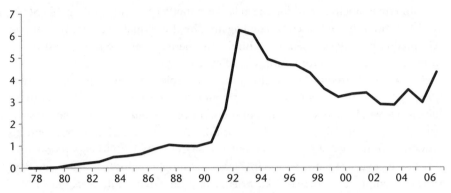

Figure 6.2. Foreign direct investment net inflows, % of GDP, 1978–2007.
Data source: World Bank, *World Development Indicators* (June 2009 edition).

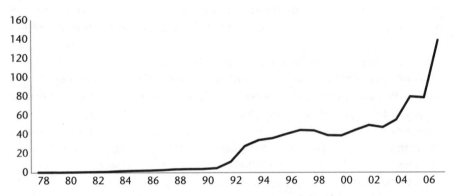

Figure 6.3. Foreign direct investment net inflows, $ billion, 1978–2007.
Data source: World Bank, *World Development Indicators* (June 2009 edition).

To address this problem, instead of the ratio of FDI inflow to GDP (*fdi/GDP*), we use the volume of inward FDI as a proxy. The trend of FDI is reflected in Figure 6.3: the net inflow was under US$10 billion before 1992, but reached US$80 billion in 2006. In the fourth column of Panel 3, we find a positive effect of the absolute volume of FDI (*fdi*) on provincial growth, that is, for a one billion RMB rise in FDI, the growth rate of GDP per capita increases by 0.008 percentage points. In order to compare the growth impacts of domestic investment and FDI, it is necessary to convert the two variables into the same units. In the third column of Panel 3, we include the absolute volume of domestic investment (*finv*$_{DOM}$) and find that a unit of FDI is about four times more important for growth than a unit of domestic investment, that is, a one billion RMB rise in domestic investment is associated with an increase in growth rate of GDP per capita by 0.002 percentage points. This is consistent with our hypothesis that an investment has a greater impact on growth if it comes from abroad, given the potential roles of FDI in export promotion, technology transfer, and productivity improvement.

6.3 Human Capital Accumulation

Human capital accumulation can be treated analogously to physical capital accumulation, and can be incorporated accordingly into growth models and their empirical testing. Whereas it is normally assumed that the relationship is between changes in human capital and changes in output, it is also possible that the stock of human capital itself contributes to economic growth through the generation, absorption, and dissemination of knowledge. Human capital is assumed to play such a role in some endogenous growth models. For instance, according to Romer (1990), human capital is an input into the research and development activity which generates technological progress.

However, research based on cross-country data has produced surprisingly mixed results about the effect of education on economic growth. For example, Barro (1991) examined the empirical relationship among growth, fertility, and investment for ninety-eight countries in the period 1960–85. His cross-sectional results show that the growth rate is positively related to the starting amount of human capital. Besides, countries with high human capital have low fertility rates and high ratios of physical investment to GDP. MRW (1992) found a significantly positive effect on output growth of secondary school enrolment as a proportion of working-age population. Nevertheless, other researchers including Benhabib and Spiegel (1994) and Pritchett (1999) claimed that output growth was not strongly related to increases in measured educational attainment (changes in the average years of schooling), especially in developing countries. One reason for this uncertainty might be that the impact of education has varied widely across countries owing to differences in institutions, labour markets, and quality of education (Temple 1999b).

There are some interesting studies of the effect of human capital on economic growth in China. Chen and Fleisher (1996) and Démurger (2001) provided evidence that education at the secondary or college level helps to explain differences in provincial growth rates. By estimating a province-level aggregate production function, Fleisher et al. (2010) found that human capital raises both output and productivity growth. Both direct and indirect effects of human capital on TFP growth are found: the direct effects are hypothesized to come from domestic innovation activities, and the indirect effects to represent knowledge spill-overs.

In this section we examine the impact of different types of human capital investment on economic growth in China. It is difficult to find a variable that adequately represents human capital. In reality, investment in human capital can take many forms, including formal and informal education, on-the-job training, health improvements, and learning-by-doing. In most empirical studies human capital is normally proxied by average years of schooling, and increments to human capital either by changes in average years of schooling or by educational enrolment rates. Thus, the quality of education and other types of human capital investment are largely ignored. Given the data availability, we use enrolment at different educational levels to measure certain aspects of human capital in China. Although enrolment is normally measured as a proportion of the relevant age group, enrolment as a proportion of the total population is a better guide to the increase in human capital and its effect on the economic growth of a province. School enrolment may conflate human capital stock and accumulation effects, and it can be a poor proxy for either.[4] Nevertheless, we make use of what information is available to us annually at the province level.

In Table 6.2 our human capital measures consist of primary school enrolment (stu_{PRIM}/pop), secondary school enrolment (stu_{SEC}/pop), regular secondary school enrolment (stu_{REGSEC}/pop), higher education enrolment (stu_{HIGH}/pop), university and college enrolment ($stu_{UNI\&COL}/pop$), and enrolment in both secondary and higher education ($stu_{SEC\&HIGH}/pop$), each expressed as a proportion of the total population.[5] To deal with the possible endogeneity of these variables, levels of human capital investment variables lagged by ten-year, fifteen-year, and twenty-year periods are used as instruments in the first-differences equations,

Table 6.2. The growth impact of human capital formation

Panel 1. Primary and secondary enrolments

	stu_{PRIM}/pop	stu_{SEC}/pop	stu_{REGSEC}/pop
Coefficients	−0.611** (0.254)	1.538** (0.326)	2.171** (0.337)
AR(2) p value	0.186	0.523	0.913
Hansen p value	0.138	0.179	0.203
Dif Sargan p value	0.895	0.706	0.905
No. of instruments	26	26	26
No. of observations	149	149	149

Panel 2. Higher education enrolments

	stu_{HIGH}/pop	$stu_{UNI\&COL}/pop$	$stu_{SEC\&HIGH}/pop$
Coefficients	3.568** (0.579)	2.201** (0.617)	1.953** (0.285)
AR(2) p value	0.286	0.155	0.803
Hansen p value	0.232	0.196	0.225
Dif Sargan p value	0.514	0.653	0.801
No. of instruments	26	26	26
No. of observations	149	147	149

Notes: Panel-data system GMM results are reported; standard errors are in parentheses, which are heteroskedasticity consistent and clustering on province; the control variables are those selected by the model selection procedures, that is, $lny_{i,t-1}$, fcf/GDP, $popngr$, $export/GDP$ and ind_{SOE}/ind_{TOTAL}, in which $lny_{i,t-1}$ is treated as pre-determined, $popngr$ is treated as exogenous, and all other variables are treated as endogenous; time dummies are included; ** and * indicate that the coefficient is significantly different from zero at the 5 or 10% significance level respectively.

and first-differenced human capital investment variables lagged by a five-year period are used as additional instruments for the levels equations in the system GMM estimation.

In line with Chen and Feng (2000) in their cross-province study, we find that the coefficient of the primary enrolment variable is insignificant in the growth regression. This is to be expected because primary education is mandatory and the negative coefficient may reflect the falling number of children as a result of the 'one-child-family' policy, introduced in the late 1970s.[6] Consistent with both the cross-country evidence[7] and the cross-province evidence,[8] we find that the secondary and regular secondary school enrolment variables have positive and significant impacts on output growth.

The higher education enrolment, and their component university and college enrolment, proportions have bigger positive effects. For instance, a one percentage point rise in the ratio of enrolment in higher education to population leads to higher GDP per capita growth by 3.6 percentage points, holding other conditions constant. The important contribution to growth made by higher education might be explained by the remarkable relative neglect of higher education, and consequent scarcity of tertiary graduates, throughout the first two decades of economic reform. Higher education enrolment remained below 0.3% of total population until 1998, and then shot up to 1.4% in 2006 as a result of a sharp change in higher education policy. Our finding is consistent with Chi (2008) who, using educational attainment to measure human capital, estimated that tertiary education had a positive impact on both GDP growth and fixed investment, and that the impact was bigger than that of primary and secondary education. He argued that China's production function therefore exhibited a degree of complementarity between physical capital and human capital. Lastly, we examine the impact of students enrolled in both secondary and higher education over population, and find that a one percentage point rise in this variable is associated with a 2.0 percentage point rise in the growth rate of GDP per capita.

To test the robustness of our human capital results, census information on the percentage of population aged 6 and above with primary, secondary, or tertiary educational attainment are adopted. These data are proxies for the stock of human capital but they are available only for the census years 1982, 1990, 1995, and 2000. We interpolate the census data to derive the observations in the years required by the analysis. For these reasons, inaccuracies and measurement errors are to be expected when these alternative human capital variables are deployed. Nevertheless, we find that the share of population with junior secondary education has a positive and significant effect on provincial growth, and that when changes in the shares are included in the growth equation, an increase in the relative stock of people with junior secondary, and also those with tertiary, education raises growth significantly. These results are consistent with our findings based on school enrolment data.

6.4 Illustrative Counterfactual Predictions

We return to the underlying question: can cross-province growth regressions help us to understand why China as a whole has grown so fast? We attempt to answer the question by means of counterfactual simulations in Tables 6.3 and 6.4. The methodology is to predict growth rates by changing mean values of key variables based on model estimation. Because these simulations contain the questionable assumption that a change in one variable would not alter the other variables in the equation, they can merely illustrate the rough orders of magnitude of the impact on the growth rate. However, insofar as an adverse change in one variable (say, human capital formation) induces an adverse change in another variable (say, physical capital formation), the simulations would understate the impact on growth.

The average value of fixed investment in relation to GDP over the full sample period was 34.3%. If instead it had been 10 percentage points lower (24.3%), the system GMM coefficient of the baseline model in Table 5.4 implies that China's annual growth of GDP per capita would have fallen by 0.9 percentage points, from 8.0 to 7.1%, holding other variables constant. Similarly, secondary school enrolment averaged 5.8% of total population. If it had been two percentage points lower, controlling for other variables, the growth rate of GDP per capita would have declined to 6.0%. Had both the physical and human capital variables been reduced in this way, China's per capita growth rate would have fallen to 5.1% per annum, holding other controls constant.

China was a low-income country at the start of economic reform.[9] The mean values of the fixed capital formation and secondary school enrolment ratios of all least developed countries (United Nations 2008 classification) over the entire period are 17.8% and 2.3% respectively.[10] Plugging these values into the baseline model, we find that China's growth rate of GDP per capita would have been only 2.9% per annum, to be compared with 1.0% for the least developed countries. On

Table 6.3. Counterfactual predictions of the growth rate of GDP per capita (baseline model)

Predicted growth rate of GDP per capita (percentage points)	stu_{SEC}/pop			
	Mean (5.79 pp)	Reduce by 1 pp	Reduce by 2 pps	Reduce to the mean of LDCs (2.26 pps)
fcf/GDP				
Mean (34.27 pps)	8.03	7.02	6.02	4.48
Reduce by 1 pp	7.94	6.93	5.92	4.39
Reduce by 5 pps	7.57	6.56	5.55	4.01
Reduce by 10 pps	7.10	6.10	5.09	3.55
Reduce to the mean of LDCs (17.76 pps)	6.50	5.49	4.48	2.95

Notes: pp(s) refers to percentage point(s); LDCs refer to the least developed countries.

Table 6.4. Counterfactual predictions of the growth rate of GDP per capita (other models)

Predicted growth rate of GDP per capita (percentage points)		stu_{SEC}/pop			
		Mean (5.79 pps)	Reduce by 1 pp	Reduce by 2 pps	Reduce to half of the mean
Innovation investment (Panel 1, Table 6.1)					
$finv_{INNO}/GDP$	Mean (6.85 pps)	8.03	6.76	5.50	4.36
	Reduce by 1 pp	7.76	6.49	5.22	4.09
	Reduce by 2 pps	7.48	6.21	4.94	3.81
	Reduce by 3 pps	7.20	5.93	4.66	3.53
	Reduce to half of the mean	7.08	5.81	4.55	3.41
Private investment (Panel 2, Table 6.1)					
$finv_{PRIV}/finv_{TOTAL}$	Mean (16.7 pps)	8.06	5.30	4.16	3.15
	Reduce by 1 pp	7.85	5.13	4.00	2.98
	Reduce by 3 pps	7.46	4.74	3.60	2.58
	Reduce to half of the mean	6.55	3.83	2.70	1.68
	Reduce to 1978 mean (5.06 pps)	6.05	3.34	2.20	1.18
Foreign direct investment (Panel3, Table 6.1)					
fdi	Mean (4.26 billion RMB)	8.06	6.62	5.20	3.94
	Reduce by 1 billion RMB	7.24	5.83	4.41	3.15
	Reduce by 2 billion RMB	6.42	5.01	3.59	2.33
	Reduce to half of the mean	6.31	4.90	3.48	2.22
	Reduce by 3 billion RMB	5.60	4.19	2.77	1.51
Higher education enrolment (Table 6.2)*					
stu_{HIGH}/pop	Mean (0.44 pps)	8.06	6.09	4.12	2.96
	Reduce by 0.1 pps	7.74	5.76	3.79	2.63
	Reduce by 0.2 pps	7.41	5.42	3.45	2.30
	Reduce to half of the mean	7.34	5.35	3.38	2.22
	Reduce by 0.3 pps	7.08	5.09	3.12	1.96

Notes: pp(s) refers to percentage point(s); * the regression that simultaneously includes both secondary and higher education enrolments is estimated but not reported in Table 6.2 to save space, but the estimated coefficients of the two variables are similar to the case when they enter the regression separately.

these assumptions, China's status as a growth outlier would have been much weaker.

Consider the effects of changes in the composition of physical investment in Table 6.4. The ratio of innovation investment averaged 6.9% of total GDP in China over the whole sample period. Our estimated coefficient shows that a reduction in this variable to half of its mean would have resulted in a one percentage point lower growth rate of GDP per capita. Combining the effect of reducing the secondary school enrolment ratio to half, the growth rate would have fallen to 3.4% holding other conditions the same. The mean value of provincial FDI over the period 1978–2007 was 4.3 billion RMB. Had the figure been held down at half of the mean, the growth rate would have been 1.7 percentage points lower, at 6.3% per annum. The joint effects of reducing both FDI and the secondary school enrolment by half would have been a growth rate of 2.2%, other things being equal. Private fixed investment averaged 16.7% of total GDP in China over the full period. If it had remained at its 1978 level (5.1%), growth would have been 2 percentage points lower, at 6.1% per annum. Combining this with the effect of reducing secondary school enrolment to half, China's growth rate would have been down to 1.2%.

How important was post-primary education to growth? Secondary and higher education enrolments averaged 5.8% and 0.4% of population respectively over the full period. Had both the secondary and tertiary ratios been half of their mean values instead, the growth rate would have fallen by 5.8 percentage points, to 2.2% per annum.

The conclusion to be drawn from these simple counterfactual exercises is that both the quantity and composition of physical and human capital formation are potentially important to China's rate of economic growth. A reduction of these inputs to levels commonly found in the countries that, unlike China, remained least developed, could have reduced the growth rate nearly to that of those countries.

6.5 How was Rapid Capital Accumulation Possible?

Two important questions flow logically from our results: how was China's rapid physical capital accumulation, and also its human capital accumulation, made possible? Each of these questions deserves a separate study on its own. Accordingly, we analyse the determinants of physical investment in Chapter 8. Suffice here to say that the rapid physical capital accumulation was the result of economic reform policies making and keeping enterprise investment highly profitable, and of powerful incentives for households, enterprises, and government to save; and that the extremely inefficient financial market did not prove to be a serious obstacle.

Educational enrolment and its growth over time has in turn to be explained. Both demand and supply factors played a role. We begin with some educational background. One success of the central planning period was the policy emphasis on primary education. Beyond primary school, however, the administrative and economic differences between rural and urban China created a rural–urban divide in education. It reflected in part the state funding of education in urban areas and the decentralized, local funding in rural areas. This divide has continued throughout the reform period, visible in both the quantity and quality of education received. For instance, in 1988 the average education of urban and rural adults was 9.6 and 5.5 years respectively. Of those (aged 14–19) who should have been in middle school, 75% of the urban and 45% of the rural sample were at school in that year (Knight and Li 1993: 303, 320). The broad base and the narrow top of the educational pyramid, combined with heavy and escalating subsidies, produced excess demand for places. It is likely that educational provision in China has been supply constrained at the upper levels. Expansion has depended heavily on the provision of additional places by the responsible tiers of government.

The private benefits of education increased as economic reform proceeded. In 1988, early in the process of urban reform, the wage premium of upper secondary education over primary education for urban residents was very low, at 4%, but with labour market reform it rose to 26% in 1995 and to 33% in 2002. The urban wage premium of higher education over upper secondary education rose from only 5% in 1988 to 17% in 1995 and to 42% in 2002.[11] In rural China, although the returns to education remained low in farming, they were higher in the non-farm activities that were opening up to rural workers, and education also improved their access to these higher-income activities (Knight et al. 2010: tables 2, 5, 6). As opportunities for local non-farm employment and rural–urban migrant employment grew, education became an increasingly important means of raising the incomes of rural workers (Knight and Song 2005: table 8.8).

These labour market reforms and changes in the structure of the economy raised the private demand for education. This demand was in any case strong on account of the respect and status commonly accorded to education, which had been embedded by Chinese history. Thus, for instance, when a sharp change in higher education policy took place in the late 1990s, the remarkable increase in the supply of college places was fully met by the pent-up demand. In 1998 enrolment in higher education was 3.4 million; in 2008 it was 20.2 million. Thus enrolment rose almost sixfold in a decade.[12] A policy of eliminating tuition fees for the nine years of basic (primary plus junior middle) education was introduced throughout rural China in 2007. However, even in 2002, the China Household Income Project (CHIP) national household survey for rural areas showed that the net enrolment rate was 95% in primary school and 90% in junior middle school; only in senior middle school, with a net enrolment rate of 55%, was rural educational drop-out a problem (Knight et al. 2010: 316).

6.6 Conclusion

Our more detailed investigation of the effects of physical and human capital accumulation was intended to throw further light on the mechanisms at work. Among the types of fixed investment, the greatest contribution was made by investment identified as 'investment in innovation' as opposed to 'investment in capital construction', whereas 'investment in other fixed assets', such as real estate, made no contribution. This result suggests that physical investment makes the greatest contribution to growth when it is most closely bound up with technological progress. Consistent with this argument, we expected that a unit of foreign direct investment would have a greater effect on growth than a unit of domestic investment. Our evidence supports this hypothesis after we solve a specification problem. Breaking down physical investment by ownership, we found that an increased share of SOEs decreases the contribution of investment to growth, an increased share of collective enterprises has a negligible effect, and an increased share of private enterprises raises the contribution. Thus, the reform process that unleashed a private sector was important for growth, and the distorted financial system which continued to favour the SOEs held back growth.

Whereas primary school enrolment has no effect on economic growth, both secondary school and higher education enrolment had a positive effect, the latter more than the former. Indeed the coefficient on higher education enrolment in relation to population implied that a rise of one percentage point would raise the growth rate of GDP per capita by 2.8 percentage points. This sensitivity might be explained by the neglect of higher education until the late 1990s: in 1998 higher education enrolment was still only 5% of the relevant age group. Our use of system GMM estimation and instrumenting of the human capital variables using lags provided the best means of estimating the causal effect of human capital on growth.

To address the underlying question—why has China grown so fast?—it was necessary to assume that the growth impact of a variable estimated on the basis of its variation among provinces would be a guide to its impact in the economy as a whole. Various counterfactual exercises were conducted on that basis. We found that a significant reduction in capital inputs could have reduced China's growth rate dramatically, indicating the important role of physical and human capital formation in determining China's remarkable rate of economic growth. Back in 1978 China was classified as a 'least developed country'. Had its physical and human capital investment rates remained at the average of the least developed country group over the following three decades, China's predicted growth rate would not have been much higher than the actual growth rate of that group.

The factors which made rapid physical and human capital accumulation possible were discussed briefly. Incentives for saving have been strong for households, enterprises, and governments over the reform period, and labour market reform, by increasing the wage premia on education, has produced rapid growth in the demand for education, to which government has responded by increasing the supply.

In this chapter we have used and extended the baseline growth equation to examine the contribution that factor accumulation has made to China's economic growth. These are the proximate determinants of growth. Underlying them, however, are the other influences on growth that enter our baseline equation. These other determinants are explored in Chapter 7.

APPENDIX 6.1

Table A6.1. Detailed Variable Definitions

Variable	Definition	Units
Dependent variable		
$g_{i,t}$	Growth rate of real provincial GDP per capita	proportion
Independent variables		
1. Physical capital formation		
(1) By national account classification		
gcf/GDP	Gross capital formation to GDP	proportion
fcf/GDP	Fixed capital formation to GDP	proportion
$inven/GDP$	Inventory investment to GDP $(inven/GDP = gcf/GDP\text{-}fcf/GDP)$	proportion
(2) By usage classification		
$finv_{TOTAL}/GDP$	Total investment in fixed assets to GDP	proportion
$finv_{CC}/GDP$	Fixed investment in capital construction to GDP	proportion
$finv_{INNO}/GDP$	Fixed investment in innovation to GDP	proportion
$finv_{OTHER}/GDP$	Fixed investment in other usage to GDP $(finv_{OTHER}/GDP = finv_{TOTAL}/GDP\text{-}finv_{CC}/GDP\text{-}finv_{INNO}/GDP)$	proportion
(3) By ownership classification		
$finv_{SOE}/finv_{TOTAL}$	Investment in fixed assets by state-owned units/Total investment in fixed assets	proportion
$finv_{COL}/finv_{TOTAL}$	Investment in fixed assets by collectively owned units/Total investment in fixed assets	proportion
$finv_{PRIV}/finv_{TOTAL}$	Investment in fixed assets by private units/Total investment in fixed assets	proportion
(4) Domestic vs foreign investment		
$finv_{DOM}/GDP$	Ratio of domestic fixed investment to GDP	proportion
fdi/GDP	Ratio of foreign direct investment to GDP (FDI converted to RMB using official exchange rate from IFS, IMF)	proportion
fdi	Volume of foreign direct investment (FDI converted to RMB using official exchange rate from IFS, IMF)	billion RMB
$finv_{DOM}$	Volume of domestic investment	billion RMB
2. Human capital formation		
stu_{PRIM}/pop	Students enrolled in primary education/Year-end total population	proportion
stu_{SEC}/pop	Students enrolled in secondary education/Year-end total population	proportion
stu_{SECREG}/pop	Students enrolled in regular secondary education/Year-end total population	proportion
stu_{HIGH}/pop	Students enrolled in higher education/Year-end total population	proportion
$stu_{UNI\&COL}/pop$	Students enrolled in universities and colleges/Year-end total population	proportion
$stu_{SEC\&HIGH}/pop$	Students enrolled in both secondary and higher education/Year-end total population	proportion
3. Other control variables		
$lny_{i,t-1}$	Logarithm of beginning-period real GDP per capita	1990 RMB
$popngr$	Population natural growth rate = birth rate – death rate	proportion
$export/GDP$	Ratio of exports to GDP (exports converted to RMB using official exchange rate from IFS, IMF)	proportion
ind_{SOE}/ind_{TOTAL}	Output value of state-owned enterprises/Gross industrial output value	proportion

Note: All the variables are calculated in 1990 constant prices and price indices are province specific. The data relate to thirty provinces in the period 1978–2007.

Notes

1. This chapter draws on Ding and Knight (2011).

2. Capital construction investment refers to the new construction projects or extension projects of enterprises and other institutions with the purpose of expanding production capacity or improving project efficiency. Innovation investment consists of the renewal of fixed assets and technological innovation of the original facilities by enterprises and other institutions. Investment in other fixed assets includes investment in real estate development, natural resource (oil, coal, ore, etc.) maintenance and exploitation, and other construction and purchases of fixed assets not listed in capital construction investment and innovation investment. See Appendix 6.1 for detailed definitions of the variables.

3. See for example Allen et al. (2005), and Guariglia et al. (2011).

4. For instance, Gemmell (1996) and Temple (1999a).

5. Secondary education includes junior and senior secondary schools, specialized secondary schools, vocational secondary schools, and technical training schools. Regular secondary schools include merely junior and senior secondary schools. Higher education includes universities and colleges as well as self-taught programmes for undergraduates.

6. The ratio of primary school enrolment to total population fell from 15% in 1978 to 8% in 2006.

7. For instance, Barro (1991), and MRW (1992).

8. For instance, Chen and Fleisher (1996), and Démurger (2001).

9. According to the *World Development Report* (1981) published by the World Bank, China's GNP per capita was $260 in 1979, ranking as the 22nd poorest country.

10. The ratio of fixed capital formation to GDP and the total population data for least developed countries come from the *World Development Indicators* (April 2008 edn.); secondary school enrolment figures come from UNESCO.

11. See Knight and Song (2005, table 3.2) and Knight and Song (2008, table 2).

12. NBS, *China Statistical Yearbook 2009*, table 20–6.

References

Allen, Franklin, Jun Qian, and Meijun Qian (2005), 'Law, finance, and economic growth in China', *Journal of Financial Economics*, 77: 57–116.

Barro, Robert (1991), 'Economic growth in a cross section of countries', *Quarterly Journal of Economics*, 106: 407–43.

Benhabib, Jess, and Mark Spiegel (1994), 'The role of human capital in economic development: evidence from aggregate cross-country data', *Journal of Monetary Economics*, 34: 143–73.

Blomström, Magnus, Robert Lipsey, and Mario Zejan (1996), 'Is fixed investment the key to economic growth?', *The Quarterly Journal of Economics*, 111: 269–76.

Bond, Stephen, Anke Hoeffler, and Jonathan Temple (2001). 'GMM estimation of empirical growth models', CEPR Discussion Paper No. 3048.

Bond, Stephen Asli Leblebicioglu, and Fabio Schiantarelli (2010), 'Capital accumulation and growth: a new look at the empirical evidence', *Journal of Applied Econometrics*, 25, 7: 1073–99.

Brandt, Loren, and Xiaodong Zhu (2000), 'Redistribution in a decentralized economy: growth and inflation in China under reform', *Journal of Political Economy*, 108: 422–51.

Caselli, Francesco, Gerardo Esquivel, and Fernando Lefort (1996), 'Reopening the convergence debate: a new look at cross-country growth empirics', *Journal of Economic Growth*, 1: 363–89.

Chen, Baizhu, and Yi Feng (2000), 'Determinants of economic growth in China: private enterprise, education and openness', *China Economic Review*, 11: 1–15.

Chen, Jian, and Belton Fleisher (1996), 'Regional income inequality and economic growth in China', *Journal of Comparative Economics*, 22: 141–64.

Chi, Wei (2008), 'The role of human capital in China's economic development: review and new evidence', *China Economic Review*, 19: 421–36.

Démurger, Sylvie (2001), 'Infrastructure development and economic growth: an explanation for regional disparities in China', *Journal of Comparative Economics*, 29: 95–117.

Ding, Sai, and John Knight (2011), 'Why has China grown so fast? The role of physical and human capital formation', *Oxford Bulletin of Economics and Statistics*, 73, 2: 141–74.

Easterly, William, and Ross Levine (2001), 'What have we learned from a decade of empirical research on growth? It's not factor accumulation: stylized facts and growth models', *World Bank Economic Review*, 15: 177–219.

Fleisher, Belton, Haizheng Li, and Min Qiang Zhao (2010), 'Human capital, economic growth and regional inequality in China', *Journal of Development Studies*, 92: 215–31.

Gemmell, Norman (1996), 'Evaluating the impacts of human capital stocks and accumulation on economic growth: some new evidence', *Oxford Bulletin of Economics and Statistics*, 58: 9–28.

Guariglia, Alessandra, Xiaoxuan Liu, and Lina Song (2011), 'Internal finance and growth: microeconometric evidence on Chinese firms', *Journal of Development Economics*, 96, 1: 79–94.

Islam, Nazrul (1995), 'Growth empirics: a panel data approach', *The Quarterly Journal of Economics*, 110: 1127–70.

Javorcik, Beata (2008), 'Can survey evidence shed light on spillovers from foreign direct investment?' *The World Bank Research Observer*, 23: 139–59.

Jones, Derek, Cheng Li, and Ann Owen (2003), 'Growth and regional inequality in China during the reform era', *China Economic Review*, 14: 186–200.

Knight, John, and Li Shi (1993), 'The determinants of educational attainment in China', in Keith Griffin and Zhao Renwei (eds.), *The Distribution of Income in China*, London: St Martin's Press.

————and Quheng Deng (2010), 'Education and the poverty trap in rural China: closing the trap', *Oxford Development Studies*, 38, 1 (March): 1–24.

Knight, John, and Lina Song (2005), *Towards a Labour Market in China*. Oxford: Oxford University Press.

——and —— (2008), 'China's emerging urban wage structure, 1995–2002', in Björn Gustafsson, Li Shi, and Terry Sicular (eds.), *Inequality and Public Policy in China*, Cambridge: Cambridge University Press: 221–42.

Levine, Ross, and David Renelt (1992), 'A sensitivity analysis of cross-country growth regressions', *American Economic Review*, 82: 942–63.

Li, Hong, Zinan Liu, and Ivonia Rebelo (1998), 'Testing the neoclassical theory of economic growth: evidence from Chinese provinces', *Economics of Planning*, 31: 117–32.

Liu, Xiaohui, Peter Burridge, and Peter Sinclair (2002), 'Relationships between economic growth, foreign direct investment and trade: evidence from China', *Applied Economics*, 34: 1433–40.

Mankiw, Gregory, David Romer, and David Weil (1992), 'A contribution to the empirics of economic growth', *The Quarterly Journal of Economics*, 107: 407–37.

Naughton, Barry (2007), *The Chinese Economy, Transitions and Growth*, Cambridge, Mass: The MIT Press.

Pritchett, Lant (1999), 'Where has all the education gone?' *The World Bank Economic Review*, 15: 367–91.

Qin, Duo, Marie Anne Cagas, Pilipinas Quising, and Xin-hua He (2006), 'How much does investment drive economic growth in China', *Journal of Policy Modelling*, 28: 751–74.

Riedel, James, Jing Jin, and Jian Gao (2007), *How China Grows: Investment, Finance and Reform*, Princeton: Princeton University Press.

Romer, Paul (1990), 'Are non-convexities important for understanding growth?' *American Economic Review*, 80: 97–103.

Sala-i-Martin, Xavier (1997), 'I just ran two million regressions', *American Economic Review*, 87: 178–83.

Scott, Maurice Fitzgerald (1989), *A New View of Economic Growth*, Oxford: Clarendon Press.

——(1993), 'Explaining economic growth', *American Economic Review, Papers and Proceedings*, 83: 421–25.

Temple, Jonathan (1999a), 'The new growth evidence', *Journal of Economic Literature*, 37: 112–56.

——(1999b), 'A positive effect of human capital on growth', *Economics Letters*, 65, 1: 131–4.

Wei, Shang-Jin (1995), 'Open door policy and China's rapid growth: evidence from city-level data', in Takatoshi Ito and Anne Krueger (eds.), *Growth Theories in Light of the East Asian Experience*, Chicago: University of Chicago Press.

Yao, Shujie (2006), 'On economic growth, FDI and exports in China', *Applied Economics*, 38: 39–51.

Ying, Long Gen (2003), 'Understanding China's recent growth experience: a spatial econometric perspective', *The Annals of Regional Science*, 37: 613–28.

7

The Role of Structural Change: Trade, Ownership, Industry

7.1 Introduction

According to Rodrik (2010), what matters for growth in developing countries is structural transformation from (traditional) low-productivity to (modern) high-productivity activities. These modern activities produce goods that are largely tradeable, and within these tradeables, mainly industrial products. He also mentions the importance of dealing with institutional weaknesses such as poor protection of property rights and weak enforcement of contracts. These ideas correspond well to the main themes of this chapter. We explore some indirect determinants of China's growth success, including sectoral change, increased openness, and institutional change.

All three forms of structural change are found to raise the growth rate. Each primarily represents an improvement in efficiency, moving the economy towards its production frontier. We conclude that such improvements in productive efficiency have been a major part of the explanation for China's growth. This highlights the potential importance of structural transformation—the transfer of resources from less to more productive activities—for accelerating growth in developing economies.

In analysing these structural variables we start with the baseline equation of Chapter 5 and then develop it, one variable at a time. We examine the growth impacts of openness (Section 7.2), institutional change (Section 7.3), and sectoral change (Section 7.4). In each of these sections we discuss the relevant theoretical and empirical literature, provide background information for China, and summarize our empirical results. Section 7.5 concludes the chapter by considering various counterfactual simulation analyses in order to throw further light on the underlying question: why has China grown so fast?

7.2 Increasing Openness

The openness–growth literature

In trade theory, the static effect of openness on the level of income can arise from specialization according to comparative advantage, exploitation of increasing returns, and spread of technology and information. The effect of openness on the growth of income is widely analysed in the endogenous growth literature.[1] If greater competition or exposure to new technologies and ideas were to increase the rate of technological progress, it would permanently raise the growth rate (Winters 2004). The channels through which openness affects economic growth may lie in access to the technological knowledge of trade partners or foreign investors and to markets with new products and inputs, transfer of multinational enterprises' managerial expertise, and greater R&D through increasing returns to innovation. It is difficult to judge empirically whether the effect on growth is transitional or permanent. In any case, since much empirical and theoretical work[2] suggests that transitional dynamics may take several decades, our research focus is on output growth rather than on output level.

The hypothesis that openness is a positive force for growth has been tested in numerous cross-country studies. For example, Dollar (1992) found for a sample of ninety-five developing countries that a measure of outward orientation, based on real exchange rate distortion and variability, is highly positively correlated with GDP per capita growth. Sachs and Warner (1995) concluded that in the period 1970–89 open economies, defined by the absence of five conditions, experienced an average annual growth rate which was 2% above that of closed economies, and that convergence occurred only in the sample of open economies. Edwards (1998) adopted nine alternative openness indices to analyse the connection between trade policy and productivity growth during the period 1980–90, and showed that openness contributed to faster total factor productivity (TFP) growth. Using geographic factors as an instrument for trade volume, Frankel and Romer (1999) examined causality between trade and income level as well as the channels through which trade affects subsequent income. They found that trade does have a quantitatively large and robust positive effect on income. Using firm-level data, Goldberg et al. (2010) produced evidence for India that the new imported inputs that are made possible by trade liberalization provide substantial growth benefits.

Empirical research on the openness–growth nexus faces at least three problems. Firstly, the appropriate definition of openness depends on the precise hypothesis to be tested. Secondly, it is difficult to measure openness. Pritchett (1996) pointed out that any single measure is unlikely to capture the essence of trade policy. Rodríguez and Rodrik (2001) argued that a low score for trade policy openness may reflect not trade impediments but other bad policies. An index which includes all the tariff and non-tariff barriers that distort international trade might be a good measure of a country's openness, and research has moved in this direction.[3] However, such indices are not relevant for examining the openness of regions within a country owing to the nationwide nature of trade policies. We therefore rely on various measures of trade volumes and changes in trade volumes to proxy openness.

Thirdly, it is difficult to establish that causality runs from openness to growth. On the one hand, openness can be endogenous. At a macroeconomic level, higher income growth may lead to more trade.[4] At a microeconomic level, efficiency and exports may be positively correlated if it is the efficient firms that export.[5] On the other hand, because trade policy is often one among a basket of growth-enhancing policies, the measure of trade policy is likely to be correlated with omitted variables in the growth regression, making it difficult to identify the causal effect of openness.[6] Baldwin (2003) argued that it is unnecessary to isolate the effects of trade liberalization on growth if it is indeed part of a broader policy package. Nevertheless, the econometric difficulties of endogeneity and omitted variables need to be resolved if we are to avoid biased or spurious estimation of the consequence of openness for growth.

Trade reform in China

China's pre-reform foreign trade regime was an extreme example of import substitution, involving both a trade monopoly and a tightly controlled foreign-exchange system. The main role of foreign trade was to make up for domestic shortages by importing and, within the planning framework, to smooth out excessive supplies of domestic goods by exporting. The initial trade reform was characterized by the decentralization of trading rights to local authorities, industrial ministries, and production enterprises. Reform started in Guangdong and Fujian through the setting up of four Special Economic Zones (SEZs) to exploit their proximity to Hong Kong and foster export-processing production. A 'coastal development strategy' was adopted in the mid-1980s to allow all types of firms in the coastal provinces to engage in processing and assembly contracts. To provide incentives for firms to embrace foreign trade, the stringent control of foreign exchange was relaxed by allowing a gradual devaluation of the renminbi (RMB). A dual exchange rate regime was introduced in 1986, in which exporters outside the plan could sell their foreign exchange earnings on a lightly regulated secondary market at a higher price.

China began to move in the direction of a genuinely open economy in the mid-1990s. A comprehensive package to reform the foreign exchange regime was introduced in 1994, including unifying the double-track exchange rate system, abolishing the foreign exchange retention system and swap system, and simplifying procedures for acquiring and using foreign exchange for current account transactions. The reforms provided a relatively stable exchange rate and a stable trading environment. China began lowering tariffs in preparation for WTO membership: the average nominal tariff was reduced in stages from 43% in 1992 to 17% in 1999 (Naughton 2007). The prospect of WTO membership was a powerful motivating factor in China's trade reform.

There is a large literature on the relationship between openness and growth in China. The hypothesis that China's growth is export led has been a subject of debate. We concentrate on the more formal tests. Wei (1995) investigated the growth impact of China's open door policy using two city-level data sets. His cross-section study suggested that, during the 1980s as a whole, exports were positively associated with higher industrial growth across the cities, while in the late 1980s, the cross-city growth difference was mainly explained by FDI. Using quarterly national data from the years 1981 to 1997 and a time-series cointegration framework, Liu et al. (2002) showed that there is a long-run bidirectional causal relationship among growth, imports, exports, and FDI. From a cross-province panel-data analysis for the period 1978–2000, Yao (2006) found that both exports and FDI have a strong, positive effect on economic growth, and concluded that the interaction among these three variables formed a virtuous circle of openness and growth in China.

Firm-level evidence is also available. Kraay (1999), using a panel of Chinese industrial enterprises over the period 1988–92, examined whether firms learn from exporting. He found that past exports led to significant improvements in firm performance, and that the learning effects were more pronounced for established exporters. Park et al. (2010), analysing panel data on Chinese manufacturers and firm-specific exchange rate shocks as instruments for exports, found that exporting increases TFP, total sales, and return on assets, so providing evidence in favour of the 'learning by doing' hypothesis. These China-specific findings are in contrast to the general argument made by Bernard et al. (2007) in a survey article that exporters are more productive not as a result of exporting but because only productive firms are able to overcome the costs of entering export markets.

Our findings

We use two groups of measures to explore the role of openness in driving China's economic growth over the reform period.[7] Both are treated as potentially endogenous variables in the system GMM estimation. The first group is calculated using trade volumes. The most basic measure of trade intensity is the simple trade share (*trade/GDP*), which is the ratio of exports plus imports to GDP. Export share and import share in GDP (*export/GDP* and *import/GDP*) are also used. Exports contribute to growth by enabling the economy to exploit its comparative advantage and exposing the exporting firms to the rigour of international competition. However, Edwards (1993) argued that too much emphasis had been placed on exports in the earlier literature. The theory of comparative advantage also predicts an efficiency gain through the import of goods and services that are otherwise too costly to produce within the country, and that producers for the domestic market can be stimulated by competition from imports. By examining four types of imports (ideas, goods and services, capital, and institutions), Rodrik (1999) even claimed that the benefits of openness lie on the import side rather than the export side. In line with Yanikkaya (2003), we hypothesize that both exports and imports are important for a country's economic development, and should be considered complements rather than alternatives.

The results for trade volume and its two components are presented in Table 7.1, Panel 1. Trade share, export share, and import share in GDP are each found to have significant and positive effects on the growth rate of GDP per capita. The similar magnitude of the coefficients of exports and imports indicates the equally important role of both dimensions of trade openness, that is, a one percentage point rise in the ratio of exports or imports to GDP in a province raises its growth rate of GDP per capita by 0.08 percentage points.

China began trade liberalization with one of the most closed economies in the world: the total trade over GDP ratio was marginally above 10% in 1978 (Figure 7.1). With its open door policy, China's degree of integration into the world economy has improved dramatically; total trade amounted to 72% of GDP in 2006. Both exports and imports as a share of GDP have climbed strongly and persistently, with two setbacks in the late 1980s and in the late 1990s. China is a

Table 7.1. The growth impact of openness

Panel 1. Trade volumes

	trade/GDP	export/GDP	import/GDP
Coefficient	0.042** (0.010)	0.083** (0.022)	0.076** (0.016)
AR(2) p value	0.368	0.421	0.335
Hansen p value	0.741	0.728	0.783
Dif Sargan p value	0.689	0.647	0.495
Num of instruments	26	26	26
Num of observations	149	149	149

Panel 2. Changes of trade volumes

	tradegr	exportgr	importgr
Coefficient	0.147 ** (0.028)	0.153** (0.024)	0.073** (0.023)
AR(2) p value	0.426	0.645	0.308
Hansen p value	0.610	0.768	0.628
Dif Sargan p value	0.474	0.450	0.404
Num of instruments	26	26	26
Num of observations	148	148	148

Note: panel-data system GMM results are reported; standard errors are in parentheses, which are heteroskedasticity consistent and clustering on province; the control variables are those selected by the model-selection procedures, that is, $lny_{i,t-1}$, fcf/GDP, stu_{SEC}/pop, $popngr$, and ind_{SOE}/ind_{TOTAL}, in which $lny_{i,t-1}$ is treated as predetermined, $popngr$ is treated as exogenous, and all other variables are treated as endogenous; time dummies are included; ** and * indicate that the coefficient is significantly different from zero at the 5 or 10% significance level respectively.

big net importer of intermediate capital-intensive and skill-intensive commodities such as machinery, electronics, and other heavy, process-technology industrial products, and a big net exporter of final labour-intensive commodities (Naughton 2007). This pattern of exports and imports corresponds well to the principle of comparative advantage given that China is a labour-rich, land-scarce, and capital-scarce economy.

The role of trade volumes in accelerating growth may not have been possible without the marked changes that occurred in the structure of trade. Figure 7.2 reflects these changes in the composition of China's exports over the period 1984–2007. There was a dramatic shift to manufacturing products and a corresponding

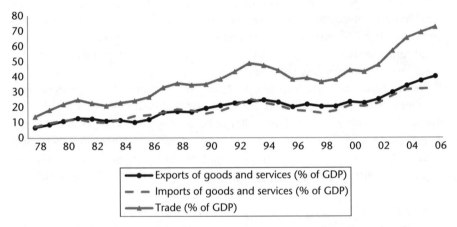

Figure 7.1. Trade volumes of the Chinese economy: exports, imports and trade, percentage of GDP, 1978–2006

Data source: World Bank, *World Development Indicators* (April 2008).

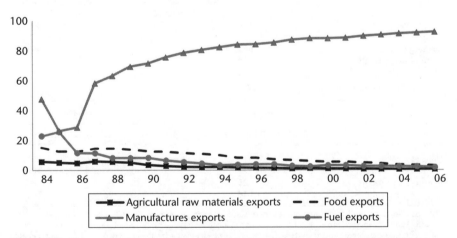

Figure 7.2. The composition of China's exports, percentage of total, 1984–2006

Data source: World Bank, *World Development Indicators* (April 2008).

decline in natural-resource-based products, for instance, agricultural raw materials, food, and fuels. This improved the prospects for rapid export growth, and for gains in productive efficiency. By contrast, some other slower-growing developing areas, such as Sub-Saharan Africa, remain heavily dependent on exports of primary commodities which are more vulnerable to adverse market conditions. The effect on growth can be a matter not only of how much countries export but also of what they export.

Our second group of openness measures is based on changes in the volume of trade. According to Dollar and Kraay (2004), trade volumes are potentially endogenous variables which may reflect a wide range of factors other than trade policy, such as geographic characteristics. They therefore regarded the proportional changes in trade volumes relative to GDP as a better measure for openness, given the fact that geography and many other unobserved country or region characteristics that drive both growth and trade vary little over time. However, Nye et al. (2002) argued that countries with the largest increase in trade volumes are likely to be those with the lowest trade volumes, and thus to be the least open. Nevertheless, we use the changes of trade volumes (*tradegr*), export volumes (*exportgr*), and import volumes (*importgr*) as additional measures of openness. We find that all variables have significantly positive impacts on the growth rate, that is, a one percentage point rise in the growth rate of exports or imports leads to an increase in GDP per capita growth of 0.2 or 0.1 percentage points respectively (Table 7.1, Panel 2).

In brief, China's foreign trade reform has been a process of shifting from import substitution towards export promotion through decentralizing foreign trade rights and liberalizing the foreign exchange system. This has led to a sharp increase in China's trade volumes. Both the level and the change of the trade share in GDP are found to raise growth, the latter more so than the former. Not only exports but also imports have a positive effect, change in the former more so than change in the latter.

7.3 Institutional Change

The institutions-growth literature

Institutions, being the rules that govern and shape the interactions of human beings, structure economic incentives (North 1990: 3). The institutional framework consists of both formal entities, like laws, constitutions, written contracts, market exchanges, and organizational rules, and informal ones, like shared values, norms, customs, ethics, and ideology (Lin and Nugent 1995). It is widely held that institutions play an important role in economic development and growth. Hall and Jones (1999) and Acemoglu et al. (2005) argue that standard economic models of factor accumulation and endogenous technical change provide only proximate explanations of economic growth, whereas differences in institutions are the fundamental causes of differential growth across countries. Lin (2007) emphasizes the role of institutional changes in driving economic development by promoting technological innovation and more efficient resource allocation.

Research on institutions and growth raises three issues—relating to concepts, measures, and causation. Acemoglu et al. (2001, 2005) examined property rights, broadly interpreted, as did Knack and Keefer (1995), Mauro (1995) examined corruption, administrative and judicial efficiency, and political stability, and Hall and Jones (1999) 'social infrastructure'. In each case proxies and instruments had to be found for these vague and potentially endogenous influences.

Market formation has been rapid in China and its timing across provinces has varied. Several cross-province studies of the effect of institutional change on growth have been conducted.[8] For instance, Lin (1992) adopted a production function approach to assess the contributions to China's agricultural growth over the reform period of institutional change (decentralizing decision making and providing incentives) and other influences. Transforming from the production team to the household responsibility system was found to improve total factor productivity and to account for about half of the output growth during the period 1978–84. Cai et al. (2002) constructed a marketization index[9] to examine the effect of market-oriented institutional reforms on economic growth, and found a significantly positive role for institutional factors, based on OLS and FGLS estimators. Hasan et al. (2009) concluded from their panel-data GMM results that the emergence of the market economy, the establishment of secure property rights, the growth of a private sector, the development of financial and legal institutions, and the representation of minor parties in province governance accelerated provincial growth over the period 1986–2003.

Ownership as a measure of institutions for China

Institutions are arguably weak in many developing countries because the rules that ensure the use and trading of property rights are absent or poorly enforced.[10] However, with its institutions devised and created for a centrally planned command economy, China at the start of economic reform was at a particularly severe disadvantage. The government committed to experimentalism and gradualism in its institutional reform. One minor reform often created the need for another, and so on. New economic institutions thus evolved by a process of cumulative causation. Compared with most developing countries, China's institutional change was fast; compared with most former communist countries, it was slow.

One distinguishing feature of China's institutional reform is the emergence of new forms of ownership. In the 1980s and early 1990s, the collectively owned 'township and village enterprises' (TVEs) experienced a significant expansion and played a catalytic role in pushing China towards a market economy. Several factors contributed to the rapid development of rural industry in China, the most important of which were access to previously protected or empty markets, their competitive advantage derived from low wages, and local government support. Jefferson et al. (1998) found empirical evidence that TVEs had institutional advantages over SOEs. Unlike SOEs, TVEs faced relatively hard budget constraints, so generating profit incentives. The entry of TVEs also provided competition for SOEs. However, when restrictions on the private sector were gradually relaxed and when the urban reforms gave SOEs more incentives to seek out profitable opportunities and to compete successfully against them, TVEs began to lose their profitability; after the mid-1990s many were transformed into private businesses.

Deng Xiaoping's southern tour of 1992 formally gave the green light for capitalist development. The Company Law of 1994 provided a uniform legal framework into which all of the ownership forms fit, signalling the introduction of more clearly defined property rights and the start of dramatic institutional change implied by the rapid downsizing of the state sector. Many SOEs and urban collective enterprises (UCEs) were shut down, and employment in SOEs and UCEs shrank by over 40% and 75% respectively between 1995 and 2006.[11] A large number of SOEs and UCEs were either privatized or turned into shareholding entities that are increasingly dominated by private owners.[12] However, SOEs remain dominant in energy, natural resources, and a few strategic or monopolistic sectors that are controlled and protected by central government.

Economic institutions comprise several elements. In the Chinese context, the allocation of decision-making rights, the motives of decision makers, the incentives faced by decision makers, and the degree of economic certainty and security within which decisions are made, have been referred to as 'property rights' (Jefferson et al. 1998). The economic environment which determines the degree of competition among producers is also relevant. The different forms of ownership are closely related to both property rights and competition. The policy of permitting privatization and encouraging private enterprises both generated incentives for profits and thus for efficiency, and also required security of property. Although urban reform provided SOEs with greater autonomy in decision making on production and investment, and a greater share of profits that could be retained, the principal-agent problem inherent in state ownership meant that efficiency and profitability in the state sector remained lower than in the non-state sector. The three main elements of institutional change—improving incentives, strengthening competition, and changing ownership—evolved together, and by their interactions pulled each other along.

It is difficult to find data that adequately measure China's institutional development at the provincial level for the entire sample period. We have good measures neither of property rights as defined above nor of the degree of competition. Instead we rely on the fact that the evolution of economic institutions has paralleled the changes in the structure of ownership. In order to proxy institutional changes, we use three groups of variables: the ownership patterns of investment, of industrial output, and of employment. We are not alone in adopting this approach: the relative size of the private sector has been widely used as a proxy for the extent of property rights protection in China.[13] All the institution measures are treated as potentially endogenous variables in our panel-data GMM estimation.

Our findings

Investment in fixed assets is classified according to ownership: investment spending by SOEs ($finv_{SOE}/finv_{TOTAL}$), collective enterprises ($finv_{COL}/finv_{TOTAL}$), and private enterprises ($finv_{PRIV}/finv_{TOTAL}$) in Table 7.2, Panel 1. As in Brandt and Zhu (2000), our estimate shows that the growth rate of GDP per capita falls as the share of investment by SOEs increases, that is, reducing the share of SOEs in total fixed investment by one percentage point is associated with an increase in GDP per capita growth of 0.1 percentage points. The recent decline in the SOE share of fixed

Table 7.2. The growth impact of institutional change

Panel 1. Institutional change of investment

	$finv_{SOE}/finv_{TOTAL}$	$finv_{COL}/finv_{TOTAL}$	$finv_{PRIV}/finv_{TOTAL}$
Coefficients	−0.089** (0.019)	−0.062 (0.069)	0.167** (0.071)
AR(2) p value	0.947	0.888	0.853
Hansen p value	0.738	0.732	0.601
Dif Sargan p value	0.295	0.681	0.211
Num of instruments	26	26	26
Num of observations	149	149	149

Panel 2. Institutional change of industrial output

	ind_{SOE}/ind_{TOTAL}	ind_{COL}/ind_{TOTAL}	ind_{PRIV}/ind_{TOTAL}
Coefficients	−0.028* (0.017)	0.012 (0.022)	0.042** (0.018)
AR(2) p value	0.421	0.738	0.899
Hansen p value	0.728	0.616	0.762
Dif Sargan p value	0.647	0.758	0.740
Num of instruments	26	26	26
Num of observations	149	124	124

Panel 3. Institutional change of employment

	wok_{SOE}/wok_{TOTAL}	wok_{COL}/wok_{TOTAL}	wok_{PRIV}/wok_{TOTAL}
Coefficients	−0.201** (0.039)	−0.039 (0.041)	0.157** (0.029)
AR(2) p value	0.543	0.685	0.284
Hansen p value	0.650	0.722	0.719
Dif Sargan p value	0.521	0.672	0.773
Num of instruments	26	26	26
Num of observations	149	149	149

Notes: panel-data system GMM results are reported; standard errors are in parentheses, which are heteroskedasticity consistent and clustering on province; the control variables are those selected by the model-selection procedures, that is, $lny_{i,t-1}$, gcf/GDP, stu_{SEC}/pop, $popngr$, and ind_{SOE}/ind_{TOTAL}, in which $lny_{i,t-1}$ is treated as predetermined, $popngr$ is treated as exogenous, and all other variables are treated as endogenous; time dummies are included; ** and * indicate that the coefficient is significantly different from zero at the 5 or 10% significance level respectively.

investment has been good for growth. The coefficient on investment by collective firms appears insignificant. The collective economy consists of both TVEs and UCEs. The former are generally said to have been dynamic, especially in the 1980s, whereas the latter are run by local governments and still suffer from the disincentives associated with soft budget constraints and principal-agent problems. We therefore had no clear hypothesis about the impact of collective firms on growth. Private sector investment affects growth positively, that is, a one percentage point increase in this variable is associated with an increased growth rate of 0.17 percentage points. This result is consistent with the evidence that the average return on investment in the private sector is higher than that in the SOEs (Riedel et al. 2007: 40–2).

We employ the share of gross industrial output value of SOEs (ind_{SOE}/ind_{TOTAL}), of collective enterprises (ind_{COL}/ind_{TOTAL}), and of private enterprises (ind_{PRIV}/ind_{TOTAL}) as proxies for institutional change in Table 7.2, Panel 2. As expected, the growth rate of GDP per capita is influenced negatively by the SOE share of output, insignificantly by that of collective firms, and positively by that of private firms. Similar results hold when measures of employment (*wok*) are adopted in Panel 3. The size of state sector has a negative consequence for growth, and the expansion of private sector is conducive to growth. It is therefore a positive development that much of the economy has been shifting from the state to the private sector.

In brief, we find that China's economic growth can be partly ascribed to the evolution of the country's economic institutions. Whether investment, output, or employment is used as the criterion, the effect of a decrease in state ownership and of an increase in private ownership is to increase growth. The private sector, with its incentives for profit and thus for efficiency, is a driving force. China's experience suggests that, through incremental changes which provide people with the right incentives, it is possible to unleash rapid growth on a weak institutional base, so permitting a successful transition from central planning to a well-functioning market economy. This is consistent with the view of Rodrik (2003) that deep and extensive reforms are not required for dynamic growth at the onset of the transition. Instead, government should encourage, and pay attention to, local and private initiatives in making institutional changes (Lin 2007).

7.4 Sectoral Change and Industrialization

The sectoral change, industrialization, and growth literature

The economic development literature has long recognized the role of sectoral change in promoting growth. Firstly, in the seminal dual economy model of Lewis (1954), transferring labour from low- to high-productivity sectors is conducive to economic growth. If the marginal product of labour is lower in agriculture, the movement of labour to sectors, such as industry, where the marginal product is higher will raise total output. Secondly, it is arguable that manufacturing benefits from more production externalities than does agriculture (Corden 1974). Production by one firm leads not only to current output but also to accumulation of knowledge which can also spread to other firms as time passes. This kind of dynamic externality can reduce industrial costs over time. Shifting the output or employment pattern from agriculture to industry can generate learning economies, thus increasing the rate of economic growth. Thirdly, if the industrial sector is more subject to economies of scale than is the agricultural sector, a relatively larger industrial sector provides scope for faster economic growth.

Robinson (1971) estimated growth regressions to assess the effect of factor transfers (both capital and labour) on economic growth in thirty-nine developing countries over the period 1958–66. The cross-section OLS estimates suggested an important role for factor reallocation in growth, and also the existence of structural disequilibrium in factor markets. Using a similar methodology, Feder (1986) constructed and estimated a disequilibrium model based on productivity differentials between agricultural and non-agricultural sectors for thirty semi-industrialized countries over the period 1964–73. He found strong evidence of sectoral differences in the marginal productivity of factors, and concluded that countries which pursued accelerated industrial growth tended to grow faster because resource allocation was improved. However, it is a shortcoming of both studies that the sectoral difference in factor marginal productivities is treated as the same across countries.

Dowrick and Gemmell (1991) used growth accounting to test the hypothesis that barriers to the transfer of labour between sectors and countries drive a wedge between sectoral marginal products. In a sample of rich and middle-income countries over the period 1960–85, their test results indicated that the degree of disequilibrium was not the same across countries, but proportional to the observed ratio of sectoral labour productivities. The ratio of labour average productivity between sectors was found to decrease with the level of development. Poirson (2001) extended the analysis of the sectoral change-growth nexus to the panel-data context. After controlling for unobserved differences in productivity growth and other omitted variables, it was found that intersectoral labour reallocation made a significant contribution to growth differences across sixty-five developing and industrial countries over the period 1960–90. Poirson confirmed the finding of Dowrick and Gemmell (1991) that the reallocation effect of labour productivity growth varied with the labour productivity in one sector relative to the other. The results proved to be robust when the endogeneity of sectoral change variables was controlled for using instrumental variable estimation methods.

Vollrath (2005) examined the static effect of factor market distortions on aggregate productivity and income level using the growth-accounting approach for a sample of forty-two countries. He showed that variation across countries in the degree of resource misallocation between agriculture and non-agriculture accounted for 30–40% of the variation in income per capita, and up to 80% of the variation in aggregate TFP. Temple and Wößmann (2006) extended Vollrath's work to a dynamic model, focusing on the relationship between sectoral change and economic growth. Changes in the structure of employment can account for a significant fraction of the observed variation in productivity growth among seventy-six countries over the period 1960–96. Moreover, the cross-section relationship between growth and the extent of sectoral change was found to be non-linear, and the extent of dualism as measured by labour productivity differentials was found to decline over time.

Dualism and sectoral change in China

At the start of economic reform China was an extreme example of a labour surplus economy. The various attempts to measure the extent of surplus labour (surveyed by Taylor 1988) produced a majority view that surplus labour represented about a third of the rural labour force, although it had been disguised by work sharing within the communes. According to official data, the agricultural labour force fell from 71% of the total in 1978 to 46% in 2000. It is very likely that the transfer of labour from rural agriculture to urban, and also rural, industry involved a sharp increase in its marginal product. For instance, Knight and Song (2005: 188–99) found that the estimated average and marginal return to rural labour were far higher in non-farm than in farm activities in 1994, the ratios being 1.5 to 1 and 10.0 to 1 respectively. Moreover, a rural household's non-farm employment had negligible opportunity cost in terms of farm work. Knight and Song (2005: 103–9) also estimated that the marginal product of migrants employed in urban enterprises in 1995 far exceeded their wage, a disequilibrium caused by official restrictions on the employment of migrants. This evidence shows why it is plausible that the transfer of labour out of agriculture had an important effect on the rate of economic growth.

The impact of sectoral change and industrialization on economic growth has received increasing research attention in the growth literature on China. Brandt et al. (2008) adopted a growth-accounting approach to examine the impact of both within-sector productivity growth and between-sector reallocation on aggregate output growth in China. Their three-sector structural growth model suggested that the non-state non-agricultural sector was the key driver of economic growth over the period 1978–2004. Evidence has also been found in the cross-province growth regression literature. In a cross-sectional analysis for the period 1978–89, Chen and Feng (2000) found that the degree of industrialization, measured as the gross output value of industry as a percentage of provincial income, had a positive effect on the growth rate of provincial GDP per capita. Cai et al. (2002) used the labour productivity of agriculture relative to non-agriculture as a measure of labour market distortion. Their panel-data estimation results for the period 1978–98 showed that labour market distortion reduced provincial growth rates. Ying (2003) examined the consequences of China's structural transformation for its post-reform growth performance. The growth of non-farm employment made the most important contribution to provincial growth in this spatial lag model.

The issue of the potential endogeneity of sectoral change variables is not adequately addressed in any of these studies, and no attempts have been made to apply a two-sector dual economy model in the growth literature for China. That is the task we set ourselves in this section.

Our findings

Sectoral change variables are not highlighted as important predictors of economic growth by either of the model-selection procedures utilized in Chapter 5, and therefore do not enter our baseline model. However, this outcome may result from the highly endogenous nature of the sectoral change variables, which cannot be accounted for at the cross-sectional model-selection stage. Accordingly, we estimate the effect of labour reallocation between sectors on provincial growth in the panel-data context and treat all sectoral change variables as potentially endogenous in our system GMM estimation. The introduction of sectoral change is based on its treatment in two cross-country empirical growth models suitable for dual economies.

Firstly, we test the hypothesis of Temple and Wößmann (2006) that changes in the structure of employment will raise total output when the marginal product of labour varies across sectors. They also hypothesized that the relationship between growth and sectoral change is convex, that is, the growth impact of a given extent of sectoral change is greater where sectoral change is faster. The intuition is that if wages are roughly equal to marginal products, the growth bonus associated with sectoral change is increasing in the size of the intersectoral wage differential. In other words, provinces with the largest wage differential are assumed to be those in which the observed extent of sectoral change is greatest, reflecting large private gains from switching sectors.

In Table 7.3, Panel 1, following Temple and Wößmann (2006), two sets of sectoral change variables are defined in a two-sector general equilibrium model of production.[14] The first set of sectoral change variables (MGROWTH and DISEQ) are derived from the assumption that the labour share in output is the same across provinces. The second set of sectoral change variables (MGROWTH2 and DISEQ2) is based on the assumption that all provinces have the same Cobb–Douglas technologies in agriculture. MGROWTH and MGROWTH2 are the linear terms reflecting changes of employment in the non-agricultural sector; DISEQ and DISEQ2 are the quadratic terms capturing the convexity effect. We find that the linear terms (MGROWTH and MGROWTH2) are positive and significant, suggesting that reallocating labour from agriculture to non-agriculture is conducive to growth of provincial GDP per capita. In contrast with cross-country analysis (for

Table 7.3. The growth impact of sectoral change

Panel 1. Sectoral change of employment

Hypothesis of Temple and Wößmann

	First set of sectoral change terms		Second set of sectoral change terms	
MGROWTH or MGROWTH2	0.854**(0.243)	1.025**(0.221)	1.977**(0.621)	2.217***(0.497)
DISEQ or DISEQ2	1.352(1.731)	4.165(2.916)	2.186(4.027)	8.267(5.929)
AR(2) p value	0.189	0.454	0.129	0.455
Hansen p value	0.791	0.720	0.791	0.619
Dif Sargan p value	0.748	0.697	0.646	0.616
Num of instruments	28	26	28	26
Num of observations	149	149	149	149

Hypothesis of Poirson

	First set of sectoral change terms		Second set of sectoral change terms
MGROWTH	1.101**(0.224)	1.025**(0.221)	0.015**(0.007)
MGROWTH * RLP	0.011*(0.006)		
AR(2) p value	0.201	0.153	0.942
Hansen p value	0.736	0.639	0.673
Dif Sargan p value	0.791	0.759	0.759
Num of instruments	28	26	26
Num of observations	149	149	149

Panel 2. Sectoral change of output

	First set of sectoral change terms		Second set of sectoral change terms
deofin	0.006 (0.026)		-0.058 (0.030)
Δdeofin		0.206** (0.041)	0.259** (0.047)
AR(2) p value	0.455	0.150	0.107
Hansen p value	0.761	0.640	0.682
Dif Sargan p value	0.613	0.720	0.619
Num of instruments	26	26	28
Num of observations	149	149	149

Notes: panel-data system GMM results are reported; standard errors are in parentheses, which are heteroskedasticity consistent and clustering on province; the control variables are those selected by the model-selection procedures, that is, $lny_{i,t-1}$, fcf/GDP, stu_{SEC}/pop, $popngr$, $export/GDP$ and ind_{SOE}/ind_{TOTAL}, in which $lny_{i,t-1}$ is treated as predetermined, $popngr$ is treated as exogenous, and all other variables are treated as endogenous; time dummies are included; ** and * indicate that the coefficient is significantly different from zero at the 5 or 10% significance level respectively.

instance, Temple and Wößmann 2006; Ding and Knight 2009; and Chapter 4 above), we find no evidence of a convex relationship. This result is robust when two sectoral change variables enter the regression either jointly or individually. It may well reflect the fact that labour mobility across provinces in China depends not only on private decisions but also on public migration controls.

We test an alternative hypothesis of Poirson (2001) that the effect of labour reallocation on growth depends on the magnitude of the labour productivity gap between sectors. In that model there are also two sectoral change terms: change in labour share in non-agricultural sector (*MGROWTH*), the same as the definition in Temple and Wößmann (2006), and change in labour share in non-agricultural sector weighted by relative labour productivity (*MGROWTH * RLP*). We find that both terms are positive and statistically significant, whether they enter the regression jointly or individually (Table 7.3, Panel 1). Therefore, our results support Poirson's hypothesis that the labour reallocation effect on growth is greater the higher is the average productivity in non-agriculture relative to agriculture.

Sectoral change can alternatively be depicted as the changing share of industry in total output. We test both the static role of the level of industrialization and the dynamic role of its change in driving economic growth (Table 7.3, Panel 2). We hypothesize that more industrialized provinces grow faster than those less industrialized. Surprisingly, we find that the degree of industrialization (*deofin*), defined as the ratio of gross industrial output value to the sum of gross industrial and agricultural output value, appears insignificant in determining provincial GDP per capita growth. Rather, it is the sectoral change in output, measured as the increase in industrialization (*Δdeofin*), that matters for economic growth, that is, a one percentage point rise in the growth rate of the ratio of industrial output to total output in a province raises its growth rate of GDP per capita by 0.2 percentage points. Thus it is the structural change of output, rather than the structure of output, that contributes to growth. Our results are consistent with the view that industrial growth, fostered by the intensification in world trade and the international division of labour triggered by globalization, is a powerful driver of China's economic growth.

In summary, China's economic growth has been intertwined with dramatic sectoral change in both employment and output. Our results indicate that transferring labour from agriculture to non-agriculture contributes significantly to economic growth. No evidence is found for Temple and Wößmann's (2006) prediction of a convex relationship between sectoral change and growth. Instead, our estimation results support the hypothesis of Poirson (2001) that the growth impact of labour reallocation is bigger for those provinces that have higher average productivity in non-agriculture relative to agriculture. Change in the structure of output from the agricultural sector to the industrial sector is conducive to economic growth. However, a higher level of industrialization itself is not associated with faster growth across China's provinces. Our results remain robust when various sensitivity tests are conducted.[15]

7.5 Conclusion

In this chapter, our research focus has been on various underlying influences on China's economic growth. Using the framework outlined in Chapter 5, we investigated in some detail the growth impact of three structural variables in China. We distinguished structure and change of structure. The structure of the economy itself affects the growth rate in the cases of trade and ownership but not of production. Having a large trade sector or a large private sector itself raises a province's growth rate. However, change in structure is even more important. China as a whole has undergone three forms of drastic structural change over the period of economic reform, and each of them helps to explain the remarkably high growth rate. Two of these changes, albeit less drastic, are likely to be shared by many developing countries; only privatization is more a feature of transition than of development.

The change of the trade share in GDP has had a positive effect, and not only exports but also imports have contributed. Posing the counterfactual, 'how would the growth rate have altered if the trade ratio had remained constant?', we find that the predicted annual average provincial growth of GDP per capita in China over the study period was 8.1%, whereas the growth of the ratio of trade to GDP was 18.1% per annum. The contribution to growth of this structural change was no less than 3.2 percentage points per annum. These results are consistent with growth benefiting from the improved resource allocation, technology, and competition that openness can bring.

The second contribution has come from the rapid privatization of the economy. Whether we use investment, output, or employment as the criterion, we find the effect of state ownership on growth to be negative and that of private ownership to be positive. Private enterprise output averaged 22.0% of total industrial output in China over the full period. If it had remained at its 1978 level (1.2%), growth would have been 0.7 percentage points lower, at 7.4% per annum. This pattern is consistent with the improvement in incentives that a greater role for profit seeking can bring.

Thirdly, it is clear that the remarkable sectoral changes have also made an important contribution to growth. The average change in the share of employment in the non-agricultural sector over the full sample period was 1.0 percentage points per annum. If instead no change had occurred, the coefficient implies that China's growth of GDP per capita would have fallen by one percentage point, from 8.1 to 7.1% per annum, holding other variables constant. This evidence is consistent with there being efficiency gains from improved sectoral labour allocation and also externalities specific to industry.

By altering mean values of key variables based on model estimation, these simple simulations contain the questionable assumption that a change in one variable would not change the other variables in the equation. It is likely that the three types of structural change are closely interrelated with each other. We therefore estimate an equation that simultaneously incorporates trade openness, private share of industrial output, and sectoral change. The full effect of structural change on growth is summed up to 4.1% per annum.[16] There remains the possibility that these structural change variables are correlated with other variables in the regression, for instance, physical and human capital formation, so that even their joint effect cannot be isolated. We thus use these figures simply to illustrate the rough orders of magnitude of the potential contribution of structural change to the growth rate.

The chapter highlights the potential importance of structural transformation—the transfer of resources from less to more productive activities—for accelerating growth in developing economies. It provides empirical support for the argument in Rodrik (2010) that high-growth economies are those that are able to transfer rapidly from low- to high-productivity sectors, that is, to production of non-traditional tradeable goods, which generate important 'learning externalities'.

Each of our three forms of structural change has involved an improvement in the efficiency of the economy by bringing it closer to its production frontier. They have also involved some outward movement of the production frontier, for instance, improvement in technology from trade openness or from greater incentives for research and development. However, the main extension of the production possibility curve has come from the accumulation of physical and human capital—an issue examined, within the same model framework, in Chapter 6.

APPENDIX 7.1

Table A7.1. Detailed Variable Definitions

Variable	Definition	Units
Dependent variable		
$g_{i,t}$	Growth rate of real provincial GDP per capita	proportion
Independent variables		
1. Degree of openness		
(1) Trade volumes		
trade/GDP	Ratio of exports and imports to GDP (Exports and imports converted to RMB using official exchange rate from IFS, IMF)	proportion
export/GDP	Ratio of exports to GDP (Exports converted to RMB using official exchange rate from IFS, IMF)	proportion
import/GDP	Ratio of imports to GDP (Imports converted to RMB using official exchange rate from IFS, IMF)	proportion
(2) Changes of trade volumes		
tradegr	Growth rate of trade volumes (Exports and imports converted to RMB using official exchange rate from IFS, IMF)	proportion
exportgr	Growth rate of exports (Exports converted to RMB using official exchange rate from IFS, IMF)	proportion
importgr	Growth rate of imports (Imports converted to RMB using official exchange rate from IFS, IMF)	proportion
2. Institutional change		
(1) Of investment		
$finv_{SOE}/finv_{TOTAL}$	Investment in fixed assets by state-owned units/Total investment in fixed assets	proportion
$finv_{COL}/finv_{TOTAL}$	Investment in fixed assets by collectively owned units/Total investment in fixed assets	proportion
$finv_{PRIV}/finv_{TOTAL}$	Investment in fixed assets by private units/Total investment in fixed assets	proportion
(2) Of industrial output		
ind_{SOE}/ind_{TOTAL}	Output value of state-owned enterprises/Gross industrial output value	proportion
ind_{COL}/ind_{TOTAL}	Output value of collective enterprises/Gross industrial output value	proportion
ind_{PRIV}/ind_{TOTAL}	Output value of private enterprises/Gross industrial output value	proportion
(3) Of employment		
wok_{SOE}/wok_{TOTAL}	State-owned enterprise workers/Total staff and workers	proportion
wok_{COL}/wok_{TOTAL}	Collective enterprise workers/Total staff and workers	proportion
wok_{PRIV}/wok_{TOTAL}	Private enterprise workers/Total staff and workers	proportion
3. Sectoral change		
(1) Temple and Wößmann's (2006) specification		
s	Agricultural share of GDP (Primary sector GDP/Total GDP)	proportion
a	Agricultural share of employment (Primary sector employment/Total number of employed persons)	proportion
m	Non-agricultural share of employment ($m = 1-a$)	proportion
p	Migration propensity ($p = -(da/dt)/a$)	
MGROWTH	Linear sectoral change term: Change of non-agricultural share of employment (dm/dt)	proportion

(continued)

Table A7.1. Continued

Variable	Definition	Units
DISEQ	Non-linear sectoral change term: Change of non-agricultural share of employment adjusted by migration propensity ($p/(1-p)*$ (dm/dt))	proportion
MGROWTH2	Linear sectoral change term: Change of non-agricultural share of employment * Average labour productivity in agricultural sector ((dm/dt)*s/a)	proportion
DISEQ2	Non-linear sectoral change term: Change of non-agricultural share of employment adjusted by migration propensity * Average labour productivity in agricultural sector ($p/(1-p)*(dm/dt)*s/a$)	proportion
(2) Dowrick and Gemmell's (1991) or Poirson's (2001) specification		
MGROWTH*RLP	Change in employment share in non-agricultural sector weighted by relative labour productivity (RLP = ratio of average labour productivity in non-agriculture to that in agriculture)	proportion
(3) Degree of industrialization		
deofin	Degree of industrialization (Gross industrial output value/(Gross industrial output value + Gross agricultural output value))	proportion
Δdeofin	Change in of degree of industrialization ($d(deofin)/dt$)	proportion
4. Other control variables		
$lny_{i,t-1}$	Logarithm of beginning-period real GDP per capita	1990 RMB
popngr	Population natural growth rate = Birth rate – death rate	proportion
export/GDP	Ratio of exports to GDP (Exports converted to RMB using official exchange rate from IFS, IMF)	proportion
ind_{SOE}/ind_{TOTAL}	Output value of state-owned enterprises/Gross industrial output value	proportion

Note: All the variables are calculated in 1990 constant prices and price indices are province specific. The data relate to thirty provinces over the period 1978–2007.

Notes

1. See, for example, Romer (1990), and Grossman and Helpman (1995).
2. For instance, Mankiw et al. (1992), Hall and Jones (1997), Barro and Sala-i-Martin (2004), Dollar and Kraay (2004), and Ding and Knight (2011).
3. For example, Yanikkaya (2003), Leamer (1988), Anderson and Neary (1992), Dollar (1992), and Sachs and Warner (1995).
4. For instance, Frankel and Romer (1999), Wacziarg (2001), and Yao (2006).
5. For example, Winters (2004), and Park et al. (2010).
6. For example, Rodríguez and Rodrik (2001), and Alesina et al. (2005).
7. The adoption of foreign technology and international business practices through the use of FDI is a potentially important channel through which openness stimulates growth. Since it is interesting to compare the growth impact of FDI with that of domestic investment, the consequence of FDI for China's economic growth is examined in Chapter 6 rather than in this chapter.
8. See Lin (1992), Chen and Feng (2000), Cai et al. (2002), Biggeri (2003), and Hasan et al., (2009).

9. Defined as an arithmetic average of the share of total commodity sales by the non-state sector, the proportion of non-state fixed capital investment in investment in total investment, the share of non-state industrial output in the total output, and foreign trade dependence.
10. For instance, Aron (2000) and Lin (2007).
11. Data come from *China Statistical Yearbook 2007*: 128.
12. See Lin and Zhu (2001), and Garnaut et al. (2005).
13. For instance, Cull and Xu (2005), and Hasan et al. (2009).
14. Variable definitions are available in Appendix 7.1 and detailed model derivation can be found in Appendix 4.2.
15. For example, according to Bernard et al. (2007), changes in the sectoral structure of both employment and output can be caused by trade liberalization. We therefore remove the openness measure and find that the growth impact of sectoral change remains intact.
16. The coefficients of all three structural change variables are significantly positive and the contributions of trade openness, privatization, and sectoral change to annual growth rate of GDP per capita are 1.9%, 1.3%, and 0.9% respectively.

References

Acemoglu, Daron, Simon Johnson, and James Robinson (2001), 'The colonial origins of comparative development: an empirical investigation', *American Economic Review*, 91, 5: 1369–401.

————————(2005), 'Institutions as a fundamental cause of long-run growth', in Philippe Aghion and Steven Durlauf (eds.), *Handbook of Economic Growth* (vol. 1A), Amsterdam: Elsevier BV.

Alesina, Alberto, Enrico Spolaore, and Romain Wacziarg (2005), 'Trade, growth and the size of countries', in Philippe Aghion and Steven Durlauf (eds.), *Handbook of Economic Growth* (vol. 1B), Amsterdam: Elsevier BV.

Anderson, James, and Peter Neary (1992), 'Trade reform with quotas, partial rent retention, and tariffs', *Econometrica*, 60: 57–76.

Aron, Janine (2000), 'Growth and institutions: a review of the evidence', *World Bank Research Observer*, 15, 1: 99–135.

Baldwin, Robert (2003), 'Openness and growth: what's the empirical relationship?', NBER Working Paper Series No. 9578.

Barro, Robert, and Xavier Sala-i-Martin (2004), *Economic Growth* (second edn.), Cambridge, Mass.: MIT Press.

Bernard, Andrew, Bradford Jensen, Stephen Redding, and Peter Schott (2007), 'Firms in international trade', *Journal of Economic Perspectives*, 21, 3: 105–30.

Biggeri, Mario (2003), 'Key factors of recent provincial economic growth', *Journal of Chinese Economic and Business Studies*, 1, 2: 159–83.

Brandt, Loren, Chang-Tai Hsieh, and Xiaodong Zhu (2008), 'Growth and structural transformation in China', in Loren Brandt and Thomas Rawski (eds.), *China's Great Economic Transformation*, New York: Cambridge University Press: 683–728.

——and Xiaodong Zhu (2000), 'Redistribution in a decentralized economy: growth and inflation in China under reform', *Journal of Political Economy*, 108: 422–51.

Cai, Fang, Dewen Wang, and Yang Du (2002), 'Regional disparity and economic growth in China: the impact of labour market distortions', *China Economic Review*, 13: 197–212.

Chen, Baizhu, and Yi Feng (2000), 'Determinants of economic growth in China: private enterprise, education and openness', *China Economic Review*, 11: 1–15.

Corden, Warner Max (1974), *Trade Policy and Economic Welfare*, Oxford: Clarendon Press.

Cull, Robert, and Lixin Colin Xu (2005), 'Institutions, ownership, and finance: the determinants of profit reinvestment among Chinese firms', *Journal of Financial Economics*, 77, 1: 117–46.

Ding, Sai, and John Knight (2009), 'Can the augmented Solow model explain China's remarkable economic growth? A cross-country panel data study', *Journal of Comparative Economics*, 37: 432–52.

————(2011), 'Why has China grown so fast? The role of physical and human capital formation', *Oxford Bulletin of Economics and Statistics*, 73, 2: 141–74.

Dollar, David (1992), 'Outward-oriented developing economies really do grow more rapidly: evidence from 95 LDCs, 1976–1985', *Economic Development and Cultural Change*, 40: 23–44.

——and Aart Kraay (2004), 'Trade, growth, and poverty', *Economic Journal*, 114: F22–49.

Dowrick, Steve, and Norman Gemmell (1991), 'Industrialization, catching up and economic growth: a comparative study across the world's capitalist economies', *Economic Journal*, 101, 405: 263–75.

Edwards, Sebastian (1993), 'Openness, trade liberalization, and growth in developing countries', *Journal of Economic Literature*, 31: 1358–93.

——(1998), 'Openness, productivity, and growth: what do we really know?' *Economic Journal*, 108, 2: 383–98.

Feder, Gershon (1986), 'Growth in semi-industrial countries: a statistical analysis', in Hollis Chenery, Sherman Robinson, and Moshe Syrquin (eds.), *Industrialization and Growth: A Comparative Study*. Washington, DC: Oxford University Press.

Frankel, Jeffrey, and David Romer (1999), 'Does trade cause growth?' *American Economic Review*, 89, 3: 379–99.

Garnaut, Ross, Ligang Song, Stoyan Tenev, and Yang Yao (2005), *China's Ownership Transformation: Processes, Outcomes, Prospects*, Washington, DC: World Bank.

Goldberg, Pinelopi, Amit Khandelwal, Nina Pavcnik, and Petia Topalova (2010), 'Imported intermediate inputs and domestic product growth: evidence from India', *Quarterly Journal of Economics*, 125, 4: 1727–67.

Grossman, Gene, and Elhanan Helpman (1995), *Innovation and Growth in the Global Economy*, Cambridge, Mass.: MIT Press.

Hall, Robert, and Charles Jones (1997), 'Levels of economic activity across countries', *American Economic Review*, 87, 2: 173–7.

————(1999), 'Why do some countries produce so much more output per worker than others?', *Quarterly Journal of Economics*, 114, 1: 83–116.

Hasan, Iftekhar, Paul Wachtel, and Mingming Zhou (2009), 'Institutional development, financial deepening and economic growth: evidence from China', *Journal of Banking and Finance*, 33, 1: 157–70.

Jefferson, Gary, Mai Lu, and John Zhao (1998), 'Reforming property rights in China's industry', in Gary Jefferson and Inderjit Singh (eds.), *Enterprise Reform in China*, New York: Oxford University Press.

Knack, Stephen, and Philip Keefer (1995), 'Institutions and economic performance: cross-country tests using alternative institutional measures', *Economics and Politics*, 7, 3: 207–27.

Knight, John, and Lina Song (2005), *Towards a Labour Market in China*, Oxford: Oxford University Press.

Kraay, Aart (1999), 'Exports and economic performance: evidence from a panel of Chinese enterprises', *Revue d'économie du Développement*, 1, 2: 183–207.

Leamer, Edward (1988), 'Measures of openness', in Robert Baldwin (ed.), *Trade Policy Issues and Empirical Analysis*, Chicago: University of Chicago Press.

Lewis, W. Arthur (1954), 'Economic development with unlimited supplies of labour', *Manchester School of Economic and Social Studies*, 22: 139–91.

Lin, Justin Yifu (1992), 'Rural reforms and agricultural growth in China', *American Economic Review*, 82, 1: 34–51.

——and Jeffrey Nugent (1995), 'Institutions and economic development', in Jere Behrman and T. N. Srinivasan (eds.), *Handbook of Development Economics (Vol. III)*, Amsterdam: Elsevier BV.

——(2007), *Development and Transition: Idea, Strategy, and Viability*, Marshall Lectures, Cambridge University.

Lin, Yi-min, and Tian Zhu (2001), 'Ownership restructuring in Chinese state industry: an analysis of evidence on initial organizational changes', *China Quarterly*, 166: 298–334.

Liu, Xiaohu, Peter Burridge, and Peter Sinclair (2002), 'Relationships between economic growth, foreign direct investment and trade: evidence from China', *Applied Economics*, 34, 11: 1433–40.

Mankiw, Gregory, David Romer, and David Weil (1992), 'A contribution to the empirics of economic growth', *Quarterly Journal of Economics*, 107, 2: 407–37.

Mauro, Paolo (1995), 'Corruption and growth', *Quarterly Journal of Economics*, 110, 3: 681–712.

Naughton, Barry (2007), *The Chinese Economy: Transitions and Growth*, Cambridge, Mass.: MIT Press.

North, Douglass (1990), *Institutions, Institutional Change and Economic Performance*, New York: Cambridge University Press.

Nye, Howard, Sanjay Reddy, and Kevin Watkins (2002), 'Dollar and Kraay on "Trade, growth, and poverty": a critique', unpublished manuscript.

Park, Albert, Dean Yang, Xinzheng Shi, and Yuan Jiang (2010), 'Exporting and firm performance: Chinese exporters and the Asian financial crisis', *The Review of Economics and Statistics*, 92, 4: 822–42.

Poirson, Hélène (2001), 'The impact of intersectoral labour reallocation on economic growth', *Journal of African Economies*, 10, 1: 37–63.

Pritchett, Lant (1996), 'Measuring outward orientation in developing countries: can it be done?', *Journal of Development Economics*, 49, 2: 307–35.

Riedel, James, Jing Jin, and Jian Gao (2007), *How China Grows: Investment, Finance and Reform*, Princeton: Princeton University Press.

Robinson, Sherman (1971), 'Sources of growth in less developed countries: a cross-section study', *Quarterly Journal of Economics*, 85, 3: 391–408.

Rodríguez, Francisco, and Dani Rodrik (2001), 'Trade policy and economic growth: a sceptic's guide to the cross-national evidence', in Ben Bernanke and Kenneth Rogoff (eds.), *NBER Macroeconomics Annual 2000*, Cambridge: The MIT Press.

Rodrik, Dani (1999), *The New Global Economy and Developing Countries: Making Openness Work*, Washington, DC: Johns Hopkins University Press.

——(2003), 'Introduction: what do we learn from country narratives?', in Dani Rodrik (ed.), *In Search of Prosperity: Analytic Narratives on Economic Growth*, Princeton and Oxford: Princeton University Press.

——(2010), 'Making room for China in the world economy', *American Economic Review: Papers and Proceedings*, 100, 2: 89–93.

Romer, Paul (1990), 'Are nonconvexities important for understanding growth?' *American Economic Review*, 80, 2: 97–103.

Sachs, Jeffery, and Andrew Warner (1995), 'Economic reform and the process of economic integration', *Brookings Papers on Economic Activity 1995*: 1–118.

Taylor, Jeffrey (1988), 'Rural employment trends and the legacy of surplus labour', *China Quarterly*, 116: 36–66.

Temple, Jonathan, and Ludger Wößmann (2006), 'Dualism and cross-country growth regressions', *Journal of Economic Growth*, 11: 187–228.

Vollrath, Dietrich (2005), 'How important are dual economy effects for aggregate productivity?', manuscript, University of Houston.

Wacziarg, Romain (2001), 'Measuring the dynamic gains from trade', *World Bank Economic Review*, 15, 3: 393–429.

Wei, Shang-Jin (1995), 'Open door policy and China's rapid growth: evidence from city-level data', in Ito Takatoshi and Anne Krueger (eds.), *Growth Theories in Light of the East Asian Experience*, Chicago: University of Chicago Press.

Winters, Alan (2004), 'Trade liberalisation and economic performance: an overview', *Economic Journal*, 114: F4–21.

Yanikkaya, Halit (2003), 'Trade openness and economic growth: a cross-country empirical investigation', *Journal of Development Economics*, 72: 57–89.

Yao, Shujie (2006), 'On economic growth, FDI and exports in China', *Applied Economics*, 38: 339–51.

Ying, Long Gen (2003), 'Understanding China's recent growth experience: a spatial econometric perspective', *The Annals of Regional Science*, 37: 613–28.

8

Why Does China Invest so Much?

8.1 Introduction

China has had a remarkably high ratio of investment to output throughout the period of economic reform, surpassing almost all other economies. This was illustrated in Table 6.1 and Figure 6.1 of Chapter 6. Although by no means the only determinant, gross fixed capital formation was found to be an important proximate determinant of China's high rate of growth in the cross-country and cross-province growth regressions of Chapters 4 and 6 respectively. It deserves to be understood.

Two basic questions are raised, relating to the demand for and the supply of investment. What drives the demand for investment? Is investment governed by the supply side? The answers to both questions can shed light on the efficiency of China's investment. This chapter gathers together the available evidence to explain why investment is so high: factors both on the demand and on the supply side, and in the latter case the availability of both resources and funds. It analyses the rate of return on capital and its evolution, and the factors that have kept it up. It draws on the literature to explain the high saving rate, and considers why the imperfect capital market and institutional deficiencies have not constrained investment. The state-owned and private sectors are treated separately because of their different objectives, behaviour, and funding.

We consider these questions in turn. Section 8.2 analyses the demand for investment. Sections 8.3 and 8.4 discuss the supply side: resources for investment and funds for investment respectively. The implications of the analysis for the efficiency of investment, and its implications in turn, are examined in Section 8.5 from the static perspective and in Section 8.6 from a dynamic perspective. Section 8.7 summarizes and concludes.[1]

8.2 The Demand for Investment

Within the framework of a competitive market economy, the implication of high investment is that it is highly profitable, and that the answer to the first question is to be found from estimates of the rate of return on capital. Within the framework of a neoclassical growth model, the implication of a high return on capital is that the economy is out of equilibrium, having a capital–labour ratio below its steady-state level. Thus, capital accumulation takes place rapidly, and the return on capital can be expected to fall as the capital–labour ratio approaches its equilibrium level.

The issue has been examined within both of these frameworks by Bai et al. (2006). The authors use data for the economy as a whole over the reform period to measure the capital stock and the rate of return on capital to answer the question: does China invest too much? They make careful use of the National Bureau of Statistics (NBS) data, along with several necessary assumptions, to derive estimates of the real rate of return on capital in the economy as a whole over the reform period. The real rate of return is obtained from figures of non-labour income and of capital stock estimated by the perpetual inventory method for 1952 and extended forward using gross fixed capital formation, assumptions about depreciation, and corrections for changes in the price of capital relative to output.

Their baseline return on capital estimated in this way was fairly steady at about 25% from 1979 until 1993. It fell over the next five years, and remained roughly constant at 20% from 1998 until 2005 (Bai et al. 2006). These high rates derive from a high capital share of income (quite close to 50% throughout), a low capital–output ratio (only 1.4 in the period up to 1993, then rising to about 1.6 from 1998 onward), and a depreciation rate of about 10% throughout. Ignoring relative price changes, these illustrative numbers do indeed produce approximate rates of return of 25% in the period 1978–93 and 20% in the period 1998–2005. In a comparison of fifty-two countries, the authors show that China's return on capital is exceptionally high, even after standardizing for output per worker.

The authors go on to modify their aggregate baseline estimates to take account of several possible complications. The most important of these are the deduction of taxes on enterprises (reducing the return substantially), the inclusion of inventories investment (also reducing the return), and the exclusion of the (urban) housing sector (raising the return). When these adjustments are combined, the return to capital is found to average 10% over the years 1993–2000 but to rise to about 14% after 2000 (Bai et al. 2006). On the basis of these results, the authors conclude that China does not invest too much.

These bold calculations are open to criticism, and indeed they were criticized by discussants of the paper. In particular, it might be queried whether all non-labour income is a return to capital. For instance, at the start of economic reform China had a centrally planned economy in which prices and wages, and therefore profits, were administered, and these controls were only gradually dismantled as urban reform proceeded. Much price reform took place in the 1980s: whereas in 1978 more than 95% of the prices of both producer goods and retail sales were fixed by the state, in 1991 the figures were 36% and 21% respectively (Dougherty and Herd 2005). Prior to market liberalization, the high share of profits was governed by the 'price scissors' policy, that is, depressed agricultural producer prices made possible low wages and relatively high industrial prices (for instance, Knight and Song 1999). The state extracted the profits of the state-owned enterprises (SOEs) to invest in planned industrial expansion; in this way it was the peasants who paid for industrialization (Knight 1995).

It was not possible from the Bai et al.'s NBS sources to disaggregate by ownership type. However, a firm-level data set (taken from OECD 2005) was used by one discussant (Blanchard 2006) to show that there is a sharp difference between private and state-controlled enterprises. In 1998 the rate of return (after tax, including inventories investment) in privately controlled industrial enterprises was 10.2%, compared with 4.8% in state-controlled industrial enterprises (Dougherty and Herd 2005). The returns were higher but the difference was maintained in 2003, the corresponding figures being 15.0% and 10.2%. However, there was much variation within their state-controlled sample: both highly profitable enterprises and sectors, such as monopolistic utilities, and many loss-making enterprises and sectors. Another source reveals wide variation in spatial profitability: in 2001 the return on net assets of local SOEs was positive in twelve and negative in nineteen provinces, and varied from 6.6% in Guangdong to –8.3% in Heilongjiang (Ministry of Finance 2009).

This general pattern of results is confirmed in the detailed study of industrial firms by Lu et al. (2008). The authors examined nine indicators of profitability using corporate accounting data. Irrespective of the indicator used, they showed a trend fall in the profit rate from 1978 to 1998 and a subsequent rise, quickening from 2002 onward. For instance, pre-tax profit over net fixed assets was 25% in 1978, 3% in 1998, 9% in 2002, and 16% in 2006. Disaggregating by ownership type, the same indicator was 1.5% for SOEs and 12% for private firms in 1998 but rose to 12% for SOEs and 20% for private firms in 2005 (Lu et al. 2008). Like Bai et al. (2006), the authors concluded from this trend in profitability that China's capital stock remained sub-optimal.

Table 8.1, derived from the *Finance Yearbook of China*, shows that the finances of the SOE sector as a whole were dire in the late 1990s but improved over the period 1998–2007 (the earliest and the latest years for which the data are available). The number of SOEs was halved in that short time; this was almost entirely due to sales and closures by local governments. In 1998 the profits of profit-making SOEs only just exceeded the losses of loss makers, whereas in 2007 the ratio was over 5 to 1.

Table 8.1. The financial performance of SOEs, 1998, 2003 and 2007

	1998	2003	2007
Number of SOEs (000)	238	146	112
of which: central	23	19	22
local	215	127	90
Total profit (00m, yuan)	214	4,796	17,442
Profit-making SOEs (% of total)	31	47	51
Profits of profit-making SOEs (00m, yuan)	3,280	7,589	21,220
Profits of loss-making SOEs (00m, yuan)	–3,066	–2,820	–3,778
Return on assets (%)	0.002	2.4	4.8
Return on net assets (%)	0.006	6.7	12.1
Profit margin on sales (%)	0.003	3.0	9.0

Note: Because there are inconsistencies in some of the published figures, we build up from the raw data.

Source: Ministry of Finance (2009: 427–9).

The return on assets rose from being negligible to 5% over the nine years, and the growth in the return on net assets and in the profit margin on sales was even more dramatic. During this period, the proportion of profit-making SOEs rose from 31 to 57%, but even in 2007 as many as 43% recorded a loss. Considering only the industrial SOEs, the losses of loss makers expressed as a proportion of pre-tax profits rose from 3% in 1980–4 to 5% in 1985–9 and then to 20% in 1990–4, and finally to a likely peak in 1995–7 (for which years the data are not available); they were as high as 160% in 1998–9 but down to 23% in 2000–4 (NBS 2005).

The sharp improvement in the profitability of the SOE sector after 1998 can be seen as a policy response to the collapse in profitability, which threatened state revenue, the banking sector with its rising non-performing loans (NPLs), and the continuation of economic growth. Budget constraints were hardened, a vast redundancy programme was imposed, and many inefficient and unprofitable enterprises were closed down or sold off. Lu et al. (2008) attributed the relative increase in SOE profitability since 1998 not only to SOE reform but also to the cancellation of bad bank debts and policies of sectoral entry restrictions favouring SOEs.

A high rate of profit on existing capital can serve as a proxy for the expected rate of profit on new investment. However, a high average rate does not necessarily mean that the expected marginal rate is also high. Moreover, even if the expected rate is high, this need not influence the demand for investment unless the profit motive is important in investment decisions. At least in the 1990s, the driver of much SOE investment could not have been expected profitability (Zou 1991; Riedel et al. 2007). The main objective of management in Chinese state-owned and state-dominated firms was to maximize not profits but the growth of investment and output. The reward to such bureaucrats takes the form of prestige, power, and the accompanying perks of commanding an organization, and the larger the organization the greater the reward. Hay et al. (1994) found that in 1988 investment was still largely determined by state planners allocating investment funds. However, investment was supplemented from the share of profits that SOEs were then permitted to retain. Additional investment was encouraged by the security that 'soft budgets' afforded. Jefferson et al. (1999) found that, by the time of their enterprise surveys in the early 1990s, over 80% of SOEs were subject to the 'contract responsibility system'. This gave them incentives to meet contracted targets, often set by local governments in terms of output. Local government officials were in turn responding to the incentives to promote local economic development that the central government had created for them. For instance, Li and Zhou (2005) used turnover data on top province leaders between 1979 and 1995 to show that their promotion and demotion depended on province GDP growth.

While China opened up to the world, and especially with entry to the World Trade Organization (WTO) in 2001, the prospects of profitably expanding exports created additional demand for investment. High export profits were possible, partly from the disequilibria that had been created by trade restrictions and partly from the undervalued Chinese currency. However, the role of exports can be exaggerated: domestic value-added constitutes no more than half of export value (Koopman et al. 2008). Thus, export value-added represented about 23% of the increase in GDP between 2001 and 2007.

Potential investors must have confidence that they will achieve an adequate return on their investment. This may well require confidence in the security of their property and of their business agreement. Such confidence can be achieved either through a formal legal system or informal substitutes. Clarke et al. (2008) examined how it was that Chinese investors had sufficient confidence in the security of property and in the enforcement of contracts to achieve such a high rate of investment. At the start of economic reform, administrative rules and interventions were adequate to resolve disputes, which were generally between parties under a common authority. With decentralization and privatization, the need grew for other, formal or informal, rules. Clarke et al. (2008) argued that, although the formal legal system had made great strides, particularly since 1992, it had developed in response to economic growth rather than being responsible for it. Instead, informal sources of security were primarily responsible for creating investor confidence. The incentive system faced by both central and local government officials rewarded economic growth, and their predictable behaviour therefore provided security of property (except in the case of farmers losing their land for urban development). The traditional system of cultivating social networks—known as *guanxi*—helped to provide security of transactions.

There is empirical evidence that security of property and enforceability of contracts are indeed important for private investment. For instance, Cull and Xu (2005) investigated the determinants of profit reinvestment by private enterprises using the World Bank's investment climate surveys of 2,400 Chinese firms in the years 2000–2. Their analysis was restricted to private firms, defined as those in which private ownership exceeded 50%. The questionnaire provided proxies for perceived security of property rights and of contract enforceability and reported the share of private ownership in the firm (mean 96%). The profit reinvestment rate for firms with positive profits (mean value 27%) was the dependent variable. Their estimates showed that, standardizing for a set of control variables, reinvestment is higher when there are perceptions of strong property rights and contract enforceability. Similarly, a greater share of private ownership—suggesting less scope for government interference—raises the reinvestment rate. These results indicate the value of protective legal, administrative, or social rules and the danger of arbitrary interventions if the objective is to promote private investment.

8.3 The Supply of Investment: Resources

In most countries an investment rate as high as China's would generate severe macroeconomic imbalance. Given their much lower national saving rates, such a claim of investment expenditure on resources would generate a combination of inflation (of both investment goods and consumption goods) and deficit in the current account of the balance of payments. The high investment rate would be unsustainable. This raises the question: how and why have the resources been available for China to invest such a high proportion of GDP? That in turn requires an analysis of the sources of and reasons for saving (defined as disposable income minus consumption).

In analysing saving and investment, we wish to distinguish three sectors: enterprises, households, and government. It is not easy to obtain this breakdown from China's official statistics. However, Barnett and Brooks (2006) compiled estimates from flow of funds accounts for the three sectors. Their annual data cover the years 1999–2005 but they report average data also for the period 1995–9. Accordingly, Table 8.2 shows averages for the periods 1995–9 and 2000–5: saving, investment (gross fixed capital formation), and saving minus investment, all expressed as a percentage of GDP. Kuijs (2005) provided similar annual data for the 1990s, but his estimates were made before the revision of GDP statistics that followed the 2004 economic census. Table 8.2 shows his estimates for 1995–9 and 1990–4. The differences in the two figures for 1995–9 represent a combination of statistical revisions and differing assumptions. The Kuijs data thus permit a comparison of 1990–4 and 1995–9, and the Barnett and Brooks data a comparison of 1995–9 and 2000–5.

The national saving rate was fairly stable at about 40% of GDP throughout the fifteen-year period, whereas investment rose, possibly by as much as 4.5% of GDP. Thus, saving actually exceeded gross fixed capital formation throughout, although the difference, when expressed as a proportion of GDP, fell over time up to the final period 2000–5.

Table 8.2. Saving, investment, and saving minus investment, national and by sector, 1990–4, 1995–9 and 2000–5

	Kuijs		Barnett and Brooks	
	1990–4	1995–9	1995–9	2000–5
National (as % of GDP)				
Saving	40.5	39.8	39.4	41.7
Investment	31.5	35.0	37.9	38.9
Saving minus investment	9.0	4.8	1.5	2.8
Saving (as % of GDP)				
Enterprises	14.0	14.4	15.8	18.4
Households	20.3	20.0	18.7	15.9
Government	6.3	5.3	2.8	4.1
Saving (as % of saving)				
Enterprises	35	36	40	44
Households	50	50	48	38
Government	15	13	12	18
Investment (as % of GDP)				
Enterprises			29.7	29.3
Households			5.4	5.5
Government			2.8	4.1
Investment (as % of investment)				
Enterprises			78	75
Households			14	14
Government			7	11
FAI (as % of GDP)				
Enterprises	29.4	29.9		
Households	5.7	5.7		
Government	2.9	3.1		
FAI (as % of FAI)				
Enterprises	77	77		
Households	15	15		
Government	8	8		
Saving minus FAI (as % of GDP)				
Enterprises	–15.5	–15.4		
Households	14.6	14.2		
Government	3.4	2.2		
Total	2.5	1.0		

Notes: Wherever possible, 'investment' is gross fixed capital formation. However, the breakdown by sector is available only for 'fixed asset investment' (FAI) in the Kuijs data. FAI includes expenditure on existing assets, such as land and buildings. 'Enterprises' are non-financial enterprises.

Sources: Kuijs (2005: table 1), and Barnett and Brooks (2006: tables A2, A2a, A3, A3a, A4, A4a).

Consider the sources of saving. In the 1990s, households contributed a higher share of national saving than enterprises but in the early 2000s the contributions were reversed. At that time enterprises saved no less than 18% of GDP, and 35% of their value-added; and households saved no less than 27% of their disposable income (Barnett and Brooks 2006). Government saving fell in the 1990s and subsequently rose. The recent rise was assisted by the improvement in government revenue-raising powers after fiscal and enterprise reforms: its revenue rose from 47% of GDP in 1995–9 to 55% in 2000–5 (Barnett and Brooks 2006).

What made such a high national saving rate possible? Households have become a major source of saving since 1978. Over the reform period China's real GDP per capita rose nearly ten times, from $165 in 1978 to $1,598 in 2006.[2] One explanation is that, with higher income, households chose to save a higher proportion of their income (Riedel et al. 2007). By contrast, Modigliani and Cao (2004) explained China's high private saving rate mainly in terms of the life cycle hypothesis. Their objective was to explain the remarkable rise in China's private saving rate, from about 3% in 1978 to approximately 33% in 2000. Rapid expected future growth of the economy can raise 'permanent income' and thus reduce saving out of current income. By contrast, the authors hypothesized that rapid long-term economic growth resulting from the economic reform policy implied rapid growth in target wealth, which would raise the saving rate. They also hypothesized that the fall in the dependency ratio resulting from the one-child family policy also implied a rise in the saving rate. Indeed, the former effect was found to explain some ten percentage points of the thirty percentage point rise in the saving rate and the latter effect another ten percentage points. Moreover, income per capita no longer played a role when added to their equation.

Wei and Zhang (2009) offered a further explanation for the rise in household saving. The saving rate and the 'sex ratio' (the ratio of boys to girls born twenty years previously) were positively correlated over time. The saving rate was higher in regions with a higher sex ratio, and households with a son saved more than households with a daughter. The authors argued that a shortage of marriageable girls created competition among households with boys, which responded by saving more on the basis that wealth and housing would help their sons in the competition for brides. Wei and Zhang (2009) estimated that marriage competition could potentially account for half of the increase in the household saving rate over the period 1990–2007.

Yet another contribution came from the new opportunities that were opened up by the economic reforms. Under central planning and the communes there was little incentive for households to save. This changed as households were given increasing scope for business and housing investment. Facing credit constraints, households responded to the new opportunities by saving for investment (Naughton 2007).

Economic insecurity grew over the reform period in both rural and urban China. Modigliani and Cao (2004) argued that the birth-control policy undermined the traditional role of children as old-age support and, in the absence of a publicly provided social security system in rural areas, so encouraged households to save for retirement. Urban economic reforms created a new motive for saving from the mid-1990s onward. As the private sector developed, as the 'mini-welfare state' provided by state-owned enterprises was withdrawn, and as large-scale labour retrenchment occurred, the heightened insecurity among urban workers could be expected to induce additional saving to replace state-funded services and to build up precautionary assets.

These arguments are supported by Chamon and Prasad (2008), who found that, contrary to the normal life cycle pattern, the relationship between the urban household saving rate and the age of its head is U-shaped. They explained the rise in the urban household saving rate by seven percentage points between 1995 and 2005 in terms of a rising future need to invest in a house and in education in the case of young households, and the need to self-insure against ill-health in the case of old households.

We saw that enterprise and government saving also contribute to China's high saving rate. On the one hand, the imperfect capital market makes firms, especially private firms, rely mainly on their own funds (that is, retained earnings) to finance investment. This provides them with a strong incentive to save. On the other hand, the profitability of firms has increased significantly since enterprise reform began in earnest in the mid-1990s. Moreover, given that the government did not seek dividends from SOEs in the period 1994–2008 and that the real interest earned in savings accounts is low, their rising profits tend to be reinvested.

Government saving has been high since 1978 as a result of a policy favouring government-financed investment over government consumption (Kuijs 2005). The Chinese government was willing and able to take a long-run view because it expected to remain in power for many years, it was not subject to democratic pressures for 'jam today, not jam tomorrow', and the rapid growth of household incomes provided a shield against social discontent.

Table 8.2 also shows the sectoral contributions to gross fixed capital formation (GFCF). The enterprise sector invested about 30% of GDP in all three periods, and the household sector (housing and household producers) 6%. The government contribution looks surprisingly small (no more than 4% of GDP) but some of the investment by enterprises, representing infrastructure investment by state-owned public utilities in sectors such as power, electricity, water, and transport, is more properly attributed to government, being both directed and funded by government. Net capital transfers were estimated to be 5% of GDP in the period 2000–5 (Barnett and Brooks 2006). Nevertheless, as the enterprise sector accounted for more than three-quarters of total investment, it is enterprise investment that holds the key to China's remarkable investment rate.

The sectoral figures provided for the 1990s by Kuijs (2005) relate to 'fixed asset investment', not GFCF, and contain expenditure on existing assets. However, Barnett and Brooks (2006) show the saving-investment balance for the period 1995–2005. We see from Table 8.2 that enterprises as a whole invested more than they saved (by 14% of GDP in the late 1990s and by 11% in the early 2000s). By contrast, households saved more than they invested (by 13% of GDP and 10% respectively), so almost precisely offsetting the enterprise sector deficit. There was a need for inter-sectoral as well as intra-sectoral financial intermediation, either through the banking system or in more informal ways. The net financial investment of the household sector was 11% of GDP in the period 2000–5, mainly (10% of GDP) in low-interest saving deposits. By contrast, the enterprise sector's net financial investment in the same period was –7% of GDP. The main (gross) sources of funding its excess of investment over saving were loans (11% of GDP) and foreign investment (3% of GDP) (Barnett and Brooks 2006).

The fact that profitability increased for all ownership categories after 1998 despite the likely trend towards greater competition in product markets suggests that macroeconomic forces were at work. One possibility is that, given the exchange rate and international price levels, the tradeable sector had comparatively high profits, and this enabled the relative expansion of tradeable goods production to raise the overall share of profits. However, there is another possibility. Because the ratio of GFCF to GDP rose from 36 to 42%, and the share of profits in national income rose from 27 to 37% over the period 1998–2007, it is feasible that the relative increase in investment was funded, at least in part, through a redistribution of income from wages to profits, that is, this additional claim on resources was met by forcing up prices relative to wages. In other words, causation might to some extent have run from investment to profits.

The underlying mechanism, attributable to Kaldor (1960), takes the following form. Assume that the propensity to save out of profits is considerably greater than the propensity to save out of wages. Thus a redistribution of national income from wages to profits raises the national saving rate. Assume that investment is determined independently of saving. Accept that there is sufficient flexibility of prices and wages to ensure that output is normally at a level corresponding to the full employment of resources. This is achieved by a movement in the profit share to a level that equates saving to investment. The equilibrium share of profits is a function of the two saving propensities and an increasing function of the investment–output ratio.

This mechanism is most likely to operate at an early stage of development, before price and wage rigidities become important and before saving becomes a function of national income, or of permanent income, rather than of factor shares. It is more likely to apply in the medium run, rather than the short run when output adjustment might dominate or the long run when competitive factor market forces might dominate. The mechanism may have relevance to China at its current stage of development.

The hypothesis is difficult to test, partly because of endogeneity issues and partly because we do not expect the relationship to hold from one year to the next. Moreover, China's data on factor shares are weak—being available only by province and being published one year at a time and not as a consistent series. Construction of a national series requires weighted aggregation.[3] Furthermore, the year 2004 is missing and there is a discontinuity in the series between 2003 and 2005, which might explain much of the rise. This is likely to reflect new information emerging from the economic census of 2004. This information can represent changes in reporting either without changes in the economy or because of changes in the economy, for example, the growth of the urban informal sector. Only in the latter case is the observed trend in the series a reliable indicator of a rising profit share. The trend in the ratio of household income to GDP is consistent with a shift to profits: the share fell from 49% to 43% over the same decade.

It is possible to tell a plausible albeit untested story. The accelerated and sustained investment boom could be financed without causing inflation, at least in part because the resultant increased claims on limited resources forced up prices relative to wages, at least in the sectors where prices were not governed by world prices and the exchange rate. This redistribution was not neutralized by 'real wage resistance' and consequent inflation because the rapidly rising productivity of the urban economy permitted sufficient growth in living standards to accommodate the relative fall in the wage share (the recorded increase of real wages in 'urban units' being 11% per annum over the period 1998–2007).

8.4 The Supply of Investment: Funds

The differences in the behaviour of different ownership types can be explained in part by the inefficient financial system. This has been the subject of considerable research, which we draw on below. Until recently, the formal financial system has been monopolized by the state-owned and state-controlled banks. Under central planning they simply acted as a conduit between government and the SOEs and did not perform the normal functions of commercial banks. As economic reform proceeded and a private sector developed, they gave priority to the state-owned sector. The private sector was forced to fund investment mainly from retained profits or from informal resources, normally at high cost. The state sector, by contrast, received easy bank loans at low interest rates. Loans were frequently made, and used, injudiciously, and this gave rise to a burgeoning burden of non-performing loans (NPLs). These in turn required the banks to engage in distress lending, which exacerbated the situation.

China can be said to have a 'repressed' financial system (Riedel et al. 2007). This repression has been a means of placing resources at the disposal of the state. The interest rates that depositors receive and borrowers pay are well below the market-clearing rate. This is shown in Figure 8.1: both real rates of interest are low in relation to the likely rate of return on investment and even negative in the late 1980s and mid-1990s because of bursts of inflation unanticipated by the rate-setting authorities. The excess demand for funds gives rise to credit market rationing. It is the state sector that benefits from the rationing process. The domestic share-issuing companies (known as legal entities) are largely state controlled—with the central or local government being the dominant shareholder—and

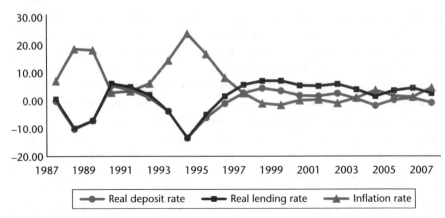

Figure 8.1. Real interest rates and inflation rate in China, annual percentages, 1987–2007

Data source: IMF, *International Financial Statistics* (August 2009 version) and World Bank, *World Development Indicators* (June 2009 version).]

Notes: Real interest rate is calculated by the authors (subtracting the current annual inflation rate from the nominal rate); Nominal deposit rate (end of period): interest rate on institutional and individual deposits of one-year maturity; Nominal lending rate (end of period): prior to 1989, rate on working capital loans to state industrial enterprises and thereafter, rate on working capital loans of one-year maturity; Inflation rate: inflation is measured by the consumer price index.

occupy an intermediate position. This is one way in which the domestic private sector continues to be the victim of policy discrimination.

Riedel et al. (2007) take the view that China's financial system is one of the weakest links in the economy and that it will hamper future investment and economic growth. In that case, it must be asked why the inadequacies of the financial system have not held the economy back in recent years, and how they have permitted such remarkably high rates of investment and growth. After all, China's formal financial system is still dominated by the state-owned banks (SOBs), lending primarily to the state sector: even in 2004 'the big four' accounted for 62% of outstanding bank loans and had an NPL rate of 16% (Allen et al. 2008). The two stock exchanges, established in 1990, played a limited and inefficient funding role, being held back by speculation and insider trading. Allen et al. (2005) argued that, in the face of formal credit rationing, the private non-listed sector relied heavily on informal financial sources: retained profits, informal intermediaries, and trade credits. The authors' explanation for the puzzlingly high investment rate that has been achieved is that the formal and informal sectors together have done enough not to constrain investment more seriously.

Table 8.3 shows the sources of enterprise investment financing of the different ownership types over the period for which data are available. We see the importance of retained earnings and informal funds ('self-raised funds and others' in the table) for all types of ownership. This is especially true of individually owned

Table 8.3. Investment financing by ownership and the distribution of loans by ownership, percentages

	1994–6	1997–9	2000–3
State-owned enterprises			
State budget	4.9	7.2	11.0
Domestic loans	24.3	23.2	24.7
Foreign investment	7.3	4.4	2.0
Self-raising funds and others	64.2	64.1	60.3
Collectively owned enterprises			
State budget	1.7	3.2	5.5
Domestic loans	24.9	15.4	11.7
Foreign investment	7.6	6.1	4.11
Self-raising funds and others	67.33	76.95	80.2
Individually owned enterprises			
State budget	0.0	0.0	0.0
Domestic loans	3.3	4.9	8.0
Foreign investment	0.0	0.1	0.1
Self-raising funds and others	96.8	95.6	95.8
Other types of enterprises			
State budget	0.6	0.6	0.8
Domestic loans	20.8	21.7	25.1
Foreign investment	37.1	31.1	11.8
Self-raising funds and others	48.7	52.0	74.5
Distribution of loans			
State-owned enterprises	62.8	64.2	42.1
Collectively owned enterprises	19.0	12.0	6.4
Individually owned enterprises	1.9	3.4	4.8
Other types of enterprises	14.9	20.4	46.7

Notes: Figures for each period are the mean values of the annual proportions; 'other types of enterprises' refers to types of ownership other than state-owned, collectively owned, and individual economic units, that is, it includes joint ownership, shareholding, foreign-funded, and Hong Kong-, Macao-, and Taiwan-funded economic units.

Source: Authors' own calculation based on NBS *Statistical Yearbook* (various issues).

enterprises, which relied on such funding for over 95% of investment. Even SOEs—not being required to pay dividends to government—raised at least 60% in this way. Bank loans ('domestic loans') and capital transfers from government ('state budget') constituted 29% of SOE funding in 1994–6, rising to 36% in 2000–3. In the former period SOEs received 63% of all bank loans and in the latter period 42%. By contrast, the corresponding shares of individually owned enterprises were 2% and 5% respectively. The corporate sector (approximated by 'other types of enterprises'), which is mostly government controlled, was on a par with SOEs by the early 2000s (receiving 25% of its funding from banks and 47% of total bank lending).

We should guard against exaggerating the uniqueness of Chinese enterprises, in particular private enterprises, in their heavy reliance on their own savings. For instance, Mayer (1988) found that in the United Kingdom in the period 1970–85 profit retentions accounted for 70% of corporate investment. Nor is it the case that a more competitive financial system necessarily involves fewer financial constraints on investment. For instance, conducting generalized method of moments

(GMM) analysis on a panel of European countries over the period 1978–89, Bond et al. (2003) found that it was only in the UK, with the most competitive financial sector, that cash flow and profit terms were statistically and quantitatively significant in explaining corporate investment. Their tests rejected the interpretation that this was due to expectations formation, and they concluded that financial constraints were relatively severe in the more market-oriented financial system. Results such as these might be explained in terms of risk aversion by borrowers and lesser information on borrowers in more competitive financial markets.

Haggard and Huang (2008) examined the policy of the Chinese government towards the private sector. They distinguished between government-controlled corporate firms and genuinely private domestic firms. They argued that the latter sector was still relatively small and subject to many controls and permissions, for instance with regard to the provision of finance and the requirement of official approval of investment projects above a certain size. Government had allowed the private sector to develop—based on its efficiency—but had not actively supported it.

This account is consistent with evidence on the changing shares of fixed asset investment (Figure 8.2). The ownership structure of investment altered dramatically after Deng Xiaoping's 'southern tour' in 1992. In the next fourteen years, the share of SOEs fell from two-thirds to one-third. However, this was largely due to the expansion of investment by shareholding companies ('other' ownerships), which were mostly companies previously classified as SOEs, with ownership and

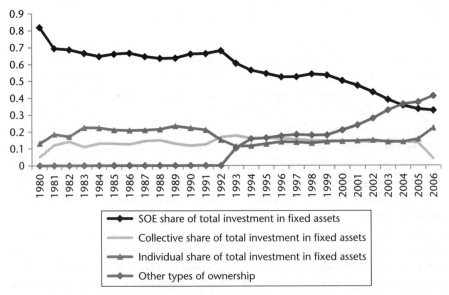

Figure 8.2. Investment in fixed assets by ownership, percentages of total, 1980–2007.
Data source: NBS, *China Statistical Yearbook* (various issues).

control still dominated by the state. We see that the contribution of individually owned enterprises was no higher towards the end than it had been towards the start of the reform period.

In explaining these results, Haggard and Huang (2008) argued that, although the SOBs became more profit oriented over the decade, private investment was constrained because licensing policies tended to confine private firms to low-profit activities. These policies were interpreted in terms of a concern to maintain power and control by the Chinese Communist Party (CCP). For instance, foreign firms, because they did not pose such a political threat, received more favourable treatment than did domestic private firms: their share of fixed asset investment rose from the low figure of 6% in 1993 to 9% in 2003 (Haggard and Huang 2008).

A rather different picture of the private sector is painted by Guariglia et al. (2011). They used a large panel of Chinese firms (all SOEs plus all large non-state firms) over the years 2000–7 to investigate the determinants of the growth rates of firms, as measured by growth of their assets. Whereas SOEs averaged proportionate asset growth of 1.1% per annum over this period (limited by the demand for rather than the supply of funds) the figure for private firms was as high as 8.5% per annum. The authors defined domestic private firms to include the corporate sector as well as individual owners. However, the main result of their analysis was found to apply also to the private individual sector on its own.

The main result concerns the coefficient on the variable cash flow as a proportion of assets. It is small and not significant in the case of SOEs but positive, significant, and close to unity in the case of private firms. The authors' interpretation is that private firms, being deprived of bank loans, are financially constrained whereas SOEs, receiving abundant bank loans, are not. This interpretation is supported by evidence that, among listed firms since 1990, the negative effect of leverage on investment is weaker, the higher is the share of state ownership in the firm (Firth et al. 2008). The standard criticism of such an interpretation is that cash flow might represent prospective investment opportunities rather than available funds (Hubbard 1998). Guariglia et al. (2011) try to guard against this possibility by using lagged values as instruments. It is notable that the cash flow (defined as income plus depreciation) of private firms averaged almost 100% of their increase in assets (both being expressed as a proportion of assets). The implication is that the high profitability and cash flow of private firms in the early 2000s made possible their high asset accumulation, notwithstanding the distortions in the credit market.

Dougherty and Herd (2005) also provide a more optimistic account of private sector development than do Haggard and Huang (2008). They estimated value-added production functions to calculate total factor productivity (TFP) by ownership type for the period 1998–2003 using a large, industrial, firm-level sample. The standardized productivity of domestic private firms was found to be at least 90% higher than that of firms more than half-owned by the state. Whereas 28% of their sample of firms was privately controlled in 1998, this figure had risen to 52% in 2003. The authors concluded that it was the superior efficiency of the private sector that had enabled it to expand rapidly over that period (Dougherty and Herd 2005).

The study by Cull and Xu (2005) of the reinvestment rates of private firms, referred to above, also contained variables representing the availability of funds for investment. Their questionnaire indicated whether the firm had received a bank loan in the previous three years (28% had), and the collateral required as a proportion of loan received (averaging 25%). The greater the collateral required for a loan, the greater is the reinvestment rate, suggesting that firms that are more risky have to be more reliant on internal funds. Having had access to a bank loan actually raises, rather than lowers, the reinvestment rate, other things being equal. This result is consistent with it being the most profitable private firms with the largest investment opportunities that receive bank loans. Indeed, an equation predicting access to a bank loan indicates that access depends on proxies for firm performance as well as proxies for the closeness of ties with government. This implies that the banking system in the early 2000s did, at least in part, apply normal commercial banking criteria in making loans, at least to private firms.

Cull et al. (2007) examined the role of trade credit in funding investment in China. Trade credit can be an important source of short-term funds because of the informational advantages that suppliers often have over financial institutions. In China, trade credit might also be a means for private sector firms to invest if they are unable to borrow from banks. In an analysis of large industrial firms, Cull et al. (2007) found that firms with better access to bank credit offered more trade credit. In the case of SOEs, profitability reduced the supply of trade credit, reflecting the investment opportunities that would be forgone. Less profitable SOEs received more bank loans, possibly reflecting financial distress, and they had the surplus funds to extend trade credit, possibly to retain their customers and suppliers. In the financially constrained private sector, by contrast, more profitable firms supplied more trade credit, reflecting their greater ability to do so. Although the authors concluded that trade credit was a likely source of funding investment by financially constrained private firms, its relatively small size meant that it could explain only a minor part of private sector investment.

Ferri and Liu (2010) use a panel-data set of 280,000 large industrial firms to examine the rate of interest paid on loans by firms of different ownership types over the period 2001–5. Even standardizing for firm size and industrial sector, they find that SOEs pay the lowest rate of interest—lower by more than two percentage points than the rate paid by private firms. Moreover, if it were required to pay the same rate of interest as the private sector, the SOE sector as a whole would make a loss. This counterfactual may be extreme because of the likely general equilibrium effects and because the standardized interest rates paid by foreign firms occupy an intermediate position, thus suggesting a role for unobserved influences.

Nevertheless, financial liberalization can be expected to reduce SOE investment. Indeed, its perceived effect on SOE profitability and investment may be a serious obstacle to the adoption of financial liberalization.

Using a panel of more than 110,000 firms over the period 2000–7, Ding et al. (2010a) confirmed that non-state firms suffer from serious liquidity constraints, as indicated by the sensitivity of their fixed investment to their cash flow. Non-state firms tend to adjust not only fixed but also working capital investment in response to fluctuations in cash flow. However, when the authors distinguished firms with relatively high and relatively low ratios of working capital to fixed capital, they found that only firms with a high ratio adjust their working capital so as to smooth their fixed capital investment. Good management of working capital can thus be a means by which China's many financially constrained firms maintain high fixed capital investment.

8.5 The Efficiency of Investment: Static

It is generally found in the literature linking financial development and economic growth that indicators of financial development foster economic growth.[4] Allen et al. (2005, 2008) see China's experience as providing a counter-example. The conventional proxies for the development of financial intermediation, such as the importance of banks and of formal lending, suggest that China's financial system is weak and undeveloped. Yet China has achieved rapid economic growth. The authors' explanation is that informal sources of finance have developed in response to a need, and that these alternative arrangements—including the use of retained profits, own savings, and informal borrowing—have proved an adequate remedy.

Does the immature financial system nevertheless impose costs on the economy, in the form of investment misallocation? Dollar and Wei (2007) examine this question, find that there is indeed misallocation, and attempt to quantify its cost. Their research is based on a sample of over 12,000 firms in 120 cities for the years 2002–4. The authors distinguish eight categories of ownership: state ownership (100%, 50–99%, and 1–49%), foreign ownership (using the same three categories), collective ownership, and domestic private ownership. State firms are found to receive more investment funding from the banking system than private firms. Regression analysis shows the conditional value of the ratio of value-added to capital to be 50% higher for private firms than wholly owned state firms. Examining the determinants of the rate of profit on capital, the authors find a similar pattern. The partly state-owned firms generally occupy an intermediate position. The inference is drawn that non-state firms are held back by financial constraints. A similar analysis of the value-added/labour ratio also reports wholly owned state firms to be different: they have the lowest returns not only to capital but also to labour. Dollar and Wei (2007) go on to conduct a heroic counterfactual simulation analysis in which the value-added/capital ratio in the state-owned sector is raised to that of the private sector, and find that misallocation of resources costs some 5% of GDP.

Guariglia and Poncet (2008) also address the issue of investment misallocation. They pose the question: how do various indicators of financial development affect the growth rates of the capital stock and of TFP growth? They use annual province data over the period 1989–2003, and attempt to solve the endogeneity issues by means of system GMM estimation and reverse causality tests. Three sorts of financial indicators are introduced: conventional proxies for financial intermediary development, such as the extent of bank loans; China-specific indicators of state intervention, such as the importance of bank loans made by the four main SOBs; and indicators of 'market-driven financing', such as the share of investment financed by self-raised funds.

In both the equation for capital accumulation and the equation for TFP growth, the conventional proxies for financial development and the indicators of state intervention have negative coefficients. Only in the case of self-raised funds is the coefficient positive. When the importance of foreign direct investment (FDI) in total investment is interacted with the financial variables, it is found to ameliorate the negative coefficients. The conclusions drawn by Guariglia and Poncet (2008) are that the formal banking sector constrained provincial growth over this fifteen-year period although inflows of FDI helped to ease the constraint; and that the availability of informal financing (from retained profits, own saving, or informal credit) promoted provincial growth.

8.6 The Efficiency of Investment: Dynamic

In Chapters 5 and 6 we examined the impact of investment in fixed assets on the growth of GDP per capita over the period 1980–2000, using system GMM estimation methods in an attempt to establish causal relationships. The effect of investment as a whole was positive and significant: a one percentage point increase in the ratio of fixed investment to GDP was associated with a 0.15 percentage point increase in the growth rate. We found a sharp contrast when investment was disaggregated by ownership status. Investment made by SOEs was wasteful: increasing the share of SOEs in total fixed investment by one percentage point was associated with a decrease in the growth rate of 0.08 percentage points. Variation in the share of investment by collective firms made no significant difference. Investment by private firms (including the corporate sector) had a powerful effect: a one percentage point rise in the investment share of the private firms was associated with a growth rate higher by 0.13 percentage points. Thus, the decline in the state's share of enterprise investment (shown in Figure 8.2) helped to raise the growth rate.

Nevertheless, it is an important question: will the high rate of investment in China carry the seeds of its own destruction? This could happen in various ways. First, the rapid accumulation of capital can lead to a fall in its marginal product. Within a competitive framework, this should reduce the rate of profit on capital and so deter future investment. That is the mechanism suggested by Bai et al. (2006), who found that the profit rate on capital had not fallen and remained high despite rapid capital accumulation. Moreover, Lu et al. (2008) found that the profit rate in industrial firms had risen substantially over the previous decade. Both studies concluded that China's high investment rate did not pose a threat to the profitability of future investment.

The high degree of self-financing in the private sector is not without its problems. According to 'agency theory', pressures from external investors and managerial ownership encourage managers to pursue value-maximizing investment policies (Jensen 1986). Without external monitoring and effective internal controls, corporate managers have incentives to expand too far and too fast by simply investing their internal funds in low-return projects and activities. Ding et al. (2010b) tested this hypothesis with a data set of more than 110,000 firms over the period of 2000–7. Using two measures of investment efficiency—the average and the marginal revenue product of capital—they found that investment efficiency overall had increased over time. There were nevertheless some over-investing firms. The authors employed two measures, found in the finance literature, to test for 'over-investment' and to identify the over-investors. Their findings supported the 'free cash flow' hypothesis, that is, firms with much free cash flow had used these funds to over-invest. The disciplinary role of debt in curbing over-investment was found to hold for collective and private firms but not for SOEs. Over-investment by firms affiliated with central or local governments was mainly due to the ready availability of bank credit.

Qin and Song (2009) attempted to measure the extent of over-investment in China using province data for the period 1989–2004. By estimating a production function they were able to predict the profit-maximizing level of investment. Defining over-investment as actual minus profit-maximizing investment, they found that there was widespread over-investment and that the coastal provinces, being more reformed and more prosperous, were technically more efficient but allocatively less efficient, that is, they tended to show a greater degree of over-investment. There is also direct evidence of underutilization of capital in certain industries, particularly heavy industries dominated by the state (European Union Chamber 2009). For instance, in 2004 the percentage rate of excess capacity was reported to be 34, 46, 73, 84, and 88% in the steel, aluminium, calcium carbide, ferroalloy, and container industries respectively.[5] Bearing in mind the shape of the short-run average cost curve, 'full capacity' is difficult to define. Nevertheless, this suggestive evidence might help to explain why a high proportion of SOEs continued to make losses despite the rising average rate of profit.

There are several possible reasons why the rapid accumulation of capital did not involve a fall in the prospective rate of profit so steep that further investment would have been deterred. One possibility is that at the start of economic reform the ratio of capital to other factors of production was far below its equilibrium level, that is, the marginal product of capital was remarkably high. In a neoclassical growth model, a higher saving and investment rate implies a higher capital–labour ratio, and a correspondingly lower marginal product of capital in the steady state: the economy has further to travel to its long-run equilibrium. The answer might thus be that the Chinese economy was initially in extreme disequilibrium.

Second, rapid capital accumulation could take place without a significant rise in the capital–labour ratio occurring. It is true that between 1978 and 2005 the capital stock rose by 10.5% per annum and the labour force rose by only 2.4% per annum, the implication being that the capital–labour ratio increased more than seven times.[6] However, it is widely accepted that at the start of economic reform China had a labour surplus economy par excellence (for instance, Knight and Song 1999, 2005). Unemployment took a disguised form, both in the cities and in the countryside. Enterprise reform, starting in earnest in the late 1990s, together with urban economic growth, released underemployed labour mainly into more productive activities. Early estimates of surplus labour on the land (surveyed in Taylor 1988) suggested that 30% of peasants could be withdrawn from farming without loss of agricultural production. Thus, the reallocation of rural labour to activities in which its marginal product was higher—initially through rural industrialization and subsequently through rural–urban migration—helped to keep down the effective capital–labour ratio.

Third, starting from a situation of dire misallocation of resources, the reform process involved drastic structural changes—from agriculture to industry, from the state sector to the private sector, and from domestic to foreign markets. We argued in Chapter 7 that each of these transfers offered profitable opportunities and moved the economy toward its production frontier. The rapid growth of the economy meant that relative resource reallocation could take place without serious excess capacity and resultant collapse in profits occurring in the relatively declining sectors.

A fourth factor helping to maintain the rate of profit on physical capital was the rapid growth of the complementary factor, human capital. The objective of compulsory basic education (six years of primary school and three years of middle school) was established in 1986, and had generally been met in the 1990s, at least in urban areas and the more prosperous rural areas. Higher education, although relatively neglected until the late 1990s, was expanded remarkably thereafter. The proportions of adults with middle school, high school, and college education in the census year 1982, along with the figures from the national samples for 1995

Table 8.4. Educational attainment of population aged 20 and above, percentages

	Higher education	Senior middle school education	Junior middle school education	Primary school education
1982	1.00	8.74	18.53	31.41
1995	2.95	10.52	31.20	35.29
2005	6.64	12.34	38.54	29.37

Source: Based on 1982 China population census and 1995 and 2005 1% sample surveys.

and 2005, are shown in Table 8.4. The proportion of adults with higher education rose from 1 to 7% between 1982 and 2005, and the proportion with more than primary education doubled, from 28 to 58%.

Both the stock of human capital (generating externalities) and its growth (increasing labour productivity) are found to be important contributors to China's rate of economic growth (Chapter 6). The availability of educated labour encourages and assists the absorption of new technology into the economy. Much fixed investment of machinery and equipment embodies improved technology, some domestic and some imported from abroad. Thus, technological progress—increasing 'efficiency units' of labour and thus decreasing the effective capital–labour ratio—has helped to keep up the profitability of investment. However, there is no consensus on the rate of technological progress in China over the reform period. The various growth-accounting exercises produce estimates ranging from 1.5 to 3.9% per annum,[7] reflecting in part the different assumptions made. In any case, if investment raises efficiency both by embodying technological progress and also by improving resource allocation, TFP is a positive function of investment and cannot be separated from it.

A fall in investment for any reason could in turn reduce aggregate demand in the economy, so further depressing investment. The virtuous circle of 'high confidence, high investment, high growth, fulfilled expectations, high investment . . .' could in this way be transformed into a vicious circle of 'low confidence, low investment, low growth, fulfilled expectations, low investment . . .'.

Gong and Lin (2008) had this mechanism partly in mind in explaining the business cycle in China. They viewed the normally high investment rate as the product of a low real interest rate and the availability of an unlimited supply of unskilled labour. However, they noted that capacity utilization had declined in certain years, and that this had deterred investment, thus generating economic recession, that is, below-trend growth. Their explanation ran as follows. A positive supply shock (the result of the relaxing of policy constraints) causes high investment. This generates inflation. The resulting anti-inflation policies create overcapacity in the capital stock, thus reducing investment and slowing economic growth. Although the account of Gong and Lin (2008) fits some of the facts well, it leaves one question unanswered. The investment function in their model depends on expected capacity utilization. This would be inconsistent with the assumption of rational expectations and would require some other assumption, such as that of bureaucratic incentives, 'irrational exuberance' or 'animal spirits', to explain the periodic over-investment.

One possible explanation for the early reform period is provided by Kim (1994). Given the powerful incentives of SOE managers to increase investment, informational weakness enabled them deliberately to understate their investment costs and capital capacities to the planners. Thus, the discrepancy between micro incentives and macro objectives could at times generate 'investment overshooting'. Soft budgets and low interest rates on loans allayed any concerns of investors about future macroeconomic corrections.

Drawing on Keynes's emphasis on animal spirits and the associated herd behaviour, some modern macroeconomic models incorporate imperfect information and the simple decision rules to which this can lead. It is possible for such rules to produce biased correlations of beliefs and so generate waves of optimism and pessimism among investors (De Grauwe 2008). Applying these ideas to China, there are reasons to expect irrational exuberance at a time of new and rapidly changing circumstances. According to Naughton (2007), Deng's famous 'southern tour' in 1992 opened the way for entrepreneurship, and set off 'a gold rush mentality and financial excess'. Much of that investment boom was due to local governments, which were responding to an exogenous shock, that is, the relaxation of constraints. The strength of their response can be explained by an incentive structure that rewarded local growth (in particular short-term growth), a lack of concern about risk on account of soft budgets, and an inability to anticipate and to see the new and emerging bigger picture.

Another explanation for China's cycles is provided by Brandt and Zhu (2000). Arguing with reference to the period prior to the drastic reform of the SOEs, the authors attributed fluctuations in investment and output to the declining profitability of SOEs combined with continued state support for them. Their growing losses required an increased transfer of both subsidies and credit. Credit allocation had been decentralized from government to the state banks early in the reform process. Despite indicative quotas, the local branches of state banks tended to collude with local governments in the pursuit of local economic development, so favouring the more profitable non-state sector beyond quota. The continued state support for SOEs resulted in rapid growth of the money supply and accelerating inflation. This forced the central government to react by recentralizing and imposing strict controls on credit, both overall and to the non-state sector, which induced periodic recessions in investment and output. An implication of the interpretation provided by Brandt and Zhu (2000) is that the subsequent reform of the SOE sector provides some protection against the virtuous circle of high investment and growth being brought to an end by this source of shocks.

Ding et al. (2010c) examined a puzzle in China's investment pattern: despite high aggregate investment, negative net investment is commonly found at the microeconomic level. Using a comprehensive firm-level data set, they tested three hypotheses to explain this phenomenon: the efficiency (or restructuring) hypothesis, the (lack of) financing hypothesis, and the (slow) growth hypothesis. Their panel-data probit estimations showed that SOEs divest mainly for inefficiency or restructuring reasons, for instance, they need to eliminate obsolete capital in the face of rising competition or other pressures to become efficient. Negative investment by private firms is mainly due to external financial constraints, for instance, they need to obtain funds before investing in new opportunities. The fact that many firms are growing fast offsets both of these forces for negative investment, particularly so in the case of the—most dynamic—private and foreign firms.

8.7 Conclusion

In economic research there is often a trade-off to be made between asking specific questions that can be tested rigorously and asking broad questions that do not lend themselves to formal tests. Despite the evidence and argument that we have mustered from the considerable literature on investment in China, we do not have a precise answer to the question posed in the title of this chapter: why does China invest so much? However, we can tell a plausible story.

Approaching the question first from the demand side, we adduced evidence that the overall rate of return on capital was initially high and remained reasonably high. Moreover, the return on capital in industry rose substantially after 1998 in both the state and non-state sectors. Although there is a potentially important difference between the observed return on capital and the perceived future return on investment, this might well be the underlying reason why investment remained so high.

Why did profitability remain promising enough to induce so much investment despite the remarkable rate of capital accumulation? It was probably maintained by rapid TFP growth, assisted by the enterprise reforms, and the ready supply of surplus labour that could be combined with the increase in the capital stock. Both would have helped to keep up the marginal product of capital. The rapid pace of spatial reallocation and urbanization, associated with structural change, increased the demand for both public and private investment in infrastructure. Starting from a situation of dire resource misallocation, economic reform and marketization achieved efficiency gains through the reallocation of resources toward more productive uses—from the state sector to the private sector, from agriculture to industry, and from domestic to foreign markets.

Entrepreneurial expectations of rapid economic growth were crucial for high investment. At the level of political economy: when the new leadership took power after the death of Mao Zedong it decided that economic development would have to be the policy priority if CCP rule was to survive. China became a 'developmental state'. Incentives were provided at all levels of governance to generate economic growth—in the country, in the province, in the city, and in the county. Bureaucrats were rewarded for promoting investment, and business-men could make investment decisions with confidence that policies for rapid growth would be pursued. The 'coordination problem', which besets enterprise in many poor countries—that each investment is unprofitable if made on its own but all can be profitable if made together—could be solved in this way.

It is arguable that the Chinese economy has been in a virtuous circle with sustaining feedback effects. High investment produced rapid economic growth and rapid growth in turn produced buoyant expectations that then elicited high investment. The fact that the economy was growing rapidly meant that relative resource reallocation could occur without the growth of huge surplus capacity and the collapse in profitability of much of the relatively declining sectors. The fact that investment, much of it embodying improved technology, was so high in turn raised the rate of technological progress. This helped to keep up the marginal product of capital and thus the rate of profit on investment.

We have produced plausible accounts of the remarkably high saving rate in each of the three sectors: enterprises, households, and government. The inefficient and repressed financial system may well have played a part: financially constrained private firms and households that saw profitable opportunities may have increased their saving to make their investments. Without a national saving rate that matched the investment rate, the investment boom could have collapsed in the face of the ensuing macroeconomic imbalances.

The supply of funds does not fit neatly into the explanation for high investment in China. Whereas a ready supply of bank loans at low interest rates has generally been available to the SOEs, non-state enterprises have had to rely on their own savings or informal loans at high interest rates. Thus, investment has been biased towards the less profitable ownership sector. Nevertheless, SOE managers were keen to invest, partly because their objectives were more growth oriented than profit oriented and partly because, until the late 1990s, they faced soft budgets and therefore had no need to be risk averse. The high investment of the private sector occurred despite the discriminatory policies that they faced: the capital market imperfections, the controls on their investment, and the legal weakness of con-tractual and property rights. This success was partly because the corporatized former SOEs were generally sufficiently state owned to be state controlled. It was also partly due to the greater efficiency of private firms, which enabled them to achieve higher profit rates than the state-owned or state-controlled sectors.

There are several necessary conditions for China's high rate of investment, although none is likely to be sufficient on its own. Our story would have been incomplete without examination of the reasons not only why the demand for investment was initially high and remained high but also why resources were available and funds could be secured for investment.

This chapter has implications also for growth research. The positive interaction between investment and efficiency gain from both technological progress and resource reallocation suggests that the endogenous growth theory offers a better theoretical framework for analysing investment in China than does the neoclassical growth theory. China's apparent virtuous circle of high investment and rapid growth suggests that conventional growth models of either type should be complemented by analysis of the underlying determinants of the rate of capital accumulation.

Notes

1. We draw on Knight and Ding (2010).
2. The data are from *World Development Indicators*, April 2008; GDP per capita is gross domestic product divided by mid-year population and is in constant (2000) US dollars.
3. We are grateful to Yang Yao for supplying the calculated national figures.
4. For example, King and Levine (1993), Levine (2005), and Wurgler (2000).
5. Derived from National Development and Reform Commission, Guofa No. 38, 2009, and other sources.
6. Calculated from Bai et al. (2006: table 1) and *China Statistical Yearbook 2006*: 60, 125, 128.
7. See Borenzstein and Ostry (1996), Hu and Khan (1997), Woo (1998), Young (2003), and Brandt et al. (2008).

References

Allen, Franklin, Jun Qian, and Meijun Qian (2005), 'Law, finance and economic growth in China', *Journal of Financial Economics*, 77, 1: 57–116.

————(2008), 'China's financial system: past, present and future', in Loren Brandt and Thomas Rawski (eds.), *China's Great Economic Transformation*, Cambridge and New York: Cambridge University Press: 506–68.

Bai, Chong-en, Chang-tai Hsieh, and Yingyi Qian (2006), 'The return to capital in China', *Brookings Papers on Economic Activity 2006*, 2: 61–88.

Barnett, Steven, and Ray Brooks (2006), 'What's driving investment in China?', International Monetary Fund Working Paper No. WP/06/265.

Blanchard, Olivier (2006), 'Comments and discussion', *Brookings Papers on Economic Activity 2006*, 2: 89–92.

Bond, Stephen, Julie Ann Elston, Jacques Mairesse, and Benoit Mulkay (2003), 'Financial factors and investment in Belgium, France, Germany and the United Kingdom', *Review of Economics and Statistics*, 85, 1: 153–65.

Borenzstein, Eduardo, and Jonathan Ostry (1996), 'Accounting for China's growth performance', *American Economic Review*, 86, 2: 224–8.

Brandt, Loren, and Xiaodong Zhu (2000), 'Redistribution in a decentralized economy: growth and inflation in China under reform', *Journal of Political Economy*, 108, 2: 422–39.

—— Chang-Tai Hsieh, and Xiaodong Zhu (2008), 'Growth and structural transformation in China', in Loren Brandt and Thomas Rawski (eds.), *China's Great Economic Transformation*, Cambridge and New York: Cambridge University Press: 683–728.

Chamon, Marcos, and Eswan Prasad (2008), 'Why are savings rates of urban households in China rising?', NBER Working Paper No. 14546.

Clarke, Donald, Peter Murrell, and Susan Whiting (2008), 'The role of law in China's economic development', in Loren Brandt and Thomas Rawski (eds.), *China's Great Economic Transformation*, Cambridge and New York: Cambridge University Press: 375–428.

Cull, Robert, and Lixin Colin Xu (2005), 'Institutions, ownership, and finance: the determinants of profit reinvestment among Chinese firms', *Journal of Financial Economics*, 77, 1: 117–46.

—— and —— and Tian Zhu (2007), 'Formal finance and trade credit during China's transition', World Bank Policy Research Working Paper No. 4204.

De Grauwe, Paul (2008), 'Animal spirits and monetary policy', CESIFO Working Paper No. 2418.

Ding, Sai, Alessandra Guariglia, and John Knight (2010a), 'Investment and financing constraints in China: does working capital management make a difference?', Department of Economics University of Oxford Discussion Paper No. 521.

—————(2010b), 'Does China overinvest? Evidence from a panel of Chinese firms', Department of Economics University of Oxford Discussion Paper No. 520.

—————(2010c), 'Negative investment in China: financing constraints and restructuring versus growth', Department of Economics University of Oxford Discussion Paper No. 519.

Dollar, David, and Sheng-jin Wei (2007), 'Das (wasted) capital: firm ownership and investment efficiency in China', International Monetary Fund Working Paper No. WP/07/9.

Dougherty, Sean, and Richard Herd (2005), 'Fast-falling barriers and growing concentration: the emergence of a private economy in China', OECD Economics Department Working Paper No. 471.

European Union Chamber Of Commerce In China (2009), 'Overcapacity in China: causes, impacts and recommendations', <www.europeanchamber.com.cn>.

Ferri, Giovanni, and Li-gang Liu (2010), 'Honor thy creditors beforan thy shareholders: are the profits of Chinese state-owned enterprises real?', *Asian Economic Papers*, 9, 2: 50–69.

Firth, Michael, Chen Lin, and Sonia Wong (2008), 'Leverage and investment under a state-owned bank lending environment: evidence from China', *Journal of Corporate Finance*, 14, 5: 642–53.

Gong, Gang, and Justin Lin (2008), 'Deflationary expansion: an overshooting perspective to the recent business cycle in China', *China Economic Review*, 19, 1: 1–19.

Guariglia, Alessandra, Xiaoxuan Liu, and Lina Song (2011), 'Internal finance and growth: microeconometric evidence on Chinese firms', *Journal of Development Economics*, 96, 1: 79–94.

—— and Sandra Poncet (2008), 'Could financial distortions be no impediment to economic growth after all? Evidence from China', *Journal of Comparative Economics*, 36, 4: 633–57.

Haggard, Stephan, and Yasheng Huang (2008), 'The political economy of private sector development in China', in Loren Brandt and Thomas Rawski (eds.), *China's Great Economic Transformation*, Cambridge and New York: Cambridge University Press: 337–74.

Hay, Donald, Derek Morris, Guy Liu, and Shujie Yao (1994), *Economic Reform and State-owned Enterprises in China, 1979–1987*, Oxford: Clarendon Press.

Hu, Zuliu, and Mohsin Khan (1997), 'Why is China growing so fast?', *International Monetary Fund Staff Papers*, 44, 1: 103–31.

Hubbard, Glenn (1998), 'Capital-market imperfections and investment', *Journal of Economic Literature*, 36, 1: 193–225.

Jefferson, Gary, Ping Zhang, and John Zhao (1999), 'Structure, authority and incentives in China's industry', in Gary Jefferson and Inderjit Singh (eds.), *Enterprise Reform in China: Ownership, Transition and Performance*, Washington DC and New York: World Bank and Oxford University Press: 43–64.

Jensen, Michael (1986), 'Agency costs of free cash flow, corporate finance and takeovers', *American Economic Review*, 76, 2: 323–9.

Kaldor, Nicholas (1960), 'Capitalist evolution in the light of Keynesian economics', in his *Essays on Economic Stability and Growth*, London: Duckworth: 243–58.

Kim, Iksoo (1994), 'The political economy of investment control in post-1978 China', in Qimao Fan and Peter Nolan (eds.), *China's Economic Reform: The Costs and Benefits of Incrementalism*, London: St Martins Press: 75–103.

King, Robert, and Ross Levine (1993), 'Finance and growth: Schumpeter might be right'. *Quarterly Journal of Economics*, 108, 3: 717–37.

Knight, John (1995), 'Price scissors and intersectoral resource transfers: who paid for industrialization in China?', *Oxford Economic Papers*, 47, 1: 117–35.

——and Sai Ding (2010),'Why does China invest so much?', *Asian Economic Papers*, 9, 3: 87–117.

——and Lina Song (1999), *The Rural-Urban Divide: Economic Disparities and Interactions in China*, Oxford: Oxford University Press.

————(2005), *Towards a Labour Market in China*. Oxford: Oxford University Press.

Koopman, Robert, Zhi Wang, and Shang-jin Wei (2008), 'How much of Chinese exports is really made in China? Assessing domestic value-added when processing trade is pervasive', NBER Working Paper No. 14109.

Kuijs, Louis (2005), 'Investment and saving in China', World Bank Policy Research Working Paper No. 3633.

Levine, Ross (2005), 'Finance and growth: theory and evidence', in Philippe Aghion and Steven Durlauf (eds.), *Handbook of Economic Growth, Volume 1A*, Amsterdam: Elsevier BV: 865–934.

Li, Hongbin, and Li-an Zhou (2005), 'Political turnover and economic performance: the incentive role of personnel control in China'. *Journal of Public Economics*, 89, 9–10: 1743–62.

Lu, Feng, Guoqing Song, Jie Tang, Hongyan Zhao, and Liu Liu (2008), 'Profitability of China's industrial firms (1978–2006)', *China Economic Journal*, 1, 1: 1–31.

Mayer, Colin (1988), 'New issues in corporate finance', *European Economic Review*, 32, 5: 1167–89.

Ministry Of Finance (MF), People's Republic Of China (2009), *Finance Yearbook of China 2008*, Beijing: Ministry of Finance.

Modigliani, Franco, and Larry Shi Cao (2004), 'The Chinese saving puzzle and the life cycle hypothesis', *Journal of Economic Literature*, 42, 1: 145–70.

National Bureau Of Statistics, People's Republic Of China (NBS) (various years), *China Statistical Yearbook*, Beijing: China Statistics Press.

Naughton, Barry (2007), *The Chinese Economy: Transitions and Growth*, Cambridge, Mass.: The MIT Press.

Organization For Economic Cooperation And Development (OECD) (2005), *OECD Economic Surveys: China No. 13*, Paris: OECD.

Qin, Duo, and Haiyan Song (2009), 'Sources of investment inefficiency: the case of fixed asset investment in China', *Journal of Development Economics*, 90: 94–105.

Riedel, James, Jing Jin, and Jian Gao (2007), *How China Grows: Investment, Finance and Reform*, Princeton: Princeton University Press.

Taylor, Jeffrey (1988), 'Rural employment trends and the legacy of surplus labour, 1928–86', *China Quarterly*, 116, 736–66.

Wei, Shang-jin, and Xiaobo Zhang (2009), 'The competitive saving motive: evidence from rising sex ratios and savings rates in China', NBER Working Paper No. 15093.

Woo, Wing Thye (1998), 'China's economic growth: sources and prospects', in Michel Fouquin and Françoise Lemoine (eds.), *The Chinese Economy*, London: Economica: 17–47.

Wurgler, Jeffrey (2000), 'Financial markets and the allocation of capital', *Journal of Financial Economics*, 58, 1: 187–214.

Young, Alwyn (2003), 'Gold into base metals: productivity growth in the People's Republic of China', *Journal of Political Economy*, 111, 1: 1220–61.

Zou, Hengfu (1991), 'Socialist economic growth and political investment cycles', *European Journal of Political Economy*, 7, 2: 141–57.

Part III
The Consequences of China's Economic Growth

John Knight

9

Economic Growth and the Labour Market

9.1 Introduction

The famous Lewis model (Lewis 1954) provides a good framework for evaluating the success of a developing economy, and for explaining the ways in which the fruits of economic development are spread. Within a competitive market economy, it is only when the economy emerges from the first, labour-surplus, classical stage of the development process and enters the second, labour-scarce, neoclassical stage that real incomes begin to rise generally. Up to that point the benefits of economic growth can accrue in the form of the absorption of surplus labour and not in the form of generally rising real incomes. Beyond that point the scarcity of labour can be a powerful force for the reduction of inequality in labour income.

The process by which an economy moves from the classical to the neoclassical stage is well illustrated by the experience of Japan (in the 1950s or 1960s) and South Korea (in the 1960s or 1970s). When economic reform commenced there is no doubt that China was an extreme example of a labour-surplus economy. There was surplus labour both in the rural areas (where it was disguised as underemployment in the communes) and in the urban areas (where it was disguised as underemployment in the state-owned enterprises). During the reform period China has achieved rapid economic growth, averaging more than 9% per annum over the three decades 1978–2008. Nevertheless, over the same period the labour force has grown by 380 million, or by 90%, equivalent to 2.3% per annum. Has the surplus labour by now been absorbed productively into the economy? The literature is divided on the answer to this question.

In Section 9.2 we briefly describe the Lewis model. Section 9.3 provides some background information on trends in the Chinese labour market. In Section 9.4 we review the literature on our research question. Section 9.5 describes the national household surveys, relating mainly to 2002 and 2007, on which we draw. Section 9.6 reports existing studies of minimum wage behaviour or migrant wage behaviour, and then makes it own contribution by analysing wage functions for the rural–urban migrant samples in order to examine and explain migrant wage behaviour in urban China. An attempt is made in Section 9.7 to measure the remaining pool of potential migrant labour in rural China by means of the rural samples and probit analyses of migration functions. Section 9.8 provides illustrative future projections of labour demand and supply. Section 9.9 concludes.[1]

9.2 The Lewis Model

The Lewis model is too well known to require formal elaboration here. Recall that the turning point comes from two possible mechanisms. One concerns the marginal physical product of labour in the rural (or agricultural, or informal) sector. As labour leaves this sector, so the ratio of land and natural resources to labour eventually improves sufficiently for the marginal product of labour to rise. The second mechanism is the possible improvement in the terms of trade between agriculture and industry as the demand for marketed food rises or the supply falls, or both, causing the value of the marginal product of farm labour to rise.

The supply price of rural labour is related to the marginal product or the average product of labour, depending on migrant objectives. Lewis assumed that the average product would be relevant until the marginal product exceeded it. A rising marginal product thus directly or indirectly increases the supply price of rural labour, and this is reflected in an eventually upward-sloping supply curve to the urban sector. Accordingly, further transfer of labour to the urban sector raises the market-determined real wage in that sector.

The process described above assists broad understanding of the way in which several of the currently developed market economies, including Japan, and some recently successful industrializing economies, such as South Korea and Taiwan, achieved generally rising living standards. However, as a description of the development process of currently poor economies, the Lewis model requires several qualifications and amendments.

First, there is unlikely to be a clear-cut distinction between the classical and the neoclassical stages, for two reasons: spatial heterogeneity and imperfect labour mobility mean that some areas experience labour scarcity before others; and the opportunity cost of migrant labour is more likely to rise gently than to jump sharply, so that the supply curve to the urban sector will curve upwards gradually.

The second qualification is that in many cases it is not possible to equate the agricultural sector with the rural sector and the informal sector, nor industry with urban and formal. Rural industry can be an important source of employment, and the urban informal sector can be an important store of surplus labour.

Third, there can be capital accumulation and technical progress in the rural sector, which raise the average and marginal product and hence the supply price of rural labour before the labour outflow itself has its effect on the supply curve. Such an increase is exogenous and not endogenous to the process of labour transfer.

Fourth, the formal sector real wage may be determined by non-market forces at a level that is above the market-clearing wage. The efficiency wage, labour turnover, and profit-sharing theories of wages, as well as institutional or bargained wage determination, are all contenders. This wage may either be set independently of the market-clearing wage or bear some positive relationship to it. If the wage relevant to migrants is set above the market-determined wage, there is a potential excess supply of migrants to the cities. This phenomenon has led to the formulation of probabilistic migration models: urban unemployment among rural migrants rises until their 'expected wage'—the urban wage multiplied by the probability of securing urban employment—equals the rural supply price.

Fifth, the development of the urban, or industrial, or formal, sector can itself lead to the creation of pressure groups and swing the balance of power towards those in that sector to the detriment of those remaining outside it. The urban bias in economic policies can harm the rural sector and thus delay its benefiting from the fruits of economic growth.

Sixth, insofar as there is reliance on the rural–urban terms of trade as the mechanism for raising rural incomes, in some countries prices may be determined more by government intervention, or by world prices and the exchange rate, than by relative supplies and demands for rural and urban goods.

Finally, the growth of the urban, or industrial, or formal demand for labour may be inadequate in relation to the growth of the labour force. If the difference between the labour force and formal sector employment increases, the economy moves away from the turning point instead of towards it.

9.3 Trends in the Chinese Labour Market

China reached the limits of its land availability decades ago. The total land area sown in 1995 was no more than 6% higher than it had been in 1952. Over the same period the rural labour force increased by 150%, to its peak in 1995. Surplus labour was present in the communes but was camouflaged by the work point system. There were numerous attempts to measure the extent of surplus labour in rural China. They produced a range of estimates but the majority suggested that surplus labour represented 30% of the rural labour force in the 1980s (Taylor 1988; Knight and Song 1999: ch. 2).

Reflecting the pro-population policies of the Maoist period, the rural labour force grew rapidly a generation later, in the 1980s. It was only in the late 1990s that the effects of the one-child family policy, introduced in the late 1970s, began to have its effects on the labour market. Table 9.1 shows various measures of labour force and employment over the period 1995–2007. The rural labour force began to decline gently in the mid-1990s. As rural non-farm employment grew (by 1.6% per annum), farm employment fell markedly (by 1.4% per annum). Urban

Table 9.1. Labour force and employment in China, 1995–2007

	Million			%	% p.a.
	1995	2007	95–07	95–07	95–07
Rural areas					
labour force	490	476	–14	–2.9	–0.03
employment	490	476	–14	–2.9	–0.03
TVEs, PEs, and self-employed	165	200	35	21.2	1.62
household farming	325	276	–49	–15.1	–1.36
employment in primary industry	355	314	–41	–11.5	–0.01
Urban areas					
labour force	196	325	131	66.8	4.43
employment	190	294	104	54.7	3.70
formal sector	149	114	–35	–23.5	–2.21
informal sector	41	180	139	339.0	13.12
unemployment	6	31	25	416.7	15.55
Rural–urban migrants	30	132	102	340.0	13.14
Yuan per annum, average (1995 prices):					
urban real wage	5,348	19,904	14,556	272.2	11.16
rural real income per capita	1,578	3,289	1711	108.4	6.31

Sources: National Bureau of Statistics (2008), tables 4-2, 4-3, 4-5, 4-8, 10-2 (and earlier versions of the same tables where necessary). For rural–urban migrants, Sheng (2008).

employment increased rapidly (by 3.7% per annum). Employment in the formal sector (including state-owned enterprises (SOEs) and urban collective enterprises (UCEs)) actually declined (by 2.2% per annum) whereas the most dynamic sector was urban informal employment (rising by 10.7% per annum).

The natural increase in the urban-born labour force was far too slow to be able to meet the growing demand for labour of urban employers, and the increasing shortfall was met by rural–urban migration. According to Sheng (2008), using data taken from a National Bureau Statistics (NBS) website, the number of rural–urban migrants rose from 30 million in 1995 to 132 million in 2006. Migrants accounted for 7% of the rural labour force in the former year but had risen to no less than 26% in the latter. It is difficult to measure the number of migrants accurately on an annual basis but these orders of magnitude are not in dispute: migrant labour was the most dynamic component of labour force activity during this decade, growing by perhaps 14% per annum.

The table also shows that average urban real wages rose by 11.2% per annum over the period 1995–2007. This rise was much greater than that of rural real income per capita (6.3% per annum). However, official sources report only the wages of urban residents and not those of rural–urban migrants. The pay of the former has been subject to institutional and politically motivated determination and, in recent years, informal profit-sharing associated with a form of efficiency wage theory, whereas the pay of the latter is often determined separately (Knight and Li 2005; Knight and Song 2005: ch. 7). Thus it cannot be inferred from this officially reported wage increase that there has been a shortage of migrant labour: information on migrant wages is required.

The 2007 national household survey of the China Household Income Project showed the ratio of the average monthly wage of urban residents to that of rural–urban migrants to be 1.49. Although migrants are more subject to market forces than are urban residents, the migrant wage is greater than the opportunity cost. The 2007 survey also asked rural–urban migrants what income they would have obtained had they remained in the village. The ratio of the average migrant wage to the average counterfactual village income per month was 2.43. According to probabilistic migration models, this urban–rural income differential should induce an influx of labour and generate substantial urban unemployment among migrants. However, the restrictions on migrant employment and settlement in the cities imposed by central government and local governments hold down migrant unemployment (Knight and Song 2005: chs. 5, 8). In 2002 the unemployment rate of workers in migrant households in urban China was only 2.8% (Li and Deng 2004).

9.4 Literature Survey

An inconclusive literature on the Lewis turning point in China is emerging. For instance, Cai et al. (2007), Park et al. (2007), and Cai and Wang (2008) argue that the turning point has been reached in China. The argument is partly based on evidence of recently rising migrant wages. However, different surveys produce different results, and the evidence requires interpretation. Both Cai (2008) and Park et al. (2007) examine the 'demographic transition' and conclude that China's labour force will begin to decline in about 2020. They see the projected deceleration of labour-force growth as a sign that the turning point has arrived or is imminent.

Kwan (2009), Islam and Yokota (2008), and Minami and Ma (2009) examine China's agricultural sector using a production function approach and conclude that, at the national level, surplus labour in agriculture has fallen but remains high. For instance, Kwan (2009) uses province-level panel data to estimate stochastic cost frontiers in Chinese agriculture and thus to calculate required labour in relation to observed labour. He finds that the labour surplus fell over the reform period as a whole but actually rose in the 2000s, on account of price changes on entry to the WTO, and was still substantial.

A paper which comes close to one of our approaches is that by Chen and Hanori (2009). The authors estimate logit equations to predict the sectoral choice of rural workers (agricultural, local non-agricultural, and migrant) and wage functions for migrants, using the China Health and Nutrition Survey for 2000. They find that the migration propensity is raised by education, being male, being under 30 years

189

of age, not having young children, if other family members have high income, and having less arable land per worker; and that the hourly wage of migrants is raised by education only if employed in a (rare) skilled job, being aged under 30, and if other family members have high income. Region of origin is relevant to both equations. The authors conclude that shortages of migrant labour could and should be eased by raising levels of rural education and by reducing artificial barriers to migration such as *hukou* restrictions.

Thus, it appears that differing methodologies provide different pointers, and that there is diverse data and evidence, resulting in conflicting conclusions. Can an explanation be provided for the puzzle that emerges from these inconsistencies?

9.5 The Data

The main source of data used in this chapter comes from two waves of household surveys conducted by China Household Income Project (CHIP) in the early parts of 2003 and 2008 and relating mainly to the years 2002 and 2007. The surveys cover three types of households: urban local households, rural households, and rural–urban migrant households. Each type of household was surveyed separately. The sample of urban local households and rural households is a part of the large sample of National Bureau of Statistics (NBS).

The 2002 survey for rural households covers twenty-two provinces with a condition that they should be representative of various regions of rural China. The number of sampled households was distributed among the twenty-two provinces roughly in proportion to their populations. In each province there had to be at least fifty households in each selected county, and counties and villages within them had to be stratified by income level. In all, 9,200 households and 37,969 individuals were surveyed in 120 counties. The 2002 survey of registered urban households was conducted in twelve of the twenty-two provinces contained in the rural survey. In all, 6,835 households and 20,632 individuals were surveyed in seventy cities. The questionnaires were designed by the members of the project research team. Income questions were posed with the objective of measuring household disposable income. Households were required to answer questions regarding wage income and other income of each working member, and also income from family business. Questions on working time inside and outside their township were asked of rural households.

The 2002 rural–urban migrant survey sampled a total of 2,000 households: 200 households in each of the coastal and central region provinces and 150 households in each of the western region provinces. A person is defined as a migrant if he or she holds a rural *hukou* (residence registration) and has been living in the urban area for more than six months. Within each province, 100 households were sampled in the capital city and fifty households in each selected middle-sized city. Within each city, rural–urban migrant households were sampled from residential communities; thus migrant workers living in construction sites and factories were excluded. The questionnaires include questions regarding wage, business income, consumption, jobs, and characteristics of households and their individual members.

Each of the 2007 CHIP surveys of rural, urban, and rural–urban migrant households was conducted in the same nine provinces. For the surveys of urban local households and rural–urban migrant households, a total of fifteen cities were selected. For the rural household survey 80 counties and 800 villages were included. The samples contained 8,000 rural households, 5,000 urban local households, and 5,000 urban–rural migrant households. As in the 2002 surveys, the 2007 surveys for rural households and urban local households took sub-samples from the national household survey of the NBS, whereas the rural–urban migrant survey was conducted separately. To ensure comparability between the 2002 and 2007 surveys, the analysis is confined to the nine common provinces.

The questionnaires for the 2007 surveys included as many as possible of the questions contained in those of 2002. In addition, some new questions on migration status and behaviour were added for the purpose of analysing migration. The two rural–urban migrant surveys involved different sampling methods. In 2007 a migrant household was selected when one of its working members was drawn from his or her workplace, whereas in 2002 migrant households were drawn from residential communities. As a result, the 2002 survey has a higher proportion of self-employed migrants. As migrants living in communities tend to have higher incomes than those living elsewhere, the difference might also produce some upward bias in the migrant wage of 2002 by comparison with 2007. To correct for this bias, we selected only those 2007 migrants whose living conditions corresponded to those of 2002 migrants.

9.6 Migrant Wage Behaviour

Other studies

We examine several sources of information on the wages of migrant workers in order to discover whether their wages have risen in recent years and, if so, whether the reason was growing scarcity of migrant labour. We start by reporting the results of Du and Pan (2009), who examined both the behaviour of migrant wages between two recent years and also the development of minimum wage regulation in China and its implications for migrant workers. Their sources were the minimum wages laid down—mainly in large and medium-sized cities—and information on migrant and urban workers provided by the China Urban Labour Surveys

(CULS), available in 2001 and 2005. These were surveys of five big cities: Shanghai, Fuzhou, Wuhan, Shenyang, and Xi'an. Minimum wage data could be traced back to 1995 but implementation was broadened and deepened by the promulgation of minimum wage regulations by the Ministry of Labour and Social Security (MOLSS) in 2004. Could rising migrant wages be due to upward adjustments in these minimum wages?

Between 2001 and 2005 the average monthly minimum wage of the covered cities rose by 45% in nominal terms and by 38% in real terms (deflating by the urban consumer price index, which rose by only 4.8%). This corresponds to 9.7% and 8.4% per annum respectively. Over the same period the average monthly wage of migrants in the CULS surveys rose by 2.6% (nominal) and by 1.4% (real) per annum. Thus, the wages of migrants actually fell relative to the minimum wage.

The ineffectiveness of the minimum wage for migrants as a whole was probably because the monthly minimum wage that employers observed did not take account of hours worked, and migrants averaged 61 hours per week in 2005. However, the wages of young migrants are of particular interest. The percentage change in the average wage of migrants showed a strong monotonic pattern by age, in favour of youth. Two explanations are possible. One is that it represents employers' responses to the need to attract new migrants in the face of growing scarcity. The other concerns minimum wages. There is also a near-monotonic rise with age in the average wage level of migrants. Thus, the larger increases for younger migrants might reflect the implementation of minimum wage levels or changes. The same pattern of wage increases is not observable for local workers, who were generally better paid and thus less likely to be affected by minimum wage adjustments. We cannot rule out the possibility that the age-selective increase in migrant wages is the result of minimum wage behaviour rather than market forces.

Zhao and Wu (2007) provided information on migrant average wages per month over the years 2003–6, obtained from the rural household survey (of 24,000 households in 314 villages in 31 provinces) conducted annually by the Ministry of Agriculture. The average nominal wage of all migrants increased by 6.9% per annum between 2003 and 2006, and their real wage increased by 3.9% per annum. However, the annual real increase was negative in 2004 and rose to 9.8% in 2006. Possibly labour scarcity began to be felt generally only in 2006.

It is helpful to compare migrant wages with rural household income per capita over the same period (NBS 2008). This actually grew more rapidly than the average migrant wage (8.0% per annum versus 3.9% per annum). Even in 2006, there was little difference between them (8.5% versus 9.8% per annum respectively). Thus, the ratio of the migrant wage to household income per capita fell over the period from 2003 to 2006. Of course, it is a prediction of the Lewis model that migration will eventually drive up both migrant wages and rural incomes. It is therefore relevant to decompose the increase in rural incomes to try to determine whether the increases were exogenous or endogenous. Some of the components of an increase in rural real income per capita are likely to be exogenous: one is the reduction in taxes and fees and another is the decline in the number of registered household members. Other components (such as farm productivity and producer price changes) could be either exogenous or endogenous to the migration process, and migrant remittance income is clearly endogenous. Unfortunately, official statistics do not permit such a decomposition.

It might be argued that the migrant labour market is changing rapidly, and that the results so far presented have been overtaken. Up-to-date evidence comes from the regular household surveys of the Ministry of Agriculture (Zhao and Wu 2007; Ministry Of Agriculture 2010). Table 9.2 provides annual data for the years 2003–9. We see that the migrant real wage increased by 10% in 2006, grew slowly during the years 2007 and 2008, but rose by no less than 17% in 2009. The evidence is consistent with there being a very recent acceleration of migrant wage growth but this change is as yet not well established.

Kong et al. (2010) made use of the 2007 CHIP survey and its 2008 continuation panel to examine the effect of the global economic recession on migrant labour. Millions of migrants lost their jobs and returned to their villages. Comparing the first halves of 2008 and 2009, the proportion of migrants fell from 25.0% to 22.8% of the rural labour force, implying a loss of about 15 million migrant jobs. Despite this, the average hourly wage and self-employment income of migrants in the urban areas rose respectively by 19% and 8% over that year, or by 15% and –5% standardizing for migrant characteristics. It is plausible, therefore, that this wage increase represents a wary and lagged response to the new, and different, demand for migrants generated by the sharp fiscal expansion emphasizing infrastructure projects, rather than an underlying shortage of rural labour.

Table 9.2. Migrant annual average wage per worker per month and its growth, 2003–9

	Nominal wage (yuan)	Nominal wage growth (%)	Real wage growth (%)
2003	781		
2004	802	2.8	–1.1
2005	855	6.5	4.7
2006	953	11.5	10.0
2007	1,060	11.2	6.4
2008	1,156	9.1	3.2
2009	1,348	16.6	17.3

Note: Real wage growth is calculated by means of the national consumer price index.

Sources: Zhao and Wu (2007) for 2003–6; Ministry of Agriculture (2010) for 2007–9.

The CHIP surveys, 2002 and 2007

The CHIP household surveys are a potentially valuable source of information on migrant wages. Our analysis takes two forms. First, we explore the determinants of migrant wages in the 2007 survey. This analysis helps us to examine the role that market forces play in migrant wage determination. Second, we combine the two surveys to examine the behaviour of migrant real wages over the crucial five years from 2002 to 2007. The purpose is to understand not only whether real wages have risen but also, if that is the case, why they have done so. Both the migrant and permanent urban resident questionnaires of the 2007 survey contain questions on monthly wage income and also on net income from self-employment. We achieve income comparability across cities by means of the PPP-adjusted deflator as calculated at province level by Brandt and Holz (2006).

It is possible to show the influence of each city's *hukou* worker income on migrant income. We do so by predicting the income that each migrant—with his or her particular characteristics—would receive if rewarded according to the relevant city income function. This variable might be interpreted as a proxy for that city's labour demand. With a perfectly elastic supply curve of migrant labour to any particular city and a segmented labour market within the city, the wages paid to permanent residents of the city need have no effect on the market wage of migrants. However, if migrant wages are responsive to city wages, this could reflect competition for jobs between migrants and city residents (i.e. incomplete segmentation) or institutional wage determination that extends also to at least some migrants. There is information on the unskilled day wage in the migrant's village and the income which the migrant reported that they would have received had they remained in the village. These variables serve as proxies for the migrant's supply price.

The proxies for migrant labour demand and supply can be helpful in interpreting migrant wage behaviour. Consider a simple demand and supply model, bearing in mind that migrants and urban workers are imperfect substitutes (Knight and Yueh 2009). A rightward shift of the demand curve elicits a small supply response in the short run, owing to informational lags, inertia, and transaction costs. We expect the migrant wage to rise and marginal employees to enjoy a wage rent. In the long run, supply responds, the marginal rent is eliminated, and the equilibrium wage is determined by the elasticities of the supply and demand curves; if the migrant supply curve is perfectly elastic, the wage in equilibrium returns to its initial level. If the labour supply curve is not perfectly elastic, we expect the proxy for city labour demand to exhibit a positive coefficient, not only in the short run but also in the long run. If instead the market shock is due to an upward (or leftward) shift of the supply curve, the wage rises only a little in the short term if supply response is lagged, and indeed there may be negative marginal rents. With time the equilibrium wage rises further, and by the full amount of the supply shock if the supply curve is perfectly elastic. In that case our proxy for labour demand does not influence the equilibrium wage.

The relative importance of the proxies for demand and supply thus provides a pointer to the market forces influencing the migrant wage. If our proxy for migrant labour demand has a relatively high coefficient, this suggests that demand is important in the determination of the wage level and of wage increases. If our proxy for the migrant supply price has a relatively high coefficient, it is likely that supply conditions are more influential in governing migrant wage behaviour. However, caution is required because our cross-section data cannot deal with lags nor distinguish equilibrium and disequilibrium situations.

Table 9.3 presents the estimates of functions for migrant wage income and for migrant self-employment income in 2007, both variables being in log form. The variables representing the migrant supply price have significantly positive coefficients: 0.161 for the reported opportunity cost and 0.046 for the village unskilled wage rate. Owing to possible co-linearity between these variables, we also estimated the coefficient on opportunity cost when the unskilled wage was excluded from the specification (the final row of the table): the effect was to raise the coefficient a little, to 0.165. When the function was estimated with income

Table 9.3. The determinants of migrant log wage income and log self-employment income, 2007

	Mean value		Coefficient	
	Wage	Self-empl. income	Wage	Self-empl. income
ln income if stayed in village	6.277	6.233	0.161***	0.197***
ln village unskilled wage	6.958	6.977	0.046**	0.173***
ln predicted city wage	7.107	7.333	0.086***	−0.006
Education (years)	9.522	8.431	0.020***	0.004
Average performance in school	0.656	0.710	−0.021	0.066
Poor performance in school	0.077	0.074	−0.038	0.070
Possession of training	0.267	0.148	0.037*	0.096*
City experience (years)	6.366	10.024	0.024***	0.022***
City experience squared	73.218	141.523	-0.001***	-0.001***
Male	0.554	0.646	0.102***	0.173***
Manufacturing sector	0.263	0.038	0.063***	0.158
Construction sector	0.072	0.022	0.165***	0.237*
Constant term			4.714***	4.677***
Adjusted R-squared			0.212	0.098
Observations			2026	980
Mean of dependent variable	7.007	7.362		
Income if stayed in village (when village unskilled wage is omitted)			0.165***	0.215***

Notes: The sample is confined to migrants who rented a house or owned a house in the city. The omitted categories in the dummy variable analyses are good performance in school, no training, female, 'other' sectors. Certain explanatory variables relating to the employer, including firm size, contact type, and ownership type, were eliminated because their coefficients were found to be generally small and insignificant. The 'predicted city wage' is the wage predicted for each migrant on the basis of her individual characteristics and the city wage (or self-employment income) function estimated for the sample of urban *hukou* residents. Nominal wages and incomes are corrected for province variation in the cost of living by means of the PPP-adjusted price indices calculated by Brandt and Holz (2006). Statistical significance at the 1, 5, and 10% level is denoted by ***, ** and * respectively.

Source: CHIP national household survey, 2007, rural–urban migrant sample.

expressed in levels and not logs (estimates not reported), this coefficient implied that an increase of ¥100 in opportunity cost would alter migrant behaviour in such a way as to raise the migrant wage by a significant ¥33. The precisely equivalent exercises for self-employment income showed the rural supply price to have larger effects (0.197 for opportunity cost and 0.173 for village unskilled wage, both significant). When the latter variable was excluded from the equation, the coefficient on opportunity cost implied that migrants with a rural supply price that was higher by ¥100 would earn self-employment income in the city that was higher by ¥73. The evidence suggests that migrants with higher village opportunity costs will only be found in city jobs which pay more. The implication is that a rise in the rural supply price will indeed result in higher migrant wages.

The predicted city wage of the migrant was introduced as a potential proxy for the pressure of demand for labour in the city. The coefficient for wage earners is positive (0.086) and significant. However, it might instead or as well reflect influences other than demand. The effect of variation among cities in the cost of living should in principle be eliminated by our use of the PPP-adjusted deflator but the province-level deflator has limitations, acknowledged by its compilers (Brandt and Holz 2006: 83), and its inaccuracy for a particular city within a province cannot be ruled out. The wage might be affected by institutional factors, in particular—because migrants are concentrated at the lower end of the city wage distribution—by the implementation of city minimum wage regulations. It is relevant, therefore, that the coefficient is not positive or significant for the self-employed (–0.006). We conducted various robustness tests on our proxy for the urban demand for migrants. The main results proved to be robust although the relative importance of the supply side and demand side effects did vary somewhat.

Several control variables—interesting in themselves—are also included in the migrant income functions: we briefly discuss those that have both significant and substantive coefficients. The return to a year of education is positive and significant but low (2.0% per annum) in wage employment, and the wage is insensitive to reported performance in school. These results might reflect the low quality of jobs that migrants generally occupy. The education variables are not significant at all in the self-employment equation. The possession of training, however, is rewarded both in wage employment and in self-employment. Similarly, city employment experience (years since migrating) has the usual inverse-U shaped relationship in both forms of migrant employment. The fact that men and construction workers receive more wage income and self-employment income than women or workers in the residual sectors (mainly sales and other services) is consistent with the arduous or unpleasant nature of some of the work performed by migrants and, in the case of self-employment, with the possibility of skill or capital barriers to entering certain activities.

Table 9.4 combines the 2007 migrant survey with the 2002 migrant survey in order to examine the change in the logarithm of the wage over time. Sampling

Table 9.4. The determinants of the proportionate change in migrant wage and self-employment income, 2002–7, combined sample

	Wage				Self-employment income			
	1	2	3	4	5	6	7	8
year 2007	0.643***	0.589***	0.531***	0.342***	0.819***	0.771***	0.737***	0.506***
education (years)		0.042***	0.030***	0.021***		0.032***	0.032***	0.019***
city experience (years)		0.025***	0.023***	0.023***		0.040***	0.038***	0.038***
city experience squared		-0.001***	-0.001***	-0.001***		-0.002***	-0.002***	-0.002***
possession of training		0.075***	0.064***	0.050***		0.066*	0.078**	0.081
male		0.212***	0.170***	0.148***		0.168***	0.159***	0.125***
manufacturing sector		0.120***	0.118***	0.096***		0.363***	0.325***	0.275***
construction sector		0.086***	0.098***	0.099***		0.208***	0.215***	0.199***
urban predicted wage			0.098***	0.085***			0.036***	0.041***
wage if stayed in village				0.158***				0.186***
constant	6.362***	5.733***	5.254***	4.648***	6.539***	6.093***	5.855***	5.026***
observations	3254	3254	3254	3254	2478	2478	2478	2478
adjusted R-squared	0.302	0.409	0.418	0.459	0.290	0.343	0.344	0.385

Notes: Columns 1 and 5 contain only the dummy variable year 2007 (with year 2002 the omitted category). Columns 2, 3, and 4 add progressively to column 1, as do columns 6, 7, and 8 to column 5. The same explanatory variables as in Table 9.3 are included except for performance in school and the unskilled wage in the village, which are not available for 2002. The omitted categories in the dummy variable analysis are female, no training, and 'other' services. Significance at the 1, 5, and 10% levels is denoted by ***, **, and * respectively.

Source: CHIP 2002 and 2007 national household surveys, rural–urban migrant samples.

procedures were different in the two surveys: the 2002 sample was drawn from residential areas and thus contains only migrants living in households, whereas that of 2007 was obtained by tracking all rural–urban migrants working in randomly selected areas. Because some of these were living in dormitories or workplaces provided by the employer, the coverage is broader. For comparability, we included 2007 migrants in the analysis only if they were living in their own houses or houses that they had rented. The Brandt–Holz (2006) PPP-adjusted deflator is used to correct both for differences in city price levels and for their rates of change.

The specifications differ from that of Table 9.3. The key variable is the year dummy, with 2007 taking a value equal to 1 and 2002 a value equal to 0. Columns 1 and 5, both including only this dummy and an intercept term, show the raw increase in migrant real income: implying growth of 10.4% and 12.7% per annum for wage and self-employment income respectively. Columns 2 and 6 add to this specification by introducing the set of individual variables available in both years. It is notable that the proportionate increases in wage and in self-employment income fall only a little, to 9.7% and 12.1% per annum respectively, when personal characteristics are held constant. This represents the income change of migrants whose characteristics make them likely to be among the least skilled. We also standardize for the urban predicted wage in columns 3 and 7: the increases come down further, to 8.9% and 11.7% respectively. Our best indicator of the rural supply price is the income that the migrant would have obtained in the village: its addition, in columns 4 and 8, reduces the increases to 6.1% and 8.5% respectively. There remains a substantial rise in wages and self-employment incomes which cannot be accounted for by the explanatory variables at our disposal.

It is possible that changes in the supply of and demand for different worker characteristics altered the migrant wage structure. In particular, if there was a growing scarcity of young and of educated migrants, this might have given them larger wage increases. We explore this possibility by distinguishing 'young' (aged up to 35 years) and 'old' (more than 35 years) workers, and workers who were 'more educated' (having completed middle school) and 'less educated' (without complete middle school). Accordingly, we re-estimate the wage functions corresponding to columns 2–4 of Table 9.4, now excluding years of education but including a young worker dummy plus a 'young worker × 2007' interaction term and a more educated worker dummy plus a 'more educated worker × 2007' interaction term. The hypothesis is that the coefficients on the interaction terms are positive. The estimates (not reported) show the coefficients on the interaction term for young workers to be significantly positive in each specification (ranging from 0.08 to 0.11). By contrast, the coefficients on the interaction term for more educated workers are not positive and indeed are significantly negative in two of the three specifications. This suggests that the young gained relatively to the old—reflecting either growing relative scarcity or minimum wage increases—whereas the wage premium on migrant education fell over the five years.

Table 9.5. Decomposition of the increase in the average real migrant wage, 2002–7, selective summary

Contribution of change in mean characteristics to the gross mean wage increase: percentage

	Wage		Self-employment income	
	2002 weights	2007 weights	2002 weights	2007 weights
education	3.3	4.1	1.3	1.9
length of city experience	−0.4	−0.4	−0.5	−0.9
predicted log city wage	31.6	42.0	8.0	30.3
log income if stayed in village	35.4	32.2	36.2	26.4
other	0.4	4.8	−0.3	2.9
total	70.3	82.7	44.7	60.6

Notes: The estimates are based on a standard Oaxaca–Blinder decomposition, using the coefficients for 2002 and for 2007 as weights. The contribution of education as a whole is based on the change in composition among four levels: primary, middle and high school, and college education. The contribution of length of city experience is based on the change in composition among five experience groups: 0–5, 6–10, 11–15, 16–20, and 21– years. The omitted categories in the dummy variable analyses are the same as those in Tables 9.3 and 9.4 plus primary education and 0–5 years of city experience. The income if stayed in village and predicted city wage are as used in Tables 9.3 and 9.4.

Source: CHIP surveys, 2002, 2007.

Over time the average migrant worker could be expected to become more educated, and to have been working in the city for a longer time: both education and work experience are productive characteristics that are rewarded by the market. A more direct way of measuring the contribution of changing characteristics to migrant wage growth is by means of decomposition analysis—permitting changes in coefficients as well as characteristics. A standard decomposition of the change in average migrant wages between 2002 and 2007, summarized in Table 9.5, shows that, of the gross mean log wage increase (0.649), a minority (less than 30%) is due to differences in the coefficients of the two wage functions and the majority can be explained by changes in mean characteristics. However, less than 5% is due to the improvement in the educational composition of migrants and no contribution is made by change in their length of city experience. The main contributions come from the increase in city demand price (32 or 42%, according to the weights being used) and rural supply price (32 or 35%), both adjusted for price changes and for differences in province price levels. Labour market forces were indeed largely responsible for the wage increase. The pattern is very similar for self-employment income, also shown in the table.

To summarize what can be learned from these wage regressions: in Table 9.3 our proxies for rural supply (the rural opportunity cost) and urban demand (employers' valuation of migrants) were indeed associated with a higher migrant wage. The rural proxy had a similar effect in the case of self-employment income, but not the urban proxy. The reward for education was only slight, probably reflecting the menial jobs which most migrants perform. We saw in Table 9.4 that the

Table 9.6. Dispersion of the migrant average city wage across cities, 2002 and 2007

	Common cities		Cities in common provinces		All cities	
	2002	2007	2002	2007	2002	2007
Gini coefficient	0.167	0.067	0.203	0.103	0.260	0.261
standard deviation of log wage	0.323	0.129	0.441	0.194	0.508	0.194
standard deviation of wage	75	134	85	165	132	170

Source: CHIP 2002 and 2007, migrant samples.

proportionate increase in the migrant real wage/income over the period 2002–7, both actual and conditioned on personal characteristics, was rapid. Table 9.5 indicated that the two variables most likely to reflect the contribution made by market forces to wage behaviour over time—the proxies for rural supply price and urban demand price—could together account for about two-thirds of the actual increase in the migrant wage.

The CHIP surveys provide some evidence suggesting that the market for migrants is becoming spatially more integrated. Table 9.6 reports the dispersion of the city average migrant wage for the seven cities that are common to the two surveys, the twenty-three cities in the seven common provinces, and for all cities in each survey. In the first of these cases, the Gini coefficient of the average city wage fell from 0.107 and 0.067, and the standard deviation of the log wage fell from 0.323 to 0.129. A similar dramatic reduction can be found for all cities in the two surveys and for all twenty-three cities in the seven common provinces, and also for migrant self-employment income. However, both of these measures of dispersion are mean dependent—falling as the mean increases, other things being equal—and the mean wage rose over this period. The standard deviation of the average real wage rose in each case. It is not clear which is the more appropriate measure of wage dispersion, but we assume that the sources of wage differences, and their costs, are likely to rise along with incomes. On that basis, these results can be interpreted in two ways: either city minimum wages became more standardized and effective or, more likely, market forces were responding to a growing spatial mobility of migrants.

9.7 The Pool of Potential Migrants

Our main concern in this section is to gauge the size of the pool of rural labour available to migrate to urban employment. Our method is to estimate migration functions using the CHIP rural sub-samples for 2002 and 2007, and then to assess how many non-migrants have high probabilities of migration. Our cut-off

Table 9.7. Probit equations predicting the probability of migrant status, 2002 and 2007

	2002		2007	
	Coefficient	Marginal	Coefficient	Marginal
male	0.552***	0.145	0.456***	0.119
married without children	−0.457***	−0.101	−0.337***	−0.079
with children aged 0–6	−0.513***	−0.113	−0.401***	−0.094
with children aged 7–12	−0.540	−0.122	−0.365***	−0.086
with children aged 13–	−0.526***	−0.136	−0.413***	−0.108
parent older than 70	0.049	0.013	−0.130***	−0.034
age group 21–5	0.172***	0.049	0.111**	0.031
26–30	0.041	0.011	−0.021	−0.006
31–5	−0.116	−0.030	−0.437***	−0.099
36–40	−0.301***	−0.073	−0.737***	−0.152
41–5	−0.530***	−0.116	−1.051***	−0.198
46–50	−0.719***	−0.150	−1.443***	−0.214
51–	−1.022***	−0.196	−1.853***	−0.298
schooling: middle	0.217***	0.058	0.081**	0.022
high	0.168***	0.047	0.014	0.004
college	0.041	0.011	−0.097	−0.025
health: good	0.181***	0.046	0.072*	0.019
poor	−0.089	−0.023	−0.271**	−0.064
arable land per hh member	−0.043**	−0.012	−0.046***	0.012
propn migrants in village	2.021***	0.541	1.493***	0.401
pseudo-R-squared	0.195		0.289	
number of observations	9321		16,094	

Notes: The omitted categories in the dummy variable analysis are female, not married, no parent older than 70, age group 16–20, primary schooling or none, normal health. The symbols ***, **, and * denote statistical significance at the 1%, 5%, and 10% levels respectively. Province dummy variables are included in the specifications but not reported.
Source: CHIP 2002 and 2007, rural samples.

probability in the probits is chosen to ensure that the number of rural workers who are predicted to migrate is set equal to the number of workers who do migrate. We use the nine provinces that are common to both surveys. In 2002 the proportion who actually migrated was 23.4% and in 2007 it was 27.3%. In 2002 14% of non-migrants were predicted to migrate and 46% of migrants were predicted not to do so; the corresponding figures in 2007 were 13% and 36%.

Table 9.7 reports the probit equations, the dependent variable being migrant status and the omitted category non-migrant status. Several of the coefficients are not only statistically significant but also economically substantial. The 'marginals' show the effect of a unit change in a variable on the probability of migration. We see that being male increases that probability by fifteen percentage points in 2002 and by twelve percentage points in 2007. Marriage reduces the probability of migration, especially if there are children. The probability peaks for the age group 21–5 in both years. It falls sharply after age 25 in 2002 and after age 31 in 2007, and thereafter it declines more sharply in the later year. We might expect the probability of older workers to rise as migrant labour becomes scarcer; on the contrary, it appears that the increased migration of younger people required a higher proportion of older people to remain at home. Age has a greater effect on the probability of migration than any other personal characteristic.

With primary education and below as the omitted category, the probability of migration after middle school is six and two percentage points higher in 2002 and 2007 respectively. High school enrolment is not significant in 2007. Although it is significant in 2002, its marginal effect on the probability of migrating (5%) is smaller than that of middle school. Consistent with the low returns to education reported in Table 9.3, education is not an important determinant of migration in 2002 and becomes even less important over the next five years. Good health increases migration in both years and poor health decreases it in 2007. The greater the area of arable land per member that the household possesses, the less chance there is of members migrating. Province dummy variables are included but not reported: province of rural residence is a notable determinant of migration.

Of great importance is the proportion of migrants among workers in the village. The mean proportion is 0.13 in 2002 and 0.22 in 2007. A one-standard-deviation increase in this proportion raises the migration propensity by 5.2 and 5.5 percentage points respectively. This result has several possible interpretations. One of them is that migration from the village sets in train a process of cumulative causation as information and support networks increase and the monetary and psychological costs of migration and job search fall. In that case the many villages which still have low proportions of migrants might be ripe to become migration villages.

What keeps the non-migrants from migrating? The 2007 survey contains a specific question asking for the reason. The distribution of replies is shown in Table 9.8. Three reasons were stressed: being too old, unable to find a job outside, and needing to care for old people or children. Each of these might prove to be flexible in the face of rising demand for migrant labour. Older workers and carers

Table 9.8. Reasons given by non-migrant workers for not migrating: distribution of replies and the relationship of the replies to the probability of migrant status

	Reason given (%)	Regression explaining the probability of migrating	
		Regression coefficient	Partial correlation coefficient
too old, under 40	17.3	−0.118***	−0.107***
too old, 40 and over	7.3	0.195***	0.161***
sick or disabled	3.2	0.000	
cannot find a job outside	22.6	0.021*	0.019*
care of elderly or children	26.0	0.021*	0.019*
has local business	10.4	0.006	0.004
other	13.3	−0.006	−0.020

Source: CHIP 2007, rural sample.

might well be willing to move if policy is revised to meet the changing circumstances, so that family migration and urban settlement are made easier. Workers will find it easier to obtain outside jobs if the demand for migrants grows, especially if migrant networks are strengthened in the process.

The table also shows the results of an OLS regression equation for non-migrants in which the dependent variable is the estimated probability of migrating, estimated from Table 9.7, and the reported coefficients are those for the dummy variables representing the different reasons for not migrating. The coefficients cannot be interpreted as denoting a causal effect: they are merely associations which indicate which subjective reasons for not migrating are associated with a high probability of migrating as predicted by the objective variables reported in Table 9.7. The higher the positive value of a regression or partial correlation coefficient, the more closely the reason is associated with a high migration probability. It suggests that such a reason is important in explaining why rural workers with high potential to migrate fail to do so. We see that the highest regression and partial correlation coefficient is the one for workers aged over 40 who say they are too old. Over and above the effect of actual age (which is already incorporated in the estimated migration probability), the perception of being too old appears to be important in deterring migration. It is an important question whether such a perception will adjust in response to improving migration opportunities and migration policies.

It was possible to use the probit estimates of Table 9.7 to predict the probability of migrating for each worker—whether in fact a migrant or a non-migrant—in 2002 and in 2007, and from that to calculate frequency distributions of workers by predicted probability. These could be expressed in millions of workers by using estimates of the number of migrants and non-migrants in the two years. Calculated on this basis, Table 9.9 and Figure 9.1 show that, in both years, there were more migrants than non-migrants among those rural workers with a predicted probability of migrant status exceeding 0.5. The disparity was small in 2002 but increased in 2007. There were many migrants (33 million in 2007) with probability between 0.3 and 0.5, indicating that migration is quite possible in that range of probabilities; there were even more non-migrants (45 million). Indeed, there were over 80 million non-migrants with a migration probability of 0.3 or higher. This figure was actually slightly higher than the 77 million in the same category in 2002.

Another method of assessing the potential pool of migrants is to find the 'expected value' of migration by non-migrants, that is, to multiply the number of non-migrants in each migration probability range by that probability (taken to be the mid-point of the range). These estimates are also shown in Table 9.9. The total expected value of migration was 74 million in 2002 and 71 million in 2007.

Because age is such an important determinant of migration, it is interesting to distinguish 'young' and 'old' non-migrants (the dividing line again being set at

Table 9.9. Frequency distribution of the number of migrants and non-migrants by predicted probability of migrating, and 'expected value' of migration by non-migrants, millions, 2002 and 2007

Predicted probability range	Migrants	Non-migrants	Migrants	Non-migrants	'Expected value' of migration by non-migrants	
	2002	2002	2007	2007	2002	2007
0–0.1	7.8	153.3	8.7	185.9	7.7	9.3
0.1–0.2	14.6	104.6	11.3	72.0	15.7	10.8
0.2–0.3	19.4	57.8	13.8	41.5	14.5	10.4
0.3–0.4	20.4	30.9	14.0	26.4	10.8	9.2
0.4–0.5	18.1	19.5	17.4	19.1	8.8	8.6
0.5–0.6	15.8	14.2	19.6	14.2	7.8	7.8
0.6–0.7	12.1	8.6	23.2	11.0	5.6	7.2
0.7–0.8	7.5	3.6	21.4	7.8	2.7	5.9
0.8–1.0	1.3	0.6	11.3	2.2	0.5	2.0
Total	117.0	393.1	140.7	380.1	74.1	71.2
Total with p > 0.3		77.4		80.7		

Note: The methods of estimation are explained in the text.

Source: CHIP 2002, 2007, rural samples.

age 35). In both years 67 million young non-migrants had a probability of migrating higher than 0.3 (most old non-migrants had probabilities lower than 0.3), and the expected value of migration by young non-migrants fell over time from 44 million to 41 million.

Our results are based on binary probit equations distinguishing migrants and non-migrants. As a robustness test we also estimated multinomial logit equations for the two years. The base category was farming and the alternatives were local non-farming and migration. The determinants of local non-farm employment and migrant employment are similar, but education is more important and age less important for local non-farm activities. Local non-farm employment is better rewarded than farming (for instance, Knight and Song 2005: ch. 8), and it might be more attractive than migration for those with access to full-time local employment. We recognize below that the number of rural workers available to migrate is likely to depend on what happens to rural non-farm employment.

A different approach to examining the extent of rural labour surplus is to measure the number of days that are actually worked in relation to the number of working days available for work. Although the 2007 CHIP survey does not contain this information, its 2008 continuation panel does record the number of days worked. Rural workers were asked to state their main economic activity. For those who said they were farmers, the average number of days worked was 183 (of which only 25 days were not in farming), and 49% of farmers worked fewer than 200 days. The corresponding figures for all rural workers (including those who classified themselves as local non-farm workers and migrant workers) were 226

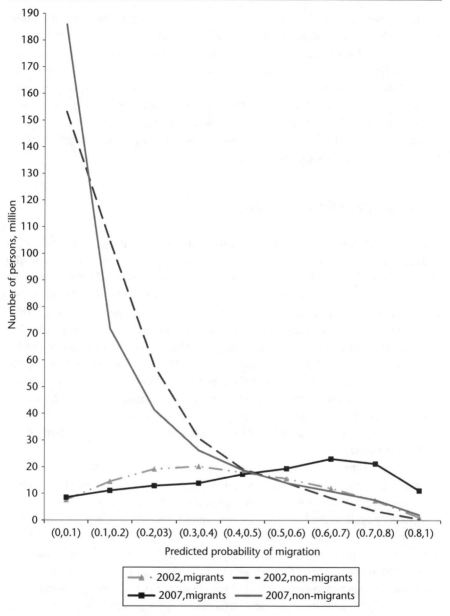

Figure 9.1. The distribution of the number of migrants and non-migrants by the probability of migrating, millions

days and 32% respectively. Clearly, rural people who obtain non-farm jobs are more fully employed than farmers. Assume that 300 days in the year are available for work. On that basis, the amount of surplus labour is 39% in the case of farmers—the group from which most potential migrants are likely to be drawn—and 25% in the case of rural workers as a whole.

Our various measures illuminate different aspects of migration potential. However, whichever measure is considered, it appears that there is a substantial supply of migrants still available in rural China. Moreover, the potential pool of migrants barely declined over the five years. In any case there are two reasons why the probabilities of migration are likely to rise as the urban economy grows. Rural workers will have better opportunities to migrate for employment, and older workers in particular will have a stronger incentive to move with their families as central government and local governments respond to the economic need for a more settled urban labour force.

9.8 Projections Into the Future

Whatever the current state of the market for migrant labour, the situation is changing rapidly. It is instructive, therefore, to project the demand for and the urban-born supply of labour into the future. Although urban and rural workers are not close substitutes, we assume that an increase in the demand for labour in the urban economy enables urban *hukou* workers to move up the occupational ladder in order to fill vacancies and rural *hukou* workers to enter the less skilled jobs that are vacated. The gap between the two can therefore be taken as an indication of the demand for migrant labour, and the evolution of that gap shows how the demand for migrant labour will grow. Table 9.10 presents our projections, necessarily based on various strong assumptions. These results are illustrated in Figure 9.2, projecting the demand for migrants up to the year 2020. We assume in these projections that the supply of migrants adjusts to equal the demand—an assumption which we discuss below.

We start on the demand side. Urban employment over the period 1980–2008 grew at an average rate of 3.8% per annum. We compare sub-periods by taking three-year averages in which the year mentioned is the middle year, so as to reduce the effect of cyclical fluctuations in employment. Growth was rapid in the 1980s (4.5% per annum), reflecting the rapid growth of the urban *hukou* labour force, in turn due to the population policies of the 1960s, and an increase in overmanning within enterprises as government sought to ensure full employment. However, there was a deceleration in the 1990s (3.6% per annum). Increased product market competition, from both urban and rural industry, involved falling profits and rising losses, and this resulted in slower growth. The policy response—privatization and reform of SOES—in the latter half involved many redundancies. Between 2000 and 2007 annual employment growth averaged 3.4%.

Peering into the future, it is plausible that China will maintain its recent trend rate of GDP growth in the first half of the next decade, although the growth rate can be expected to fall as the rate of structural change slows down and resources become more fully employed. Indeed, the rise in migrant wages that would occur

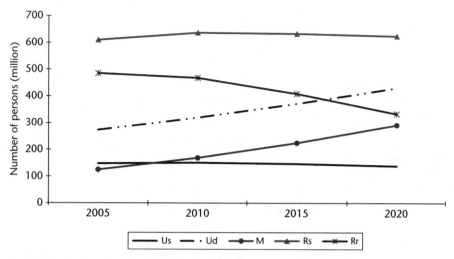

Figure 9.2. Projections of the labour force, urban, rural, and migrant, millions, 2005–2020

U_s natural increase or decrease of labour force in urban areas
U_d projected urban demand for labour
M demand for and supply of rural–urban migrants ($U_d - U_s$)
R_s natural increase or decrease of rural labour force
R_r residual rural labour force ($R_s - M$)

beyond the Lewis turning point would also curb the demand for labour, by encouraging employers to substitute away from unskilled labour and from unskilled-labour-intensive products. We project urban employment from 2008 to 2020 on a conservative assumption: that it grows by 3% per annum. This projection is shown as the curve U_d in Figure 9.2.

The projection of the urban *hukou* labour force is complicated by the need to separate urban *hukou* workers from rural *hukou* workers, and by the changing age structure of urban citizens. The baseline for our projections is provided by the official 1% Population Survey of 2005, and the projections are made over the period 2005–20. The survey provides detailed information for cities, towns, and rural areas on population by age, on age-specific mortality rates, and on age-specific labour force participation rates (all for five-year age groups). We estimate the number of entries to and retirements from the urban-born labour force in each year from 2005 onwards. People are assumed to enter at age 18 and to retire on turning 60. The five-year age-specific mortality rates in 2004 are used to estimate deaths in each age-group each year. The age-specific participation rates of 2005 are used to convert from population of working age to labour force.

The projections of the natural increase in the urban labour force are shown as the curve U_s in Figure 9.2. The projections imply an average rate of natural increase

Table 9.10. Projections of the labour force, urban, rural and migrant, millions, 2005–2020

	Urban						Rural						
	Demand		Labour force		Migrants		Labour force		Migrants		Non-migrants	
	index	million	index	million	index	million	index	million	index	million	index	million
2005	100.0	273	100.0	148	100.0	125	100.0	610	100.0	125	100.0	485
2010	115.9	320	101.8	151	135.2	169	104.4	637	135.2	169	96.5	468
2015	134.3	372	99.1	147	180.0	225	104.0	634	180.0	225	84.3	409
2020	156.7	431	93.6	139	233.6	292	102.6	626	233.6	292	68.9	334

Note: The method of projection is explained in the text.
Sources: NBS (2006) data; Sheng (2008).

by −6.4% (equal to −0.44% per annum) over the fifteen years 2005–20. There is a rise (of 1.8%) over the five years 2005–10, then a fall (−2.7%) over the years 2010–15, and an acceleration in fall (−5.5%) in the period 2015–20.

This remarkable demographic behaviour is to be explained by the violent changes in China's population policies in the past. Mao's exhortations produced a baby boom in the 1960s and early 1970s, after the Great Famine. This resulted in a rapid increase in the labour force in the 1980s and early 1990s. It also generated an echo baby boom in the decade 1985–95, as the large age cohort born in the 1960s reached their most prolific child-bearing age. Thus it was only from the mid-1990s that the low fertility rate (of the female population of child-bearing age)— starting in 1978 as a result of Deng's one-child family policy and applied particularly harshly in urban China—came to dominate the birth rate. In 2005, the number of urban children in the age groups 15–19, 10–14, 5–9, and 0–4 decreased in the proportions 100, 81, 66, and 56 respectively. This decrease, combined with the continuation of the draconian family planning policy, is the main explanation for the fall in the labour force after 2010.

The NBS's 2005 survey defined the urban population simply as those who had lived in the place for more than six months. It includes many but not all of the rural *hukou* migrants. We therefore use the estimate of the number of rural–urban migrant workers made by Sheng (2008), also taken from NBS sources, to indicate the 'excess demand' of urban labour demand over urban *hukou* labour supply in 2005. The growth in the number of migrants in urban employment is shown in the figure by the curve M. Migrants represented 46% of the urban labour force at the start of our projection period. By 2010 the excess demand is 53%, by 2015 60%, and by 2020 68%. In that year the number of rural–urban migrants working in China's cities and towns is projected to be 292 million. Thus, on the assumption that something like the past rate of urban economic growth can be maintained in the future, rural–urban migrants (that is, workers with rural origins) will become increasingly important in the urban economy, and indeed will be predominant from about 2010 onwards.

We conducted the same projection exercise for rural areas, using precisely the same methodology. The results are also shown in Table 9.10 and in Figure 9.2. The curve R_s represents the natural increase of the population resident in rural China in 2005. The family planning policy was not applied as strictly in rural as in urban China: in many provinces parents were, and are, permitted to have a second child if the first was a girl. However, rural China was subject to the same violent swing in population policy. Again, there was a precipitous fall in births, albeit starting five years later: in 2005 the numbers in the age groups 15–19, 10–14, 5–9, and 0–4 fell in the proportions 100, 104, 79, and 68 respectively. Thus the rural labour force is projected to rise by only 2.6% over the fifteen years, equivalent to 0.2% per annum. There is a rise of 4.4% in the first five years, an almost constant labour force in the next five years, and a fall of 1.6% in the final five years. The curve R_r is the residual labour supply, that is, the rural natural increase minus the projected migrant labour outflow. There is a dramatic fall in employment in rural China over the projection period: by 31%, or by 2.5% per annum, up to 2020. Our projection is from 485 million in 2005 to 468 million in 2010, to 409 million in 2015 and to 334 million in 2020. The Lewis turning stage—stage rather than point—is unlikely to be far off.

These projections are of the demand for migrant labour. We have assumed thus far that the supply will match that demand. However, the projected fall in rural employment over the period under consideration is likely to raise the supply curve of migrants and thus the migrant wage, which in turn will curb the growth in labour demand. The wage response will be strengthened if the current institutional deterrents to migration remain in place.

The rate of increase in migrant wages will depend also on the growth of rural non-farm employment. There is evidence that the average, and particularly the marginal, returns to non-farm employment exceed those to farm employment in rural China, and that the average and marginal returns to local non-farm are not far below those to migrant employment (Knight and Song 2005: ch. 8). Another study (Zhao 1999) found that rural workers prefer local non-farm employment to migration despite receiving lower wages. Thus, it is likely that the faster the future growth of non-farm employment, the more rapidly will the market for migrant labour tighten. However, the growth of employment in rural industry appears to be decelerating: TVE employment grew annually by 11.9% in the 1980s, by 3.3% in the 1990s, and by 2.3% in the 2000s up to 2007 (NBS 2008: table 7–2).

9.9 Conclusion

We have produced evidence of simultaneous surplus labour in rural areas and rising migrant wages in urban areas. The two phenomena appear to be inconsistent with the predictions of the Lewis model, and yet they are both observed in China. Our interpretation of the puzzle is that there is segmentation in the labour market—the result of constraints on rural–urban labour migration (for instance, Knight and Song 1999: chs. 8–9; 2005: chs. 5–7; Lee and Meng 2010: 41–4). The institutional constraints create difficulties for migrants living in urban areas—in respect of good and secure jobs, housing, and access to public services—and these deter or prevent migrant workers from bringing their families with them. This in turn makes many rural workers reluctant to leave the village, at least for long periods. The institutional arrangements that prohibit the ownership, and thus sale, of rural land also serve as a deterrent to permanent urban settlement. Although there is evidence that the Chinese market for migrant labour is becoming more integrated, it is possible that the two phenomena will continue to coexist for several years: there will not necessarily be a neat Lewis turning point in a country as large and as regulated as China is. In their revision of the Lewis model, Ranis and Fei (1961) formally incorporated a turning stage that reflects a gradually rising marginal product of rural labour. We envisage an even longer turning stage—the result not only of rural sector heterogeneity but also of China's factor market institutions.

We adduced evidence that migrant wages have indeed risen in real terms in very recent years, and that their wages are sensitive to urban labour market conditions and to rural supply prices. Much of the increase could be explained by rising rural household incomes, although it was not possible to distinguish the increases that were exogenous (such as the abolition of agricultural taxes and of fees for basic education) and the increases that were endogenous to the migration process. We had expected that the increased migrant wage was partly due to the improving human capital of migrant workers—both their educational attainment and their urban work experience—but this effect turned out to be surprisingly small, at least over the years 2002–7.

Our analysis of the CHIP 2002 and 2007 rural surveys showed that there is a large pool of non-migrants with fairly high probabilities of migrating. Much depends on how far the three main perceived reasons for not migrating—being too old, needing to care for dependants, and failing to find migrant work—will fade as work opportunities for migrants improve and labour market policies adjust endogenously.

Our heroic projection of future trends indicates that the number of rural–urban migrants will grow rapidly and the number of workers remaining in the rural areas will fall rapidly. By 2020 migrants will constitute about two-thirds of urban employment and the residual rural labour force will be about one-third lower than in 2005. Before that date, however, it is likely that there will be an endogenous response both of the market and of the government. In the labour market, the competitively determined wages of unskilled workers can be expected to rise generally. The government response is likely to involve retirement policy, birth control policy, and urbanization policy.

One policy variable open to government is the normal age of retirement. In China people generally retire young, reflecting the low life expectancy of past times. The 2002 survey contains information on age of retirement. The median male retirement age was 59, and 90% of men had retired by the age of 61; the median female retirement age was 51, and 92% of women had retired by the age of 56. A case can be made for raising the retirement age on account of the currently higher, and rising, life expectancy. A tightening of the labour market might well provide the impetus for such a move. The impending labour scarcity and the remarkable fall in the number of births might induce government also to relax the one-child family policy. However, this could affect the number of new entrants to the labour market only with a median lag of about eighteen years.

If our projections are broadly correct, future trends in the labour market are likely to encourage both the urban settlement of migrants and the weakening of the *hukou* system. As more of the skilled jobs become vacant and migrants accordingly move up the job ladder, so the economic imperative will be for their permanent settlement. Skill and its associated training cost bring the need for long-term employment. The Chinese system of 'floating'—temporary migration—will increasingly become economically inefficient. The solution to this problem which employers in many countries have adopted is to try to stabilize their labour forces by improving the rewards for staying. If long service becomes economically more efficient, governments have an incentive to permit and encourage it, employers have an incentive to reward it, and migrants have an incentive to acquire it. Long service in turn encourages migrants to settle with their families.

Long-term residence in the city leads to the adoption of urban attitudes and the transfer of migrant social reference groups from the village to the city (as shown in Knight and Gunatilaka 2010). This process may well give rise to feelings of relative deprivation in relation to urban *hukou* residents. As more and more former peasants make the transition to urban living, so the pressure on Chinese central and local governments to treat them on a par with urban-born residents is likely to grow, and *hukou* privilege accordingly likely to be eroded. Increasingly, migrants will become proletarians.

There are other far-reaching implications of our findings about the effects of economic growth on the market for relatively unskilled labour. General scarcity of unskilled labour is probably the most powerful market force for reducing the inequality of income in China—inequality that has grown over the period of economic reform. It is likely to be the main market mechanism for narrowing the still widening income divide between rural and urban China. Rapidly rising returns to unskilled labour will also require a change in development strategy towards more skill-intensive and technology-intensive economic activities, and this requires long-term planning and investment in human capital. There is little evidence that these changes in the economy are taking place as yet, other than the remarkable expansion of higher education enrolments that has occurred since 1998. However, given continued rapid growth of urban employment and the rapid demographic transition that we predict, it is likely that they will increasingly be found in the coming years.

Note

1. This chapter draws on Knight et al. (2011).

References

Brandt, Loren, and Carsten Holz (2006), 'Spatial price differences in China: estimates and implications', *Economic Development and Cultural Change*, 55 (October): 43–86.

Cai Fang (2008), 'Approaching a triumphal span: how far is China towards its Lewisian turning point?', WIDER Research Paper, February.

——Du Yang, and Zhao Changbao (2007), 'Regional labour market integration since China's WTO entry: evidence from household-level data', in R. Garnaut and Song Ligang (eds.), *China: Linking Markets for Growth*, Canberra: Asia Pacific Press: 133–50.

——and Wang Meiyun (2008), 'A counterfactual of unlimited surplus labour in rural China', *China and the World Economy*, 16, 1 (January–February): 51–65.

Chen Guifu and Shigeyuki Hanori (2009), 'Solution to the dilemma of the migrant labour shortage and the rural labour surplus in China', *China and World Economy*, 17, 4 (July–August): 53–71.

Du Yang and Pan Weiguang (2009), 'Minimum wage regulation in China and its application to migrant workers in the urban labour market', *China and World Economy*, 17, 2 (March–April): 79–93.

Islam, Nazrul, and Kazuhiko Yokota (2008), 'Lewis growth model and China's industrialization', *Asian Economic Journal*, 22, 4: 359–96.

Knight, John, Deng Quheng, and Li Shi (2011), 'The puzzle of migrant labour shortage and rural labour surplus in China', *China Economic Review*, 22, 4: 585–600.

——and Ramani Gunatilaka (2010), 'Great expectations? The subjective well-being of rural–urban migrants in China', *World Development*, 38, 1 (January): 113–24.

——and Li Shi (2005), 'Wages, profitability and labour market segmentation in China', *China Economic Review*, 16, 3: 2005–28.

——and Lina Song (1999), *The Rural–Urban Divide: Economic Disparities and Interactions in China*, Oxford: Oxford University Press.

————(2005), *Towards a Labour Market in China*, Oxford: Oxford University Press.

——and Linda Yueh (2009), 'Segmentation or competition in China's urban labour market?', *Cambridge Journal of Economics*, 33, 1 (January): 79–94.

Kong, Sherry Tao, Xin Meng, and Dandan Zhang (2010), 'The global financial crisis and rural–urban migration', paper presented at the Beijing Forum, November.

Kwan Fung (2009), 'Agricultural labour and the incidence of surplus labour: experience from China during reform', *Journal of Chinese Economic and Business Studies*, 7, 3 (August): 341–61.

Lee, Leng, and Xin Meng (2010), 'Why don't more Chinese migrate from the countryside? Institutional constraints and the migration decision', in Xin Meng and Chris Manning (eds.), *The Great Migration: Rural–Urban Migration in China and Indonesia*, Cheltenham: Edward Elgar: 23–46.

Lewis, W. Arthur (1954), 'Economic development with unlimited supplies of labour', *The Manchester School*, 22 (May): 139–92.

Li Shi and Deng Quheng (2004), 'Re-estimating the unemployment rate in urban China', *Economic Information*, 4, 44–7 (in Chinese).

Minami, Riaxin, and Xinxin Ma (2009), 'The turning point of Chinese economy: compared with Japanese experience', Conference paper, ADBI, Tokyo, June.

Ministry of Agriculture (2010), 'Steady augmentation of employment of out-migrants and faster increase of wage of migrant workers', website (in Chinese) <http://www.moa.gov.cn/sjzz/jianchaju/xxjb/201001/t20100114_1829425.htm>.

National Bureau of Statistics (2006), *One Per Cent Population Survey 2005*, Beijing: China Statistics Press, and online.

——(2008), *China Statistical Yearbook 2008*, Beijing: China Statistics Press.

Park, Albert, Cai Fang, and Du Yang (2007), 'Can China meet her employment challenges?', Conference paper, Stanford University, November.

Ranis, Gustav, and John Fei (1961), 'A theory of economic development', *American Economic Review*, 51, 4 (September): 533–65.

Sheng, Laiyun (2008), *Floating or Migration? Economic Analysis of Floating Labour from Rural China*, Shanghai: Shanghai Yuan Dong Press (in Chinese).

Taylor, Jeffrey (1988), 'Rural employment trends and the legacy of surplus labour', *China Quarterly*, 116 (December): 736–66.

Wang Dewen (2008), 'Lewisian turning point: Chinese experience', in Cai Fang (ed.), *Reports on Chinese Population and Growth No. 9: Linking up Lewis and Kuznets Turning Points*, Beijing: Social Sciences Academic Press (in Chinese).

Zhao Changbao and Wu Zhigang (2007), 'Wage issues of rural migrants', Working Paper, Research Centre of Rural Economy, Ministry of Agriculture (in Chinese) <http://www.rcre.cn/userArticle/ArticleFile/2007121015627344.doc>.

Zhao Yaohui (1999), 'Labor migration and earnings differences: the case of rural China', *Economic Development and Cultural Change*, 47, 4 (July): 767–82.

10

Economic Growth and Inequality

10.1 Introduction

In 1978 China had a communist government in substance as well as name, a centrally planned economy, low productivity, widespread poverty, and extremely low inequality. Such inequality as then existed was spatial in character, reflecting the lack of factor mobility among localities and between rural and urban areas. The last three decades have witnessed three great and closely related events: a gradual-ist transition from central planning towards markets, a remarkable rate of economic growth, and a dramatic rise in economic inequality.

Of course, it is not surprising that inequality rose from its initial low level, as the economy became marketized and as egalitarianism ceased to be a central plank of economic policy. But China now has an unequal society—not rivalling the extreme inequality found in (say) Brazil or South Africa, but nevertheless worse than or on a par with other parts of developing Asia. For instance, a study by the Asian Development Bank (2007: figure 1) finds China's income inequality to be the joint highest (with Nepal) among the twenty-one Asian countries that are compared.

There is a vast literature, both theoretical and empirical, on the relationships between economic development and economic inequality, summarized in Chapter 2. Kuznets (1955) postulated an inverted U-shaped relationship: as mean income grows, so the inequality of income per capita first rises, eventually peaks, and then declines. The main theoretical reasons for expecting an initial rise are the growth in the importance of the modern, or urban, sector of the economy, with its higher income and greater inequality, and the emergence of inequality based on possession of financial, physical, and human capital. The main reasons for expecting an eventual decline are that the low-income rural sector becomes a minority, that market scarcity drives up the returns to relatively unskilled labour, and that the broad socio-economic groups that emerge with economic development acquire the political power to press for redistribution and the creation of a welfare state. The cross-country evidence for the inverted U-shaped relationship is actually very weak (Anand and Kanbur 1993a, 1993b). Kanbur (1997) has argued for country case studies as a better way of understanding the complex relationships between economic development and economic inequality. It is therefore an important question: has China's inequality now peaked and started to fall?

Is China's economic growth responsible for its rise in inequality? The fact that economic reform and economic growth have gone hand in hand means that it is difficult to distinguish their effects on inequality. Indeed, it is arguably not sensible even to attempt to separate their effects, because the rapid economic growth was itself largely a consequence of the reform policies.

There are many dimensions of inequality besides household income per capita. Other contributors to economic welfare include wealth, housing, education, health care, social security, subjective well-being, and what Sen (1984) has called people's 'capabilities' to be and to do things of intrinsic worth. We choose to concentrate on income inequality but refer occasionally to other dimensions of inequality.

In Section 10.2 we examine the extent to which the inequality of income has risen. Section 10.3 analyses the rising inequality of wealth. Section 10.4 asks how the rise in income inequality affects poverty alleviation. We explore the main components of rising inequality by focusing on urban inequality (Section 10.5), rural inequality (Section 10.6), and spatial inequality (Section 10.7). This leads on in Section 10.8 to an examination of some policy issues. Section 10.9 concludes.[1]

10.2 The Rise in Inequality

The annual nationwide household income and expenditure survey conducted by the National Bureau of Statistics (NBS) is not available to researchers at disaggregated household and individual level. Measures of income inequality such as the Gini coefficient, when derived from official statistics, therefore have to be based on province-level or percentile data. However, there is another source: a national household survey designed and conducted by the Institute of Economics, Chinese Academy of Social Sciences (CASS), in conjunction with foreign scholars including one of the authors, with research hypotheses in mind. This has been conducted periodically: in 1988, 1995, 2002, and 2007. We draw heavily on the results of research done within this China Household Income Project (CHIP) and based on these surveys.

Because of the sharp administrative and economic divide between urban and rural China, and the need for different survey questionnaires, Table 10.1, based on the CHIP surveys, presents three Gini coefficients for each year, corresponding to urban, rural, and total households. Recall that the Gini coefficient is an aggregate measure of income inequality, varying in value from 0 (complete equality) to 1 (complete inequality); it is sometimes expressed as a percentage. There are many

Table 10.1. Gini coefficients of disposable income per capita, urban, rural and all households, China, 1988, 1995, 2002, and 2007, CHIP surveys

	Urban	Rural	National
1988	0.244	0.325	0.398
1995	0.339	0.364	0.469
2002	0.322	0.365	0.468
2002	0.328	0.358	0.456
2007	0.338	0.363	0.481

Note: the first three rows are taken from the former source and the last two from the latter.
Source: Gustafsson et al. (2007c: table 2.2); Li et al. (2011: tables 2, 4, 7).

other measures of income dispersion but the Gini coefficient suffices for our purposes. Being very commonly estimated, it has the advantage that it can be used for comparative analysis.

The first three rows of Table 10.1 are taken from Gustafsson et al. (2007b). This permits a comparison across fourteen years using consistent data. Only those provinces present in the urban samples of each survey are included, and correspondingly for the rural samples; there is careful weighting of provinces and of rural and urban areas to obtain representative measures of inequality. The definition of income, again consistent over time, follows the NBS definition but adds housing subsidy and imputed rents. Only urban *hukou* residents are included in the urban survey and rural *hukou* residents in the rural survey.

In 1988 the urban Gini coefficient was very low by international standards (0.244), the rural Gini was higher (0.325), reflecting regional income disparities, and the national Gini was higher than either (0.395), reflecting the high ratio of urban to rural income per capita. Over the seven years 1988–95, all three Gini coefficients rose; the national Gini was 0.469 in 1995. However, the trend was not continued over the next seven years. In 2002 the urban Gini (0.322) was nearly two percentage points lower than in 1995, the rural Gini (0.365) was effectively the same as it had been in 1995, and the national Gini also remained constant, at 0.468.

The final two rows of Table 10.1, drawn from Li et al. (2011), make a consistent comparison of the years 2002 and 2007. Accordingly, we show two sets of Gini coefficients for 2002, taken from the two different sources. The second estimate is slightly higher for the urban sample but slightly lower for the rural sample and for China as a whole. The differences arise because of differences in the weighting of the samples and the use, in the second estimate, of a deflator to adjust for spatial differences in the cost of living. We see that the urban Gini rose by one percentage point to 0.338 over the five years, and the rural Gini rose half a percentage point to 0.363. The national Gini (0.481) was no less than 2.5 percentage points higher in 2007 than in 2002, partly on account of the continued rise in the ratio of urban to rural mean income.

Table 10.2. Gini coefficients of income per capita, urban, rural and all households, China, 1988, 1995, and 2001, NBS surveys

	Urban	Rural	Total	
			Adjustment for COL difference:	
			Without	With
1988	0.210	0.297	0.330	0.295
1995	0.283	0.340	0.415	0.365
2001	0.323	0.365	0.447	0.395

Source: Ravallion and Chen (2007: table 10).

Whether income inequality stopped rising in China after the mid-1990s is clearly an important question. Both fact and feeling are relevant. The public perception of urban inequality is that it continued to rise. Respondents in the 2002 urban survey were asked how inequality had changed in their city over the previous five years. Offered a choice of five answers, over 90% reported that it had widened, 48% saying 'slightly' and 43% 'notably' (Gustafsson et al. 2007c: 44). Moreover, Ravallion and Chen (2007), of the World Bank, having partial access to the NBS micro-level data, found that the Gini continued to rise in the years 1995–2001 (Table 10.2). Over those six years, all three Gini coefficients increased, by four percentage points in the urban case, over two percentage points in the rural case, and over three percentage points in the national case; their estimate of the national Gini in 2001 was 0.447. The authors show two estimates of national inequality—one without and one with income adjusted for differences in the cost of living. They adjust on the basis of the estimated cost of the basket of goods purchased by poor people in urban and rural areas and the official urban and rural price indexes. The adjustment reduces national inequality in each year because it squeezes the urban–rural income ratio. However, it makes very little difference to the size of the increase in the Gini coefficient over the period.

The annual *China Statistical Yearbook* of the NBS provides information on income shares of household income quintiles in urban China, from which it is possible to explore whether inequality (as measured in the NBS surveys) continued to rise beyond 2001. Table 10.3 confirms that inequality grew in the late 1990s and suggests that it did so again in the 2000s. The share of the first three quintiles falls monotonically over the period 2000–8, whereas that of the highest quintile grows sharply: its share increases by 5.9 percentage points. There is no indication here that urban inequality stopped rising.

Why do the CHIP and NBS data sources produce different answers? The main reason is that they have different concepts of income. The NBS definition excludes the imputed value of owner-occupied housing and undercounts subsidies, including housing subsidies, whereas the CHIP definition includes housing-related income components and more fully captures subsidies. These components of income disproportionately accrue to urban households, which are relatively rich.

Table 10.3. Income by household income quintile, urban China, 1995, 2000, 2008, percentage of total, NBS surveys

Quintile	1	2	3	4	5
Percentage share:					
1995	11.1	15.2	18.5	22.6	32.6
2000	9.7	14.2	18.1	23.0	35.0
2008	8.5	13.3	17.2	22.5	38.5
Change in share:					
1995–2000	−1.4	−1.0	−0.4	+0.4	+2.4
2000–08	−2.6	−1.9	−1.3	−0.1	−5.9

Notes: We obtain quintile income shares by multiplying income per capita in each quintile by household size. It is not possible to provide similar information for rural China without making several assumptions.
Source: NBS (annual), various issues.

This explains why the CHIP-based estimates of the national and urban Gini coefficients tend to be higher than the NBS-based estimates. Moreover, the importance of these income components has declined in recent years. This helps to explain why the CHIP-based Gini did not rise between 1995 and 2002. A recalculation of the CHIP data using the NBS definition does indeed produce an increase in the Gini between 1995 and 2002 of 1.6 percentage points; and a value in 2002 of 0.452—very close to the NBS-based estimate for 2001 (Gustafsson et al. 2007b: 20–1).

The withdrawal of subsidies has a misleading implication. The most important urban subsidy, the housing subsidy, was merely capitalized: the housing subsidy was reduced after 1995 because urban houses were sold to their occupants at prices well below the prices that would have prevailed had there been a housing market. Zhao and Ding (2007: tables 5.5, 5.7, and 5.8) show that, in 2002, the ratio of current market price to purchase price of houses averaged over 7 to 1, and that the net value of housing represented 64% of total wealth and contributed 67% to the inequality of net wealth per capita in urban China.

The various estimates of income discussed above are for disposable income, that is, after taxes paid to and benefits received from central and local governments. In fact, net taxes do nothing to remedy factor income inequality and little to remedy its growth, either between rural and urban China or within these two sectors. Khan and Riskin (2007) show that net taxes reduced rural income per capita by 2.6% in 2002. However, although regressive in 1995 (accounting for 2% of total rural inequality as measured by the Gini coefficient) net taxes became slightly progressive (contributing –1%) in 2002. By contrast, subsidies exceeded taxes in urban China, despite the greater prosperity of urban-dwellers. Net subsidies (mainly housing) accounted for 11% of income per capita in 1995 but fell to 2% in 2002. The contribution of net subsidies to urban inequality was 16% of the total in 1995 but only 1% in 2002: from being strongly regressive, fiscal intervention became only mildly so. However, there remains great scope for a more progressive fiscal policy.

10.3 Inequality of Wealth

During the period of central planning there was almost no personal wealth in China. Starting from scratch, economic reform brought with it, in just a few years, not only the rapid accumulation of wealth but also considerable inequality of wealth. China thus provides an excellent case study of the processes that generate inequality of wealth. We draw on the research in Zhao and Ding (2007), which used the CHIP data sets.

Urban real (net) wealth grew at a rate of no less than 19% per annum between 1995 and 2002. In the latter year urban wealth per capita was 4.7 times urban income per capita, and the equivalent rural figure was 3.9. The ratio of urban to rural wealth per capita was 3.6:1.

The Gini coefficient of wealth per capita in China as a whole in 2002 was 0.550—considerably higher than that of income per capita. The rural Gini had risen from 0.351 in 1995 to 0.399 in 2002. The main contribution to this inequality was housing (accounting for 49% of the total in 2002). Although the imputed value of land (held on long leases) contributed a further 20%, the policy of allocating village land equitably ensured that the inequality of land reflected spatial differences in land endowments rather than localized inequality. The Gini coefficient of urban wealth per capita was 0.496 in 1995 and 0.475 in 2002. The most important contribution came from housing (accounting for 68% of the inequality in 2002) and financial assets (24%). We see the great importance of housing both for accumulating wealth (urban housing wealth grew by 22% per annum over the seven-year period) and also for generating inequality of wealth.[2] Urban-dwellers who acquired ownership of the houses that they had occupied (paying nominal rents) made huge capital gains. The inequality of wealth in turn feeds the inequality of income through the returns to wealth assets such as imputed rents of owner-occupied houses.

More generally, the acquisition or appropriation of state assets at below-market prices was a powerful disequalizing force, which central and local governments in some cases aided and abetted and in other cases failed to prevent (Yu 2008). The divergence of wealth was also assisted by the fact that the household saving rate rises sharply with income. For instance, the 1995 CHIP survey showed the urban saving rate to rise monotonically from –2% in the lowest income per capita decile to 35% in the highest; the corresponding rural rates were 3% and 41% respectively (Shi 2007).

10.4 The Rise in Inequality and the Relation to Poverty

In the twenty years between 1981 and 2001 real household income per person increased on average by 5.8% per annum in urban China, 5.4% in rural China, and

Table 10.4. Measures of poverty for urban, rural, and all households, per cent, 1981, 1988, 1995, and 2001, NBS surveys

	Urban		Rural		Total	
	HC	PG	HC	PG	HC	PG
1981	6.0	1.0	64.7	20.0	52.8	16.2
1988	2.1	0.5	23.2	5.5	17.7	4.2
1995	0.9	0.2	20.4	5.7	14.7	4.1
2001	0.5	0.2	12.5	3.3	8.0	2.1

Note: The headcount measure of poverty (HC) is defined as the percentage of households that fall below the official set poverty line, and indicates the relative number of poor people. The poverty gap measure (PG) is defined as the ratio of income needed to get all poor people up to the poverty line to income as a whole, and provides an indication of the relative resources required to eradicate poverty. The poverty line is officially set at 850 yuan per person per year in 2002 prices for rural China, and at 1,200 yuan for urban China.

Source: Ravallion and Chen (2007: tables 2, 3, 4).

(with reweighting) 6.5% overall (Ravallion and Chen 2007: table 1). On the one hand, this rapid growth of incomes had the power to reduce poverty dramatically. On the other hand, the rising inequality tended to increase poverty. There were two counteracting forces, the rise in mean income and the rise in dispersion of income around the mean. In fact, the former proved much more powerful.

Table 10.4, taken from Ravallion and Chen (2007), shows poverty (as defined by government) declining sharply over the years, whether we use the headcount measure (HC) or the poverty gap index (PG). HC is the proportion of households that fall below the income per capita equal to the poverty line; it indicates the human scale of the problem. PG is the income needed to get all poor households up to the poverty line expressed as a ratio to income as a whole; it indicates the relative resources needed to eliminate poverty.

The great fall in rural poverty occurred in the early period of decollectivization and rural reform, from 1978 to 1985. However, rural poverty incidence and intensity continued to fall beyond 1985, despite rising inequality. Urban poverty has been low, reflecting the protected and privileged status of urban-dwellers. Nevertheless, research based on a 1999 CASS urban household survey that examined the effects of the massive redundancy programme in the state sector, commencing in the mid-1990s, shows that urban poverty became closely associated with unemployment or layoff. Individuals who were unemployed or *xia gang* (laid off), or whose household heads suffered that status, had a predicted probability of falling into poverty that was between three and six times higher on that account (Li 2006).

10.5 The Components of Rising Inequality: Urban Income

There are several dimensions of rising inequality, and various forms of decomposition analysis are required to measure their contributions. We start with urban income inequality. Under central planning the work unit (*danwei*) served as a mini welfare state, providing lifetime employment, housing, pensions, and medical care to its members. Workers were allocated to work units bureaucratically and wages were determined administratively. The urban wage structure was highly egalitarian. Movement from one work unit to another was extremely rare, and rural–urban migration was very limited. The slow evolutionary movement towards the formation of a labour market is analysed and explained in Knight and Song (2005).

The 1988 survey, conducted near the start of the urban reform process, reflected the administered and egalitarian labour system of the time. The Gini coefficient of urban wages grew continuously as reform progressed. It rose from the low value of 0.23 in 1988 to 0.31 in 1995 (Knight and Song 2007: 222). Table 10.5 shows the percentage changes from one survey to the next. Whereas the median real wage rose by 6% per annum over this period, the corresponding percentages for the (lowest) tenth and ninetieth percentiles were 1 and 8% respectively. Wage inequality continued to grow over the period 1995–2002: the Gini coefficient increased by an additional five percentage points, to 0.37. Between those years the hourly real wage rose by 7% per annum at the median, 5% per annum at the tenth percentile, and 8% per annum at the ninetieth percentile. Given extreme disequilibrium in the urban labour market in 1988, this rise in wage inequality probably represented a move towards the market equilibrium rather than a movement of the market equilibrium.

The wage premium of a college degree over primary schooling was 9% in 1988, 39% in 1995, and 88% in 2002; for completion of secondary school the corresponding figures were 4, 17, and 42% respectively. A very similar story can be told about occupation-specific skills. Some of the widening wage structure represents rewards for productivity and incentives for efficiency. Thus, for instance, the rising returns to education, the greater premia in skill-based occupations, and the more bowed inverse-U-shaped wage-experience profile may well represent the stirring of market forces rewarding productivity.

Table 10.5. Measures of central tendency and dispersion of the wage per worker at constant prices, urban China, 1988, 1995, and 2002, CHIP surveys

	Annual wage 1995 (1988 = 100)	Hourly wage 2002 (1995 = 100)
Mean	152	168
Median	148	158
10th percentile	106	137
90th percentile	175	175
Gini coefficient	134	114

Source: Knight and Song (2007: table 9.1).

On the other hand, there is evidence of greater wage discrimination (against women, and in favour of CCP members) and also of considerable wage segmentation, which is difficult to justify in terms either of efficiency or of equity. The segmentation takes three main forms: segmentation by province, segmentation by type of ownership (with foreign firms paying most, then state enterprises, and local private firms paying least), and segmentation by profitability of enterprise. This last form can be explained in terms of the *danwei* sharing profits informally with its urban employees (Knight and Li 2005). Although many urban *hukou* workers are members of trade unions, the trade unions are subordinate to government and controlled by government: they have few of the rights and powers that trade unions in most countries possess. Nevertheless, it is possible that workers or their trade union representatives within an enterprise press for a share of rising profits, and that their employers see informal profit sharing as a way to secure cooperation and maintain morale.

A decomposition of the growth of wage inequality between 1988 and 1995 showed that increased wage segmentation by province made the greatest contribution to that growth. An equivalent decomposition for the next seven years found that segmentation by province, although still important, made a negative contribution to the growth of wage inequality. However, another form of segmentation—by ownership type—did make a positive contribution (Knight and Song 2007: table 9.5).

In summary, there is a good deal of support for the hypothesis that the rewards for productive characteristics rose during this period of growing labour market competition. However, the evidence also suggests that, owing to institutional arrangements and immobility of labour, the labour market became more segmented—across firms, across regions, and probably also between urban and rural *hukou* workers. Both trends have contributed to rising inequality in the urban labour market.

A rich entrepreneurial class has emerged remarkably rapidly in China—there were large supernormal profits to be earned. The combination of semi-marketized economy, weak legal system, and ill-defined or insecure property rights provides great scope for corruption, cronyism, rent-seeking, and appropriation of state assets. Corruption is a major concern of Chinese citizens as reported in public opinion surveys, especially where people are directly affected, such as in the provision of health services or the inadequately compensated loss of land. However, not all income derived from rent seeking or corruption is detectable in the household surveys. Both the NBS and CHIP surveys may understate incomes at the top of the income distribution. One reason is the tendency for rich households to avoid inclusion in the NBS samples, either because of their higher opportunity cost or because they have more things to hide. The other is the tendency for rich households, if they are included, to under-report their incomes.

An ingenious method has been devised to measure the latter effect (Wang and Woo 2011). The argument is that people have an incentive not to report 'grey income', that is, illegal, corrupt, or dubious income, often reflecting the rents accruing to people with power over resource allocation in a semi-marketized economy. The hypothesis is that households with high legitimate income have greater opportunities to obtain grey income. To test this hypothesis, professional interviewers were employed to interview 2,000 households in the normal way in several cities in 2005. The methodological trick was to get them to select only households whom they knew, either as relatives or friends, in the expectation that such people would be more honest in their answers to interviewers who were close to them. The authors also had access to the corresponding income and expenditure information in the 2005 NBS urban household survey. The latter sample, ranked by income per capita, was divided into seven groups. The Engel coefficient (food consumption as a proportion of total consumption) and the mean income per capita of households in each group were calculated. It was assumed that the Engel coefficient could be measured without bias. The expected monotonic inverse relationship between the Engel coefficient and mean income per capita was found across the groups. Wang and Woo divided their own sample, ranked by income per capita, into seven groups so that each group had the same Engel coefficient as the corresponding group in the NBS sample. They then compared mean income per capita of the corresponding groups. The ratio of income per capita in the small survey to that in the NBS survey rose monotonically, from 1.1 in the lowest income group and to 3.2 in the highest. It is in the highest income group in particular that under-reporting occurs. Income inequality among urban households is likely to be underestimated for this reason. Although the methodology is open to criticism (Li 2008: 160), an alternative estimate implies that correction for the under-reporting of high incomes would raise the urban Gini by eight percentage points and the national Gini by five percentage points (Li et al. 2011: fn. 14)

Estimates of urban income inequality in China are much complicated by the presence of rural–urban migrants. Ever since urban economic reform commenced in the mid-1980s, China has experienced what has come to be known as 'the greatest migration in human history'. In 1990 there were probably about 20 million rural migrants present in the urban areas, whereas in 2006 there were probably about 130 million. The driving force was the rapid growth of demand for labour in urban areas and the slow growth of the urban-born supply of labour. The residence registration (*hukou*) system ensured that migration was generally channelled and controlled to meet the growing urban demand. It was difficult for rural *hukou* holders to acquire urban residence rights. Much of their migration, especially to the large cities, was temporary and based on one-year employment contracts. Many of these migrants retained close links with their rural households, expecting to return, and normally returning, to the village after their urban sojourn.

Temporary migration poses a problem for the estimation of household income per capita and of income inequality among households. Rural–urban migrants who are not accompanied by their families can be regarded as remaining part of their rural households. Their income should accordingly be attributed to that household. In fact, it is likely that only income remittances can be accurately measured in the rural survey. In the past, the population censuses recorded temporary migrants as resident in their place of *hukou* registration. Only in recent years have migrants who were resident for a certain period (now more than six months) been recorded as part of the urban population. Following NBS practice, the CHIP surveys relating to 1988 and 1995 excluded rural *hukou* households from the urban sample. Breaking with NBS practice, the CHIP surveys of 2002 and 2007 added separate samples of rural–urban migrants. However, their sampling methods differed: in 2002 the sampling was household based and confined to migrant households, whereas in 2007 it was employment based and so representative of all rural–urban migrants.

These complications limit our ability to measure changes in urban income inequality. In principle the inclusion of migrants should increase the measure of urban inequality as they tend to be among the poorest in the cities. Moreover, the increasing number of migrants in urban China should raise urban income inequality.

The average income per capita of rural–urban migrant households in 2002 was higher—nearly double—that of rural households, but about 35% lower than that of urban households (Gustafsson et al. 2007c: 47). Using a six-province urban survey of 1999, Appleton et al. (2004: table 1) found that the median wage of migrants was 54% of the median for (non-retrenched) urban *hukou* workers. However, a measure of the extent of labour market segmentation between urban and migrant workers requires standardization for productive characteristics. On that basis, Appleton et al. (2004: table 3) estimated that migrants received 75% of the urban wage. With the migrants being at an economic disadvantage, the presence of migrant households raises urban inequality—provided, of course, that they are included in the urban household surveys. The 2002 CHIP survey is the first national survey to permit estimation of urban inequality with migrants both excluded (the usual practice) and included. Khan and Riskin (2007: tables 3.6, 3.7, 3.10) estimate the urban Gini coefficient for household income per capita to be 0.318 when rural–urban migrant households are excluded and 0.338 when they are included; migrant households themselves have a Gini of 0.380. However, these figures understate the effect of migrants in raising urban income inequality because most of the rural–urban migrants—those not living in households— were not recorded in the 2002 survey. A comparable or even similar exercise is not available for 2007.

10.6 The Components of Rising Inequality: Rural Income

Evidence from the 1995 CHIP survey shows the importance of non-farm employ-ment for rural household incomes and for rural income inequality. Wages ac-counted for 21% of rural income inequality in 1988 (contributing seven percentage points to the Gini) and for 44% (contributing nineteen percentage points) in 1995 (Knight and Song 2001: table 4.6). Wages rose from being 11% to being 26% of rural incomes over the seven years. The contribution of wages to the rise in the Gini actually exceeded the total rise. It is clear that access to individual labour income was then the key to higher income for the household.

Rural income inequality either grew more slowly (according to the NBS data of Table 10.2) or stagnated (according to the CHIP data of Table 10.1) between 1995 and 2002. Why the deceleration or stagnation? Over that period the share of wages in rural income rose again, to 30%. However, the contribution of wages to rural inequality fell slightly, from 40% to 37% of the total (Khan and Riskin 2007: table 3.3). Thus, wages became less disequalizing. The authors suggest that this is because the growth of wage employment reduced spatial, especially provincial, inequality of access to wage employment, and regard it as an important reason why they found no rise in the rural Gini coefficient.

Whereas the main absorber of the growing rural labour force in the 1980s was rural industry, since 1990 it has been rural–urban migration, much of it temporary in nature. Temporary migration has two main effects on rural income inequality. Migrant remittances should raise rural incomes and thus reduce the urban–rural income disparity. Within rural areas, the effect on inequality depends on who migrates. The really poor may not have the education, or the funds, or the con-tacts, to migrate. However, such studies as have been made of this issue suggest that, in the Chinese case, migration has an equalizing effect on rural income distribution (for instance, Knight and Song 1999: ch. 9).

Luo and Yue (2010) used the 2007 CHIP survey to examine the effect of migra-tion on rural poverty. Equations were estimated to predict whether a household was in poverty, including as an explanatory variable whether the household contained a migrant worker. Being potentially endogenous, this variable was instrumented with village migration intensity. Household membership of mi-grants was weighted by the proportion of the year that the migrant spent at home. It was found that migrant households had higher average consumption per capita, and that households with a migrant were significantly less likely to be in poverty. The more time the migrant spent working away, the greater this effect. It is likely that migration helps to reduce not only rural poverty but also rural income inequality.

A comparison of the 2002 and 2007 CHIP rural surveys shows that real income per capita from migration grew at 17% per annum, and that its share of rural household income increased from 11% to 18%. Its contribution to rural income inequality increased from 9% to 15%, whereas that of local wage income fell from 35% to 26% (Li et al. 2011: tables 1, 2). Because the former income source has a more equal distribution than rural income as a whole, the effect of its expanding share is actually to reduce rural inequality. Because the latter source has a less equal distribution than rural income as a whole, its declining share also reduces rural inequality. By contrast, the growing importance and high inequality of property income helps to explain the slight rise in the rural Gini coefficient over those five years.

The effects of the newly introduced 'harmonious society' policies were also observable. The rural tax rate fell from 2.9% in 2002 to 0.3% in 2007, and became less regressive. Poor households were three times more likely than the non-poor to receive 'minimum living level' payments (*dibao*) in 2007. Nevertheless, coverage was limited: over 90% of the poor did not receive *dibao* (Luo and Sicular 2011: tables 13, 18).

10.7 The Components of Rising Inequality: Spatial Income

We begin with the rural–urban divide, studied in Knight and Song (1999). There has been a very wide ratio of urban to rural income per capita throughout the communist period. It narrowed during the period of decollectivization and rural reform 1978–85, but since urban economic reform commenced in the mid-1980s the ratio (with rural income = 100) has grown, and it was greater (at 331) in 2008 than it had ever been (Table 10.6). This is the ratio based on the NBS annual household surveys. The table also shows the ratio derived from the CHIP household surveys, which is higher on account of their broader definition of income. However, it also rises over time, reaching no less than 410 in 2007.

Table 10.6. The ratio of urban to rural household income per capita, rural = 100, 1978–2008, NBS and CHIP surveys

	NBS	CHIP
1978	257	
1985	186	
1988	217	269
1990		
1995	271	308
2000	278	
2002	311	335
2007		410
2008	331	

Sources: NBS (2004: 357); Gustafsson et al. (2007c); Li et al. (2011: tables 1, 3).

Table 10.5 shows the simple ratios of nominal income per capita. However, the cost of living differs across provinces and it is higher in urban than in rural China. For instance, Ravallion and Chen (2007: table 1) report that the urban cost of living was 19% higher than the rural in 1981, and that this rose to 40% in 2001. Brandt and Holz (2006) estimated province, rural and urban costs of living, and on that basis adjusted the NBS income ratio. The urban cost of living was 24% higher in 1990, and 40% in 2000. The real ratio was 178 in 1990 (when the nominal ratio was 220) and it was 199 in 2000 (nominal ratio 278).

Using the CHIP 2002 data set, Sicular et al. (2005: table 1) show that the ratio of urban to rural household income per capita (rural income = 100) is reduced from 335 to 240 by introducing Brandt–Holz purchasing power parity. However, Li (2008: 159) points out that the additional inclusion of in-kind subsidies such as subsidized pension schemes and health care, which are received largely by urban residents, raises the ratio to 435, so bringing it back to more than the initial figure of 335. Thus in-kind subsidies effectively neutralize the narrowing effect of cost of living differences on urban–rural income inequality.

The upward trend in the ratio of urban to rural income per capita has helped to increase the contribution that the ratio makes to national income inequality. The contribution rose from 37% in 1988, to 41% in 1995, to 46% in 2002, and to a remarkable 54% in 2007, far higher than for other developing countries in which similar decompositions have been conducted (Gustafsson et al. 2007b: table 1.2; Li et al. 2011: table 8). About half of China's income inequality would vanish if mean income per capita in rural and urban China were equal.

How is the rural–urban divide to be explained? The high ratio was understandable under central planning, when the CCP built an institutional framework which divided China into two compartments, separate in terms of administration, financing, and resources. The policy of 'price scissors' kept down the price of food in relation to manufactures. In that way the peasants paid indirectly for urban industrialization. Part of the investible surplus was diverted to enable urban workers to enjoy a higher standard of living than their rural counterparts. Worker discontent, low morale, and threat to political stability are all aspects of the power—latent rather than overt in the case of China—which residentially concentrated, interacting workers appear to possess.

The rural–urban divide survived and even grew as the 'invisible Great Wall' which separated rural and urban China was partly dismantled. As the economy became more marketized, why were the returns to factors not equalized across space? Why did the rural–urban income gap not get competed away? The answer lies mainly in the government control of migration. Migrant workers were permitted to meet the growing needs of the urban economy but urban workers continued to receive preference—in employment, wages, housing, social security, etc.—while migrants were treated as second class citizens. The real wages of urban *hukou* residents have increased rapidly along with urban economic reform and rapid urban economic growth, being shielded from the labour market competition of rural labour.

Income divergence across regions of China is another source of growing inequality. Two counteracting forces are in operation. Processes of cumulative causation can create 'growth poles' and so increase spatial inequality, whereas processes involving 'spill-overs' and 'spread effects' can reduce it. The former is likely to hold sway in the initial stages of development but will eventually give way to the latter, as competitive advantages are eroded by rising costs.

Regional inequality in China has attracted a good deal of research, using conventional tests of absolute or conditional convergence or divergence. The results have been rather mixed, depending on the data set, the dependent variable, the unit of observation, and the time period. Nevertheless, there is much evidence of absolute divergence among provinces. Standardizing for the other determinants of income growth, conditional convergence—a prediction of economic growth theory—is also commonly found, as it was in Chapter 5 above. For instance, Lau (2010), testing for absolute and conditional trends in income per capita among provinces over the period 1978–2005, found absolute divergence and conditional convergence. However, economic welfare—the common objective of economic policy—is dependent on absolute trends.

Consider first the urban economy. There is evidence of powerful absolute divergence in urban income per capita and in urban wages among provinces and among cities over the period 1988–95 (Knight et al. 2001). This is partly the result of regional comparative advantage, but it also reflects weak government regional equalization policy, imperfect capital markets, and continued restrictions on the mobility of labour. The coastal provinces gained not only from their advantageous location but also from initial preferential policies on FDI and exports and from the growth of tax revenues as their development proceeded. There is some indication that there have been elements of spatial convergence or at least stability since 1995. The same exercise is not available for the 1995–2002 period, but Gustafsson et al. (2007c: table 2.9) found that the percentage of inequality in urban China that is due to between-province inequality fell from 29% in 1988 to 26% in 1995 and to 19% in 2002. The main gain came from within eastern China, where this more developed regional economy was becoming more spatially integrated.

Turning to the rural economy, Gustafsson et al. (2007c: table 2.9) find that the contribution of between-province inequality to rural income inequality rose from 22% in 1988 to 39% in 1995 and remained at 39% in 2002. We learn about the mechanisms at work from a microcosm of rural society, the village. A small survey of seven villages in two counties in Hebei province raised a fascinating question: how can villages which are so close together geographically be so far apart economically? Knight and Li (1997) developed an answer in terms of factor immobility and processes of cumulative causation. People cannot move freely among villages: each village is self-contained. Insiders have property rights, broadly interpreted, to village resources, and preclude others from sharing those rights. Institutional and informational problems segment capital markets, making the village itself the main source of funds for investment. Informational imperfections limit business and technical skill acquisition from outside. The village cannot rely much on the receipt of external public funds.

It is possible for a minority of villages to develop on the basis of fertile land that permits a prosperous agriculture, but the majority must rely on non-agricultural sources of development. One possibility is migration, but the opportunities may be limited owing to the costs and risks involved. They can be expanded if the village can build up a social network of migrant contacts, which reduce informational and transaction costs. In that way migration from the village breeds more migration. The other possibility is the development of village industry. Here the important thing is to overcome the entrepreneurial and capital constraints. A good natural resource base helps. However, the development of village industry is very much a process that builds on itself through the generation of profits for reinvestment and of new skills via learning by doing. Funds for infrastructure investment depend on village taxable capacity, which in turn depends on the extent of village industry. Path-dependent processes thus operate to propel some village economies forward and to hold some back.

At some point spread effects take over. The further growth of the more developed villages will be retarded by shortages of labour and land and rising costs, and the less developed villages may benefit from the consequent positive feedbacks. With the rapid growth of urban China, the greater opportunities for rural–urban migration may also have assisted the poorer villages to kick-start the development process.

10.8 Rising Inequality: the Policy Issues

Some of the rise in inequality was inevitable as the central planning system was dissolved and marketization occurred. However, some of the rise was due to the government's policy stance. Partly as a reaction to the egalitarianism of the past, wherever there was a trade-off, efficiency considerations took priority over equity considerations. Government long-term strategy is well summed up in the words of a high official, Du Runsheng (1989: 192): 'prosperity to few, then to many, then to all'.

We give three examples of how government has chosen to trade equity for efficiency. One is regional policy. The most efficient location for most foreign direct investment is on the eastern seaboard. However, for a long time. FDI was required to locate there and prohibited from locating elsewhere. This gave the initially favoured areas a head start. Under central planning there was a substantial progressive provincial tax and transfer system that redistributed revenue from the richer to the poorer provinces. This redistribution was much weakened under economic reform, as each province relied increasingly on its own so-called 'extra-budgetary' revenue and expenditure (Knight and Li 1999). There was a reform of the fiscal system in 1994, intended to strengthen central government control of tax revenues. Nevertheless, public resources continued to be closely related to the level of local economic development. Richer areas have more revenues and are better able to provide public services and invest in local infrastructure. This worsens the spatial distribution of income. At the local rural level, villages, townships and counties are generally expected to 'pull themselves up by their own bootstraps'. This degree of fiscal decentralization contributes to spatial inequality, and can produce poverty traps, for instance with regard to the quantity and quality of primary and secondary education (Knight et al. 2009, 2010). Spatial inequalities could be reduced if the national and the provincial governments were to adopt less decentralized and more equalizing fiscal arrangements. In this case, apparent efficiency is preferred to equity, but the playing field may not be sufficiently level to ensure efficiency.

A second example is the powerful urban bias which is apparent in much government policy, and which sustains and promotes the rural–urban divide (Knight et al. 2006). It is arguable that urban bias exists in China, in two senses. First, government allocates fewer resources to the rural sector than it would if it were concerned only with improving economic efficiency, as determined by shadow prices. Second, rural-dwellers receive less priority than they would if the government social welfare function made no distinction between rural and urban residence per se, and placed a greater value on additional income, the poorer the person. Underlying urban bias is the greater potential threat to political stability and government survival that urban people constitute.

Being separately administered, the rural areas are at a great fiscal disadvantage: they are largely expected to find their own revenue. Agriculture has received little policy support, and rural industry—the great success of the early reform period—has grown relatively slowly in recent years as it has lost out to urban industry. This suggests that a low weight is implicitly attached to the welfare of rural people in the government's social welfare function. It is also partly the result of both fiscal and financial market arrangements. The high degree of fiscal decentralization within the rural economy makes it difficult for poor rural people and communities to better themselves, even if there are good opportunities for them to do so. The deliberately repressed financial system, which rations credit and allocates it mainly to large state-controlled firms and does so inefficiently, imposes tight credit rationing on rural people (Chapter 8). Rural investment may therefore be sub-optimal even if judged solely by the criterion of efficiency. In this case, the urban bias policy may harm both efficiency and equity in the interests of social and political stability.

The third example is the large-scale redundancy programme in the state sector that was introduced in the mid-1990s. This was forced on government by the declining profits and rising losses of state enterprises, as a result of growing competition, which threatened economic growth and state revenues. It did not herald the end of urban bias. Indeed, the urban workers who retained their jobs enjoyed a real wage increase of some 8% per annum throughout the period of the redundancy programme. The redundant workers—more than 40 million of them—received little support and were thrown on the very tough residual labour market. These losers from economic reform were neglected: the social security previously provided by the *danwei* was tardily and inadequately replaced by more centralized systems. In this case, efficiency was achieved but without accompanying equity.

10.9 Conclusion

Our objective in this chapter has been to examine the relationship between economic growth and economic inequality. There was little point in attempting to distinguish the effects of economic reform and economic growth on inequality because economic growth was itself largely a consequence of economic reform. However, because the nature of the reform process shaped the degree of inequality, there was no mechanical relationship between economic growth and inequality. China's experience is not necessarily a guide for other countries.

On the basis of international experience, it is plausible that, with economic growth, China will eventually reach the peak of the inverted-U of the Kuznets curve, beyond which the Gini coefficient will fall. It was predictable that income inequality would grow rapidly in the early stages of economic reform, and indeed it did. The evidence for the period after 1995 is more ambiguous. The CHIP data suggested that income inequality, already high, stagnated and then rose a little, whereas the NBS data implied that inequality continued to grow. The difference may be due to the choice of income definition. Neither source provides a sure guide to the future of inequality in China.

Whether inequality in China rises or falls will depend on the balance of countervailing forces. It is clear that among the forces raising inequality in recent years are the growing importance of the rural–urban income disparity and the growth of urban wage inequality, themselves to be explained mainly by continuing labour market segmentation and by greater rewards for human capital. Among the forces reducing inequality are spread effects: the diffusion of non-farm wage employment in rural areas and some convergence in household income per capita among provinces, especially among those in the eastern region. We argued in Chapter 9 that the impending scarcity of relatively unskilled labour will be a powerful driver of inequality reduction in the future, in both rural and urban China. The government response to rising inequality when it poses a threat to social and political stability—already discernible in the recent policies to promote a 'harmonious society'—can also be a powerful force for reducing inequality.

In this chapter we have not addressed the second issue raised in Section 2.4: how does income inequality affect economic growth? China began its reform journey with very low income inequality, and yet it was able to grow rapidly. Some rise in inequality was necessary to get and to keep the process going. In the new millennium China has maintained its remarkable growth rate but with high income inequality. Some of the inequality was unnecessary to keep the process going. China's experience over the reform period suggests that the effect of inequality on growth is a very complex one, even within countries let alone across countries. Detailed country case studies are required to advance understanding of the relationship. In Chapter 12 we make a start on this, when we examine whether and how China's future economic growth is threatened by its high degree of inequality.

Notes

1. We draw on parts of Knight (2008).
2. These figures are all taken from Zhao and Ding (2007: 130, tables 5.3, 5.4, 5.8).

References

Anand, Sudhir, and Ravi Kanbur (1993a), 'The Kuznets process and the inequality-development relationship', *Journal of Development Economics*, 40: 25–52.

————(1993b), 'Inequality and development: a critique', *Journal of Development Economics*, 41: 19–43.

Appleton, Simon, John Knight, Lina Song, and Qingjie Xia (2004), 'Contrasting paradigms: segmentation and competitiveness in the formation of the Chinese labour market', *Journal of Chinese Economic and Business Studies*, 2, 3: 185–205.

Asian Development Bank (2007), *Inequality in Asia*, Manila: ADB.

Brandt, Loren, and Carsten Holz (2006), 'Spatial price differences in China: estimates and implications', *Economic Development and Cultural Change*, 5 (October): 43–86.

Du, Runsheng (1989), *China's Rural Economic Reform*, Beijing: Foreign Languages Press.

Gustafsson, Bjorn, Li Shi, and Terry Sicular (eds.) (2007a), *Inequality and Public Policy in China*, New York and Cambridge: Cambridge University Press.

—————(2007b), 'Inequality and public policy in China: issues and trends', in Gustafsson et al. (2007a), ch. 1.

—————and Yue Ximing (2007c), 'Income inequality and spatial differences in China, 1988, 1995 and 2002', in Gustafsson et al. (2007a), ch. 2.

Kanbur, Ravi (1997), 'Income and development', World Bank, word-processed, January, 1–100.

Khan, Ajit, and Carl Riskin (2007), 'Growth and distribution of household income in China between 1995 and 2002', in Gustafsson et al. (2007a), ch. 3.

Knight, John (2008), 'Reform, growth, and inequality in China', *Asian Economic Policy Review*, 3, 1 (June): 140–58.

——and Li Shi (1997), 'Cumulative causation and inequality among villages in China', *Oxford Development Studies*, 25, 2: 149–72.

————(1999), 'Fiscal decentralisation: incentives, redistribution and reform in China', *Oxford Development Studies*, 27, 1: 5–32.

————(2005), 'Wages, firm profitability and labor market segmentation in urban China', *China Economic Review*, 16: 205–28.

————and Deng Quheng (2009), 'Education and the poverty trap in rural China: setting the trap', *Oxford Development Studies*, 37, 4 (December): 311–32.

—————(2010), 'Education and the poverty trap in rural China: closing the trap', *Oxford Development Studies*, 38, 1 (March): 1–24.

————and Lina Song (2006), 'The rural–urban divide and the evolution of political economy in China', in J. Boyce, S. Cullenberg, P. Pattanaik, and R. Pollin (eds.), *Human Development in the Era of Globalization*, Cheltenham, UK and Northampton, Mass.: Edward Elgar.

——and Lina Song (1999), *The Rural–Urban Divide: Economic Disparities and Interactions in China*, Oxford: Oxford University Press.

————(2001), 'Economic growth, economic reform and rising inequality', in Carl Riskin, Zhao Renwei, and Li Shi (eds.), *China's Retreat from Equality: Income Distribution and Economic Transition*. Armonk, NY: M. E. Sharpe: 84–124.

————(2005), *Towards a Labour Market in China*, Oxford: Oxford University Press.

————(2007), 'China's emerging wage structure, 1995–2002', in Gustafsson et al. (2007a), ch. 9.

——Zhao Renwei, and Li Shi (2001), 'A spatial analysis of wages and incomes in urban China: divergent means, convergent inequality', in C. Riskin, R. Zhao, and S. Li (eds.), *China's Retreat from Equality: Income Distribution and Economic Transition*, Armonk, NY: M. E. Sharpe: 133–66.

Kuznets, Simon (1955), 'Economic growth and income inequality', *American Economic Review*, 45 (March): 1–28.

Lau, C. K. M. (2010), 'New evidence about regional income divergence in China', *China Economic Review*, 21: 295–309.

Li, Shi (2006), 'Rising poverty and its causes in urban China', in S. Li and H. Sato (eds.), *Unemployment, Inequality and Poverty in Urban China*, London and New York: Routledge.

——(2008), 'Comment on "Reform, growth and inequality in China"', *Asian Economic Policy Review*, 3, 1 (June): 159–60.

——Luo Chuliang, and Terry Sicular (2011), 'Changes in the levels, sources, and distribution of household income in China, 2002–2007', mimeo.

Luo, Chuliang, and Terry Sicular (2011), 'Inequality and poverty in China', mimeo.

——and Ximing Yue (2010), 'Rural–urban migration and poverty in China', in Xin Meng and Chris Manning (eds.), *The Great Migration: Rural–Urban Migration in China and Indonesia*, Cheltenham: Edward Elgar.

National Bureau of Statistics (NBS), People's Republic of China (annual). *China Statistical Yearbook*. Beijing: China Statistics Press.

Ravallion, Martin, and Shaohua Chen (2007), 'China's (uneven) progress against poverty', *Journal of Development Economics*, 82, 1: 1–42.

Sen, Amartya (1984), 'Rights and capabilities', in *Resources, Values and Development*. Oxford: Basil Blackwell.

Shi, Y. (2007), 'Why is China's post-1978 household saving rate so high?', M.Phil. thesis, Oxford University.

Sicular, Terry, Yue Ximing, Bjorn Gustafsson, and Li Shi (2005), 'The urban–rural gap and income inequality in China', Paper presented at the UNU-WIDER Project Meeting, 'Inequality and Poverty in China', Helsinki, August.

Wang, Xiaolu, and Wing Thye Woo (2011), 'The size and distribution of hidden household income in China', *Asian Economic Papers*, 10, 1: 1–26.

Yu, Yongding (2008),'Comment on "Reform, growth and inequality in China"', *Asian Economic Policy Review*, 3, 1 (June): 161–2.

Zhao, Renwei, and Ding Sai (2007), 'The distribution of wealth in China', in Gustafsson et al. (2007a), ch. 5.

11

Economic Growth and Happiness

11.1 Introduction

China's remarkable rate of economic growth since the start of economic reform is generally assumed to have raised the economic welfare of the Chinese people dramatically. This is regarded as self-evident from the facts that, in less than three decades, average real income per capita rose more than six times and that more than 300 million people have been lifted out of 'dollar-a-day' poverty (Ravallion and Chen 2007). Moreover, within a quarter of a century China's 'human development index' rose from 0.37 to 0.68 (UNDP 2010: table 2). For us to question whether economic growth has raised happiness in China appears either absurd or disingenuous.

Nevertheless, starting from the pioneering work of Easterlin (1974), economists have increasingly asked this question of advanced economies. It has been shown that, in several advanced economies—including the United States, Japan, the United Kingdom, France, Germany, Italy, and the Netherlands—income per capita rose consistently over one or more decades and yet the mean subjective well-being score remained roughly constant (for instance, Blanchflower and Oswald 2004; Easterlin 1995, 2001). By contrast, Stevenson and Wolfers (2008) report a cross-country equation indicating that, within countries over time but given a common slope, happiness increases with income. However, a re-specification allowing country slopes to differ produces an average value of the country coefficients that is negative albeit not significantly so (Krueger 2008: 99). There is indeed something odd to be explained.

Very few such studies have apparently been made for developing countries, probably owing to a lack of relevant time-series data on subjective well-being. However, one would expect that the happiness of people in poor countries is determined in a different way. For instance, it is arguable that the greatest concern of poor people is to meet their basic physical needs for food, shelter, and clothing, whereas non-poor people are more concerned with their position and achievement in relation to society. Thus, absolute income might be important to happiness at low levels of income but relative income might be more important at higher levels.

Could the findings for the advanced economies be true also for China? Although the lack of appropriate data prevents us from exploring the issue directly, we approach it indirectly on the basis of four papers reporting research on subjective well-being in China by means of a national household survey (Knight et al. 2009; Knight and Gunatilaka 2009, 2010a, 2010b).[1] We begin with some background evidence on subjective well-being (we use the terms subjective well-being, happiness, and satisfaction with life interchangeably).

11.2 Background on Subjective Well-Being

Kahneman and Krueger (2006) present a graph obtained from the Gallup Organization, which had conducted surveys of respondents in China in four years ranging from 1994 to 2005. The percentage of respondents who were somewhat satisfied or very satisfied with life fell monotonically by 15% over that period, and the proportion of respondents who were somewhat dissatisfied or very dissatisfied thus rose monotonically. Yet over that period household real income per capita rose annually on average by 3.7% in rural China and by 5.4% in urban China. Easterlin and Sawangfa (2010) provide evidence of the trend in reported life satisfaction or happiness in China from three sources: the Gallup survey, the Asiabarometer survey, and the World Values survey. The results are shown in Table 11.1. In each case the average life satisfaction score fell: from 2.82 in 1997 to 2.67 in 2004; from 3.73 in 2003 to 3.68 in 2007; and from 6.83 in 1995 to 6.76 in 2007, respectively (each survey used different units). The happiness score in the World Values survey also fell, from 3.05 in 1995 to 2.94 in 2007. Unfortunately,

Table 11.1. Mean life satisfaction or happiness in China over time

	About 1995	About 2000	About 2005
Life satisfaction score			
Gallup survey (1–4 scale)	2.82	2.78	2.67
Year:	1997	1999	2004
Asiabarometer survey (1–5 scale)		3.73	3.68
Year:		2003	2006
World Values survey (1–10 scale)	6.83	6.53	6.76
Year	1995	2001	2007
Happiness score			
World Values survey (1–5 scale)	3.05	2.87	2.94
Year:	1995	2001	2007

Notes: An earlier World Values survey is excluded because it was confined to the urban population. The 1995 World Values survey covered central China (two-thirds of the national population) and the 2001 and 2007 surveys were intended to be nationally representative. The 1994 Gallup survey is excluded because it had five rather than four response categories.

Sources: Easterlin and Sawangfa (2010); *World Values Survey,* data for China.

these time-series data sets are not rich enough to permit direct analysis of the reasons for their trends.

The question being posed therefore cannot be dismissed out of hand. It is worth exploring further. To do so, it is necessary to review the reasons that have been put forward for what has come to be known as the 'Easterlin paradox' (Easterlin 1974, 1995). Easterlin's own explanation, both in his original paper and subsequently, is that subjective well-being is a positive function of income but a negative function of aspirations, and that aspirations rise along with income, so cancelling out the positive effect of income. Moreover, the reason why aspirations tend to rise with absolute income is that they are influenced by relative income.

Any explanation would have to deal with the obvious fact that nearly everyone, in rich as well as poor countries, if asked, would say they wanted more income, other things being equal; and, if offered more income, would reveal their preference for it. Easterlin's explanation provides an answer: people want more income because they wish to raise their relative income, or they recognize that the incomes of their comparator groups will rise, or they fail to recognize that their aspirations will rise as well as their income. Thus, people run on a 'hedonic treadmill'.

Is the Easterlin paradox trivial? At least three arguments might be put. The most basic criticism is that happiness scores are meaningless. However, this is not difficult to refute on account of the widespread success in estimating happiness functions from sample surveys. The individual happiness score is the dependent variable and various personal, household, and community characteristics are the explanatory variables. Many functions produce significant coefficients with predictable signs and powerful regularities across different countries and contexts.

A second criticism is that subjective reports of happiness are not comparable across people. This would be important if the object was to compare two individuals, but in large samples, comparing groups such as men and women or young and old, the problem is much reduced. Issues of unobserved heterogeneity remain but they merely warrant caution in the interpretation of suspect coefficients.

A third criticism is that people redefine their happiness scores over time. For instance, if people adjust their aspirations to the utility they normally experience, an improvement in their normal utility would lead them to report no higher happiness than previously, even if they were experiencing higher utility than previously. People are thus on an 'aspirations treadmill' and not a 'hedonic treadmill'. A test of this argument requires separate measures of 'experienced utility' ('net affect', or feelings) and of subjective well-being (life satisfaction). Kahneman and Krueger (2006) present evidence suggesting that measures of net affect show as much adaptation as do measures of life satisfaction, and accordingly reject this criticism. In any case, there is no consensus that there is such a thing as utility independent of aspirations, that is, that the utility which a person experiences can be separated from their perception of happiness, however formed.

In contrast to these arguments, there is now a considerable literature providing evidence—largely for advanced economies—that happiness is sensitive to relative income (for instance, Frank 1997; Clark and Oswald 1998; Frey and Stutzer 2002; Luttmer 2004; Di Tella and MacCulloch 2006; Graham and Felton 2006; Clark et al. 2008). The effect of reference group income is normally negative but a couple of studies have shown it to be positive (Senik 2004; Kingdon and Knight 2007). There is also evidence-based research showing that aspirations are important to subjective well-being (Stutzer 2004; Di Tella et al. 2003; Di Tella et al. 2007). The research provides the justification for examining the effect of economic growth on happiness within the framework of Easterlin's explanation for his paradox.

11.3 Survey, Data, and Method

The data used in this chapter come from the national household survey, relating to 2002, of the China Household Income Project (CHIP). This is the third CHIP cross-section national household survey, containing rich socioeconomic information. This and the previous two surveys (1988 and 1995) were designed by the same research team, with hypotheses in mind, but only the 2002 survey contained questions on subjective well-being.

There were just a couple of subjective well-being questions in the questionnaires for the sub-samples of (registered) urban resident households and rural–urban migrant households, but the questionnaire for rural households contained a specially designed module on subjective well-being. The analysis has to be based on a snapshot picture with no panel element. The paper pioneers the analysis of the question being posed but it can only be a suggestive beginning.

The subjective well-being question that is available for all three sub-samples can be translated as 'how happy are you nowadays?' Five answers were offered: very happy, happy, so-so, unhappy, and not at all happy. This forms the dependent variable in much of the analysis. It was treated either as an ordinal or as a cardinal measure, involving either ordered probit or OLS estimation. In line with the methodological study by Ferrer-i-Carbonell and Frijters (2004), we found no substantive differences between the results using the two measures, and accordingly we report only the cardinal results since they are easier to interpret. The household head, or its main member present, was asked the question; the respondent is identified.

The explanatory variables in the happiness equations are a set of individual, household, and community socioeconomic characteristics. We distinguish what we term basic variables, conventional economic variables, comparison variables, insecurity variables, and attitudinal variables. We retain the specifications taken from the four papers but, to simplify, generally report in the tables only those variables that are discussed in the text.

The coefficients in the happiness functions represent associations and not necessarily the hypothesized causal relationships. They might instead reflect the influence of unobserved variables on both the dependent and the independent variable, or reverse causation. In some cases we shall suggest reasons why the independent variable might have a causal effect on happiness but without establishing causation, either because the variable is not germane to the main argument or because a valid instrument is not available. If the interpretation is important to our story—as in the case of income—we try to isolate the effect of exogenous variation in the independent variable by means of instrumenting. Owing to the difficulty of finding persuasive instruments in a cross-section analysis, we present the relevant statistical tests in each table and discuss the theoretical and contextual plausibility of the instruments in notes.

11.4 Rural Happiness

We begin with rural happiness, drawing on the paper which analyses its determinants (Knight et al. 2009). Despite the fact that rural-dwellers have relatively low incomes and have been left behind in China's economic development, it appears that rural China is not a hotbed of dissatisfaction with life. No less than 62% of the sample reported to be happy or very happy, and only 9% not happy or not at all happy. With very happy having a score of 4, happy 3, so-so 2, unhappy 1, and not at all happy 0, the mean score was 2.67. Nevertheless, there is much variation in happiness scores, and this variation can be well explained by the variables in the survey.

The happiness functions for rural households are reported in Table 11.2. The first and second columns show the basic and the full OLS equations respectively, and the third and fourth columns the basic and the full IV equations, in which ln income level is instrumented. Many of the coefficients are statistically significant, have predictable signs, and display the regularities that are common to many happiness studies around the world. For instance, the age-happiness profile has a U-shaped pattern, and being female, being married, and being in good health all raise happiness. The conventional economic variables affect happiness, in line with basic economic theory, but the contributions of log income and net wealth (positive), and of working hours (negative) are weak. We instrumented the income variable in case it was endogenous.[2] The effect was to raise the coefficient on log income. We had expected unobserved characteristics, such as a happy disposition, to raise both income and happiness, so producing upward bias in the OLS equation. The downward bias suggested either that high aspirations raise income but lower happiness or that there is attenuation bias resulting from measurement error. Even then, the effect of a doubling of income was to raise the happiness score by only 0.4 points (column 3).

Table 11.2. Determinants of happiness in rural China: OLS and IV estimates

	Mean or proportion	(1) OLS	(2) OLS	(3) IV	(4) IV
Basic variables					
Age	45.41	-0.011771**	-0.016635**	-0.021543**	-0.026927***
Age squared	2174.09	0.000179***	0.000231***	0.000233**	0.000311***
Male	0.74	-0.066897***	-0.053657**	0.002762	-0.090826
Married	0.95	0.133205**	0.114782		
Divorced	0.00	-0.397782***	-0.709748***		
Widowed	0.02	-0.244595***	-0.17365		
In good health	0.74	0.411764***	0.289433***	0.393000***	0.304549***
Conventional economic variables					
Log of per capita household income	7.68	0.160237***	0.070470***	0.968701***	0.507371
Net wealth ('000 yuan)	37.68	0.001785***	0.000507*	-0.003990**	-0.001893
Working hours ('00 per year)	17.09	-0.003352***	-0.001504	-0.008953***	-0.003703
Comparison variables					
Household income much above village average	0.02		0.216251***		0.172576*
Household income above village average	0.19		0.110135***		0.103991**
Household income below village average	0.20		-0.270085***		-0.192513***
Household income much below village average	0.03		-0.843016***		-0.727418***
Current living standards better than five years ago	0.61		0.181139***		0.163433***
Current living standards worse than five years ago	0.05		-0.181702***		-0.182926***
Expect big increase in income over next five years	0.10		0.189245***		0.138659**
Expect small increase in income over next five years	0.68		0.088255***		0.059321
Expect decrease in income over next five years	0.04		-0.087432		-0.071144

(continued)

Table 11.2. Continued

	Mean or proportion	(1)	(2)	(3)	(4)
		OLS	OLS	IV	IV
Gini Coefficient of household income per capita at county level	0.28		0.725110***		0.772551**
Attitudinal variables					
Degree of harmony among lineages	2.82		0.037985**		0.037119
Degree of harmony in village	2.83		0.073600***		0.064207**
Agree that money is important	2.33		-0.032230**		-0.029007
Importance of family	3.90		0.046659		0.074325*
Importance of friends	3.35		0.049534***		0.014856
Constant		0.786090***	0.879206***	-4.514834***	-1.818563
R-squared/Centred R-squared		0.215	0.340	-0.141	0.227
Number of observations		8872	7000	5198	4228
Significance of exclusion restrictions in first stage equation					
Father's years of education				*	**
Spouse's education				***	
F-test of excluded instruments (p val)				0.0000	0.0054
Sargan test/Hansen J statistic, for over-identification of all instruments (p val)				0.9788	0.9696
Anderson–Rubin–Wald, F test (p val)				0.0004	0.3834

Notes: Dependent variable: Score of happiness based on cardinal values assigned to qualitative assessments as follows: very happy = 4; happy = 3; so-so = 2; not happy = 1 and not at all happy = 0. Independent variables with cardinal values assigned to qualitative assessments so that greater intensity is represented by a higher value are: level of harmony among lineages, level of harmony among villagers, agreement that money is important; importance of family; importance of friends; importance of religion. The omitted categories in the dummy variable analyses are: female sex; single; current living standard the same as five years ago. ***, **, and * denote statistical significance at the 1%, 5%, and 10% levels respectively. Instrumented variables regression results are generated using the Baum et al. (2003), ivreg2.ado programme for Stata. Variables related to marital states have been excluded from the IV specifications because spouse's years of education is used as an instrument. Models (2) and (4) have been clustered at village level for robust standard errors. Net wealth is defined as household financial assets, productive assets and consumer durables less debts.

Source: Knight et al. (2009): tables 6 and 11. Not all explanatory variables contained in those tables are reported here.

Despite the apparent unimportance of income for happiness, 64% of the unhappy gave lack of income as the reason for their unhappiness. A possible explanation for these discrepant results is that happiness is not only a positive function of income but also a negative function of aspirations, and that the latter can be governed by the income of the reference group. The reference group is likely to be determined by information sets and by social interactions. Most rural people report confining their reference groups to the village: 68% make comparisons with their neighbours or fellow-villagers.

Happiness is sensitive to respondents' perceptions of their household's position in the village income distribution (since only ten households were sampled in each village, it is not possible to use actual instead of perceived position). Five categories are distinguished: income perceived to be much above, above, at, below, and much below the village average, with the middle category being the omitted variable in the dummy variable analysis. The coefficients are large: that of the highest income category is greater than that of the lowest by 1.05 (column 2). The notion of relative deprivation, as developed by sociologists such as Runciman (1966), appears to be relevant. Thus, a rise or fall in income tends to be offset if there is a simultaneous rise or fall in village income. Aspirations appear to adjust to the income of the community, so producing a hedonic treadmill.

By contrast, income inequality in the county (as measured by the Gini coefficient of income per capita of the sampled households) is found to raise happiness. Hirschman's (1973) 'tunnel effect'—the analogy of two lines of cars jammed in a tunnel—might provide the explanation: initially at least, the movement of one line raises expectations that the other will also move. Thus, county income inequality might serve as a 'demonstration effect' of possible progress in the future.

Reference time is relevant as well as reference income. Respondents who consider their current living standard to be higher than five years ago are happier than those who consider their living standard now to be lower. By comparison with static expectations, those who expect an increase in income over the next five years have a higher current happiness score while those who expect a decrease have a lower score, other things being equal. This is inconsistent with the standard assumption that current utility depends on current consumption and not on expected future consumption; it suggests that people internalize their future states into their current happiness. That being the case, it is consistent with the psychological research findings (for instance, Rabin 1998) that people tend to base their aspirations on current incomes, and that they are better able to project their income into the future than their aspirations.

We distinguish those whose comparators are within and those whose comparators are beyond the village. Relative income within the village appears to be less important, and the coefficients showing the effect of future income on current happiness all have lower values, in the case of those with reference groups beyond the village (Knight et al. 2009: table 9). This suggests that the aspirations, relative to current income, of villagers with wider horizons are raised by the higher incomes of their comparators.

We introduced a set of attitudinal variables into our happiness functions, in an attempt to explore otherwise hidden influences. The significant coefficients suggest that rural people who derive their satisfaction with life more from personal relationships and less from material goods and services are happier, other things being equal, although reverse causation is also possible.

11.5 Urban Happiness

Our discussion of urban happiness draws on another paper (Knight and Gunatilaka 2010b). Happiness functions for households with urban *hukou* (residence registration) are shown in Table 11.3. Again, there are four columns: basic and full OLS, basic and full IV equations respectively. The full equations cover only respondents who were employed (64% of the total), the reason being that we could then include a set of variables representing urban insecurity.

We obtain the conventional results for some of the standard variables. The coefficients on the log income variable are roughly twice the size of the coefficients in the corresponding functions for rural residents (columns 1 and 2): it appears that urban people may be more materialistic, in the sense that either aspirations for or need for income are raised by urban living. When the income variable is instrumented, its coefficients lose their significance—but instrumenting might not be necessary.[3]

Our hypothesis is that urban people also experience relative deprivation. We find two indicators that relative income is important for happiness. First, households in each city were grouped into four income per capita quarters. Given the highest quarter as the reference category, the coefficients on the quarters become monotonically more and more negative, and the effect is both statistically significant and substantively important. City mean income per capita across the cities varies sufficiently for this variable not simply to reflect the variation in household incomes. Second, the log of average urban income per capita in the province of residence has a negative coefficient (but significantly so only in the OLS equation). In the urban case, unlike the rural case, the effect of surrounding prosperity on aspirations may arouse feelings of relative deprivation.

Those who consider income distribution, both in the nation and in the city, to be fair are happier, *ceteris paribus*, although it is unclear which way causation runs. As with rural-dwellers, expected future income is important to current happiness, possibly because people internalize their future states but they also assume that their aspirations in the future will be the same as their current aspirations.

Table 11.3. Determinants of happiness in urban China: OLS and IV estimates

	Mean or proportion	(1) OLS	(2) OLS	(3) IV	(4) IV
Basic variables					
Age	46.66	-0.047289***	-0.018598	-0.045127***	-0.016762
Age squared	2304.15	0.000505***	0.000233	0.000491***	0.000297**
Male	0.45	-0.078728***	-0.075042**	-0.090342*	-0.136904***
Married	0.94	0.192927**	0.063989	0.173121	-0.015554
Divorced	0.02	-0.212924*	-0.390620*	-0.236712*	-0.459314***
Widowed	0.03	-0.019126	-0.251903*	-0.046513	-0.430463***
In good health	0.60	0.272303***	0.162378***	0.273752***	0.167731***
Conventional economic variables					
Log of per capita household income	8.83	0.322386***	0.180122***	0.250968	-0.430686
Net wealth ('000 yuan)	45.99	0.000209**	0.000189	0.000309	0.000609***
Working hours ('00 per year)	15.29	-0.001066	-0.001214	-0.00111	-0.004428*
Comparison variables					
Extent of fairness, income distribution in China	0.77		0.073321**		0.063782**
Extent of fairness, income distribution in city	0.82		0.100717***		0.117929***
Living standard in second highest quarter in city	0.32		-0.235025**		-0.261292**
Living standard in third highest quarter in city	0.56		-0.439412***		-0.610865***
Living standard in lowest quarter in city	0.11		-0.925256***		-1.311817***
Expect big increase in income over next 5 years	0.02		0.280757**		0.289570***
Expect small increase in income over next 5 years	0.46		0.102234**		0.115980***
Expect decrease in income over next 5 years	0.19		-0.238048***		-0.214846***
Ln average per capita urban income in province	8.94		-0.166284**		0.348818
Insecurity variables					
Unemployed	0.05	-0.291062***	-0.095000***	-0.320859***	-0.105792**
Corruption is most important social problem	0.21		-0.088776*		-0.157433***
Unemployment or *xiagang* is most important problem	0.32		-0.193750**		-0.186774***
Social polarization is most important social problem	0.06				

(continued)

Table 11.3. Continued

	Mean or proportion	(1) OLS	(2) OLS	(3) IV	(4) IV
Immorality is most important social problem	0.01		-0.384379*		-0.321259**
Enterprise made high profit	0.09		0.029279		0.094054**
Enterprise made loss	0.08		-0.080067*		-0.166492***
Laid off work some time in 2002	0.37		-0.134122**		-0.235986***
Constant		0.372521*	2.990434***	0.906496	3.554063***
R-squared/Centred R-squared		0.117	0.242	0.115	0.138
Number of observations		6495	4152	6495	4151
Significance of instruments in first stage equation					
Number of labour force participants				*	
Parents' membership of Communist Party				***	
Father's years of education					***
Mother's years of education					***
F-test of excluded instruments (p val)				0.0000	0.0000
Sargan test, for over-identification of all instruments (p val)				0.1274	0.6905
Anderson–Rubin test of joint significance of endogenous regressors in main equation, F test (p val)				0.2172	0.2269

Notes: Dependent variable: score of happiness is based on cardinal values assigned to qualitative assessments as follows: very happy = 4; happy = 3; so-so = 2; not happy = 1 and not at all happy = 0. Models (2) and (4) are limited to sub-sample of employed respondents. Omitted categories in the dummy variable analyses are: female sex; single; employed or labour force non-participant; not healthy; living standard in highest quarter in city; no change in income expected in next 5 years; environmental degradation most important social problem; enterprise made marginal profit; employed all of 2002. Independent variables with cardinal values assigned to qualitative assessments so that a higher value denotes greater intensity are: extent of fairness, income distribution in China, extent of fairness, income distribution in the city. Models (2) and (4) are clustered at province level for robust standard errors. Instrumented variables regression results are generated using the Baum et al. (2003), ivreg2.ado programme for Stata.

Source: Knight and Gunatilaka (2010b): tables 7 and A7. Not all explanatory variables contained in those tables are reported here.

There was a high rate of retrenchment from state-owned enterprises in the years prior to the survey, and retrenched workers faced great difficulties in finding re-employment. The social security system was in transition from being employer based to insurance based, and unemployment benefits were not reliable, so that many unemployed workers received very little. We expected the new uncertainties of urban living to depress happiness. We therefore explored the effect of insecurity on urban-dwellers' happiness.

The experience of current unemployment, and of having been laid off in the past, had a significant negative coefficient, as also did the dummy variable denoting that a worker's employing enterprise currently made a loss: this would increase the employee's chances of being made redundant. Emil Durkheim's (1897) notion of *anomie* might be relevant. He defined *anomie* as normlessness, when social rules break down and people do not know what to expect of each other. The remarkable economic progress, the rapid creation of markets, the withdrawal of institutional support, and the demise of ideology might have created a state of *anomie*. The survey does not possess good attitudinal questions to identify *anomie*. However, respondents were asked what they considered to be the most important social problem. Three suggestive pointers are the negative coefficients on corruption, on social polarization, and on immorality in the happiness function.

11.6 A Rural–Urban Comparison

We went on to make a comparison of rural and urban China (Knight and Gunatilaka 2010b). As we discussed in Chapter 10, China has a remarkable rural–urban divide. The ratio of urban to rural household income per capita has exceeded 2.0 to 1 throughout the period of economic reform, and actually rose in recent years despite the economic reforms and marketization that partly integrated the rural and urban sectors. In 2002, the year of the survey, the ratio obtained from the survey stood at 3.1 to 1. We would therefore expect a corresponding large divide in subjective well-being. Yet the survey also shows that, when happiness is converted into a cardinal value, the urban score is no higher than the rural score. Indeed, the reported mean urban happiness (2.5) is actually lower than the mean rural happiness (2.7). How can this result be explained?

We first calculated a standard 'Oaxaca decomposition' of these mean differences in happiness using those variables in the equations that are identical in the two sub-samples. The difference in income of course simply added to the puzzle. What raised the happiness of rural people was their superior happiness generation function. Unfortunately, much of the work was being done by the difference in the intercept terms, which remained unexplained. It was necessary to produce an explanation from the separate and non-identical rural and urban happiness functions.

It is possible that in some societies there is a cultural unwillingness to report happiness, or alternatively unhappiness, and that comparisons made across culturally distinct groups might be misleading as a result. Thus a greater willingness of urban than of rural people to report being less than happy might explain our results. We cannot reject the hypothesis, but one piece of evidence points against it. As we shall see, rural migrant households living in the cities reported having lower average happiness than did urban households. A culture of not wishing to admit to being unhappy is not observable among households that were recently part of rural society.

Our preferred explanation, based on Tables 11.2 and 11.3, runs as follows. On the one hand, rural China is not a hotbed of dissatisfaction with life, despite the relative poverty and low socioeconomic status of its people in Chinese society. The basic reasons are that they have limited information sets and narrow reference groups, they expect their income to rise in the future, and they place a high value on personal and community relationships. On the other hand, the relatively low happiness of urban people despite their relatively high income and their expectations of higher income in the future has to do with the nature of the urban society that has emerged in recent years. High aspirations, governed by reference groups, appear to give rise to the relative deprivation that makes for unhappiness. In addition, the greater insecurity associated with redundancy, unemployment, and various other urban social ills also makes city-dwellers unhappy.

11.7 Migrant Happiness

Rural–urban migration in China has grown remarkably in recent years: the number of rural–urban migrants probably exceeded 130 million in 2002. Many of the migrants are temporarily in the cities but settlement is increasingly permitted. The higher income to be obtained in the city than in the village appears to provide a strong incentive to migrate. The 2002 CHIP survey contained a unique feature—a nationally representative sub-sample of rural–urban migrants, that is, rural *hukou* households living in the urban areas. Their subjective well-being is analysed in Knight and Gunatilaka (2010a). The average happiness score of these, fairly settled, migrants is lower than that of rural residents. This appears to be inconsistent with the economic theories of rural–urban migration based on utility maximization. We looked at three main possible explanations: in terms of the hardships of urban life that they experience, in terms of self-selection, and in terms of revised aspirations.

We proceeded by estimating migrant happiness functions (Table 11.4), both OLS (columns 1 and 2) and IV (columns 3 and 4). Again we found the usual results for several of the basic variables. The coefficient on log income per capita is significantly positive but its values indicate that a doubling of income raises the

Table 11.4. Determinants of happiness of rural–urban migrants: OLS and IV estimates

	Mean or proportion	(1) OLS	(2) OLS	(3) IV	(4) IV
Basic variables					
Male	0.61	-0.268374**	-0.198893*	0.897308	0.871168
Married	0.90	-0.05981	0.046933	1.270881	1.164349
Male and married	0.55	0.349128***	0.243219**	-0.696701	-0.690339
In good health	0.90	0.123086***	0.129427	0.076211	0.098606
Duration of urban residence (years)	7.51	0.013580*	0.008731	0.019486*	0.016416
Duration of urban residence, squared	84.83	-0.000547*	-0.000391	-0.000848**	-0.000768*
Conventional economic variables					
Log of per capita household income	8.55	0.208102***	0.186286***	0.634208***	0.635487***
Net financial assets ('000 yuan)	16.51	-0.000247	0.000349	-0.001622*	-0.001719*
Working hours ('00 per year)	31.94	0.000093	0.000581	0.001842	0.003424*
Comparison variables					
Expect big increase in income over next 5 years	0.07	0.298398***	0.245207**	0.272629**	0.212345*
Expect small increase in income over next 5 years	0.55	0.026176	0.005977	0.031948	0.013430
Expect decrease in income over next 5 years	0.10	-0.403299***	-0.383004***	-0.341623***	-0.324785***
Log of average per capita urban income in city of current residence	8.97	-0.120432	-0.134564	-0.326767**	-0.325644**
Harshness of city life variables					
Living with family members	0.88	0.134726	0.147542*		
Number of relatives and friends in city	7.19	0.003869*	0.002658	0.001810	0.001581
Child still in village	0.32	-0.124977**	-0.127723**	-0.210346***	-0.213707***
No heating	0.65	-0.149865**	-0.138521**	-0.182631***	-0.196890***
Satisfaction with job	1.98		0.073527*		0.066589**
Index of discrimination	5.35		-0.032196***		-0.029696***
Can find another job in two weeks	0.11		-0.099676		-0.181578**
Can find another job in one month	0.23		-0.121339**		-0.221834***
Can find another job in two months	0.10		-0.147820*		-0.170080*

(continued)

Table 11.4. Continued

	Mean or proportion	(1)	(2)	(3)	(4)
		OLS	OLS	IV	IV
Can find another job in six months	0.13		−0.191704**		−0.200813**
Need more than 6 months to find another job	0.17		−0.214012***		−0.208395**
Constant		1.024808	1.536916	−1.349415	−0.720115
R-squared		0.100	0.129	0.046	0.070
Number of observations		1850	1715	1115	1100
Significance of instruments in first stage equation					
Mother's years of education				**	**
Spouse's years of education				***	***
Earnings per month before migrating				***	***
F-test of excluded instruments (p val)				0.0000	0.0000
Sargan test, for over-identification of all instruments (p val)				0.5207	0.6300
Anderson–Rubin test of joint significance of endogenous regressors in main equation, F test (p val)				0.0130	0.0283

Notes: Dependent variable: score of happiness based on cardinal values assigned to qualitative assessments as follows: very happy = 4; happy = 3; so-so = 2; not happy = 1 and not at all happy = 0. Models 1 and 2 are for the full sample. Models 3 and 4 are for the sub-sample of employed persons. The omitted categories in the dummy variable analyses are: single female; not healthy; no change in income expected in the next five years. ***, **, and * denote statistical significance at the 1%, 5%, and 10% levels respectively. Models have been clustered at city level for robust standard errors. Instrumented variables regression results are generated using the Baum et al. (2003). ivreg2.ado programme for Stata.

Source: Knight and Gunatilaka (2010a): tables 2 and 3.

happiness score by only 0.13 points (column 2). Although the coefficient is raised, the inference that income level is unimportant is not altered by instrumenting the income variable.[4] The coefficient tends to rise with length of stay, suggesting either that there is a process of self-selection or that migrants may become more materialistic as they lay down deeper urban roots. Although current income is not important to happiness, expectations of income over the next five years enter powerfully and significantly into the current happiness score. Again, this suggests that anticipated future happiness is absorbed into current happiness, but also that people are bad at forecasting how their aspirations will change if income changes and that they judge their future happiness on the basis of their current aspirations. An alternative interpretation is that expected future income determines current consumption, in line with the 'permanent income' theory of consumption, and that the relationship would therefore not survive if current income were replaced by current consumption in the happiness function. However, this substitution made no notable difference to the coefficients on expected income (Knight and Gunatilaka 2010a: 117); moreover, the same result was found for the other two sub-samples.

When migrants who reported that they were unhappy or not at all happy were asked the reason for their unhappiness, over two-thirds said that their income was too low. This pointer to the possible importance of perceptions of relative deprivation is confirmed by the negative, large, and significant coefficient on per capita income of urban residents in the destination province. This effect is stronger for the migrants who had been in the city for more than the median length of time, 7.5 years (Knight and Gunatilaka 2010a: table 2). The migrants appear to compare their own situations with those of others living in their new surroundings, and increasingly to do so as they become more settled.

China's political economy accords urban *hukou* people a set of rights and privileges that are denied to rural *hukou* people residing in the cities (Knight and Song 1999, 2005). The migrants are generally 'second class citizens'. When we included various proxies for these disadvantages in the happiness function, job dissatisfaction, perceptions of discrimination against migrants, and measures of job insecurity had significant negative coefficients. The unsatisfactory conditions in which migrants live and the unpleasant and insecure nature of their employment depress happiness.

We explored the reasons why migrants were on average less happy than peasants by conducting a decomposition analysis using happiness functions with identical determinants for the migrant and rural sub-samples (Table 11.5). The objective was to explain the migrant shortfall in mean happiness score, equal to 0.31, distinguishing between the contributions of the different mean values of the explanatory variables and those of their coefficients. The effect of characteristics was actually to increase the difference in mean happiness scores: in particular, the migrants had higher mean income. The explanation was therefore to be found in

Table 11.5. Decomposition of the difference in mean happiness score between rural–urban migrants and rural residents: percentage contributions to the difference

	Using the rural happiness function		Using the migrants' happiness function	
	Due to characteristics	Due to coefficients	Due to characteristics	Due to coefficients
Ln income per capita	−55.51	1.13	−55.39	1.01
Health	−26.39	114.99	−5.81	94.41
Income expectations	14.71	32.98	11.34	36.36
Age	13.97	−138.82	6.69	−131.54
Education	−2.55	22.61	−0.13	20.18
Male	−4.70	−23.87	0.74	−29.30
Marital status	2.49	−1.82	0.89	−0.22
Ethnicity	1.10	2.12	0.13	3.10
CP membership	5.01	1.38	0.40	5.99
Unemployment	0.09	0.02	0.10	0.02
Working hours	16.65	−23.94	5.53	−12.81
Net financial assets	−13.43	21.28	0.29	7.56
Constant term	0.00	140.48	0.00	140.48
Sum (percentage)	−48.56	148.56	−35.23	135.23
Sum (score)	−0.1485	0.4544	−0.1078	0.4137

Notes: The mean happiness scores are 2.6764 in the case of rural residents and 2.3703 in the case of migrants, creating a migrant shortfall of 0.3061 (set equal to + 100%) to be explained by the decomposition. Thus the combined contributions of characteristics and coefficients sum to 100%. The composite variables are age and age squared for age, married, single, divorced, and widowed for marital status, and big increase, small increase, and decrease for income expectations.

Source: Knight and Gunatilaka (2010a): table 5.

the superior happiness function of rural people. Here the expectations of future income were crucial. With static income as the reference category, the coefficients of the migrants were uniformly lower, suggesting that migrants had higher income aspirations relative to their current income. This can be expected if aspirations depend on the income of the relevant comparator group. The rural respondents are representative of rural society and so their mean income is close to the mean income of their likely comparator group. But the migrant sub-sample is unrepresentative of urban society: migrants tend to occupy the lower ranges of the urban income distribution. If migrants make comparisons with urban-born residents as well as with other migrants, their aspirations will be high in relation to their current income.

An equivalent exercise was conducted to decompose the difference in mean happiness between migrants and urban *hukou* residents (Table 11.6), the migrant shortfall in happiness score being 0.11. In this case the difference in coefficients makes no net contribution to the explanation. Two differences in mean characteristics can explain all of the difference: the higher mean income of urban residents and their superior position in the urban income distribution. Position in the city income distribution has a powerful effect on happiness, and this is true for both samples. A far higher proportion of migrants than of urban residents fall into the

Table 11.6. Decomposition of the difference in mean happiness score between rural–urban migrants and urban residents: percentage contributions to the difference

	Using the urban happiness function		Using the migrants' happiness function	
	Due to characteristics	Due to coefficients	Due to characteristics	Due to coefficients
Ln income per capita	43.20	457.57	28.15	472.62
Income expectations	−47.03	66.43	−39.92	59.32
Living standard in second highest quarter in city	−16.81	9.40	−33.68	26.28
Living standard in third highest quarter in city	−8.19	74.32	−11.71	77.84
Living standard in lowest quarter in city	194.35	−26.79	175.93	−8.37
Age	1.52	−562.72	32.85	−594.05
Male	11.53	−62.39	−4.08	−46.78
Education	−8.65	8.22	−11.54	11.11
Marital status	0.18	2.63	−1.96	4.77
Ethnicity	−2.12	3.19	−0.34	1.40
CP membership	15.69	1.00	7.63	9.06
Unemployment	−6.68	−2.01	−0.68	−8.01
Health	−54.21	78.08	−28.01	51.89
Working hours	−1.08	22.20	10.50	10.62
Net financial assets	1.69	3.85	−2.46	8.01
Constant term	0.00	−96.38	0.00	−96.38
Sum (percentage)	123.41	−23.41	120.67	−20.67
Sum (score)	0.1372	−0.0260	0.1342	−0.0230

Notes: The mean happiness scores are 2.4845 in the case of urban residents and 2.3703 in the case of migrants, creating a migrant shortfall of 0.1143 (set equal to + 100%) to be explained by the decomposition. Thus the combined contributions of characteristics and coefficients sum to 100%. The composite variables are age and age squared for age, married, single, divorced, and widowed for marital status, and big increase, small increase, and decrease for income expectations.

Source: Knight and Gunatilaka (2010a: table 4).

lowest quarter of city households in terms of living standards. If the income of the relevant comparator group influences aspirations, the inferior position of migrants in the city income distribution can thus explain why they appear to have higher aspirations in relation to their current income.

There might be selection on the basis of unobserved characteristics. For instance, migrants might be inherently unhappy people who have unsuccessfully sought happiness through migration. Our test was to use the residual (actual minus predicted) happiness score as a proxy for inherent disposition and to introduce this variable into a probit equation predicting that the migrant reported urban living to yield more happiness than rural living. The coefficient was significantly positive and large, implying that the unobserved characteristic was acquired after migration. Thus, this explanation lacked empirical support (Knight and Gunatilaka 2010a: 121–2).

11.8 Aspiration Income and Happiness

The argument of this chapter has centred on peoples' aspirations in relation to their income, and yet the evidence has been only indirect. We should ideally measure aspirations, or at least aspirations for income. There is a proxy for 'aspiration income' in the rural data set, which is analysed in Knight and Gunatilaka (2009).

Respondents were asked: 'What is the minimum income needed to sustain the household for a year?' It was possible to justify this as a proxy for income aspirations. The strategy was first to analyse its determinants and then to include income aspirations as an additional argument in the happiness functions that had previously been estimated for the rural sample.

Table 11.7 reports the determinants of income need, with log of household income need as the dependent variable. Column 1 shows the OLS and column 2 the IV estimation with log of household income instrumented. Among the demographic and physiological determinants of income need, we see that good health (reducing income need), satisfaction with the village clinic (reducing income need), and size and composition of the household are important, and that the age, sex, and marital status of the respondent may be. The equations contain several variables that might influence aspirations for income. In particular, the coefficient on log of household income is both positive and significant. The coefficient is 0.19 (OLS) and 0.57 (IV), that is, a doubling of actual income increases the perceived minimum income by 19% or 57% respectively.[5] Years of education also has a significantly positive coefficient: the more education the respondent had received, the higher the income needed. With static living standard as the base category, those whose current living standard is worse than five years ago have a significantly higher aspiration for income. By contrast, financial assets may have a negative effect, that is, more wealth appears to provide security rather than to raise aspirations. Those whose main reference group is outside the village have higher aspiration income, as do households whose income is below their village's average household income.

At the second stage, we added the aspiration income variable to the function estimating happiness, again converted into a cardinal score. Table 11.8 shows OLS and IV estimates, columns 1 and 3 having log per capita income need as the only aspiration variable and columns 2 and 4 having a full list of aspiration variables respectively. Both log income per capita and log income needed per capita are instrumented. When other variables that are likely to represent aspirations are introduced as well as minimum income need, they generally have significant coefficients. However, our particular interest here lies in aspiration income. As expected, the coefficient on log household income per capita is significantly positive in the OLS specifications, with an average value of about 0.20; the

Table 11.7. Determinants of rural income need: OLS and IV estimates

	Mean or proportion	OLS	IV
		(1)	(2)
Log of total household income	8.97	0.189531***	0.568303***
Aspiration variables			
Net financial assets ('000 yuan)	5.52	−0.001471	−0.005687***
Current living standards better than 5 years ago	0.60	−0.002653	−0.024994
Current living standards worse than 5 years ago	0.05	0.200728***	0.209451***
Education (years)	7.14	0.025571***	0.023523***
Main reference group beyond village	0.11	0.100161**	0.085029*
Household income much above village average	0.02	0.070678	0.009413
Household income above village average	0.18	0.052439*	0.004858
Household income below village average	0.20	0.053649*	0.125806***
Household income much below village average	0.03	0.188881**	0.365798***
Conditioning variables			
Age	45.26	0.023823***	0.009860
Age squared	2159.52	−0.000281***	−0.000121
Male	0.75	−0.052313**	−0.013750
Married	0.95	0.176272**	0.183060*
Divorced	0.00	0.225053	0.257623
Widowed	0.02	0.13155	0.068548
In good health	0.74	−0.080823***	−0.085976***
Satisfaction with clinic	2.34	−0.049787***	−0.058235***
Senior citizens, male, aged 65 +	0.10	0.174814***	0.165848***
Senior citizens, female, aged 65 +	0.11	0.116292***	0.099134**
Adult males of 18 to 64 years	1.48	0.128360***	0.083446***
Adult females of 18 to 64 years	1.39	0.142299***	0.101945***
Teenaged males of 11 to 17 years	0.36	0.107355***	0.067175***
Teenaged females of 11 to 17 years	0.31	0.105044***	0.079474***
Children, males less than 11 years	0.27	0.024714	0.005915
Children, females less than 11 years	0.22	0.034355	0.022870
Constant		5.410067***	2.491840*
R-squared		0.14	
Number of observations		6231	5356
Significance of exclusion restrictions in first stage equation			
Father's years of education			*
Productive assets			***
F-test of excluded instruments (*p* val)			0.0000
Hansen J test for overidentification of all instruments (*p* val)			0.7236
Anderson–Rubin test of joint significance of endogenous regressors in main equation, F test (*p* val)			0.0296

Notes: Dependent variables: logarithm of minimum income needed (mean 8.455, standard deviation 0.731). Independent variables with cardinal values assigned to qualitative assessments so that greater intensity is represented by a higher value are: satisfaction with clinic. The omitted categories in the dummy variable analyses are: female sex; married; not healthy; current living standard the same as five years ago; main reference group within village; household at average village income. ***, **, and * denote statistical significance at the 1%, 5%, and 10% levels respectively. Instrumented variables regression results are generated using the Baum et al. (2003), ivreg2.ado programme for Stata. The models have been clustered at village level for robust standard errors.

Source: Knight and Gunatilaka (2009): tables 3 and 4. Not all explanatory variables contained in those tables are reported here.

Table 11.8. Aspirations-augmented determinants of rural happiness: OLS and IV estimates

	Mean or proportion	(1) OLS	(2) OLS	(3) IV	(4) IV
Log of per capita household income ('000 yuan)	7.58	0.234759***	0.153428***	1.104873	0.307646
Aspiration variables					
Log of per capita minimum income needed	7.07	-0.081381***	-0.063265***	-0.346743	-0.094068
Agreement with statement that money is important	2.35		-0.036981***		-0.051366**
Household income much above village average	0.02		0.259189***		0.194926**
Household income above village average	0.18		0.082069***		0.054872*
Household income below village average	0.20		-0.321823***		-0.292942***
Household income much below village average	0.03		-0.802952***		-0.737081***
Current living standards better than 5 years ago	0.60		0.201302***		0.179919***
Current living standards worse than 5 years ago	0.05		-0.089702**		-0.07863
Basic variables					
Age (years)	45.26	-0.009889	-0.015145**	-0.022530*	-0.019203***
Age squared	2159.52	0.000170**	0.000232***	0.000263***	0.000274***
Male	0.75	-0.083351***	-0.082530***	-0.028222	-0.066467***
Married	0.95	0.148818**	0.139821**		0.133112
Divorced	0.00	-0.423336**	-0.477544***		-0.483547**
Widowed	0.02	-0.299207***	-0.220053**		-0.228856**
Working hours ('00 per year)	17.07	-0.003072***	-0.002391**	-0.007579	-0.002877**
Net financial assets ('000 yuan)	5.52	0.001576***	0.001384*	-0.01088	-0.000811
In good health	0.74	0.423018***	0.344800***	0.378415*	0.344245***
Constant		0.701449***	1.467268***	-3.143911	0.689295
R-squared		0.231	0.308		5620
Number of observations		6617	6538	3896	5620
Significance of exclusion restrictions for ln of per capita household income in first stage equation					
Father's years of education				*	**
Spouse's years of education				***	***
Senior citizens, male, aged 65 +					***
Senior citizens, female, aged 65 +					***

Adult males of 18 to 64 years		***
Adult females of 18 to 64 years		***
Teenaged males of 11 to 17 years		***
Teenaged females of 11 to 17 years		***
Children, males less than 11 years		***
Children, females less than 11 years		***
F-test of excluded instruments (p val)	0.0000	0.0000
Significance of exclusion restrictions for ln of need minimum income in first stage equation		
Father's years of education	ns	
Spouse's years of education	***	
Senior citizens, male, aged 65 +		ns
Senior citizens, female, aged 65 +		***
Adult males of 18 to 64 years		***
Adult females of 18 to 64 years		***
Teenaged males of 11 to 17 years		***
Teenaged females of 11 to 17 years		***
Children, males less than 11 years		***
Children, females less than 11 years		***
F-test of excluded instruments (p val)	0.0000	0.0000
Sargan test for over-identification of all instruments (p val)		0.2213
Anderson–Rubin test of joint significance of endogenous regressors in main equation, F test (p val)	0.0009	0.0011

Notes: Dependent variables: score of happiness based on cardinal values assigned to qualitative assessments as follows: very happy = 4; happy = 3; so-so = 2; not happy = 1 and not at all happy = 0. The mean value of happiness is 2.63, standard deviation 0.88, and coefficient of variation 0.33. Independent variables with cardinal values assigned to qualitative assessments so that a higher value denotes greater intensity; agreement that money is important. The omitted categories in the dummy variable analyses are: female sex; married; not healthy; household at average village income; current living standard the same as five years ago. ***, **, and * denote statistical significance at the 1%, 5%, and 10% levels respectively. Variables related to marital states have been excluded from the IV specification in Model (3) because spouse's years of education is used as an instrument. Instrumented variables regression results are generated using the Baum et al. (2003), ivreg2.ado programme for Stata.

Source: Knight and Gunatilaka (2009): tables 5 and 6. Not all explanatory variables contained in those tables are reported here.

coefficients are higher but not significantly positive in the, less precise, IV estimates. Log minimum income needed has a significantly negative coefficient, averaging –0.07 in the OLS estimates; it is more negative but not significant in the IV estimates.[6] Although the conventional statistical tests of good instruments are passed, it is not possible to find a set of instruments which reliably identify the separate effects of the two income variables. Nevertheless, this set of results provides direct, albeit only suggestive, evidence that, other things being equal, having higher aspirations for income can reduce happiness. Moreover, a comparison of the positive and negative coefficients suggests that people run on a partial 'hedonic treadmill'.

11.9 Conclusion

We are now in a position to consider whether these sets of results, all based on cross-section evidence, can provide an answer to and explanation for the time-series question posed in this chapter: does economic growth raise happiness in China?

First, in all three data sets—the rural, the urban, and the migrant—current income has a positive and significant effect on happiness. However, in none of these sub-samples is the coefficient on current income substantively large. Clearly, there are other, more important, determinants of individual subjective well-being. Second, this pure effect of individual income level is further weakened by the fact that economic growth will tend to raise incomes generally. Insofar as the income of the reference group rises as well as own income, the decline in relative income reduces individual happiness. As the economy grows, it is important to 'keep up with the Zhous'.

Third, the higher the incomes to which people aspire, the lower is their subjective well-being. Fourth, aspirations are influenced by peoples' reference groups and reference times. For rural people, the reference group is generally their fellow-villagers, for urban people it is their fellow-citizens within the city, and for rural–urban migrants, it is also other people living in the city, urban as well as rural *hukou* holders. It is not the income of 'any old Zhou' that produces feelings of relative deprivation but the income of the 'Zhous you know'—those who fall into a person's reference group. Fifth, China's national Gini coefficient of household income per capita rose from 0.39 in 1988 to 0.47 in 2002 (Gustafsson et al. 2008: 19). It is likely that this rising income inequality reduced happiness, but the relationship is complicated by the importance of local reference groups and the possibility of demonstration effects as well as relative deprivation effects.

Sixth, aspirations for income are much influenced by reference time income, and this is governed mainly by the present. It is current income—both absolute and relative—that mainly determines aspirations for income. However, there appears also to be a 'ratchet effect': previous income can also influence aspirations, so that experience of a past fall in income reduces happiness, other things being equal. In general terms, the analysis highlights the important role that aspirations play in peoples' perceptions of their own well-being. Seventh, expectations of future income are important for current happiness. This suggests that a gloomier view of the economy's prospects could be serious for well-being, and maybe even for political stability.

Using this framework of empirical findings, we can see that the changes in the economy and in the society that stem from, or go along with, economic growth are likely to have implications for overall happiness in China. The effects of income growth itself are limited because of the resultant growth in aspirations, this being a function of both own and relative income. The importance of relative income for subjective well-being in all three sub-samples, together with rising income inequality over time, helps to explain the failure of happiness scores to rise with income levels. The new urban insecurities and uncertainties generated by economic reform and marketization have a negative impact on the subjective well-being of the growing number of urban residents. In particular, rural–urban migrants—rapidly expanding in number—suffer both from their second-class status in the cities and from the widening of their reference groups to include the more affluent urban *hukou* population. By extending the reference groups of rural-dwellers beyond the village, migration can also have the effect of reducing rural happiness. These findings help to explain why mean happiness in China appears not to have risen, and may even have fallen, in recent years.

Our analysis raises, and also illuminates, some basic normative and policy issues. To what extent should subjective well-being enter into the social welfare function, and be accepted as one of the criteria for policy making? Ultimately, a value judgement is required. Powerful and plausible regularities were observed in the analysis. Thus, in making that value judgement, it is difficult simply to dismiss as irrelevant peoples' reported perceptions of their own welfare. There are some difficult policy trade-offs between the gains from economic growth and the losses from the socioeconomic changes accompanying growth, and these have not been sufficiently recognized.

For over a quarter of a century China's reformist policy makers gave the highest priority to the achievement of rapid economic growth. In the last five years, however, the balance of policy objectives has moved somewhat in the direction of creating a 'Harmonious Society', for instance, showing greater concern for reducing income inequality and for improving social security. That move can be seen as a response to the issues that underlie this chapter. The leadership has also begun to talk about a new policy goal: one of raising happiness rather than just income. Our evidence shows that this might be the harder goal to achieve.

Notes

1. We draw also on a summary paper (Knight and Gunatilaka 2011).
2. The task was to find variables that were well correlated with the income variable but for which it was plausible that they made no direct contribution to happiness. The instruments chosen (father's education and spouse's education, in years) were unlikely to affect own happiness (even own education had a significant positive effect only in the most basic specification). The F-test of excluded instruments shows that the instruments are not weak (p values 0.000 and 0.0054), the Sargan–Hansen over-identification test (if one instrument is exogenous then at least one other is exogenous) is passed (p value > 0.96), and the Anderson–Rubin–Wald test (of joint significance of the endogenous regressors) suggests that instrumenting is necessary (p value = 0.0004) in column (3) but may not be necessary (p value = 0.3834) when more regressors are added in column (4).
3. The instruments listed in the notes to the table (combinations of parental or household characteristics) were unlikely to affect happiness directly; they are not weak; they pass the Sargan test; however, the Anderson–Rubin test fails to provide evidence of endogeneity.
4. The instruments for ln household income per capita (mother's education, spouse's education, and earnings per month before migrating) were unlikely to affect current happiness; they passed the statistical tests of relevance and validity and, according to the Anderson–Rubin test, they were needed.
5. The instruments for ln total household income (father's education and productive assets, that is, rural household machinery and equipment) were in themselves unlikely to influence the household's perceived need for income. According to the test results shown in the table, they were relevant and valid, and instrumenting was necessary.
6. In our view, the instruments (combinations of father's education, spouse's education, and household composition) were unlikely to affect happiness directly. They were highly correlated with both ln household per capita actual income and needed income: in each case the F-test of excluded instruments was highly significant (p value = 0.000). The Sargan test for over-identification of all instruments was passed, and the Anderson–Rubin test indicated that instrumenting was needed.

References

Baum, C. F., M. E. Schaffer, and M. Stillman (2003), 'Instrumental variables and GMM: estimation and testing', *Stata Journal*, 3, 1: 1–31.

Blanchflower, David, and Andrew Oswald (2004), 'Well-being over time in Britain and the USA', *Journal of Public Economics*, 88, 7–8: 1359–86.

Clark, Andrew, and Andrew Oswald (1998), 'Comparison-concave utility and following behaviour in social and economic settings', *Journal of Public Economics*, 71, 1: 133–55.

——Paul Frijters, and Michael Shields (2008), 'Relative income, happiness and utility: an explanation for the Easterlin paradox and other puzzles', *Journal of Economic Literature*, 46, 1: 95–144.

Di Tella, Rafael, John Haisken-DeNew, and Robert MacCulloch (2007), 'Happiness, adaptation to income and to status in an individual panel', NBER Working Paper 13159.

——and Robert MacCulloch (2006), 'Some uses of happiness data in Economics', *Journal of Economic Perspectives*, 20, 1, Winter: 25–46.

——Robert MacCulloch, and Andrew Oswald (2003), 'The macroeconomics of happiness', *Review of Economics and Statistics*, 85, 4: 809–27.

Durkheim, Emile (1897 [1952]), *Suicide: A Study in Sociology*, trans. J. A. Spaulding and G. Simpson, London: Routledge and Kegan Paul.

Easterlin, Richard (1974), 'Does economic growth improve the human lot? Some empirical evidence', in P. David and M. Reder (eds.), *Nations and Households in Economic Growth: Essays in Honor of Moses Abramovitz*, New York and London: Academic Press: 98–125.

——(1995), 'Will raising the incomes of all increase the happiness of all?', *Journal of Economic Behaviour and Organization*, 27, 1: 35–48.

——(2001), 'Income and happiness: towards a unified theory', *Economic Journal*, 111, 473: 465–84.

——(2008), 'Lost in transition: life satisfaction on the road to capitalism', *Journal of Economic Behavior and Organization*, 71, 2: 130–45.

——and Onnicha Sawangfa (2010), 'Happiness and economic growth: does the cross section evidence predict time trends? Evidence from developing countries', in Ed Diener, Daniel Kahneman, and John F. Helliwell (eds), *International Differences in Well-Being*, Oxford: Oxford University Press: 166–246.

Ferrer-i-Carbonell, Ada, and Paul Frijters (2004), 'How important is methodology for estimates of the determinants of happiness?', *Economic Journal*, 114, 497: 640–59.

Frank, Robert Frank (1997), 'The frame of reference as a public good', *Economic Journal*, 107 (November): 1832–47.

Frey, Bruno, and Alois Stutzer (2002), 'What can economists learn from happiness research?', *Journal of Economic Literature*, 40, 2: 402–35.

Graham, Carol, and Andrew Felton (2006), 'Inequality and happiness: insights from Latin America', *Journal of Economic Inequality*, 4, 1: 107–22.

Gustafsson, Bjorn, Li Shi, and Terry Sicular (eds.) (2008), *Inequality and Public Policy in China*, Cambridge: Cambridge University Press.

Hirschman, Albert (1973), 'The changing tolerance for income inequality in the course of economic development', *Quarterly Journal of Economics*, 87, 4: 544–66.

Kahneman, Daniel, and Alan Krueger (2006), 'Developments in the measurement of subjective well-being', *Journal of Economic Perspectives*, 20, 1 (Winter): 3–24.

Kingdon, Geeta, and John Knight (2007), 'Community, comparisons and subjective well-being in a divided society', *Journal of Economic Behavior and Organization*, 64: 69–90.

Knight, John, and Ramani Gunatilaka (2009), 'Income, aspirations and the hedonic treadmill in a poor society', University of Oxford, Department of Economics Discussion Paper No. 468, December.

————(2010a), 'Great expectations? The subjective well-being of rural–urban migrants', *World Development*, 38, 1 (January): 113–24.

————(2010b), 'The rural–urban divide: income but not happiness?', *Journal of Development Studies*, 46, 3 (March): 506–34.

————(2011), 'Does economic growth raise happiness in China?', *Oxford Development Studies*, 39, 1 (March): 1–24.

——and Lina Song (1999), *The Rural–Urban Divide: Economic Disparities and Interactions in China*, Oxford: Oxford University Press.

————(2005), *Towards a Labour Market in China*, Oxford: Oxford University Press.

————and Ramani Gunatilaka (2009), 'The determinants of subjective well-being in rural China', *China Economic Review*, 20, 4 (December): 635–49.

Krueger, Alan (2008), 'Comment', *Brookings Papers on Economic Activity 2008* (Spring): 95–100.

Luttmer, Erzo (2004), 'Neighbors as negatives: relative earnings and well-being', *Quarterly Journal of Economics*, 120, 3: 963–1002.

Rabin, Matthew (1998), 'Psychology and economics', *Journal of Economic Literature*, 36 (March): 11–46.

Ravallion, Martin, and Shaohua Chen (2007), 'China's (uneven) progress against poverty', *Journal of Development Economics*, 82, 1: 1–42.

Runciman, W. G. (1966), *Relative Deprivation and Social Justice*, Berkeley: University of California Press.

Senik, Claudia (2004), 'When information dominates comparison: learning from Russian subjective panel data', *Journal of Public Economics*, 88: 99–123.

Stevenson, Betsey, and Justin Wolfers (2008), 'Economic growth and subjective well-being: reassessing the Easterlin Paradox', *Brookings Papers on Economic Activity 2008* (Spring): 1–87.

Stutzer, Alois (2004), 'The role of income aspirations in individual happiness', *Journal of Economic Behavior and Organization*, 54, 1: 84–109.

United Nations Development Programme (2010), *Human Development Report 2010*, New York, UNDP.

Part IV
Conclusion

John Knight

12

Economic Growth in China: Prospect

This concluding section contains two chapters, in what might appear to be an illogical order. The first is concerned with China's growth in prospect and the second with China's growth in retrospect. Our justification is that, in Chapter 12, we are able to base our discussion of China's future growth prospects on the analysis of previous chapters. Then, in Chapter 13, where we try to explain China's remarkable economic growth at different levels of understanding, we base our summary and conclusion on all that has gone before.

12.1 Introduction

Over the period of economic reform the size and nature of the Chinese economy have changed out of all recognition. Real GDP in 1978 was only 7% of its size in 2007. This is an economy in which output has on average doubled every eight years. Its structure, also, has changed remarkably. In 1978 the primary sector accounted for 70% of employment, whereas the corresponding figure for 2007 was 40%. A Chinese consumer of three decades ago would have been overwhelmed by the range of goods now available in the shops, and by the infrastructure now visible in city and countryside. All these and many other changes—none of them predictable back in 1978—transformed Chinese society and social attitudes as well as the economy. What might the next three decades bring?

In considering China's growth prospects we are treading on dangerous ground. Economists cannot make long-term forecasts with confidence: there are too many imponderables. Any forecasting model that might be developed has to make many assumptions that certain variables will change in particular ways and that other variables will not change. However, quantitative economic relationships that have held in the past often break down, in unpredictable ways, in the future. Economies are subject to unpredictable shocks, some shocks internal to the economy and some external, some economic in nature and some social or political, some based on current events and some on expectations about the future. Our approach, therefore, is to examine the more predictable determinants of China's future growth and to discuss some of the possible shocks that might derail that growth. We approach this chapter on China's growth prospects with the diffidence that it is due.

Can China's remarkable economic growth be maintained in future years? There are various reasons why we might expect the growth rate inevitably to decline from its current very high level as the Chinese economy matures. This is a process through which many economies have passed. For instance, Japan, South Korea, and Taiwan each had growth spurts over two or three decades, which were followed by slower growth. In addition, however, there can be shocks to the Chinese economy which dislodge it from its current virtuous circle of rapid growth. These might be financial, fiscal, or external shocks, shocks arising from macroeconomic imbalances, or shocks which are inherently political or social and which then affect the growth rate through their effects on confidence in the economy. It is all too likely that one form of shock will generate others. Economic recession might foment mass protests, or social instability might retard economic growth. We consider the different possible shocks in turn.

12.2 The Maturing Economy

We saw in Chapter 7 that a major part of the growth rate is to be explained by structural change—from agriculture to industry, from the public sector to the private sector, and from production for the domestic market to production for exports. It is inevitable that the growth rate will decline somewhat as the economy matures, that is, as the scope for further structural change diminishes. A large part of the economy is still within the production frontier, and some of China's growth is the result of its approaching the frontier. As the gap between potential and actual output narrows, so this source of growth will become less important.

Another source of growth has been the availability of abundant and relatively cheap unskilled labour. We saw in Chapter 9 that China is likely to experience an increasing scarcity of unskilled labour over the coming decade. This, also, is likely to put a brake on economic growth. The extent to which it does so will depend on the institutional response of land and labour markets and on the ability of the Chinese economy to move towards more skill- and technology-intensive production. An important consideration here is the rate of growth in the quantity and quality of human capital. The remarkable and sudden expansion of higher education, starting in 1999, might be interpreted as a preparation for China's predictable movement of production up the 'value chain'. Between 1998 and 2008, higher education enrolment increased from 3.4 million to 20.2 million (NBS 2009: 795). This expansion posed problems of absorption into the labour market in the short run, giving rise to social discontent among young people, but it might well prove to be important in sustaining rapid economic growth in the long run.

It is possible that the further marketization of the economy will slow down the growth rate. Huang (2009) argues that the failure to reform factor markets as far and as fast as product markets has assisted China's growth rate in the past but now poses a threat to continued rapid growth in the future. We examined in Chapter 3 how, as part of the strategy to promote economic growth, each of the factor markets remains undeveloped, regulated, and distorted, and how in aggregate these distortions might represent a subsidy to production of as much as 7% of GDP. It is the author's argument that the eventual correction of these distortions will slow down the growth rate.

We begin with the labour market, examined in Chapter 9. So long as the influx of rural–urban migrants is into relatively unskilled jobs requiring little training, the system of temporary migration—however inequitable—is economically efficient and growth enhancing. The impending shortage of migrant labour and the predictable urbanization of migrants are likely to reduce the degree of labour market segmentation, raising migrant wages and extending social security provision to them. The resultant higher labour costs can be expected to slow down the growth of the urban economy. In Chapter 8 we argued that the capital market remains distorted. China has a 'repressed financial system' with highly regulated interest rates, credit rationing, and government influence on credit allocation. However, the effect of further financial reform on the growth of the economy is difficult to predict. Reform will probably reduce the amount of investment as interest rates rise, but improve its efficiency. Land is owned by the state in the cities and by the local community in the countryside. In order to attract investment, it is common for local governments to underprice land for sale or use, as a subsidy for industrial development. The confiscation of land without adequate compensation is a source of political discontent, to which China's leaders are sensitive. This might provide the impetus to the future introduction of land markets, which are in turn likely either to increase (by providing greater security) or to decrease (if there is withdrawal of subsidies) the incentives to invest.

The environment is utilized in production and can thus be viewed as a scarce resource. China has introduced a series of environmental laws and regulations, and there is in place a State Environmental Policy Agency (SEPA) with ministerial status. However, enforcement has been weak because governments have prioritized economic growth. There is severe environmental damage in many areas of China. Environmental problems take two forms: pollution and the depletion of resources. China's heavy use of water and of coal contributes to both. The pollution of air, water, and land is a visible sign of the economy's rapid growth. China contains six of the world's ten most polluted cities, acid rain affects a third of Chinese territory, grassland degradation continues, taking the form of erosion and desertification. Desertification is moving east at a rate of 3,900 square miles a year (Woo 2009: 82–3). A World Bank report estimated in 1997 that the costs of air and water pollution corresponded to 8% of GDP (Naughton 2007: 493). Since producers generally do not fully compensate for the damage they do to the environment, their production costs are lowered and short-term growth is promoted. There is growing public concern about environmental damage, fostered by rising prosperity and the spread of information through the internet. This can be predicted to lead to more stringent environmental policies, more effectively enforced, but that will be costly and may well reduce economic growth in the long term.

Water shortage appears to be the most immediate environmental threat. Two-thirds of total water use is for irrigation. A fifth of water in the main river systems is so toxic that it cannot be used for anything (Naughton 2007: 492). On current trends, by 2030 China may need to use all of the water that is available. Because water is unevenly distributed, the majority of China's 660 cities already experience water shortage, and 110 of them experience 'severe shortage' (Woo 2009: 82). Water tables are falling, and some cities have experienced land subsidence as a result. In the 1960s the Yellow River annually fed 50 billion cubic metres of water into the sea; currently it feeds 5 billion cubic metres. A water transfer project of unprecedented magnitude—three canals to move water from the wet south to the dry north—is under construction, at great cost. Because water is underpriced, Chinese producers are profligate in their use of it. Policies to raise the price to its marginal social cost would increase firms' costs of production. Environmental limits, or the cost of extending them, may come to constrain China's future economic growth.

Some of the growth analysis in this book has been of GDP and some of GDP per capita. The distinction is important for projections into the future. Over the reform period China has derived a 'demographic dividend' from the rise in the 'support ratio', that is, the ratio of labour to population. Whereas output growth is related to the growth of labour as a factor of production, output per capita growth is related to the growth of population. The rise in the support ratio represents the contribution made by the demographic dividend to the growth of output per capita. According to Wang and Mason (2008), China's support ratio rose annually by 1.28% over the period 1982–2000, reflecting the sharp fall in fertility. They expected this rise then to slow down to 0.28% per annum over the period up to 2013—the projected peak year—and to decline by an annual 0.45% over the period 2013–50. Thus, it is arguable that the demographic dividend raised the growth of output per capita by as much as 1.28% per annum in the first two decades of economic reform. However, in future decades its effect will be to slow down the growth of output per capita, and thus the rise in living standards.

12.3 Macroeconomic Imbalances

Whereas the growth-retarding mechanisms discussed in Section 12.2 are long-term issues, Section 12.3 addresses problems that might require resolution in the short term—say, over a period of five years.[1] We have argued in several chapters that China's rapid growth has been primarily due to its growth-oriented political economy. This has generated a virtuous circle of high confidence, high expectations, high investment, high growth, high confidence, high expectations, and so on. In what circumstances might the virtuous circle be broken? Such a break would require a shock of either an economic or a political nature. Here we consider the economic shock that might arise from China's macroeconomic imbalances.

The Chinese economy is remarkable in at least two respects: its rate of economic growth and its macroeconomic imbalances. Over the last two decades of rapid growth, the economy has developed two forms of severe macroeconomic imbalance: an 'expenditure imbalance', by which we mean very high investment and very low consumption, giving rise to rapid capital accumulation; and an imbalance between expenditure and production, implying 'external imbalance', that is, a huge surplus in the current account of the balance of payments. How did these two forms of imbalance come about? What are their consequences? Can the imbalances be sustained or will they unwind in a way which threatens continued rapid economic growth? These are among the most important issues facing the Chinese macroeconomy.

We first describe the nature of China's macroeconomic imbalances and their interrelationships, and then explore in more detail how the current account surplus arose. We examine the disposal of the external surplus and the problems to which it gives rise, which leads on to a discussion of policies to deal with the imbalances. We are then in a position to consider whether the imbalances are sustainable and whether they threaten continued rapid economic growth. Finally, we examine the separate but related issue of the fragility of China's banking system.

China's macroeconomic imbalances

Consumption, investment, and net exports are the three components of expenditure on the GDP. Table 12.1 provides data on these components for China and other important or comparable economies over the latest five years for which comparable data are available, 2004–9. In the other countries, consumption generally comprises two-thirds or more, and investment one-third or less, of GDP. By contrast, we see that in China consumption is close to 50% and investment is over 40% of GDP. China's net export ratio (almost 9% of GDP) is exceeded only by that of Russia. China is indeed an international outlier in the composition of its

Conclusion

Table 12.1. The components of GDP in selected economies, percentage of GDP, 2004–9

	Consumption	Investment	Net exports	Saving
China	50.3	41.2	8.6	49.7
Brazil	80.5	16.9	2.6	19.5
Germany	76.7	18.1	5.2	23.3
India	68.6	31.5	–0.1	31.4
Japan	75.9	22.7	1.4	24.1
Korea	68.6	29.0	2.4	31.4
Russia	67.6	19.9	12.5	32.4
United Kingdom	86.2	16.6	–2.8	13.8
United States	86.6	18.3	–4.8	13.4

Notes: The period percentages are calculated by averaging annual percentages. Saving is derived as GDP – consumption. Investment – saving is by definition equal to net exports but with opposite sign.

Source: World Bank, *World Development Indicators*.

expenditure: its consumption is lower and investment higher than in the other economies, and net exports are large and positive.

China's macroeconomic imbalances grew remarkably over the decade 1999–2008, and particularly after 2004 (Figure 12.1). Consumption fell monotonically after 2000, from 62% of GDP in that year to 48% in 2009, a fall of fourteen

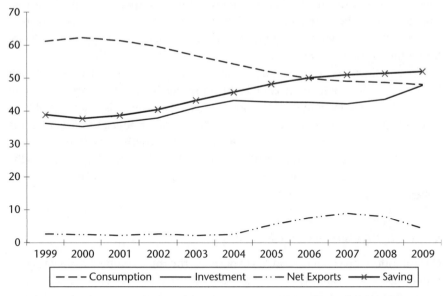

Figure 12.1. The components of GDP in China, percentage of total, 1999–2009, annual
Source: NBS (2010).

Notes: Consumption is household consumption + government consumption, investment is gross fixed capital formation + change in inventories, and net exports are obtained as a residual. By definition, saving equals GDP – consumption; and investment – saving equals net exports but with opposite sign.

percentage points. There was a sharp rise in investment between 2002 and 2004, from 38% to 43% of GDP, and thereafter the share remained at a high level and reached a thirty-year high of 48% in 2009. The export surplus was stable from 1999 to 2004, at between 2% and 3% of GDP. As the share of consumption continued to fall, net exports rose sharply, from less than 3% of GDP in 2004 to a peak of 9.9% in 2007, and then declined on account of the global economic recession.

It is a national income-accounting identity that $(X - M) + (I - S) + (G - R) = 0$ where X is exports, M is imports, I is investment, S is saving, G is government expenditure, and R is government revenue. As $(G - R) = (I_g - S_g)$, the government balance can be subsumed into $(I - S)$, Thus, the internal balance $(I - S)$, that is, net investment, is necessarily equal to the external balance $(X - M)$, that is, net exports, but with opposite sign. Equivalently, $(S - I) = (X - M)$, that is, net capital outflow equals the external balance. It is clear from the figure, therefore, that $(I - S)$ was consistently negative throughout the decade 1999–2009, and in size became an international outlier after 2004. Despite the high investment rate, the saving rate was even higher.

Any realistic macroeconomic model makes these balances a function of many variables, some of which are themselves endogenous: a complicated simultaneous equation model is required. It is sufficient for our purposes, however, to consider the likely causal effects of certain key variables on the external imbalance in the short run. To do this, we distinguish between national accounting identities and equilibrium conditions in which there are no involuntary changes in inventories. At a very simple level, and given a fixed exchange rate, an exogenous investment boom is likely to raise demand and thus a combination of output and prices. As saving is unlikely to increase by as much as investment, the investment boom increases $(I - S)$. The increased demand is likely to raise imports and so lower $(X - M)$. Output and prices adjust to ensure that in equilibrium the imbalance between expenditure and income arising from the decisions of economic agents is equal but opposite to the external imbalance also arising from their decisions. Consider the short-run consequences of an exogenous export boom. This is liable to generate an increase in $(X - M)$. Although it also produces higher output and prices, the ensuing increase in imports is unlikely to be as great as the initial increase in exports. The increase in output is likely to raise saving and so to lower $(I - S)$. Output and prices adjust so that in equilibrium the increase in net exports $(X - M)$ desired by economic agents is equal to the desired decrease in net investment $(I - S)$.

Applying this analysis to China, the rising value of $(X - M)$ and falling $(I - S)$ of the last decade would be consistent with rapid growth in both exports and saving. It appears that China's investment boom, with its capacity to reduce external imbalance, was more than offset by its export boom and by saving growing even more rapidly than investment. We explore the reasons for this outcome below.

There is considerable evidence, based on differing methodologies, that gross fixed capital formation is an important proximate determinant of economic growth in China (Kuijs and Wang 2005; Shane and Gale 2004). Moreover, in Chapters 4, 5, and 6 we estimated cross-country and cross-province growth regressions by means of system GMM analysis and reached this conclusion.

The impact of investment has two components. One is China's remarkably high ratio of investment to GDP, as was shown in Figure 6.1 of Chapter 6. Gross fixed capital formation as a proportion of GDP rose above 30% after 1991 and above 40% after 2003. This investment ratio far exceeds that of the industrialized countries and exceeds even that of Japan (32% in the period 1960–85) and South Korea (30% in the period 1970–95) during their growth heydays. The other component is the high coefficient on investment in the cross-province growth equations. This is partly because of the embodiment of technological progress in capital goods and the complementarities of physical capital with human capital and with abundant unskilled labour (Chapter 6) and partly because investment made possible various structural changes in the economy towards more productive activities and sectors (Chapter 7).

The predominant source of China's high investment ratio was the enterprise sector. Household investment rose slightly after 2002, possibly because of the emergence of urban residential investment, but was only 8.7% of GDP in 2008. Government investment (excluding capital transfers to enterprises) was even lower, being under 5% in 2008. By contrast, enterprise investment was consistently above 27% of GDP after 1992 and was responsible for most of the annual fluctuation in the investment rate. It is the enterprise investment rate that is the international outlier (Kuijs 2005).

The underlying reasons for China's high investment were examined in Chapter 8. Research shows that the rate of profit on capital remained high despite the remarkable increase in the capital–labour ratio. There was a trend fall in the corporate profit rate up to 1998 and a subsequent rise, especially from 2002 onwards. The same pattern was found in both state-owned enterprises (SOEs) and private firms, although SOE profits were lower and more heterogeneous.

Movements in the profitability of SOEs can be explained by the growing competition facing the inefficient and increasingly unprofitable SOE sector, which then forced SOE reform, beginning in the late 1990s. The ensuing greater managerial autonomy and incentives, including permission to retrench surplus labour, the retention of profits, and the scrapping or disposal of some loss makers, raised the profitability of the SOE sector. In the early part of the period, SOE managers, facing soft budgets, and local government owners were more concerned with growth than with profits. In more recent years, as profitability became a more important concern, the high and rising profit rate helped to maintain high investment.

The underlying political economy is conducive to investment. The incentive and patronage system facing government officials has rewarded economic growth, and their predictable behaviour has provided investment security. The 'developmental state' ensures that entrepreneurial expectations of rapid growth are created and, through subsequent economic growth, are maintained (Chapter 8).

We see in Table 12.1 that China's saving rate is considerably higher than that in the other economies listed, and in Figure 12.2 that China's saving rate increased from an already high value of 39% in 1999 to 53% in 2009, a rise of no less than fourteen percentage points. In the latter year saving actually exceeded consumption: a remarkable statistic for such a poor country.

We examined the reasons for China's high saving rate in Chapter 8. Here we concentrate on the reasons for its rise in recent years, distinguishing household, government, and enterprise saving. Figure 12.3 shows saving as a proportion of GDP in these three sectors over the years 1990–2008. The 1990s and 2000s are different: the three components of saving individually remained fairly constant as a proportion of GDP until about 2000, soon after which each of them began to rise. Their combined saving rate increased by fifteen percentage points between 2000 and 2008.

The household saving rate (by definition equal to 1 – the household consumption rate) expressed as a proportion of household income over the period 1990–2009 is shown in Figure 12.3. The urban household saving rate trended

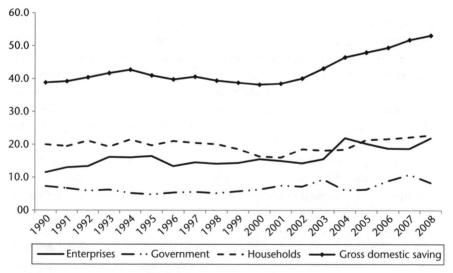

Figure 12.2. Saving by different sectors as percentage of GDP, 1990–2008, annual
Source: 1992–2008: NBS (various years), flow-of-funds tables; 1990–1: Kuijs (2005).
Notes: GDP is the total value added in the corresponding flow-of-funds table.

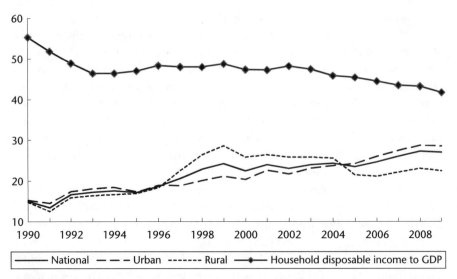

Figure 12.3. Household saving rates, and household income as percentage of GDP, 1990–2009, annual

Source: NBS (various issues, 1991–2010), household survey tables.

Notes: Saving rate of urban households = (1 − per capita consumption expenditure)/per capita disposable income. Saving rate of rural households = (1 − per capita total consumption expenditure)/per capita net income.

upwards, from 15% in 1990 to 29% in 2009, a rise of fourteen percentage points. The rise might reflect credit constraints and the greater incentive to save for business opportunities, house purchase, education, retirement, and health care as the urban economy became marketized, the 'iron rice bowl' was removed, and city life became less secure; also, rising income inequality among urban households. Similarly, the rural saving rate increased from 15% to 23% over the same period, an increase of eight percentage points. All of this occurred in the 1990s: the rural saving rate actually fell slightly after 2000. The rise in the 1990s might reflect improving opportunities for various forms of investment and the monetization of the rural economy, as well as increasing marriage competition among sons. The combined urban and rural household saving rate had reached 27% in 2009: a rate so high as to make Chinese households an international outlier—all the more remarkable in such a poor country.

Figure 12.3 also shows that household income as a proportion of GDP fell from 55% in 1990 to 42% in 2009. The thirteen percentage point decline occurred between 1990 and 1993 and again between 2003 and 2009. That redistribution of income would raise the national saving rate if the propensity to save income of the non-household (enterprise plus government) sector exceeded that of the household sector. This argument, also, has been adduced to help explain the rise in China's saving rate.

Consider government saving. Figure 12.4 presents government revenue (proxied by government disposable income), government expenditure and government balance $(R - G)$ as a proportion of GDP, and government saving $(S_g = R - C_g)$ as a proportion of government revenue, over the period 1990–2008. Government revenue was consistently higher than government expenditure, that is, the government balance was positive; and indeed the balance rose after 2004. Government saving out of revenue exceeded 30% throughout and was as high as 40% in 2007. Government saving was generally high as a result of a policy that favoured government-financed investment over government consumption.

Of the three sources of saving, enterprise saving is the most remarkable for its high and rising level. This is seen in Figure 12.5 for the period 1993–2008. From 2001 to 2008 the share of profits, expressed as a proportion of GDP, was both high and rising. We explored the reasons for this rise in Chapter 8. Enterprise saving as a proportion of GDP also rose, being lowest in 1996 and highest in 2008. The enterprise saving rate out of profits was consistently high, but varying between 60 and 80%.

In the case of the non-state sector, the high enterprise saving out of profits is to be explained in terms of the imperfect credit market. The 'repressed financial

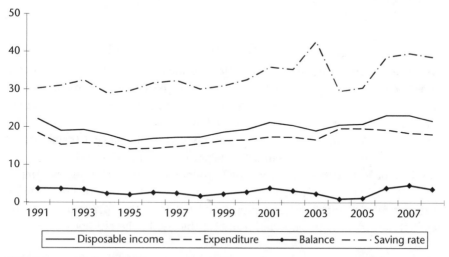

Figure 12.4. Government revenue (disposable income), expenditure, and balance as percentage of GDP, and saving rate as percentage of revenue, 1990–2008, annual

Source: 1992–2010: NBS, flow-of-funds tables; 1990–1: Kuijs (2005).

Notes: Government expenditure includes government consumption and government investment.

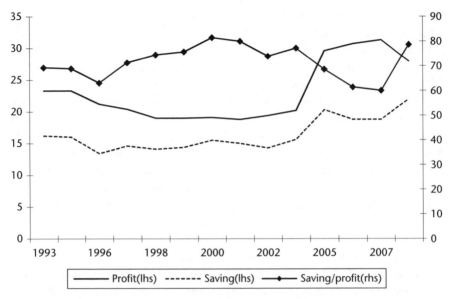

Figure 12.5. Enterprise profit and saving as percentage of GDP, and saving rate as a percentage of profit, 1993–2008, annual

Source: NBS (1992–2010).

Notes: Enterprise profit is calculated using the income approach whereas saving is calculated using the expenditure approach. The GDP in profit/GDP is the value added using the by-income approach and GDP in saving/GDP is taken from the expenditure approach.

system' channelled funds to the state sector and starved private firms of finance for investment: they were heavily reliant on ploughing back profits for investment. In the case of SOEs, the facts that firm growth was an important managerial objective, that lenders' interest rates were fixed at low levels, and that for many years government did not require SOEs to pay dividends, encouraged them to save and reinvest their profits; even in 2010 the proportion of profits paid in dividends was 10% or less. In the 2000s, retained profits represented 60% of investment funds in the case of SOEs but no less than 96% in the case of private firms (Chapter 8). The rising share of profits and the incentive to retain profits for reinvestment is thus an important cause of the rise in the ratio of total saving to GDP.

Figure 12.6 reports the net saving rates (S – I) of households, government, and enterprises. On a minor scale, government was consistently a net saver. On a major scale, households were consistently net lenders and enterprises consistently net borrowers. The 'repressed financial system' garnered savings from households, paying low depositor interest rates, and the state-owned banks made the funds

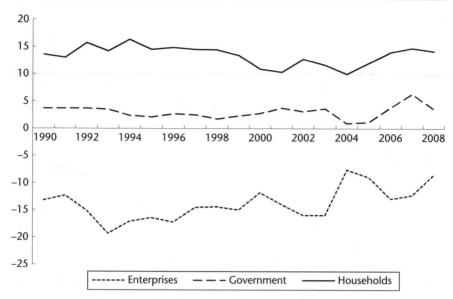

Figure 12.6. Saving minus investment as percentage of GDP by sector, 1990–2008, annual

Source: 1992–2010: NBS (various years), flow-of-funds tables; 1990–1: Kuijs (2005).

Notes: GDP is the total value added in the corresponding flow-of-funds table.

available to the SOE sector, and more recently to the corporate sector—much of which remained state controlled.

China's external imbalance

Research on the relationship between exports and economic growth in China has produced encouraging results. Yao (2006) found that exports have a strong positive effect on the growth rate of output. In Chapter 7, using system GMM estimation to establish causal effects, we found that both export share and import share raised the growth rate in China over the period 1978–2006; and that the growth in export share and in import share had the same-sized effect. Both the level of trade and its expansion are good for economic growth.

It is China's external surplus, with its implication of external deficit for its trading partners as a group, that is of particular concern to the world. How did it arise? Figure 12.7 reports the annual data on exports, imports, and net exports as a proportion of GDP over the period 1990–2009. We see that both exports and imports rose steadily, and that after 2001 net exports, here defined as the current account surplus of the balance of payments, began to trend upwards. The trend became an explosion after 2003: it rose from $46 billion in 2003 to a high point of $372 billion in 2007. In that year net exports amounted to 10.6% of GDP. By

277

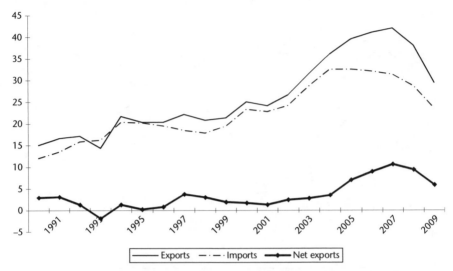

Figure 12.7. Exports, imports, and net exports as percentage of GDP, 1990–2009, annual

Source: NBS (various years), balance of payments tables.

contrast, the current account of Japan during its period of rapid growth (1960–85) was 4.3% of GDP, and that of Korea (1976–95) was negligible (–0.86%).

The current account of the balance of payments is made up of trade in goods and services, income to and from abroad, and current transfers. The big increase in the current account surplus occurred between 2004 and 2008, rising from $67 billion to $426 billion (the surplus suffered a small setback relative to GDP in 2009 on account of the world economic recession). Some 85% of the increase was contributed by trade in goods and services.

Why did the trade surplus in goods increase? Figure 12.8 shows that exports and imports both grew rapidly in the period from 2001 to 2004 and that there was little change in the trade balance. However, the subsequent rapid growth of exports (29% per annum between 2004 and 2007) exceeded that of imports (22% per annum) and caused the balance of trade in goods to increase almost tenfold. Moreover, the growth in imports was partly due to the growth in exports because of the processing nature of much of China's exporting industries: only 50% of export value represents domestic value added (Koopman et al. 2008).

Why did exports of goods surge so remarkably after 2004? China joined the WTO at the end of 2001, so integrating the economy more closely with global markets. Tariffs had already been reduced in anticipation of WTO accession, and the subsequent effect in increasing imports was not large. The WTO agreement required that conditions imposed on foreign direct investment in China be ended. Together with the assurance of 'most favoured nation' treatment and of China's inclusion in the 2005 termination of quotas on textiles and clothing exports, this

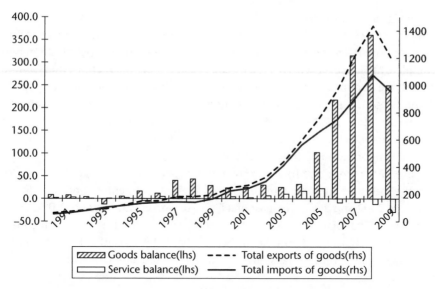

Figure 12.8. Trade surplus on goods and services, US$billion, 1990–2009, annual
Source: NBS (various years), balance of payments tables.

improved the attractiveness of China's investment climate for export-oriented production (Rumbaugh and Blancher 2004; Athukorala 2009). By 2008 'foreign-funded enterprises' accounted for no less than 55% of China's exports. Perhaps the main effect of WTO entry on the current account came through the increased competitive impetus for domestic reform and thus faster productivity growth in the tradeable goods sector.

The export surplus would not have grown so remarkably had China not enjoyed potential comparative advantage, and indeed absolute advantage, in the export industries. What was the basis of this advantage? Manufactures accounted for more than 90% of the growth of goods exports after 2001. Therefore, it is instructive to investigate the main types of manufactures. In the 1990s, conventional labour-intensive manufactures (the 'miscellaneous manufactured products') such as footwear, clothing, toys, and sports goods accounted for almost half of manufacturing exports. Though labour-intensive exports continued to grow impressively (by 15% per annum) in the decade after 1999, there was a structural shift in composition towards seemingly more sophisticated product lines, in particular machinery and transport equipment: their share of manufactured exports increased from 30% to 49% over the decade.

This suggests that technology and/or capital have played an increasingly important role. However, Athukorala (2009) argues that China is merely the assembly centre for machinery and transport equipment, contributing the most labour-intensive operations of a production process spread over several countries: the share of components in total machinery imports increased from 33% in 1992/3 to 63% in 2004/5; by contrast, final goods continued to dominate China's export composition. It appears that China's main role in international specialization is to complete the labour-intensive final assembly stage. Sung (2007) finds that China's exports are dominated by low-value-added processing by foreign affiliates: exports involving processing with imported materials as a proportion of total exports rose to a peak of 44% in 2004, and declined marginally thereafter. Since nearly half of China's manufactured exports are in the processing category, low labour cost remains important for China's trade competitiveness.

Table 12.2 reports the hourly compensation per worker in manufacturing for China, both absolutely and relative to its trading competitors and the United States, in 2002 and 2007. The cost of a Chinese worker was only US$1.0 in 2007, about 3% of that of a US worker. Even by comparison with its export competitors, China's labour cost is still low, being 'bettered' only by Sri Lanka. This labour cost advantage comes from China's huge labour supply and abundance of rural–urban migrants.

Despite the high and rising rate of return on capital in China's corporate sector, documented in Chapter 8, there is evidence to suggest that China developed excess capacity in certain industries in the early 2000s. These tend to be heavy industries dominated by SOEs. Table 12.3 shows that their capacity utilization rates were 75% or below. Take the steel industry for example: in 2005 China's steel output was 350 million tons but its excess capacity (120 million tons) was said actually to exceed the output of the world's second-largest steel producer, Japan (113 million tons); and 70 million tons of capacity was 'in building'.

Excess capacity in various industries had implications for China's surge in net exports after 2004. First, it provided China with enough capacity to satisfy the external demand. According to Anderson (2007), the rising trade surplus came largely from heavy industrial products including aluminum, machine tools, cement, key chemical products, and steel products—a list which corresponds well with the industries listed in Table 12.3. Secondly, the existence of spare capacity meant that additional production would drive firms down their short-run average cost curves, thus enabling them to lower their prices and so increase relative demand. For instance, in 2006 when China's exports of steel surged and the international steel price kept rising, the domestic price was 10% lower than in 2005.[2] Third, the increase in net exports was as much about import substitution as about exports. The underutilization of capacity in heavy industry enabled firms to switch from foreign sources of intermediate products for export production to cheaper and more reliable domestic sources.

Irrespective of the exchange rate, we would expect China to have adapted further to its comparative advantage in trade after its preparation for and entry to the WTO reduced trade uncertainties and restrictions. However, the low and relatively stable value of the renminbi (RMB) provided an additional impetus to

Table 12.2. Hourly compensation costs/wages in manufacturing, US$, 2002 and 2007

	China	Brazil	Mexico	Philippines	Eastern Europe	India	Sri Lanka	Indonesia	Pakistan
2002	0.6	2.6	2.5	0.7	3.6	0.5	0.5	0.9	1.5
2007	1.0	6.0	2.9	1.1	7.3	1.7*	0.6	1.8	—

Notes: For India, Indonesia, and Pakistan, the compensation costs are wages and do not include the social welfare payments by employers and are therefore undervalued.
*The later Indian figure relates to 2006.

Source: Department of Labor, United States (2009); China NBS (2008); and International Labour Organization (India, Indonesia, and Pakistan).

Table 12.3. Excess capacity in different industries, million tons, 2005

	Output capacity	Output	Excess capacity	In building	Capacity utilization (%)
Steel	470	350	120	70	75
Aluminium	10.3	7.0	3.3	—	68
Ferroalloy	22.1	12.0	10.1	2.8	54
Calcium carbide	10.4	6.0	4.4	12.0	58
Containers	4.5	2.4	2.1	1.3	53

Note: Container output is measured in twenty-foot equivalent units.

Source: 'China's overcapacity in thirteen industries', *China Economic Weekly Journal*, 19 May 2006 (in Chinese).

exports. Makin (2007) argued that, by reducing exchange rate uncertainty for the export sector, China's exchange rate management encouraged exports. Goldstein and Lardy (2006) used the 'underlying balance' approach to estimate the equilibrium exchange rate. The approach is to estimate the real effective (trade-weighted) exchange rate that would produce an equilibrium in which the 'underlying' current account is approximately equal, and opposite in sign, to 'normal' net capital flow. They took the average capital account surplus as a proportion of GDP in the period 1999–2002 (when there was no expectation of RMB appreciation) as the normal net capital flow and found that to return to that balance in 2005, the RMB should be appreciated by 20–40%. Cline and Williamson (2008) provide a comprehensive survey of eighteen studies that estimated China's equilibrium exchange rate in the 2000s. The studies varied considerably in data, methodology, and conclusions. However, the simple average of the estimates of the RMB appreciation that would be required to produce equilibrium in the real effective exchange rate was 19%. The estimates implied that the RMB had become more undervalued over time: the studies based on the period 2000–4 required an average appreciation of 17%, and those based on 2005–7 an average of 26%.

The rapid growth of foreign exchange reserves in the 2000s indicates that the Chinese government intervened to maintain the undervaluation of the RMB. In 2005 the People's Bank of China (PBC) carried out a reform of the exchange rate regime. However, this minor RMB appreciation did not alleviate expectations of further appreciation. To prevent the currency appreciating sharply, the PBC had, on the one hand, to purchase a great amount of foreign currency and, on the other hand, to sterilize much of the reserve accumulation through open market operations and by increasing commercial bank reserve requirements. The PBC began to require commercial banks to hold US dollar reserves in 2005, and it increased the reserve requirement ratio three times in 2006 and eight times in 2007. The continued strengthening of the current account balance implied that the RMB was becoming further undervalued. This was exacerbated by the response in capital markets. Not only did the one-way bet on the currency attract hot money inflows but also it inhibited private capital outflows.

Figure 12.9 shows the nominal and real exchange rate of the RMB with the dollar and a trade-weighted basket of currencies over the period 1990–2009, where 2005 = 100. A rise indicates that the RMB appreciated. Although the exchange rate with the dollar is politically more sensitive, it is the real trade-weighted exchange rate that is the best indicator of changing competitiveness. Between 2002 and 2007, the nominal (NEER) and real (REER) effective exchange rates both stayed relatively low. The RMB peaked at 113 in 2001, fell to 100 in 2005, and then rose to 119 in 2009.

We are now in a position to review the reasons for China's rising external imbalance. The explanation requires the identification of the exogenous changes in a simultaneous equation system. These can arise either in $(S - I)$ or in $(X - M)$.

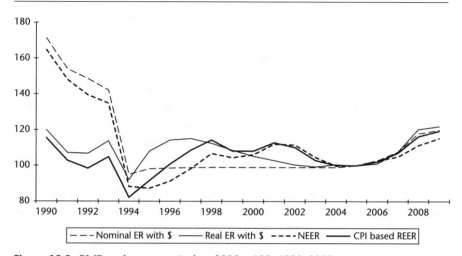

Figure 12.9. RMB exchange rate index, 2005 = 100, 1990–2009

Source: NEER and CPI-based REER indices are from IMF, *International Financial Statistics*.

The $(S - I)$ approach is the appropriate framework for applying the 'saving glut' theory of Bernanke (2005). Bernanke argued that global imbalances had grown as a result of a rise in saving relative to investment in various countries, including China.

It is very likely that two sets of forces were at work to increase China's export surplus, in turn responding endogenously to each other. On the one hand, there was an exogenous increase in S relative to I, for the reasons that we have outlined. On the other hand, there was an exogenous increase in X relative to M, again for the reasons set out above. Following Corden's (2009) application to China of the familiar Swan diagram depicting the requirements for both external and internal balance, and assuming initial equilibrium, the export surplus can be interpreted as follows. The increase in export surplus was partly due to a rise in competitiveness—itself the result of economic reform and new export opportunities (both in part associated with WTO accession), together with a fairly fixed exchange rate. It was also due partly to a fall in expenditure relative to output—the rise in saving, linked to rising profitability (itself associated with economic reform). Thus, both $(X - M)$ and $(S - I)$ rose exogenously, in addition to their endogenous interaction; both contributed to the external imbalance.

The external surplus and the foreign exchange reserves

We examine the disposal of the external surplus and the problems, actual and potential, to which it gives rise. We do so under four headings: exchange rate policy, excess liquidity and sterilization, the accumulation of foreign assets, and the effect on international trade relations. This analysis enables us then to pose the question: is the external imbalance sustainable?

In July 2005 the Chinese government appreciated the RMB by 2.1%. The government announced that the external value of the currency would be set with reference to a basket of currencies rather than being pegged to the dollar, allowing a movement of up to +/– 0.3% in bilateral exchange rates within any given day, and that it would be determined more on the basis of market supply and demand than in the past. It was natural for the markets to expect further appreciation. However, in order to maintain the growth of output and employment in the export sectors and to protect China's immature and fragile financial system, the PBC intervened in the market to control the pace of appreciation. In theory the new regime would permit an upward trend of 6.6% per month but in practice by the end of 2008 the RMB had appreciated at an annual average rate of 5% against the dollar.

Nor did it appear that the rate was being set by reference to a basket of currencies. Frankel and Wei (2007) regressed changes in the value of the RMB against those of the dollar, euro, yen, and other currencies that should be in the basket, and found that the RMB was still largely linked to the dollar over the years 2005–7. We see in Figure 12.10 that between July 2005 and July 2008 the RMB gradually appreciated against the dollar but, because the dollar depreciated sharply against other major currencies, the RMB depreciated against the euro. We also see that after July 2008 the RMB was pegged to the dollar while it fluctuated against the

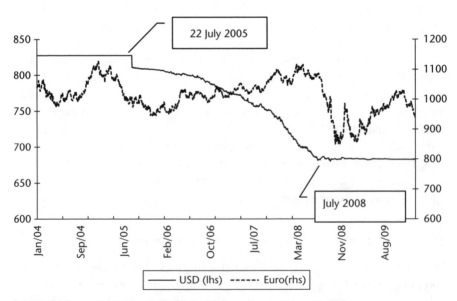

Figure 12.10. US$/RMB and €/RMB exchange rates, 2004–10, daily
Source: <www.finance.yahoo.com>.

euro. Rather than preventing the growth of the export surplus, the new exchange rate policy brought several problems.

While the RMB was expected to float upwards, the private sector was reluctant to accumulate dollar assets. Thus the PBC had to purchase dollars if it wished to prevent large upward movement in the RMB. This rapid accumulation of foreign exchange was accompanied by the release of domestic currency, which caused a rapid increase in the domestic money supply. In 2007 the year-on-year growth rate of M1 reached 21%, the highest rate since 1998. From an analysis of monthly data since 2000, Wang (2010) concluded that the increase in the foreign exchange reserves had not been fully sterilized.

The sharp increase in liquidity generated serious asset bubbles. The real estate market boomed: between 2004 and 2009 house prices in China's thirty-five main cities tripled. Take Beijing for example: the average price of newly built flats rose from 4,747 in 2004 to 13,799 yuan/sq.m in 2009. Stock markets boomed astonishingly: the Shanghai comprehensive stock index started from 998 in July 2005 and reached 6212 in October 2007. Then the impact of excess liquidity shifted from financial assets to the real economy. The excess liquidity now came from the decrease in money demand owing to the rise in asset prices (Yu 2008).

From the start of 2006 the inflation rate accelerated despite price controls on petrol and electricity. As Figure 12.11 shows, the CPI peaked at 8.7% in February 2008. The real interest rate (proxied by the nominal rate minus the current inflation rate) became negative in March 2007, although the central bank increased interest rates five times over the next thirteen months. The negative real interest rate in turn stimulated investment and added to inflation.

In its attempt to maintain price stability and prevent asset bubbles, the PBC carried out a large-scale sterilization operation to mop up excess liquidity. This

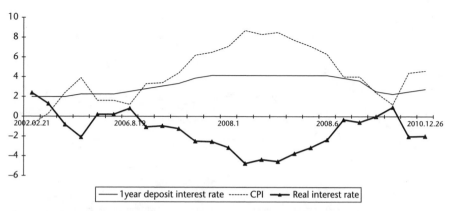

Figure 12.11. Nominal interest rate on one-year deposits, CPI, and real interest rate, per cent per annum, 2002–10

Source: NBS (various years) and PBC data.

involved selling within three years all the government bonds that it had accumulated since 1998, and increasing the bank cash reserve requirement ratio eleven times in 2006–7. Commercial banks were also required to hold some US dollars as deposit reserves. The central bank used directives to control commercial banks' release of credit. The PBC wished also to issue central bank bills. Since the large-scale issue of such bills would push up market interest rates, the danger was that this would attract capital inflows, so increasing the pressure for RMB appreciation. The only solution was to force the commercial banks to buy bills. In the course of 2010 the inflation rate rose and the real interest rate became negative. The PBC had to raise the banks' reserve requirement to 19%, its highest-ever level. China's exchange rate policy continued to restrict the scope for monetary and stabilization policy.

The large-scale sterilization through involuntary purchases of central bank bills and the other credit control methods produced at least three deleterious consequences for the commercial banks (Yu 2008). Their profitability was reduced by the fact that low-yield assets accounted for more than a fifth of their total assets. The attempt to maintain profit margins led commercial banks to increase lending to riskier borrowers willing to pay higher interest rates. Moreover, the forced purchase of central bank bills compromised the process of financial reform.

We see in Figure 12.12 that the current account, consistently positive over almost the entire period 1990–2009, increased sharply after 2004. Gross FDI inflows were also positive throughout, peaking in 1994 at 7% of GDP after Deng Xiaoping's southern tour which encouraged FDI, and running at about 3.5% of GDP in the period 2004–8; net FDI was only very slightly lower. The current

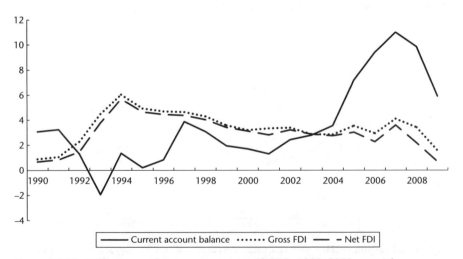

Figure 12.12. Different surpluses as percentage of GDP, 1990–2009, annual
Source: NBS (various years), balance of payments tables.

account and net FDI combined indicate the rate at which foreign financial assets were accumulating: at its peak in 2007 this represented no less than 14% of GDP.

China's foreign exchange reserves were mainly held in the form of dollar-denominated US government bonds, earning a low rate of interest. Assume that one-year bonds are the main asset in the portfolio. From July 2005 until the December 2008 the average annual return on one-year bonds was 3.0%, whereas the dollar depreciated against the RMB by an average annual rate of 6.1%. The huge increase in PBC purchases after 2004 was sufficiently important to help keep US interest rates low. Indeed, some have argued that this contributed to the US housing bubble which precipitated the banking crisis that in turn created the world economic recession. There is a great irony to an arrangement in which one of the poor countries of the world (in 2008 GDP per capita PPP, $5,962) lends to one of the rich countries (GDP per capita PPP, $46,716). The arrangement required China to live within its means and permitted the United States to live beyond its means. It implied a low rate of time preference in China and a high rate in the US: China was postponing consumption and the US was bringing it forward.

Despite the security that US government bonds possess if held until maturity, China's reserve portfolio strategy was extremely risky. This took the form of foreign exchange risk: China was becoming increasingly boxed in. Leightner (2010) estimated the marginal effect on the exchange rate of a reduction in China's foreign reserves. The estimates implied that the US dollar would fall by 0.44% if China were to sell 1% of its dollar holdings. Although the effect will depend on whether central banks stabilize or speculate, this potentially sensitive relationship is likely to serve as a deterrent both to substantial sales and to further accumulation of dollar reserves.

Should the reserves have been invested in more profitable assets such as shares, property, and structured instruments? With the proportion currently less than 1%, China has scope to increase the share of its foreign assets held in the form of equities. Several developing countries hold more than 10%. However, this needs sophisticated expertise and experience, and China's initial failures (for instance, the Blackstone fiasco) made it hold back. Because of the risks, most developing countries—including India, Brazil, and Russia—have kept the ratio below 2%. Nor does the holding of equities reduce foreign exchange risk.

Although it is the current fashion for the currencies of the major economies to be allowed to float, it is only a modern practice even for the major economies and it is still not the rule for developing countries, nor necessarily is it in their interests. To accuse China of 'currency manipulation', as some have done, is merely rhetoric. The serious issues are whether China on balance benefits from its policy of RMB undervaluation, and whether other countries lose from it. Although consumers in the advanced economies have benefited from the flood of relatively low-priced imports from China, it is possible that some of their countrymen have suffered through the loss of jobs in manufacturing and the structural problems of switching labour and resources into other activities. As China's export surplus has grown, so the major countries—in particular the US and the EU—have begun to put pressure on China to change its policies.

Trade disputes have broken out. From July 2000 to June 2007, there were 375 anti-dumping investigations of China's export products, equivalent to 25% of the total. A WTO secretariat report in May 2009 showed that products exported from China were increasingly picked out, and they accounted for almost half of all measures in the latter half of 2008. Since 2006 the US and the EU had imposed anti-dumping and anti-subsidy import restrictions on China in more than 100 cases. It is understandable that most of these occurred in 2009 when the major economies were in serious recession and China's currency peg with the dollar had been restored. The measures were concentrated on China's exports of shoes, clothing, steel, tungsten, tyres, and machinery. In 2010 there was further political pressure from the US for RMB appreciation, and many other countries extended the terms of their anti-dumping tariffs. As the world economy recovers, and China's export surplus begins to grow again—as it is likely to do given current Chinese policies—political pressures and trade restrictions against China can be predicted to grow.

Policies to correct the imbalance

Just as the explanation for the export surplus is two-pronged, so also the policy to address the problem can be two-pronged. External and internal policies to achieve external balance cannot be neatly separated. Basically, if a high value of $(X - M)$ is to be reduced, this implies that the equally high value of $(S - I)$ is also reduced. However, policies to reduce X or to raise M might affect both S and I. There is also a policy choice between attempting to lower S or to raise I. Policies to lower S or to raise I can impinge also on X and M. Although recognizing the importance of these interrelationships, we analyse first external policies and then internal policies for correcting imbalance.

In the past China had in place a number of trade policies intended to encourage exports. After WTO entry the government reversed or lessened these policies. All forms of export subsidy inconsistent with WTO rules, including grants and tax rebates linked to export performance, were eliminated (Rumbaugh and Blancher 2004: 8). It had also been the practice for the state-owned banks to provide loans at favourable interest rates to some export-oriented SOEs; the policy was ended in 2007.

Having reduced the weighted average tariff rate from 38% in 1993 to 9% in 2001 (Rumbaugh and Blancher 2004: table 8), the Chinese government appeared reluctant to go much further, basically because several of the import-substitute industries, such as vehicles, were not ready to meet competition from abroad. In 2007 it relaxed the import rights for some products including vegetable oil, alumina, and stainless steel, reduced the import tariffs for some high-technology and advanced manufactured products, and increased the annual personal foreign exchange purchasing limit. However, since these changes were minor in size and scope, their effect on imports was very limited.

Net inward FDI raises profit remittances and so decreases the current account surplus whereas net outward FDI increases that surplus. The government became keener on outward FDI: enterprises were encouraged to invest abroad through merger or acquisition or by making strategic investments in natural resources—not only to raise the average return on overseas assets but also to acquire high technology, management expertise, and strategic reserves. Chinese direct investments abroad jumped from about US$16 billion in 2006 to US$54 billion in 2008. However, the policy of encouraging inward FDI was maintained. Under a scheme introduced in 2006, securities firms and mutual fund management companies are allowed to make overseas portfolio investments. The portfolio stock at the end of 2006 was US$229 billion, or 14% of China's foreign assets (Wang et al. 2007); and in 2008 US$252 billion, or 9% of the total. The expectation of RMB appreciation, boom in the domestic stock market, and the poor performance of the first group of overseas investments produced a damp squib.

The policies so far adopted to influence China's external surplus have failed to prevent its rapid growth. In 2008 and 2009 China's external surplus was reduced by the fall in demand that resulted from the world economic recession. However, the external surplus was merely temporarily reduced, and it could be predicted to bounce back. Would more rapid appreciation of the RMB restore external balance? The appreciation of 2005–8 clearly failed to do so, partly because it was small. Some researchers have argued that appreciation would have rather limited effects on the current account. For example, Shu and Yip (2006), using data for the period 1995 to 2006, found that change in relative price has only a small effect on exports and trade balance; this was attributed to China's role as a processor of intermediate products.

A further pointer is the behaviour of exports to the US and to the EU in response to changes in the exchange rate between the dollar and the euro between start-2005 and end-2008 (Figure 12.10). From July 2005 and June 2008 the RMB appreciated continuously against the dollar. By contrast, the RMB fell against the euro from January 2006 to March 2008 but rose otherwise. The growth of exports to the US fell throughout the period; the growth of exports to the Eurozone increased when the RMB depreciated but otherwise decreased. This analysis, although simplistic, suggests that the trend rate of growth of exports is sensitive to the external value of the RMB: appreciation should help to reduce the external surplus.

Mckinnon and Schnabl (2009) were concerned that RMB appreciation would not be effective because of the indirect effects of reducing the current surplus $(X - M)$ on domestic S and I. In particular, they argued that investment would fall because appreciation would make China a more expensive production location, thus raising $(S - I)$, *ceteris paribus*, and so tending to offset the fall in $(X - M)$. However, while it is true that FDI in particular may be footloose, FDI accounts for only a small part of investment: it averaged 8% of total fixed capital formation over the years 2000–8. Moreover, another possible indirect effect is through the effect of appreciation on the distribution of factor income in China. Insofar as the appreciation redistributes income from enterprises in the tradeable sector to households, this is likely to reduce the saving rate, thus reducing $(S - I)$, *ceteris paribus*, and so assisting external rebalancing. In any case, government has the power to raise government consumption expenditure or to encourage private consumption expenditure so as to counteract a rise in $(S - I)$.

If exports grow rapidly as the world economy recovers, a large appreciation might be feasible without causing exports to fall. The PBC faces a dilemma on exchange rate policy: a large sharp appreciation might allay expectations of further appreciation but cause a collapse of producers reliant on exports, whereas a small gradual appreciation might not threaten exporters but cause a speculative inflow of capital, so either forcing further appreciation or risking loss of control over the money supply. The danger of too great and too swift and appreciation and the likely response lags suggest the need for gradualism. The danger of speculative short-term capital flows based on expectations of further appreciation, with consequent overshooting, suggest the need for a sharp, single, and substantial appreciation. Much depends on the adequacy of short-term capital controls. It is true that China has maintained controls on capital mobility, and in principle it has the means to prevent inflows of short-term funds. Using monthly data for the 2000s, Wang (2010) examined their effectiveness. It was found that capital controls were not fully effective, and became less so over the decade, as the economy opened up. For instance, current account convertibility provided opportunities for illegal capital flows.

Unless currency speculation can be curbed sufficiently, the least bad exchange rate policy might be a significant one-off appreciation followed by a pegging of the RMB to a trade-weighted basket of currencies. The appreciation should have an immediate effect in reducing the external surplus and probably reducing income inequality, and the peg should help to reduce trading risks. Their combination should diminish expectations of a one-way bet on the currency and speculative flows of funds. This would permit a more independent monetary policy and a more effective stabilization policy, not fettered by the need to sterilize the inflow of foreign exchange and to keep down interest rates. The choice of peg, however, requires the weighing up of risks to China's trade against risks to China's wealth: a peg to the US dollar would help to reduce foreign reserves risks.

The Chinese government has so far been reluctant to appreciate the RMB significantly, for two main reasons. One is a concern that China's rapid economic growth is dependent on the continued even more rapid growth of exports. There are worries that social stability would be threatened by an economic slowdown and job losses in the export sector, if they are not compensated by job gains in the import-substitution sector. However, the government has some leeway given the remarkable growth of exports from 2004 to 2007 and its likely continuation once the world economy recovers. Moreover, government might prefer RMB appreciation to the trade restrictions that might be imposed by trading partners if the external surplus continues to grow. The second reason for resisting a currency appreciation is the fall in the domestic value of China's foreign exchange holdings. Some fall in national wealth is inevitable but it can be alleviated to some extent by gradual realignment of the portfolio away from dollars.

The great monetary expansion of 2008 and 2009 was intended to protect the Chinese economy against the consequences of the world recession. It had the effect of stimulating investment, particularly that of state-owned and state-controlled enterprises and on infrastructure projects. However, the sheer size and speed of the expansion—M1 rose by 32% between December 2008 and December 2009—made it likely that the proportion of non-performing bank loans would rise. The short-run policies to deal with world recession did nothing to help rebalance the economy.

The main policy tool for raising private consumption is likely to be through the public finances. Government can effect an internal rebalancing by increasing government consumption and so reducing its net saving. One reason for the high saving rate of rural and urban households, and the rising urban saving rate, has been their lack of security. Greater public provision and funding of social services, including health care, education, welfare, and pensions would have the effect of reducing not only government saving but also household saving. We saw in Figure 12.5 above that government has the potential to increase its current expenditure without reducing its capital expenditure. Reform of public provision and funding of health care, education, welfare, and pensions is necessarily a complicated and long-drawn-out process. It requires dealing with interest groups and careful experimentation and planning, but there is a good case for policy to move in that direction.

Rebalancing might also require financial sector reform. A more competitive financial market should relax the borrowing constraints on private firms, so encouraging them to redistribute more profit as dividends and to save less. Against this, a more competitive financial market—without interest rate caps—might also reduce the margin between deposit rates and lending rates and encourage households to save. Requiring SOEs to pay dividends should reduce their saving and probably also their investment. Similarly, the encouragement of free entry and product market competition in the sectors where SOEs continue to enjoy protection should reduce profit mark-ups and redistribute income from profits to wages. An appreciation of the RMB might have the same redistributive effect in the tradeable sectors.

291

Are the imbalances sustainable?

The Chinese government has so far failed to reduce the rocketing external surplus, to reduce the foreign exchange reserves from a level which is now difficult to justify, to ease the increasingly tense relationship with its trade partners, or to rebalance the pattern of economic growth. This failure might indicate a lack of concern for these objectives. It might instead represent a deliberate weighing up of the benefits and costs of the current policies against alternatives. However, it might simply reflect the sheer speed with which the economy moved into external imbalance in the period 2004–7—which would inevitably involve lags in policy making—and the subsequent policy priority that was given to the effects of the world recession in 2008–10.

Macroeconomic imbalance has two aspects. One is expenditure imbalance and the other is external imbalance. In both cases the underlying issue is the inter-temporal distribution of consumption. More investment relative to consumption in the present raises consumption in the future. An external surplus involves an increase in foreign assets, so making resources available for consumption in the future. China's macroeconomic imbalances imply that the society and its government have a low rate of time preference. How can this be explained?

Since the start of economic reform, the Chinese government has given the highest priority to promoting economic growth. The leadership considered rapid growth to be the best strategy for maintaining CCP rule: China became a develop-mental state. The growth strategy was behind the government's decision to join the WTO and to embrace globalization. In conjunction with the undervalued currency, this was partly responsible for the rising export surplus. It improved China's export prospects and induced domestic reforms that forced up productivity growth. The leadership chose to keep the value of the RMB down in order to encourage the growth of exports. It was correct in recognizing that the growing proportion of exports and imports to GDP raised the growth rate (Chapter 7). The rate of appreciation against the US dollar that was permitted after 2004 was insufficient to prevent the export surplus from rocketing. Another contribution came from the sharp rise in domestic saving relative to investment, implying that expenditure fell relative to output. The economic reform policies were important in explaining the rise in business and household saving.

For as long as economic growth remains the Chinese government's central objective, the stage is set for a continuance of policies that create macroeconomic imbalances. But are the macroeconomic imbalances sustainable? Consider the remarkably high investment rate. There is a danger that the rapid accumulation of capital will carry the seeds of its own destruction. Competitive economic theory predicts that the rate of return on capital will fall as the capital–labour ratio rises. Although there is evidence for China that there has been serious excess capacity in some industries, there is also evidence that the rate of profit on physical capital in industry as a whole has risen over the last decade. This rise might be due to the rapid growth of human capital along with physical capital, and to both the technological progress and the structural shifts towards more productive activities that the high investment rate and economic reform policies brought about. There is some danger that the great expansion of credit in 2008–10 will generate more excess capacity. However, when excess capacity emerged in the mid-2000s it appears that it was then absorbed by the rapid expansion of net exports; this might happen again. There is no persuasive evidence so far that maintaining the current investment rate at the expense of consumption will bring China's rapid economic growth to an end.

Is the export surplus sustainable? Although it fell as a proportion of GDP in 2008 and 2009—down to 4% on account of the world recession—given current policies the export surplus might well rise again as the world economy emerges from recession. This is liable to give rise to three problems. First, the PBC will have difficulty in curbing the rise in liquidity as it purchases foreign exchange from net exporters. Failure in this regard may contribute to asset bubbles, which in turn can endanger the financial system and investor confidence. The experience of Japan in the late 1980s is a spectre to avoid. Just as the ensuing financial crash did in Japan, so a financial crash might break China's current virtuous circle of high confidence, high investment, and high growth.

Secondly, the current policies imply that China's foreign exchange reserves will continue to grow, and that the rate of return on the reserves will be low and might even prove to be negative in real terms. If as much as two-thirds of the reserves are held in the form of US government debt, Chinese policy will become increasingly boxed in. According to the US Treasury, at the end of June 2009 China held $1,473 billion US securities, out of which $915 billion was long-term and short-term treasuries, $454 billion was government agency debt, and the rest were corporate bonds; in the meanwhile China's foreign exchange reserves were $2.13 trillion. The reserves are now large enough—reaching $2.40 trillion at the end of 2009—to mean that any substantial sale of US dollars by PBC would depreciate the dollar, especially if it created expectations of further sales. That would in turn reduce the value of China's remaining dollar-denominated reserves.

Thirdly, China's current account surplus implies an export deficit for its trading partners as a group. For instance, in 2007, when China's current account surplus represented about 11% of GDP, its surplus with the US represented 22% of the US current account deficit. If China's current account surplus is maintained, and particularly if it begins to grow, it is likely that the major trading partners will take more drastic action against imports from China, in the form of additional trade restrictions. If China does not itself take measures to correct its external imbalance, other countries may do so instead. Given the risks of trade retaliation and political repercussion, these ways may be more harmful to all parties, including China.

Bank vulnerability

Whether separate from China's macroeconomic imbalances or interwoven with them, it is possible that China will have a banking crisis. The fragility of the banking system stems from the roles that it was required to play in the command economy and the transition economy. Under central planning the state-owned bank (later, banks) simply served to implement the planners' directives, without the need for applying commercial criteria. As marketization took place and the SOEs came under greater competition, the state-owned banks (SOBs) protected ailing SOEs and their workers. The banking system thus ensured that there could be continued 'reform without losers'. Moreover, some unproductive activities were funded for reasons of patronage, or worse. China possessed a banking system 'woefully unsuited for the demands of a sophisticated market economy' (Naughton 2007: 460).

The number of non-performing loans (NPLs) rose dramatically. One estimate puts the value of NPLs of the SOBs at 53% of their total loans in 1997 (Matthews et al. 2007: 5). Bank reform began in the late 1990s, when government recognized that things would have to change. The policy makers had to tackle both a stock problem and a flow problem. To reduce the stock of NPLs, substantial funds were injected to recapitalize the banks. The most important vehicle for this was four state-run asset management companies (AMCs). The AMCs purchased pre-1996 NPLs at face value, which were sold or auctioned but with only a small proportion of the purchase costs being recovered. Further infusion of capital to the big four banks took the form of foreign exchange reserves. Thus, ultimately it was the Chinese government and its central bank that was to bear the burden of the insolvent banking system.

The recapitalization of the banks greatly reduced their NPLs. The scale of the problem is difficult to gauge on account of the poor information on NPLs—itself possibly a strategic choice. However, Matthews et al. (2007: 5) show the NPLs as a proportion of total loans of the SOBs falling from 53% in 1997 to 32% in 2000 and to 9% in 2006. Naughton (2007: 462) provides information implying that NPLs in the banking system fell from 28% of loans in 2002 to 9% in 2005. The website of the China Banking Regulation Commission (CBRC) has the NPLs of the commercial banks falling from 6% of loans at end-2007 to under 2% at end-2009. China's fiscal and foreign exchange reserves had thus resolved much of the NPL stock problem. They would probably be harnessed to do so again if the need were to arise in the future.

There remained the flow problem. On the one hand, the opening up of competition for Chinese banks from international banks under China's WTO accession agreement and their acquisition of shares in the big banks (after the latter's entry to the stock market in 2005–6) provided incentives for improved efficiency. On the other hand, the resolution of the NPL stock problem exacerbated the flow problem by creating 'moral hazard'. The experience of being rescued created disincentives for banks to reform their lending policies. This, together with the government's continued close involvement in the economy and its need for patronage resources, implies that the problem of NPLs might well recur.

Probably the greatest danger to the banking system comes from the possibility of speculative asset bubbles bursting, especially a real estate bubble (Allen et al. 2008: 559). Such a crash could create many bad debts for the banking system. It is linked to China's macroeconomic imbalances, already examined in this section. Given the limited success of capital controls, the need to prevent speculative inflows of short-term funds has forced the monetary authorities to keep interest rates low (Allen et al. 2008), as also has the need to support the less profitable SOEs (Ferri and Liu 2010). Even in 2006, the net interest margin of the four big banks was only 2.5% and their average return on assets was only 0.67% (Matthews et al. 2007: 5). China's export surplus has presented a problem of sterilizing the foreign exchange inflow—which is needed to prevent uncontrolled increases in the money supply. The scope for asset bubbles to emerge was increased by the huge monetary expansion of 2008 and 2009 in response to the global economic crisis. It is likely that many of the hastily introduced bank-financed public infrastructure projects will prove to be misguided. Insofar as the stimulus programme will produce an increase in NPLs—albeit with a lag—that will weaken the banking system and make a banking crisis more plausible.

12.4 Political Shocks

In common with leaders of many countries, China's leaders are primarily concerned with their own political survival. Their nightmare is a national protest movement of discontented groups united against the regime. Hence, the leaders' fixation on what they call 'social stability' (Shirk 2008: 6–7). The CCP has followed policies intended to diminish both social discontent and its expression. The most important policy weapon against the emergence of social discontent has been rapid economic growth. The most important policy weapons against its expression have been the inculcation of nationalistic feelings, the control and selection of public information, and political repression.

Sources of social discontent

Consider the possibility of a political shock arising from social discontent. Economic reform has not been accompanied by political reform. The party still retains a monopoly of power and control. Economic growth has enabled China to maintain the political institutions of old-style communism while dropping the ideological framework that inspired them. The communist political system and the capitalist economy have been merged, although it is an uneasy merger, giving rise to its own problems (Mcgregor 2010). Will the CCP be able to adjust and adapt sufficiently to maintain its power over a rapidly changing and increasingly complex society? We consider the more obvious possible sources of social discontent: economic inequality, unemployment and layoffs, insecurity, and corruption.

The CCP's failure to prevent the sharply rising inequality in many dimensions—examined in Chapter 10—that has accompanied economic reform and economic growth signals a danger of rising social discontent. The increase in income inequality takes three main forms: inequality among households, across regions, and between urban and rural areas. It is not clear how far these forms of inequality generate social discontent. The estimates of the determinants of subjective well-being—which were the subject of Chapter 11—suggest that relative deprivation is an important determinant: low relative income reduces happiness. There is evidence that 'relative poverty' has risen. Defining the poor as those whose household income per capita is no more than half the national median income per capita, poverty rose as a percentage of the population between 2002 and 2007 (Li et al. 2012).

The research on subjective well-being also showed the importance of the chosen reference group. Rural people have narrow orbits of comparison: it is their position in the village income distribution that matters most. Urban residents and also rural migrants settled in the city are sensitive to their position in the income distribution of their city. In particular, the rapidly growing migrant population of the cities—normally at the bottom of the city income distribution, being treated as second class citizens, and having the lowest average subjective well-being—poses a political threat.

Note the rise in the Gini coefficient of inequality in income per capita among households, which was analysed in Chapter 10. The rise occurred in rural China, in urban China, and at the national level, this last being raised also by the increase in the ratio of average income per capita in urban and rural China. Although inequality has appeared to rise throughout the three decades of economic reform, it is not inevitable that this trend will continue. We suggested in Chapter 9 that the most important market mechanism for halting the rise in inequality would be the impending scarcity of relatively unskilled labour.

Comparisons with the national income distribution, or across regions, or with urban (if the person is rural) or rural (if urban) income levels may not be important. It may instead be important for a government concerned about social discontent to remedy the causes of income inequality within the village and within the city. In any case, unhappiness does not necessarily translate into social discontent. This might depend on the extent to which people perceive their unhappiness to be man-made and capable of being remedied by government.

Chapter 11 provided evidence that insecurity diminishes subjective well-being. Thus, not only actual unemployment itself—reducing income—but also the expectation of unemployment reduces the happiness of people in the cities. The retrenchment programme in the SOEs, starting in the mid-1990s and continuing into the early 2000s, created much unemployment and hardship, which was discussed in Chapters 3 and 10. The end of the 'iron rice bowl', with the loss of much job security and social security, and the introduction of fees for public services such as health care and some education, made urban life less safe and less satisfying. This helps to explain our finding that the average happiness score of rural people actually exceeded that of urban people, despite the much higher average income of urban people. Perhaps the most prevalent cause of widespread social unrest in rural China is anger over the appropriation of farm land by local officials—often in collusion with developers—with little or no compensation being paid to the displaced. The unchecked abuse of power by local officialdom appears to be a general source of complaint.

Another finding to emerge from the analyses of Chapter 11 is the importance for current happiness of expectations about future income. In all three sub-samples, if people expected their income to be higher, and especially if they expected it to be much higher, in five years' time, the happiness score would be raised, *ceteris paribus*. The majority of respondents did indeed expect their future income to rise. If there were to be a crisis in the economy which depressed expectations of future income, this could have a significant effect on levels of happiness, and therefore potentially on social discontent.

Corruption is a potentially serious source of social discontent. The CCP has wanted to maintain close control of the economy as well as of the society, and this has hindered the creation of a fully marketized economy operating under the rule of law. China's partially marketized economy requires economic actors to secure government permissions and approvals in many spheres of economic activity. This system is a breeding ground for rent seeking and corruption of bureaucrats and party officials, especially at local levels and especially now that a restraining ideology no longer prevails.

Transparency International, an independent body, measures the perceived levels of public sector corruption around the world, on a scale from 0 (utterly corrupt) to 10 (not at all corrupt).[3] The corruption perception index aggregates data on each country from thirteen possible sources using well-informed business and international agency reports. China's index is based on nine sources, several of them being country risk agencies. China's score in 2010 was 3.5, ranking it the 78th least corrupt among 178 countries—better than India (3.3) and Egypt (3.1) but worse than Singapore (9.3), Hong Kong (8.4), Taiwan (5.8), and South Korea (5.4). China's score had stayed roughly constant, being 3.5 in 2002 as well. An alternative measure is calculated by the World Bank in its 'worldwide governance indicators'. The World Bank combines several independent evaluations to produce six different indicators of the quality of governance in each of 235 countries, one of the six being 'control of corruption'. In 1996, 42% of countries had a better score on this measure than China, and in 2009 the proportion was 63%, so that China ranked as low as 148th out of 235 countries.[4]

It is the perceptions of China's people that better indicates the threat that corruption poses to the regime. There are widespread perceptions of graft in high places and throughout the bureaucracy down to the lowest ranks. The issue is not played down by government: Hu Jintao is said to have described corruption as 'rampant' (Shirk 2008: 32) and to have stated that the resolute punishment and effective prevention of corruption is essential for the survival of the CCP (Wedeman 2009a, 2009b). Respondents in the urban sub-sample of the Chinese Household Income Project (CHIP) survey relating to 2002 were asked what they considered to be the most serious social problem. Corruption (mentioned by 21%), along with lack of social security (also 21%) was placed second, after unemployment and layoff (32%).

The central leadership is able to cast itself as an opponent of corruption and defender of its victims. It has launched a series of high-profile anti-corruption campaigns. According to Yao (2010: 333), 104 officials of the rank of vice-minister (such as provincial governor) or above were prosecuted in the period 2001–8, of whom 40 were sentenced to death or to more than ten years' imprisonment. Although this action is by no means sufficient to stop corruption, it gives people some confidence in the government's handling of the issue.

However, the underlying problem is that China's institutional arrangements and political system make it prone to corruption: officialdom has unbridled power to permit or refuse the applications of business in China's much regulated economy. There are things that the latter want to get, or to buy, and the former have those things to give, or to sell. However, the problem facing the CCP is that the system of patronage, which is prone to corrupt practices, helps to maintain its power; and corruption, by distributing rents among the powerful, can also help to do so.

An indication that China's system of governance makes it vulnerable to self-interested collusion and predation by elite groups is provided by the World Bank's 'worldwide governance indicators'. The indicators include 'government effectiveness' and 'voice and accountability', as well as 'control of corruption', which was discussed above. China scores best among the six indicators on government effectiveness, ranking 94th in 2009. Needless to say, had the World Bank also provided an indicator of 'reform strategy', that is, the creation of incentive structures to promote economic reform and create a 'developmental state', China would probably have ranked very high by that criterion. By contrast, China's worst score is on voice and accountability, ranking 220th out of 235. The voice and accountability score effectively measures the ability of citizens to shape, monitor, and check government behaviour. In 1996 no fewer than 93% of countries scored better than China on voice and accountability, and in 2009 the proportion was 94%. The avoidance of social discontent requires enhanced accountability and transparency in China's governance, such as might be achieved through an independent judiciary or an anti-corruption agency reporting directly to the central leadership.

Control of social discontent

These are all reasons why even continued rapid growth might not be sufficient to prevent the rise of social discontent. In the absence of accommodating democratic processes that can serve as a guide, and a response, to public opinion, rising social discontent might become a tinderbox which ignites a political shock that could bring rapid economic growth to an end. The CCP, by its words and actions, appears to be well aware of this fragility. Shirk (2008: 53) notes that the term 'social stability' had figured 700–800 times a year in the *People's Daily* over the previous decade. The public emphasis placed on the need for social stability can be seen as a way of persuading the people that CCP rule is essential for maintaining order and prosperity (Shirk 2008: 52).

There is evidence that social unrest has risen in China in recent years. It is possible to piece together from official sources the number of 'mass incidents' that have occurred. Mass incidents are the official term used for protests, demonstrations, strikes, and riots. According to Wedeman (2009a), the number of mass incidents grew steadily from a trivial number of 8,700 in 1993 to 74,000 in 2004 and to 127,000 in 2008. However, his analysis suggested that the expressions of discontent normally remained incoherent and disorganized, and were mainly about specific local grievances rather than broader political issues. In his view, although the remedy often lay with local officials—who had disregarded legitimate complaints—it was frequently sought in more effective police control.

More generally, how have economic complaints been dealt with? In Chapter 3 we discussed the retrenchment programme that was imposed on state-owned enterprises (SOEs), starting in the mid-1990s and continuing for several years. This episode provides understanding of how the government, in the pursuit of economic growth and fiscal health, was willing first to create and then to deal with worker discontent. The reform of the SOEs was forced on government by the decline in their profitability which threatened both government revenue and economic growth. As part of the reforms the top leadership ordered the privatization or closure of many smaller SOEs, the hardening of soft budget constraints, and the retrenchment of redundant workers. Previously, government had preferred urban unemployment to be disguised, in the factories, rather than open, on the streets, but that option was no longer available. Official statistics are difficult to interpret but it is possible that the accumulated gross number of laid-off workers was as much as 60 million (Knight and Song 2005: 118). The policy posed a serious threat to social stability.

The unemployment insurance system was in flux, moving from being enterprise based to being city based: it could not be relied upon to protect retrenched workers. The social discontent arising from both the actual and the threatened redundancies was addressed also by means of the *xia gang* policy that was introduced. Eligible redundant workers—those who had previously enjoyed lifetime employment rights—were supported for several years by means of payments from the government and the enterprise (if it remained in existence and was not bankrupt). There is much evidence of resulting hardship owing to both the inadequate public support and the difficulty of becoming re-employed (for instance, Appleton et al. 2002). Nevertheless, the political threat proved not to be serious: protest was confined to localized expressions, especially in those areas, such as the northeast, with many ailing SOEs.

By the time that Hu Jintao and Wen Jiabao acceded to the top leadership positions of party and state in 2002, it was evident that the policy emphasis on economic growth had brought with it the numerous social problems listed above. The new leadership attempted to redirect policy somewhat from the sole concern about economic growth towards what was termed 'the harmonious society'. In effect, it wished to redress some of the social problems that were giving rise to social discontent. Among the objectives listed were strengthening the legal system, according greater respect to people's rights, narrowing income inequalities among households, across regions, and between urban and rural areas, placing greater emphasis on rural development, improving the social security system, and attending to environmental damage. The new policy became official CCP doctrine in 2006.

Certain policy initiatives can be traced to the harmonious society objectives. In particular, rural society benefited from the abolition of the agricultural tax in 2005, the abolition of school fees for rural basic education which became universal in 2007, an increase in rural infrastructure investment as part of the fiscal stimulus of 2008–9, the introduction of a subsidy on rural purchase of home appliances in 2008, and the extension of social security provision to some provinces through a rural counterpart of the urban minimum income subsidy system (*dibao*).

There is evidence that the policies for the 'new socialist countryside' have had a noticeable effect (Michelson 2011). Small surveys conducted in about thirty villages across six provinces in 2002 and in 2010 made it possible to compare villagers' attitudes before and after the reforms. The 2010 survey showed that at least two-thirds of respondents felt that government at each administrative tier cared about the well-being of villagers, and the provision of local public goods was important to that perception. The majority said that villager–cadre relations had improved, and more than four-fifths said that government investment in public goods had increased. The proportion who did not respect government fell from 21% to 8% over the eight years. The implication is that the potential sources of rural discontent had been diminished by the pro-rural policy shift.

The property law of 2007 in principle gave owners greater security of property, and the labour contract law of 2008 gave workers greater rights and more job security. No doubt many other policies, less attributable or noticeable, were also influenced by the redirection of objectives. However, it appears that the growth objective was not watered down, and rapid growth continued—with potentially disequalizing consequences. The harmonious society objectives had to contend with the incentive structure for local government officials, which continued to reward local economic growth achievements.

The emphasis on the growth objective had led the state to prioritize public investment projects over public consumption projects. The extreme macroeconomic imbalance, examined in Section 12.3, means that the government has the fiscal resources to expand the provision of public services—on health care, education, social security, etc.—that have been neglected in the past, particularly in the countryside. Such a redirection of policy emphasis might require also the amendment of the incentive structure facing local cadres.

A helpful insight into how the Chinese government would deal with an economic recession that threatened social and political stability is provided by its response to the global financial crisis of 2007–8 and the global economic recession of 2008–10. The global economic recession had a dramatic effect on China's exports: $US export value fell by no less than 40% from the third quarter of 2008 to the first quarter of 2009, and then began gradually to recover.[5] The collapse of employment in the export sector—largely labour-intensive processing of manufactures—threatened to produce a wave of social discontent. The government responded promptly and powerfully to protect the economy against the economic recession that the export shock would otherwise create; it did so by means of reflationary monetary and fiscal policies (Xu 2010).

The PBC lowered reserve requirements and the bank deposit rate and other interest rates several times. In consequence the money supply (M2) increased by 18% in 2008 and by 28% in 2009; bank loans grew by 33% in 2009. A vast fiscal expansion plan was also launched by central government, with 60% to be spent in 2009 and 40% in 2010. The great majority (80%) was allocated to expenditure on infrastructure, partly because its effects would be immediate. Local governments in turn planned an even larger infrastructure package, funded mainly by bank loans to companies set up for that purpose. The public sector balance of expenditure over revenue grew rapidly.

The effect of the stimulus package was quickly felt. Having been 10% per annum during 2008, GDP growth fell to 6% per annum in the first quarter of 2009 but thereafter began to rise, reaching 9% per annum in the fourth quarter of that year. Fixed asset investment was 31% higher in 2009 than in 2008. The flood of bank lending precipitated speculative asset bubbles and speculative inflows of capital. For instance, the price of real estate in Shanghai rose by 42% in 2009, and the Shanghai stock composite index rose by 75% in four months (Xu 2010: 134), although some reversals took place in 2010. In summary, the swift policy response to the fall in exports ensured that the danger of a collapse of entrepreneurial confidence was averted, and indeed the problem soon became one of inflationary expectations.

Kong et al. (2010) made use of a rural household panel survey to compare employment in the first halves of 2008 and 2009. They found that at least 15 million rural migrants (more than 10% of the total) had made a net return to the rural areas over that period. They also estimated that, through a multiplier effect on demand, 38 million rural workers had lost their rural non-farm jobs. Rural agriculture had to take in 53 million workers (10.5% of the rural labour force). Agriculture thus acted as a sponge to absorb unemployment—in the form of underemployment—and the new poor. Kong et al. (2010) concluded that rural incomes fell because the average income of agricultural households is significantly lower than that of households with access to local non-farm or migrant employment. Rural migrants returning to village agriculture, being dispersed and not at all organized, do not pose as great a social and political threat as they would do had they remained in the cities. Nevertheless, government wanted to provide new opportunities for the retrenched migrants. Many of them subsequently found new urban jobs as the macroeconomic stimulus programme got under way and expanded, mostly in construction of infrastructure or self-employment activities and no longer in export industries. An official estimate found that the total number of rural migrants in the cities increased substantially in the course of 2009 (Ministry Of Human Resources and Social Security 2009, 2010). Thanks to active government intervention, the employment of rural migrants had more than recovered by the end of that year.

Propaganda is important to social stability in China, and it is the more effective because the CCP now harnesses and channels public opinion rather than directly controlling it. However open the debate might be behind the closed doors of the party, it has been concerned to present economic successes and to play down failings. Its 'Publicity Department' exercises censorship in all matters that are perceived to be threatening, for instance, news about social unrest in other authoritarian countries. The power to control public opinion in China has been weakened by the development of the internet as a source of information, and as a means of organizing dissent. The internet, too, has been subject to censorship. For instance, controversial postings are erased, although this might take an hour or more.[6] However, the internet can also be used as a source of information about public opinion, which in turn gives government the option to adjust its policies so as to reduce discontent.

China's sense of nationhood is partly a reflection of the predominance of people of Han ethnicity: minorities account for less than 10% of the population. Collier (2007: 49–50) argues that in many ethnically diverse developing countries the government has a narrow, ethnic support base. This is especially the case if its rule is autocratic. The narrower the base of social and political support, the stronger is the incentive for government to sacrifice economic growth in order to redistribute income to the support group. Thus, according to this reasoning, China's ethnic homogeneity has been good for its economic growth.

It is nevertheless arguable that the CCP has attempted to diminish social instability and political discontent by subtly encouraging a sense of popular nationalism among its people (Kim 2009). His argument, supported by many examples, is that tight control and direction of the mass media, including television and films, enables the government to shape public sentiment towards the revival of China's greatness. The school system is another vehicle for promoting nationalism. By these means the party and the state are identified with the society, and it is regarded as unpatriotic to criticize policies or to question patriarchal authority.

This strategy might yet carry its own dangers. Internet readings suggest that nationalistic fervour has grown, especially among young people, as China's economy has become more important in the world. This growth might yet work against the government rather than for it. Indeed, the two previous dynasties fell to nationalistic movements (Shirk 2008: 7). In the face of rising nationalism, it is predictable that the CCP would adopt a more nationalistic stance and be tough in its dealings with other countries, so as to identify itself with popular sentiments. Any consequent deterioration in China's international relations might pose a threat to its continued rapid growth—particularly if it leads to military action, for instance against Taiwan. The remarkable expansion of China's international trade makes it economically more vulnerable not only to a fall in exports but also to a fall in imports, especially of raw materials.

The CCP retains its powers of coercion. Its control of the courts, for instance through the appointment of judges, is important for this purpose. Any activity that is considered as a threat to, or subversive of, the CCP is forbidden. This involves outlawing even some religious groups which decline to come under the aegis of party control. Having been negligible in the past, non-governmental organizations (NGOs) have been allowed to proliferate in recent years, but only if they are ultimately subordinate to government.

The labour contract law of 2008 gave workers more individual rights and greater job security but it did not give workers the right to form their own trade unions. Only the official, government-controlled, trade union is permitted. The official union speaks for workers with a muted voice and effectively curbs expressions of worker discontent. There is official encouragement of elections at village level, which have been shown to improve the quality of village economic governance (Luo et al. 2007). However, the effect is confined to the village; at a broader level, effective farmers' lobbies are not permitted.

The massacre of the student protestors in Tiananmen Square in 1989, and the subsequent policies of punishment and indoctrination, showed that the CCP would be willing to use coercion by deploying the military in the face of calls for democracy. Similarly, two instances of political resistance based on ethnic nationalism—in Tibet and Xinjiang—were put down forcefully. It is important to the continuation of party rule that the military be on-side. This is achieved, for instance, by controlling all top military appointments and by ensuring that the People's Liberation Army (PLA) is well funded.

China's political evolution

China's future economic growth may depend on its future political evolution. The political future cannot be predicted with any confidence: suffice that we present contrasting views. The inevitable evolution of society and economy, of people's aspirations and demands, and of powerful interest groups makes it unlikely that the political system will remain unchanged. One view is that the political system is set to deteriorate, and that this will threaten continued rapid growth. Another view is that the political system will gradually evolve both to accommodate the demands of rising prosperity and to facilitate continued rapid growth.

Pei (2006) argues that China is 'trapped in transition'. The lack of accountability in the political system leads to pervasive corruption and collusion among the ruling elite. The developmental state is becoming a predatory state. For instance, he reports the following argument, attributed to Zhao Ziyang while under house arrest: when ownership of property becomes legitimate, it is inevitable that those with unaccountable power over resources use their power to transfer resources or resource rents into private hands (Pei 2006: 8). Attempts by the political leadership, fearing the threat to its rule, to restore political accountability and so curb predation, will meet resistance from its beneficiaries in this partially reformed economy. The use of political power to amass private wealth contributes to rapidly rising inequality. That in turn produces sharply rising social discontent which, in its manifestation, will eventually bring rapid economic growth to an end.

Zheng (2009) notes that the CCP is not a political party in the western sense. The party stands above and dominates the state; indeed, through its party organization it created the Chinese state in its current form. It appears to be an obstacle to the creation of a modern state built on the rule of law. Given that China will continue to be a one-party state, the author argues that this rule can be legitimized and sustained only if the CCP adapts and renews itself vigorously by reconnecting with the common people and reconnecting its ideological base with the rapid socioeconomic changes.

In contrast to Pei (2006), Naughton (2008) argues that the top leadership has shown increasing decisiveness in its pursuit of economic growth. Many economic interest groups remained or were created in the process of reform but any obstacles they presented were generally overcome once the top leadership recognized that there was a compelling reason for doing so. For instance, the leadership has attempted to deal with the threat to efficiency and dynamism posed by the monopolistic state-owned sectors by developing a system of oligopolistic competition among these SOEs. Naughton (2008) recognizes that continued authoritarian rule will depend not only on good economic performance but also on a broadening of support for the CCP. The leadership needs to create a reform coalition that is a counterweight to the winners from partial economic reform. He expects it to do so by means of policies that reallocate resources towards weaker and excluded groups, using its formidable patronage resources.

Yao (2010) presents a political scenario which carries an optimistic growth prospect. He poses the question: why has China's rapid economic development not produced demands for democratization? One reason is that the state has relaxed its hold on daily life, so that people have greater freedom in their private lives. Since Deng Xiaoping's southern tour in 1992, making money has been more exciting than asking for democracy. Submission to authority is part of Confucian doctrine, which in recent years the Chinese government has helped to revive. Another reason is that the CCP has tried to widen its bases of support in order to enhance its political legitimacy.

Yao (2010) recognizes, however, that although the CCP now wants to be an all-people's party, there remains a danger that officialdom will be captured by strong interest groups. His notion of the 'disinterestedness' of the Chinese government, discussed in Chapter 3, would be threatened were a strong alliance to be formed between holders of private capital and the CCP. However, he argues that the party has taken steps to avoid this happening. Many functions of the party and the government have become institutionalized. The party presents itself as the enemy of corruption, and it has introduced laws to protect people against actions that cause social discontent. For instance, both the local government appropriation of land with only nominal compensation and the shabby treatment of workers by employers are threats to social stability to which central government has responded. The property law of 2007 was intended to enable citizens to protect their property, including real estate, and the labour contract law of 2008 improved the rights and job security of workers. Village elections, introduced from 1988 onwards, have enhanced the accountability of village governance, and there are now experiments with township elections. In these various ways, the government has been able to curb social discontent and its expression, and thus the threat to continued rapid economic growth. Yao expects the CCP to remain sufficiently adaptable in the future.

Of course, the expression of social discontent might itself drive the CCP towards democracy. Yao (2010) argues that economic growth and educational expansion have created a growing middle class, and that this has generated a more assertive civil society. For instance, the internet has democratized news and ideas, and it has become a powerful tool by which people can make their voices heard and become organized. Unless internet postings can be effectively censored, they impose a constraint on government behaviour. The author envisages a gradualist and endogenous democratization of the Chinese political system from these small beginnings. No doubt the crucial condition for such an evolution will be that the CCP retains sufficient political legitimacy to expect to be successful in a democratic arena.

12.5 Conclusion

Several forecasts of China's future economic growth project a declining rate in the long term, in line with the experience of other countries. For instance, Hofman and Kuijs (2008) use a growth-accounting exercise and various assumptions to forecast the annual growth rate of GDP to fall from 8.3% in 2005–15 to 6.7% in 2015–25 and to 5.6% in 2025–35. This fall is due partly to a decline in employment and partly to slower growth of labour productivity, in turn shared between a rising capital–output ratio and decelerating total factor productivity growth. In our view, such projections are no more than informed guesswork influenced by the experience of other economies. Several complications have to be recognized. For instance, it is likely that the abundant supply of unskilled labour that has permitted the remarkable growth will dry up within a decade, the eventual reform of factor markets might slow down growth, and environmental damage and impending water shortage will probably raise the costs of continued rapid growth. Nevertheless, we share the judgement that China's growth rate will decline in the long run as the economy matures, and that it is unlikely to exceed 6% per annum in two decades' time.

One reason why we stopped short of producing growth projections is that China's rapid growth has been supported by a virtuous circle of high confidence, giving rise to high expectations, contributing to high growth, which has then fed back into high confidence, and so on. Underlying this virtuous circle is China's political economy. For understandable reasons, the Chinese government became a developmental state. Chinese economic history itself shows that it is by no means inevitable for an autocratic government to espouse growth objectives, but that has been the case in China over the period that began in 1978. It may well continue.

Nevertheless, there are certain potential hazards in the road ahead that could break the virtuous circle. In this category we have discussed the potential unravelling of China's macroeconomic imbalances, the possibility of a banking crisis, and the chances of social instability, including the big issue of whether China's society is heading towards polarization of power and wealth rather than gradual institutionalization and democratization. Each of these is merely a danger that might never materialize—carrying a probability that cannot be measured—but they should each be acknowledged. If there is a political shock, an economic shock will become more likely, and vice versa.

Notes

1. This section draws on Knight and Wang (2011).
2. Price Inspecting Center, National Development and Reform Commission, 'Analysis of steel price of 2006 and forecast for 2007', 16 February 2007 (in Chinese).
3. Transparency International, Corruption Perception Index <transparency.org/policy research/surveys indices/cpi/2010>.
4. Governance Indicators of the World Bank Group, country data report on China <info.worldbank.org/governance/wgi/sc_country.asp>.
5. IMF, *International Financial Statistics*, April 2010.
6. For instance, there are western press reports that a confidential PBC document was mistakenly uploaded to an official website, where it appeared briefly. The document estimated that over a fifteen-year period some 18,000 corrupt officials had smuggled over $US100 billion out of China.

References

Allen, Franklin, Jun Qian, and Meijun Qian (2008), 'China's financial system: past, present and future', in Loren Brandt and Thomas Rawski (eds.), *China's Great Economic Transformation*, Cambridge and New York: Cambridge University Press.

Anderson, Jonathan (2007), 'Is China export-led?', UBS Investment Research, September, <http://www.allroadsleadtochina.com/reports/prc_270907.pdf>.

Appleton, Simon, John Knight, Lina Song, and Qingjie Xia (2002), 'Labor retrenchment in China: determinants and consequences', *China Economic Review*, 13: 252–75.

Athukorala, Premachandra (2009), 'The rise of China and East Asian export performance: is the crowding out fear warranted?', *The World Economy*, 32: 234–66.

Bernanke, Ben S. (2005), 'The global saving glut and the US current account deficit', Lecture, Washington, DC: Federal Reserve Board.

Cline, William R., and John Williamson (2008), 'Estimates of the equilibrium exchange rate of the renminbi: is there a consensus, and if not, why not?', in M. Goldstein and N. R. Lardy (eds.), *Debating China's Exchange Rate Policy*, Washington, DC: Peterson Institute for International Economics: 131–54.

Collier, Paul (2007), *The Bottom Billion*, Oxford: Oxford University Press.

Corden, W. Max (2009), 'China's exchange rate policy, its current account surplus and the global imbalances', *The Economic Journal*, 119, 541: F430–41.

Department Of Labor, United States (2009), 'International comparisons of hourly. compensation costs in manufacturing, 2007'.

Ferri, Giovanni, and Li-gang Liu (2010), 'Honor thy creditors beforan thy shareholders: are the profits of Chinese state-owned enterprises real?', *Asian Economic Papers*, 9, 3: 50–69.

Frankel, Jeffrey A., and Shang-jin Wei (2007), 'Assessing China's exchange rate regime', *Economic Policy*, 22: 575–627.

Goldstein, Morris, and Lardy, Nicholas (2006), 'China's exchange rate policy dilemma', *American Economic Review*, 96, 2: 422–6.

Hofman, Bert, and Louis Kuijs (2008), 'Rebalancing China's growth', in M. Goldstein and N. R. Lardy (eds.), *Debating China's Exchange Rate Policy*, Washington, DC: Peterson Institute for International Economics: 109–22.

Huang, Yiping (2009), 'China's great ascendancy and structural risks: consequences of asymmetric market liberalization', Peking University, China Center for Economic Research, Working Paper No. E2009003, June.

Kim, Kwong Ok (2009), 'Reflections on China's power', in Keun Lee, Joon-han Kim, and Wing Thye Woo (eds.), *Power and the Sustainability of the Chinese State*, London: Routledge: 11–30.

Knight, John, and Lina Song (2005), *Towards a Labour Market in China*, Oxford: Oxford University Press.

——and Wei Wang (2011), 'China's macroeconomic imbalances: causes and consequences', *The World Economy*, 34, 9: 1476–1506.

Kong, Sherry Tao, Xin Meng, and Dandan Zhang (2010), 'The global financial crisis and rural–urban migration', paper presented at the Beijing Forum, November.

Koopman, Robert, Zhi Wang, and Shang-jin Wei (2008), 'How much of Chinese exports is really made in China? Assessing domestic value added when processing trade is pervasive', NBER Working Paper No. 14109, June.

Kuijs, Louis (2005), 'Investment and Saving in China', World Bank Policy Research Working Paper No. 3633.

——and Tao Wang (2005), 'China's pattern of growth: moving to sustainability and reducing inequality', World Bank Policy Research Working Paper No. 3767.

Leightner, Jonathan E. (2010), 'How China's holdings of foreign reserves affect the value of the US dollar in Europe and Asia', *China and the World Economy*, 18, 3: 24–39.

Li Shi, Luo Chuliang, and Terry Sicular (2012), 'Overview: income inequality and poverty in China, 2002–2007', in Li Shi, Hiroshi Sato, and Terry Sicular (eds.), *Rising Inequality in China: Challenges to a Harmonious Society*, New York: Cambridge University Press, forthcoming.

Luo, Renfu, Linxiu Zhang, Jikun Huang, and Scott Rozelle (2007), 'Elections, fiscal reform and public goods provision in rural China', *Journal of Comparative Economics*, 35: 583–611.

Mcgregor, Richard (2010), *The Party: The Secret World of China's Communist Rulers*, London: Allen Lane.

Mckinnon, Ronald, and Gunther Schnabl (2009), 'The case for stabilizing China's exchange rate: setting the stage for fiscal expansion', *China and the World Economy*, 17, 1: 1–32.

Makin, Tony J. (2007), 'Does China's huge external surplus imply an undervalued renminbi?', *China and the World Economy*, 15, 3: 89–102.

Matthews, Kent, Jianguong Guo, and Nina Zhang (2007), 'Non-performing loans and productivity in Chinese banks: 1997–2006', Cardiff Economics Working Paper E2007/30, November.

Michelson, Ethan (2011), 'Public goods and state-society relations: an impact study of China's rural stimulus', Indiana University Center for Chinese Politics and Business, Working Paper No. 4, February.

Ministry Of Human Resources and Social Security (2009), 'Series of reports on China's employment strategies against the global financial crisis', unpublished manuscript (in Chinese).

——(2010), 'An investigation of employment demand of enterprises in spring 2010 and employment status of rural migrants in 2009', unpublished manuscript (in Chinese).

Naughton, Barry (2007), *The Chinese Economy: Transitions and Growth*, Cambridge: The MIT Press.

——(2008), 'A political economy of China's economic reform', in Loren Brandt and Thomas Rawski (eds.), *China's Great Economic Transformation*, Cambridge and New York: Cambridge University Press: 91–135.

National Bureau Of Statistics Of China (NBS) (various years), *China Statistical Yearbook*, Beijing: China Statistics Press.

Pei, Minxin (2006), *China's Trapped Transition: The Limits of Developmental Autocracy*, Cambridge, Mass.: Harvard University Press.

Rumbaugh, Thomas, and Nicolas Blancher (2004), 'China: International trade and WTO accession', IMF Working Paper WP/04/36.

Shane, Mathew, and Fred Gale (2004), 'China: A study of dynamic growth', electronic Outlook Report from the Economic Research Service.

Shirk, Susan L. (2008), *China: Fragile Superpower: How China's Internal Politics Could Derail its Peaceful Rise*, Oxford and New York: Oxford University Press.

Shu, Chang, and Raymond Yip (2006), 'Impact of exchange rate movement on the mainland economy', Hong Kong Monetary Authority, China Economic Issues 3/06.

Sung, Yun-wing (2007), 'Made in China: from world sweatshop to a global manufacturing centre?', *Asian Economic Papers*, 6, 3: 43–72.

Wang, Feng, and Andrew Mason (2008), 'The demographic factor in China's transition', in Loren Brandt and Thomas Rawski (eds.), *China's Great Economic Transformation*, Cambridge and New York: Cambridge University Press: 136–66.

Wang, Yajie, Hui Xiaofeng, and Abdol Soofi (2007), 'Estimating renminbi equilibrium exchange rate', *Journal of Policy Modelling*, 29, 3: 417–29.

Wang, Yongzhong (2010), 'Effectiveness of capital controls and sterilization in China', *China and the World Economy*, 18, 3: 106–24.

Wedeman, Andrew (2009a), 'Enemies of the state: mass incidents and subversion in China, paper presented at the APSA 2009 Meeting, Toronto.

——(2009b), 'Corruption in China: crisis or constant?', background paper for China Balance Sheet Project, Washington DC: Peterson Institute for International Economics.

Woo, Wing Thye (2009), 'Assessing China's capability to manage the high-probability risks to economic growth: fiscal, governance and ecological problems', in Keun Lee, Joon-han Kim, and Wing Thye Woo (eds.), *Power and the Sustainability of the Chinese State*, London: Routledge: 75–99.

Xu, Mingqi (2010), 'The role of macroeconomic policy in China's high economic growth amidst the global financial crisis', *Seoul Journal of Economics*, 23, 1: 123–44.

Yao, Shujie (2006), 'On economic growth, FDI and exports in China', *Applied Economics*, 38, 3: 339–51.

Yao, Yang (2010), 'A Chinese way to democratization?', *China: An International Journal*, 8, 2 (September): 330–45.

Yu, Yongding (2008), 'The new challenges of inflation and external imbalances facing China', *Asian Economic Papers*, 2, 7 (June): 34–50.

Zheng, Nongnian (2009), 'Can the Communist Party sustain its rule in China?', in Keun Lee, Joon-han Kim, and Wing Thye Woo (eds.), *Power and the Sustainability of the Chinese State*, London: Routledge: 186–210.

13

Economic Growth in China: Retrospect

13.1 Introduction

We begin with a summary of the argument of the book, examining the causes of China's rapid growth in Section 13.2 and the consequences in Section 13.3. We then turn to the more general conclusions to be drawn from our argument: methodological, substantive, and policy oriented. Lessons for growth research are discussed in Section 13.4, lessons for China in Section 13.5, and lessons for other developing countries in Section 13.6.

13.2 The Causes of China's Growth

In Chapter 4 we placed China in a cross-country perspective—an issue that has received very little quantitative attention in the literature on China's growth. Reflecting in part the limited data available for cross-country studies, we used a neoclassical framework relating factor inputs to output. Starting with the conventional Solow model, we augmented the basic equation first with human capital and then also with a measure of resource transfer from the agricultural to the, more productive, non-agricultural sector. The dependent variable was growth of output per worker. We found that the extended version of the augmented Solow model provided a good explanation of China's growth success. China's annual growth rate of output per worker (7.2%) falls within the 95% confidence interval for its predicted growth rate (6.3%). The unexplained residual might represent efficiency gains from economic reform and marketization that are not captured by the structural change terms.

The model proved to be a valuable means of understanding the large and persistent differences in growth rates between China and other countries. China's relatively good performance can be attributed to several factors. First and foremost, China accumulated physical capital more rapidly than did other major country groups. Starting our period at a lower level of output per worker and thus further away from its long-run equilibrium, China benefited from conditional convergence. The slow convergence rate predicted by our model implied that, despite diminishing returns to capital, the role of capital accumulation in driving economic growth could persist for decades during China's transition to the long-run equilibrium predicted by neoclassical growth theory.

Also related to capital accumulation is the contribution made by China's more rapid structural change, as labour moves from the low-productivity agricultural sector to the high-productivity non-agricultural sector. The slower population growth in China than in other developing countries helps to explain its faster growth of output per worker. The level of human capital contributes to the growth difference between China and other developing counties, but not the growth of human capital as China's educational expansion was generally matched.

In addition to the cross-country analysis we conducted a cross-province analysis. All provinces are subject to central government policies with regard to foreign trade, family planning, macroeconomic management, financial policies, etc. However, some provinces reformed and marketized earlier and further than others, and there are differences in openness to foreign trade, natural increase in population, level of economic activity, investment–output ratio, etc. Our method was to explain the province differences in growth rates in terms of their differences in explanatory variables, as a means of explaining why China as a whole and indeed all its provinces have grown so fast.

The dependent variable was the growth rate of real GDP per capita. We adopted the informal growth regression approach, so permitting the introduction of many explanatory variables. Our task in Chapter 5 was to estimate a basic equation. We had to solve the problem of model uncertainty, that is, to construct an empirical model based on robust predictors. The first stage model selection results identified a role for conditional convergence, physical and human capital formation, rate of population growth, degree of openness, and institutional change in determining growth rates across China's provinces. At the second stage we estimated the baseline model using panel-data system GMM techniques.

Three major findings of the baseline model form the basis of our story. There is conditional convergence among provinces, and both physical and human capital accumulation promote economic growth. Conditional convergence occurred despite continuing absolute divergence: the rich provinces were becoming relatively richer. The findings are consistent with the implications of the transitional dynamics of neoclassical growth theory. Such transitional movement is indeed to be expected given the likely extreme disequilibrium of the Chinese economy at the start of economic reform. Our evidence of conditional convergence suggests that each province is converging towards its equilibrium steady state. It might, however, have other explanations, for example, that convergence reflects the effects of fiscal transfers from the central government to poor provinces and minority areas. The growth impacts of physical and human capital are in line with the disequilibrium growth/conditional convergence argument. However, an alternative interpretation of the positive effects of both types of investment is that capital accumulation is closely bound up with technological progress.

The baseline model was extended in Chapters 6 and 7 to examine the roles of particular variables. Chapter 6 was concerned with factor inputs, in particular physical and human capital accumulation. Our more detailed investigation of the effects of these two forms of investment was intended to throw further light on the mechanisms at work.

When we distinguished different types of physical capital, the greatest contribution was made by expenditure classified as 'investment in innovation' as opposed to 'investment in capital construction'; 'investment in other fixed assets', such as real estate, made no contribution at all. Physical investment appears to make the greatest contribution to growth when it is most closely bound up with technological progress. Because foreign companies can be a source of knowledge and technology, we expected that a unit of foreign direct investment would have a greater effect on growth than would a unit of domestic investment. Our evidence supported this hypothesis after we solved a specification problem.

Firms under different types of ownership face different incentives, experience different government policies, and have different opportunities. Breaking down physical investment by ownership, we found that an increase in the investment share of SOEs decreases the contribution of investment to growth, an increased share of collective enterprises has a negligible effect, and an increased share of private enterprises raises the contribution. Thus, the reform process that unleashed a private sector was important for growth, and the distorted financial system which continued to favour the SOEs held it back.

Our results illustrate the importance of distinguishing the growth effects of education at different levels. The differences in these effects depend on the nature of the economy's production function and how it changes, and on the policy emphasis that was previously placed on primary, secondary, and tertiary education. Whereas primary school enrolment has no effect on economic growth, both secondary school and higher education enrolment have a positive effect, the latter more than the former. Indeed, the coefficient on higher education enrolment in relation to total population implies great sensitivity of the growth rate. This might be explained by the neglect of higher education until the late 1990s: in 1998 higher education enrolment was still only 5% of the relevant age group.

To answer the question—why has China grown so fast?—it was necessary for us to assume that the growth impact of a variable estimated on the basis of its variation among provinces would be a guide to its impact in the economy as a whole. Various counterfactual exercises were conducted on that basis. We found that a significant reduction in capital inputs could have reduced China's growth rate dramatically—so indicating the great importance of physical and human capital formation in explaining China's remarkable growth. However, that begs the question: why was capital accumulated so rapidly?

In the case of education, labour market reform, by increasing the (initially negligible) wage premia on education, produced rapid growth in the private demand for education, to which government responded by increasing the supply. In the case of physical investment, the strong incentives both to save and to invest (examined in Chapter 8) will be discussed below.

Factor inputs and their growth can be viewed as the proximate determinants of output and its growth. Underlying these technical relationships, however, are other, less direct, influences on growth. These were explored in Chapter 7. Starting again from the baseline model, we examined three such determinants of China's growth success: increased openness, ownership change, and sectoral change. Each effect primarily represents an improvement in efficiency, moving the economy towards its production frontier.

The structure of the economy itself—level rather than change—affects growth in the cases of trade and ownership but not of sectoral composition. Having a large trade sector or a large private sector itself raises a province's growth rate. However, change in structure is more important. China as a whole has undergone three forms of drastic structural change over the period of economic reform, and each of them helps to explain the high growth rate.

At the start of economic reform, China had a closed economy, and its industrial structure, based on the Soviet model, did not reflect its comparative advantage. The subsequent increase in the share of trade in GDP had a positive effect, and not only exports but also imports contributed. The contribution to growth exceeded 3 per cent per annum. These powerful results are consistent with growth benefiting from the improved resource reallocation, technology, and competition that openness brings.

Whether we use investment, output, or employment as the criterion, we find the effect of an increase in the share of private ownership on growth to be positive, and that of state ownership to be negative. Had privatization, with the resulting improvement in productive efficiency, not occurred, growth would have been lower by 0.7 percentage points per annum.

The remarkable sectoral change also made an important contribution to growth. Had the share of employment in the non-agricultural sector not increased, annual growth would have been slower by one percentage point. The evidence is consistent with there being efficiency gains from improved sectoral labour allocation and also with externalities specific to the industrial sector.

When we estimated an equation that simultaneously incorporated openness, privatization, and sectoral change, the full effect of structural change on growth exceeded 4% per annum. This figure illustrates the rough order of magnitude of the contribution made by structural change to China's growth rate. There was not only economic growth but also economic transformation, and that transformation accounted for much of the growth rate. China provides a vivid illustration of the importance of structural evolution, and the new incentives and institutions that it creates, in promoting economic growth in developing countries.

China's experience shows that rapid growth is possible despite starting with inappropriate institutions. Government was able to address the institutional obstacles to growth as they became apparent. The reform of institutions loosened various binding constraints on growth and helped to unleash previously untapped market forces. Although our growth regressions captured increasing openness and privatization, other institutional changes were not observable. Alternative approaches were required to capture these other processes.

The growth regressions highlighted the great importance of capital accumulation for China's rapid growth. That raises deeper, underlying questions. Why does China invest so much? What drives the demand for investment? How can resources and funds be supplied for so high a rate of investment? Chapter 8 tried to answer these questions, drawing on the considerable literature about investment in China. A plausible story emerged.

We adduced evidence that the overall rate of return on capital was initially high and remained reasonably high. Moreover, the return on capital in industry rose substantially after the late 1990s, in response to industrial reform. Despite the remarkably high rate of capital accumulation, profitability remained promising enough to induce high investment. This was facilitated by rapid TFP growth and the ready supply of surplus labour that could be combined with the growing capital stock.

Entrepreneurial expectations of rapid economic growth were crucial for high investment. China became a 'developmental state': incentives were provided at all levels of government to generate economic growth, bureaucrats were rewarded for promoting investment, and businessmen could make investment decisions with confidence that policies for rapid growth would be pursued. The Chinese economy entered a virtuous circle with sustaining feedback effects. High investment produced rapid growth and rapid growth in turn produced buoyant expectations that elicited high investment. The fact that investment—mainly in the relatively high productivity sectors and much of it embodying improved technology—was so high in turn accelerated the growth of TFP.

Without a national saving rate that matched the high investment rate, the investment boom would have collapsed in the face of the ensuing macroeconomic imbalances. We were able to provide plausible accounts of the remarkably high saving rate in each of the three sectors: enterprises, households, and government. The inefficient and repressed financial system may well have played a part: financially constrained firms and households that saw profitable opportunities may have increased their saving to make their investments.

The supply of funds could have been a constraint on aggregate investment but this proved not to be the case. Whereas a ready supply of bank loans at low interest rates was generally available to SOEs, non-state enterprises had to rely on their own savings or on informal loans at high interest rates. Despite the lower profitability of the SOE sector, its managers were keen to invest, partly because their objectives were more growth oriented than profit oriented and partly because, until the late 1990s, they faced 'soft budgets' and therefore had no need to be risk averse.

High investment of the non-state sector was possible, partly because the corporatized former SOEs were generally sufficiently state owned to be state controlled, and partly because of the greater efficiency of private firms, which enabled them to achieve higher profit rates and thus higher retained profits than the state-owned or state-controlled sectors.

China's high investment relative to consumption and high excess of saving over investment, that is, current account surplus (discussed in Chapter 12), both imply a low rate of time preference on the part of society and government. This in turn is assisted by rapid economic growth: fast-rising consumption dissipates political discontent, and the ensuing political stability encourages the CCP to take a long-term, dynastic view. It is another example of the positive feedback that keeps China in a virtuous circle of rapid economic growth.

We argued in Chapter 3 that its underlying political economy was central to China's growth success. From the start of reform, the decentralization of economic powers to local governments gave them incentives to raise revenue by owning, encouraging, and taxing local economic activities. Governments could raise and retain 'extra-budgetary revenue' for their own purposes. This was particularly important in promoting rural industrialization in the 1980s. More generally, the fiscal incentives gave each tier of local government—from the province downwards—incentives to pursue local economic development. The fiscal reform of 1994 altered the structure of incentives somewhat but the thrust of incentives was unaltered.

Early in the reform process the leadership embarked on a reform of the cadre system towards greater professionalism and towards an incentive system that rewarded the achievement of state objectives. This involved performance evaluation in career promotion. Over the years, the party and state bureaucrats and SOE managers were moulded to meet CCP objectives, to which the achievement of economic growth was central. Not only did the bureaucracy not hold back economic reform but also it was often willing and able to push economic reform.

Given the growth objectives of the top leadership, there remained an immense problem of implementing policies for growth in a country as vast as China. The leadership resorted to the engineering of appropriate incentives for decision makers. The combination of fiscal incentives for local governments and career incentives for officials was a powerful, indeed crucial, means of creating a developmental state.

13.3 The Consequences of China's Growth

China's economic growth has had dramatic effects on its labour market. At the start of economic reform China was an extreme example of a labour-surplus economy. The abundance of relatively unskilled labour assisted the process of physical capital accumulation, itself so important for economic growth. The combining of additional capital with relatively costless additional labour delayed the onset of diminishing returns to capital.

We argued that the famous Lewis model provides a helpful framework for explaining the ways in which the fruits of economic development are spread: within a competitive market economy, it is only when the economy emerges from the first, labour-surplus, classical stage of the development process and enters the second, labour-scarce, neoclassical stage that real incomes begin to rise generally. Up to that point the benefits of economic growth can accrue in the form of the absorption of surplus labour; beyond it, the scarcity of labour can be a powerful market force for the reduction in inequality of labour income.

Has economic growth propelled the Chinese economy into Lewis's second stage? In Chapter 9 we produced evidence of simultaneous surplus labour in rural areas and rising migrant wages in urban areas. Our interpretation of the puzzle posed by this evidence is that there is segmentation in the labour market. On the one hand, migrant wages have indeed increased in real terms in very recent years, and their wages are sensitive to both urban labour market conditions and rural supply prices. Most of the increase can be explained by rising rural household income, much of which is likely to be exogenous to the migration process. On the other hand, institutional constraints create difficulties for migrants living in urban areas, and these deter or prevent migrant workers from bringing their families with them. Together with the inalienability of rural land, this in turn makes many rural workers reluctant to leave the village, at least for long periods. There will not necessarily be a neat Lewis turning point in a country as large and as regulated as China is. We envisage a turning stage, resulting not only from rural sector heterogeneity but also from China's factor market institutions.

Our heroic projection of future trends indicates that the number of rural–urban migrants will grow rapidly over the coming decade and the number of rural workers remaining in the rural areas will fall rapidly. Before the decade is out, however, there is likely to be an endogenous response both of the market and of the government. In the labour market the market-determined wages of unskilled labour can be expected to rise rapidly. The government response is likely to involve retirement policy, birth control policy, and urbanization policy. The labour market trends can be predicted to encourage the permanent urban settlement of migrants and the weakening of the *hukou* system that currently discriminates against migrants. Rapidly rising returns to unskilled labour will also require a change in development strategy towards more skill-intensive and technology-intensive activities. The continued growth of the Chinese economy can thus be expected to bring about far-reaching changes in both the economy and the society.

Chapter 10 dealt with the rising inequality that accompanied economic growth in China. It is of course not surprising that income and wealth inequality rose from the remarkably low level that was imposed under central planning—as the economy was marketized, economic incentives were created, and egalitarianism ceased to be a central plank of economic policy. However, income inequality was shown to rise dramatically: the Gini coefficient was 0.35 in 1988 and 0.48 in 2007. A 2007 study found China's income inequality to be the joint highest among twenty-one Asian countries.

There are reasons why the early economic growth of a poor country can itself raise inequality. However, the fact that economic reform and economic growth went hand in hand makes it difficult to distinguish their effects on inequality. Insofar as there is a trade-off between efficiency and equity, government was willing to sacrifice greater equality in order to achieve faster growth. Nevertheless, there are instances in which rising inequality was not the inevitable consequence of economic reform or economic growth. These might include the urban bias in policies, and the rent seeking and corruption that reflected the lack of accountability in China's system of governance. There are inevitable tensions surrounding China's economic transformation. They derive from the uneven benefits of growth, and from the pressures for a different distribution of those benefits. Various forms of inequality—including the rise in regional inequalities, in the rural–urban divide, and in the inequality of pay, the emergence of a wealthy entrepreneurial class, the public perception of corrupt gains, the uneven effects of SOE reform, the rise in urban unemployment, and the weakening of social protection—are all potential sources of discontent.

When in the late 1980s one of us joined the, now still ongoing, China household income project (CHIP) investigating income inequality, there was little official interest in it. Now our Chinese colleagues are in much demand in government circles. The introduction of the 'harmonious society' policies in the mid-2000s was aimed at reducing some of the inequalities, and in particular at redressing rural poverty. However, new business interest groups are forming and their influence on policy is probably growing. This might serve as a counterweight, so as to weaken the policy response to rising inequality. The most powerful market force for reducing income inequality is likely to be China's impending scarcity of relatively unskilled labour, examined in Chapter 9.

In Chapter 11 we explored a question that is original for China: does economic growth raise happiness? Evidence was presented from the available surveys which indicated that China's average happiness score had declined over the previous decade. In several rich countries it has been found that happiness scores have remained fairly constant while real incomes have trended upwards. The conventional explanation is in terms of aspirations. People's aspirations increase as well as their incomes, and rising aspirations tend to neutralize the effect of rising incomes on happiness. Nevertheless the finding for China comes as a surprise: firstly, because we expect happiness in poor societies to depend more on the fulfilment of basic needs than is the case in rich societies; secondly, because happiness appears actually to have fallen despite the remarkably rapid rise in living standards.

We used our data to suggest an explanation, distinguishing three samples of households. Rural people have the highest average happiness score—ironically so, as they are the poorest group. We explained their happiness in terms of their limited 'information sets' and narrow 'reference groups', their optimism about the future, and their non-materialistic attitudes. Urban people report lower happiness despite having much higher incomes. Our evidence suggested that this is due to their concern about their relative income in the city and feelings of 'relative deprivation', together with the greater insecurity that urban reforms have brought to their lives. Settled rural–urban migrants have the lowest average happiness, which we explained in terms of the transfer of their reference group from the village to the city, the perception of being among the poorest in their new environment, and city discrimination against migrants.

It was therefore possible to produce a plausible story for the apparent fall in subjective well-being in China—in which rising aspirations, perceptions of relative deprivation, changing reference groups, and increasing insecurity each play a part. Rising income inequality has probably reduced happiness, although it is inequality within a person's reference group that counts. People in all three samples derived happiness from the expectation that their income would rise in the future. This finding carries a warning that happiness in China might fall, and even political stability might be threatened, if an economic shock were to lead people to expect that economic growth would slow down.

13.4 Lessons for Growth Research

The distinctive methodological characteristic of this book is that it takes a broader approach to understanding economic growth—its causes and consequences— than is conventional for economists. Insofar as there is a trade-off between specificity and generality in approach, we have veered towards generality. An answer to a single specific research question—however good that answer might be—cannot provide a full explanation for China's remarkable economic growth. Many, often interrelated, questions have to be posed. Our encompassing approach—that of informing with economic theory and econometric evidence a country study of the causes and processes of economic growth—is similar to the 'analytic narrative' research that Rodrik (2003) recommends.

Much of the literature about economic growth is based on theoretical models. A second strand of literature involves empirical estimation of the quantifiable determinants of economic growth. A third strand explores the connections between institutions, and the associated policies, and growth. Our position is that all three approaches are required to understand why China has grown so fast. Nevertheless, we conclude that the least rigorous of the three approaches may well be the most fruitful. It is ultimately the evolution of institutions, and the incentives to which they give rise, that makes China's growth so remarkably high. The relative emphasis that we place on the three approaches contrasts with that to be found in modern graduate textbooks on economic growth (such as Acemoglu 2009; Aghion and Howitt 2009), where growth theories appear to take pride of place and most space.

Consider the methodological lessons to be gleaned from our use of the three approaches, beginning with growth theory. Our application of neoclassical growth theory in a cross-country context was reasonably successful after it had been augmented by human capital and a structural change term. In the cross-country and the cross-province analyses there was evidence both of capital accumulation being important for growth and of conditional convergence. This suggests that China—and no doubt other developing countries—is characterized by disequilibrium rather than equilibrium growth. The fact that 'investment in innovation' had a greater effect on growth than other forms of physical investment suggests that technical improvement is partly embodied in plant and machinery, in which case it is difficult to distinguish investment and technical progress. The important role that structural change was found to play illustrates the danger of applying growth models to developing countries that omit the TFP-enhancing effects of institutional and policy changes, such as greater openness and privatization, or of resource reallocation towards more productive activities. Positive interaction between investment and efficiency gain from technical progress and resource reallocation suggests that endogenous growth theory offers a helpful framework for analysing the effects of capital accumulation.

All three of the main approaches to the quantitative analysis of economic growth deserve to be explored: neoclassical growth equations, informal growth regressions, and growth-accounting exercises. The choice of approach depends on the context and might vary with the research question being posed, the availability of data, and one's theoretical priors. Various considerations led us to adopt the first two and not to attempt the third. The estimation of informal growth regressions encounters the problem of model uncertainty. Our solution was to employ two recently developed methods of model selection, 'Bayesian model averaging' and 'general-to-specific' methodologies. System GMM estimation proved in all cases to be the best way of identifying causal relationships. This was appropriately executed by dividing our period into five-year sub-periods.

It is difficult to include good proxies for institutions, and their change, in growth regressions. The relationships between institutions and economic growth are likely to be complex, involving lags and with causation running in both directions. It was therefore helpful also to provide a, necessarily non-rigorous, account of institutions: their evolution, functions, causes, and consequences.

A potentially important but rather unexplored research topic concerns the underlying political economy that gives rise to a developmental state, that is, a state which accords overriding priority to the achievement of rapid economic growth. Johnson (1982) explained the Japanese developmental state as a national response to a series of crises. For South Korea and Taiwan, external threats may well have been the driving force—threat from North Korea in the former case and from China in the latter. They produced a firmity of purpose that is lacking in many developing countries: political survival required economic strength. In China's case, the developmental state appeared to arise from the need of the ruling party to restore and maintain the political legitimacy that it had lost. Comparative studies would be valuable.

13.5 Lessons for China

The main lessons for China that arise from our research concern the need to reduce the social costs of rapid economic growth. A start was made with the introduction of policies for the 'harmonious society' in the mid-2000s. However, much more can be done. This includes policies to reduce China's currently high and possibly rising income inequality—among households, among regions, and between rural and urban areas—and policies to avoid and reverse the degradation of the environment. It also requires reform of the system of governance that can easily give rise to rent seeking and corrupt behaviour, especially at the local level. The lack of accountability in China's system of governance presents a serious risk for the maintenance of social stability and for the continuance of rapid economic growth.

If such a package of reforms involves a trade-off with economic growth, it might nevertheless be justified. Justification can be found either in a social welfare function that reflects concern to maintain social and political stability or in one that reflects concern about people's economic welfare and society's notions of equity.

It is clear from our projections that, if rapid growth continues, China will soon enter the 'Lewis turning stage', if it has not done so already. This has implications for future planning. As the cost of relatively unskilled labour rises, so China's comparative advantage in trade will move up the 'value chain' towards more skill-intensive and technology-intensive products. The education system should be prepared for that change. The government has taken dramatic steps in higher education. There was a sharp policy change in 1999: in 1998, 3.4 million students were enrolled in higher education; in 2008, there were 20.2 million—almost a sixfold increase in a decade. The remaining educational weakness lies in the quantity and quality of rural education, for which we cited evidence of a 'poverty trap'. Yet most of these children will grow up to be urban workers, many of them in skill-demanding jobs. Our projected great increase in the number of rural–urban migrants implies that there will be a case, on both economic and social grounds, for policies to permit urban settlement and to end *hukou* discrimination against migrants.

A novelty of this book was the analysis of subjective well-being in China. The analysis proved to be academically promising because happiness scores could be well predicted and well understood. The happiness functions reveal a good deal about people's perceptions of their own welfare, although what can be inferred from that remains a subject of debate. The most striking result was the evidence that the average happiness score in China had not risen, and may even have fallen, despite rapid economic growth. This should be a matter of concern for government. The study of subjective well-being is new to China and only just beginning. People's happiness deserves further monitoring and investigation.

In Chapter 12 we examined the rise of China's current account surplus in recent years. The rise was due partly to the effect of enterprise reforms in raising industrial efficiency and partly to the policy of holding down the value of the RMB. The surplus may well rise again as the world economy emerges from economic recession. We argued that it is probably in China's own interests to take measures to correct its external imbalance. The imbalance might otherwise pose a threat to China's medium-term economic growth.

A continuing export surplus is liable to give rise to three problems. First, the central bank will have difficulty in curbing the rise in liquidity as it purchases foreign exchange from net exporters. Failure in this regard might contribute to asset bubbles, which in turn can endanger the financial system and investor confidence. A financial crash might break the virtuous circle that sustains China's growth rate. Secondly, the current policies imply that China's foreign exchange reserves will continue to grow, and that their rate of return is likely to be low or even negative in real terms. China's foreign exchange policy will become increasingly boxed in: any significant sale of dollar reserves is likely to reduce the value of China's remaining dollar-denominated assets. Thirdly, a continuation of the current account surplus poses the threat of trade restrictions. It is possible that trading partners will take action against China's exports. Given the risks of trade retaliation and political repercussion, this way may be more harmful to all parties, including China.

13.6 Lessons for Other Developing Countries

We address two issues: how does China's rapid growth affect the development prospects of other developing countries, and what lessons do China's growth policies provide for other developing countries?

In broad terms, China's growth and openness offer opportunities for trade. In recent years China has tended to dominate the labour-intensive processing of manufactures for export. Economies with a similar comparative advantage face intense competition from China. This will continue until China's growth success, technological advance, and rising labour costs move its comparative advantage towards more technology-intensive and skill-intensive products. However, those countries—including many in Africa—which have a comparative advantage in the production of primary products, such as energy, minerals, and raw materials for manufacturing, gain from the growth of the Chinese economy. The rising Chinese demand expands the market for these products and—with other rapidly growing countries like India—raises their market prices. The scale and speed of China's impact through trade requires its trading partners to plan ahead in the expectation of China's continued rapid growth.

At first glance it would appear obvious that the success of China's policies for economic growth should carry important policy lessons for other developing countries. However, we hesitate to draw specific conclusions from Chinese experience for economic policies elsewhere. Many features of China's experience over its period of economic reform are very different from the standard features of developing countries. For one thing, China's vast population size marks it off from the many developing countries that are small: China can achieve economies of scale in production and governance, and the average ability of the upper echelons of officialdom can be very high. For another thing, China's initial factor endowment—much labour in relation to land and natural resources—distinguishes it from the developing countries that have plentiful land and/or natural resources.

Another obvious difference is that China began its economic reform from a situation of huge misallocation of resources and great inefficiency in their use. The economy was operating far within its production frontier. Rapid growth was therefore made possible simply by the process of marketization and the greater economic efficiency that it induced.

A further example of China's specificity is the spectacular rural industrialization that accompanied rural economic reform in the 1980s. Rural industrialization was due to a number of specific factors: there was unmet demand for light manufactured consumer goods; TVE production faced socially efficient (low labour cost, high capital cost) factor prices in an otherwise distorted industrial sector; and local governments had a strong fiscal incentive to develop township- and village-owned enterprises at a time when private enterprise remained largely unacceptable.

China's rural industrialization is therefore unlikely to be a model for other developing countries to follow unless they face similar distortions. The nearest case would be one in which factor markets were distorted against industrial development (for instance, on account of high wages) but the distortion was confined to the urban economy.

The fact that China's rate of population growth has been slower than that of other developing country regions was shown in Chapter 4 to contribute to its faster growth of output per worker. Again, the policy lessons are unclear. China reduced its population growth dramatically by means of the draconian and compulsory 'one-child family' policy. Faced with much existing surplus labour at the start of economic reform, the government was willing to sacrifice the wishes of one or two generations in order to accelerate the rise in living standards. Democratic countries, and even many authoritarian ones, would reject that example. Most already have policies intended to reduce the birth rate by voluntary means. However, in the light of the evidence for China they might wish to strengthen these policies through increased birth control subsidies and additional general and specific female education.

Is China's remarkably high investment rate, in turn made possible by its high saving rate, the most important policy lesson for other poor countries? It is clear that rapid capital accumulation was central to China's growth, and it is likely that faster capital accumulation, if only it could be achieved, would accelerate growth elsewhere. Again, our explanations for these phenomena are rather specific to China. Saving is high for several reasons: the growing economic insecurity and the low dependency ratio of households; credit constraints forcing up household and enterprise saving; the high share of profits in national income; and the high government saving rate, reflecting its low rate of time preference. Investment is high because the rate of profit has risen despite rapid capital accumulation, assisted by the reform policies that improved enterprise efficiency. Moreover, the underlying political economy of China has created a developmental state and produced self-fulfilling expectations of rapid growth and profitable investment. This combination of circumstances is rarely to be found in other poor countries.

China's most important distinguishing feature concerns the objectives of its rulers. The reform leaders gave economic growth their highest policy priority, essentially to restore and maintain political legitimacy for the authoritarian ruling party and to stave off social and political instability. In pursuing this objective, the leadership created an incentive structure—based on both career incentives and fiscal incentives at all levels of government—that would promote local and national economic growth.

The creation of a developmental state in this way is not unique to China, but it is not common. For instance, it is arguable that the governments of both South Korea and Taiwan have single-mindedly pursued growth objectives and have achieved rapid growth (Amsden 1989; Wade 1990). By contrast, many governments of developing countries, whether democratic or authoritarian, appear from their deeds if not their words to place low priority on the pursuit of economic growth. Rent-seeking activities by elite groups divert attention from growth objectives. The 'helping hand' observable at different levels of government in China becomes a 'grabbing hand' elsewhere (Frye and Schleifer 1997).

On a normative plane, it is easy to recommend China's growth policies to other countries wherever their own conditions make the policies appropriate. On a positive plane, however, the crucial thing is that the government accords high priority to economic growth. It is necessary for the leadership to build the institutions that will create growth incentives throughout the country's decision-making structures. These are the preconditions for establishing a developmental state.

The overwhelming priority given to growth objectives in China has had various side effects, including rising income inequality, lack of social security, and environmental degradation. Another government might regard these adverse consequences as being politically too costly. The dictatorial nature of the Chinese government has provided protection against political pressures that could slow down growth, for instance pressures to avoid those adverse consequences. However, this authoritarianism also means that there is a lack of political accountability, which in turn produces a breeding ground for rent seeking and corruption, especially at the local level. We saw in Chapter 12 that, on the World Bank's governance indicators, China ranked well among 235 countries on 'government effectiveness' but poorly on 'corruption' and very badly on 'accountability'.

Those who present China's growth as providing a 'China model' for other developing countries to follow should recognize that the China model contains flaws. The front cover of this book depicts a rampant dragon, representing China's remarkable economic growth. It should ideally also depict some dragon droppings, representing the social costs of the exclusive pursuit of growth objectives. However, it is perhaps symbolic that the detritus has been swept under the carpet.

The political system that has helped to create a developmental state and to drive economic growth thus has its drawbacks. Although these drawbacks have not impeded China's growth, they pose a difficult question. Can other countries follow China's example in creating a developmental state while avoiding the disadvantages that accompany it in the Chinese case? The most important lesson that China's experience offers other countries lies in the answer that they can find to this question.

References

Acemoglu, Daron (2009), *Introduction to Modern Economic Growth*, Princeton: Princeton University Press.

Aghion, Philippe, and Peter Howitt (2009), *The Economics of Growth*, Cambridge: The MIT Press.

Amsden, Alice (1989), *Asia's Next Giant: South Korea and Late Industrialization*, New York and Oxford: Oxford University Press.

Frye, Timothy, and Andrei Schleifer (1997), 'The invisible hand and the grabbing hand', *American Economic Review*, 87, 2: 354–8.

Johnson, Chalmers (1982), *MITI and the Japanese Miracle: The Growth of Industrial Policy, 1925–1975*, Stanford, Calif.: Stanford University Press.

Rodrik, Dani (2003), 'Introduction: what do we learn from country narratives?', in Dani Rodrik (ed.), *In Search of Prosperity: Analytic Narratives on Economic Growth*, Princeton: Princeton University Press.

Wade, Robert (1990), *Governing the Market: Economic Theory and the Role of Government in East Asian Industrialization*, Princeton: Princeton University Press.

Index of Names

Index of Subjects

Index of Subjects